Handbook for Shooters & Reloaders

Volume 1

Parker O. Ackley

Published by Echo Point Books & Media
Brattleboro, Vermont
www.EchoPointBooks.com

Copyright © 1962, P. O. Ackley

ISBN: 978-1-62654-101-6

Cover design by Rachel Boothby Gualco,
Echo Point Books & Media

Editorial and proofreading assistance by Christine Schultz,
Echo Point Books & Media

Printed and bound in the United States of America

CONTENTS

	Page
Foreword	v
Acknowledgments	vi
Around the World With Wildcats – Warren Page	1
Allyn H. Tedmon – P. O. Ackley	11
Reflections of a Rifleman-Hunter – Allyn H. Tedmon	13
Africa Safari – J. R. Buhmiller	27
Killing Power – P. O. Ackley	45
Reduced Loads – P. O. Ackley	91
Wind Drift – P. O. Ackley	109
Shooting in the Wind – Homer S. Powley	110
Pressure – P. O. Ackley	131
Headspace – P. O. Ackley	151
Bore Capacity – P. O. Ackley	165
Sectional Density – Paul C. VonRosenberg	179
A Simple Chronograph – P. O. Ackley - A. E. Ellinger	191
Rimmed vs. Rimless Cartridges – P. O. Ackley	197
Barrel Steel – P. O. Ackley	203
The Lowdown on Loading Dies – P. O. Ackley	219
Loading Data - Rifle – P. O. Ackley	256
Loading Data - Pistol and Revolver – P. O. Ackley	508
Powder – B. E. Hodgdon	523
Questions and Answers – P. O. Ackley	538

P. O. ACKLEY

FOREWORD

The author, P. O. Ackley, has been associated with the development of high velocity "wildcat" cartridges for over a quarter of a century, and is one of the foremost authorities on "wildcat" cartridges. He is also a well known rifle barrel maker and custom rifle builder.

P. O. Ackley is a native of Granville, New York. He was graduated from Syracuse University, Magna cum laude, in 1927 and entered the full-time gunsmith business in Roseburg, Oregon in 1936. This enterprise flourished, but in 1942 war work beckoned and he became attached to the Ordnance Department and was with the small arms section in Ogden, Utah, until 1944.

He re-established his gunshop at Trinidad, Colorado in 1945 and had one of the largest custom gun shops in the nation. He was instructor in theory of gunmaking and metallurgy at Trinidad State Junior College in 1946 to 1951, and carried on extensive experimental work at the college and in his own shop which had been incorporated in 1947.

Mr. Ackley has been a regular contributor of magazine articles. He is a member of the Technical Staff of "Guns and Ammo" and is the Gunsmithing Columnist of "Shooting Times". He has built a reputation for "always telling the truth" in his writings.

His line of "wildcat" cartridges represents superlative engineering and unfailing adherence to standards of uncompromising quality. They are, in fact, no longer true "wildcats", for they have been accepted by the shooting public and have proven themselves in game fields all over the world.

Ackley rifle barrels have been in constant demand over the years not only for experimental work but by other custom rifle makers who proudly advertise "Barrels by Ackley". Experimenters almost unfailingly call on P. O. Ackley for their exacting demands in rifled tubes, knowing that through them will be delivered the last potential of their ideas. Many of his barrels have been used in the experiments which have resulted in the success of our missile program.

The author's opinion of the various "wildcat" cartridges is given in the description of each cartridge as it is found in this book. This opinion is based on many years experience. However, this is personal opinion and should be considered as such.

Paul W. Cox

ACKNOWLEDGMENTS

The loading data for cartridges shown in this book has been gathered from various sources including the personal work and experiments of the author and from the originators of various "wildcat" cartridges.

Sources of data other than above include loading manuals by Speer, Lyman Gun Sight Corporation, Belding and Mull and Norma's "Gunbug's Guide." These books are distributed by Speer Products Company, Lewiston, Idaho; Lyman Gun Sight Corporation, Middlefield, Connecticut; Belding and Mull, Phillipsburg, Pennsylvania; Norma by Precision Products, South Lansing, New York. These books are desirable additions to any handloaders library and each contains information not found in the others.

Some of the information contained in this book has been taken from "Reloading Simplified" by Cyril Waterworh, and is published by Afco Printing, Limited, 9 Bligh Street, Sydney, Australia. This is a book which all Australian, Canadian and New Zealand shooters should have since it contains a great deal of information of particular interest to shooters of the British Commonwealth of Nations. Other handloading books are "Complete Guide to Handloading" by the late Phil Sharpe, "Why Not Load Your Own," by Townsend Whelen and "The Principles and Practices of Loading Ammunition," by Earl Naramore. The DuPont charts included with this book are reproduced through the courtesy of E. I. duPont de Nemours and Co., Inc., Penns Grove, New Jersey.

The aid and contributions of the following persons is acknowledged with thanks by the author:

Jack O'Connor — Gun Editor of "Outdoor Life"
Warren Page — Gun Editor of "Field and Stream"
Les H. Bowman — Wyoming Guide and Outfitter
J. R. Buhmiller — Custom Barrel Maker and big game hunter
Homer S. Powley — Ballistic engineer
Capt. John J. O'Hara
Allyn H. Tedmon

Bruce Hodgdon — Loading Component Supplier
Paul VonRosenberg — Ballistic Engineer
Robert Hutton — Technical Editor of "Guns and Ammo"
Les Womack — National Park Ranger
A. E. Ellinger — Ballistics Engineer

and the many others who have contributed to making this book possible.

Photography — Vaun G. Severson, Salt Lake City, Utah

AROUND THE WORLD WITH WILDCATS

by Warren Page

Tourist manuals, books on hunting and riflery, outfitter's instructions to their oncoming customers—about ninety percent of them read the same way. They consistently suggest, be the hunt planned for the tundra-floored valleys of Alaska or the thornbush-dotted sands of Kenya's Northern Frontier, that the visiting hunter bring along rifles in standard calibres. This is a lot of malarkey. The confirmed reloader and wildcat fan can have more fun, kill his game certainly as well and very likely better, whether he's hunting deer forty miles from home or ten thousand miles away and ten thousand feet up in Baluchistan. I know. I've done it.

Matter of fact, over a handful of years in which the bulk of my hunting whether domestic or foreign has been done with wildcats, or if with standard calibres with reloads, the only problem I've ever run into has been that of transportation. On long hauls extra airplane weight, in the form of cartridges can run into a pile of shekels. Opposed to that is the fact that you can buy a box of 180 grain Silvertips for your .30/06 in half a dozen stores in Anchorage, or in Nairobi enough .375's to get you by. But the man smart enough to load his own is also presumably smart enough to ship heavy ammo and rifles ahead, to do his trophy-taking with a minimum amount of fodder. Furthermore, in many of the odd backwaters of this world, where the really fine hunting is, you'll find no store where you can buy even a box of .22 rim-fires, let alone game loads. You had better have your own rifle fodder along, and it might well be your own fodder in every sense.

There has been a lot of dire warning in print to the effect that tropical heat jumps up pressures, so may shove past the danger point loads that functioned handsomely back home in Kalamazoo. The basic theory is correct, in that temperature hikes markedly above a norm of, say 70 degrees Fahrenheit do cause a lift in the pressures created by burning powder. The commonest rule of thumb is that one degree jacks velocity an average of one foot per second—find that with your chronographs, friends—and increases pressures somewhat more.

The first time I headed for the tropics with wildcats—a 7mm Mashburn Magnum and a .375 Weatherby, the latter at that time a true wildcat and even now primarily a reloader's cartridge, surely—I had visions of letting hellfire loose though my loads were clearly at a practical maximum when fired at normal U.S. temperatures, say sixty to seventy degrees. But it didn't happen. This hunt first involved chasing Asiatic wild boar in the sun-struck marsh edges of Tigris in Iraq. No hellfire appeared, not even a stiffened bolt lift. Next stop was India; and for more than two weeks of hunting in southern Chanda province, the midday thermometer reading ranged from 110-120 degrees. Really hot. But the tigers and the sambur and the gaur and the leopards all tumbled, and nary a sign of over-built pressures did I get from either wildcat.

In the course of hunting all manner of game on six of the world's continents, probably ninety per cent of the time with handloads of either factory calibres or wildcats, I have yet to run into a situation where extremes of temperature or humidity had any discoverable effect on the ammunition. Back in '59, before the political roof blew off in the Belgian Congo, I hunted elephant there for a month before moving over into Mozambique. We ran into days of torrential downpour on the tusker-crowded Rutshuru Plain. Everything was soaked and stayed soaked in steaming humidity. The trusty old .375 wildcat I toted much of the time continued to function perfectly, to kill elephant at from a hundred yards to a tenth as many feet, with ammo that had already been toted half across the world several times, through every extreme of weather—then it went on through some superheated days in Portuguese East, when the real heat begins just before the rains, to perform in absolutely normal fashion.

And in hunting the tropics, in Asia or Africa, where your rifles are likely to be pointed at dangerous game, beasts that may run over you and stand or claw your carcass into hamburger, the ammo has to perform. A mis-fire, or a pressure swelled cartridge case that sticks in the chamber to halt or even slow your reloading, might just mean your finish. But somehow or other, even when crawling through wall-solid jungle after Cape buffalo known to be wounded and ready to charge, the thought of failure of a reload or hand-assembled wildcat has never entered my mind. Not likely to, since they've never given trouble when they were given thought beforehand.

Which doesn't mean, of course, that you can take along loads that under standard North American temperatures are already giving you case head expansion, already opening primer pockets, then let them bake for hours in direct tropical sun, and not expect rather disastrous evidence of excess pressure—but you can't do that at home in Kalamazoo, either! Not for long you can't.

The warning has further been made that a reload, be it factory or wildcat in case shape, is more likely to give you misfires than a factory cartridge, more likely to cause hang-ups in feeding and chambering just at that crucial moment when the buffalo is bearing down or the prize kudu scooting off. Seems doubtful, somehow. The hunter-rifleman who is interested enough in his weapon and its ammunition to put up his loads by hand is also interested enough to be precisely methodical in his loading, to inspect his brass for flash hole size beforehand, to keep his primers free of oil and seat them to proper depth, to weigh or throw his charges exactly. He's certainly interested enough to run every round through the magazine and chamber of his rifle before he leaves home. The smart hunter would make that feed check even with store-bought ammo for a store-bought rifle, and he'll find that even such "standard" combinations will give him function hang-ups more often than once in a blue moon.

The prime reason, of course, for using wildcats or handloads anywhere, be it in Maine or Ethiopia, is the added personal satisfaction we get from clobbering a trophy with a load of our own devising, a bullet of our own careful selection over a powder charge that was arrived at after thoughtful personal experiment. This has been likened to catching a trout with a self-tied fly, but the satisfaction goes a lot further. After all, there's usually another trout ready to bite five minutes later, and I've never heard of a man's being chewed up by a trout because the fish wasn't presented the right fly.

In the spring of 1958 I hunted for some seven weeks in New Zealand, which pair of southern hemisphere island has more game than you can shake a stick at--European red deer or hirsch, elk and whitetail from our own continent, pigs from heaven knows where, fallow deer from England, Japanese and Axis deer from eastern Asia, sambur deer from India, chamois from the Austrian Alps and Himelayan tahr from the crags on the roof of the world —and all of it on a no-season, no-limit, no license basis. The government even hires "cullers"—which term should actually be killers —to hack away at the burgeoning herds of these animals at the rate of from sixty to one hundred thousand each year.

Had I been a conventional thinker visiting this rifleman's paradise, I'd have brought down under a sporterized SMLE chambered .303 British because that ammo is common as dirt in New Zealand—they'll even give you four free cartridges for every Himalayan tahr you shoot, which is mighty poor pay because those characters live up where the chamois fear they may fall off, or I might have settled for a .30/06 because sporting fodder is reasonably available in that calibre. Either would have been adequate and then some. But no, being an unconventional gink, as half my arsenal I lugged down a little featherweight 6mm rifle, chambered .240 Page Sooper Pooper, and for it four boxes of home-grown loads. What load? In Remington fire-formed cases the Federal 210 primer, 48 grains of 4831, some Nosler 100 grain and some Speer 105 grain spitzers. The two bullets shot to the same place, punched tackhole groups. The pigs and Jap deer and big red deer stags that I dropped with this combination might possible have been just as dead had I slammed them with pinkie-sized pills from a .303—but which way did I have more fun? Which way would I have gained greater personal satisfaction? And come to think of it, I'm not sure that the .303 would have killed as well after all. It certainly wouldn't have been as easy or as sure to hit with.

On one hunt in British East Africa, I had a chance to kill two rhino up in Northern Kenya. One was a sick beast, maddened with the pain of ulcerous skin sores so that it was beating up on the natives in a remote shamba. He was not a big rhino so no trophy, but he was threatening the very lives of the blacks, so counted no score against my license. The other was a fine trophy, a bull of 27 inches of horn, taken in fair combat. One of these rhino I shot most immediately dead with a .458 Winchester and factory solids. The other was shot just as immediately dead with the .375 Weatherby and loads personally concocted with 82 grains of 4064 and the 300 grain Kynock-made steel jacket. Quite aside from the circumstances of shooting, quite aside from the relative length of horn, which do you suppose gave me the bigger personal bang, the one Mr. Winchester's combination killed for me, or the one I killed by and for myself?

The pleasure we get out of any hunting trip is made up of many things, not just a matter of the size of the elk or the horn length on the goat—and the feeling that rifle and cartridge are personal possessions or creations, not just tools off-handedly picked up in a store, is a good part of that pleasure.

Surprising how effective these personal loads, or these personally chosen wildcats can be, too. Or perhaps it isn't such a surprise, because the chances are good that the wildcat rifleman, like the reloader, has put extensive thought and experiment into his gun gear.

In making up the loads to take to East Africa for a 7mm short Magnum wildcat, I had a long backlog of experience with the 180 grain Barnes and 175 grain Hornady bullets—all of it to that date on North American critters like goat, elk, caribou, several moose. But I'd heard tell that the African beasts of like weight and size were mighty tough, took more killing and demanded more bullet penetration. So one-half, and the other half of it, matched for point of impact with a bit of load jugglery which worked out at one grain less of 4831, with the Nosler 175 grain partition-jacket. They'd hang together if anything would.

And it worked out. The Hornady slug seemed to have just the right balance of expansion and penetration for antelope on the order of the oryx, four hundred pounders made tough by the inch-thick hide they carry on their forequarters as protection against the stabbing horns of other love-minded bull oryx. This combination did as well on the topi and kongoni clan. But when it came to zebra—and remember that a stud Burchell's zebra, chunky and muscular, will heft as heavy as a really big bull elk and has great affection for life—the slightly more frangible Hornady bullet gave me a little trouble when the shot had to be taken at a bad angle. Not enough penetration, not every time. Since we had to drop a number of zebra for lion baits for two hunters, I switched to the tough Nosler. That settled the zebra hash.

The conclusion here isn't so much that there's a performance different in the two like-diameter bullets as it is that only the true gun-bug, the chap who loads his own and very likely loads wildcats, would have gone to the trouble of job-selecting bullets in the first place, and tailoring loads in the second place.

For one trip into Yukon territory I wanted to work out the fullest potential of a .270, a factory cartridge, but certainly a wildcat in basic origins since it's nothing but the old '06 necked down. We anticipated shots on four types of game. True, Dall sheep and caribou, are "soft" animals in that they are not hard to kill, do not offer stiff resistance of hide, heavy bone, or massive muscle to a bullet. A frangible 130 grain pointed for long shots, would do well on them, so load #1 employed over 49.5 grains of 4064 and Remington's bronze-point. Also on the game list were very heavy Yukon moose, the *alces gigas* type that pushes a ton and takes a lot of bullet penetration if you can't get in for that classical broadside chest shot, and grizzly. For these the 150 grain Nosler and, since from my rifle it gave the same impact center at a hundred yards and would follow the trajectory of the 130 grain closely enough for practical purposes, 53.5 grains of 4350. Considerable thought and some titivating with loads went into those combinations. I don't know that the Yukon trophies ran any longer in the horn or silkier in the hair because they were killed with those loads. Maybe they'd have been magically transformed into records if straight store-bought loads had been used—but I somehow doubt it, and spending a couple of weekends working up the combinations extended the pleasures of the Yukon trip just that long!

One of the better-known trophy hunters in these United States, though he has never sought publicity for his exploits, is a Spokane gent named Don Hopkins. Don has about as many entries in the Boone and Crockett Club North American big game records as any one, and a darned sight more Dark Continent biggies for the Rowland Ward list. I doubt that more than a hand-count of these have been shot with a "standard" ammo. The great bulk of his trophies both here and overseas—and Hopkins has combed the African game list so carefully during the past fifteen years that he no longer goes hunting for a mere elephant, but seeks only a 1500 pounder—have bitten the dust from the punch of wildcats. The .285 OKH, his short and long .33's a big .424—quite a family of wildcats, each thoughtfully designed and bullets prepared for specific hunting jobs. If he's had wildcat troubles, I haven't heard about them and Don is a scrupulously truthful man.

We have a wildcat list, we U.S. gun cranks, as long as a gorilla's arm. Probably we have too many, and a lot of them are of very doubtful virtue, or at least of virtue too loudly protested. In some areas and types of use the oddball cartridge doesn't do a darned thing that a factory-made item won't do as well or better. But this isn't true where the "blow job" or the use of larger case-per-calibre develops velocities two, three, or even four hundred feet per second greater than the factory equivalent. Such speed build-ups, with attendant energy increases, must increase killing power *if* the proper bullets for the speed, and for the game, are available for use. It isn't true where the wildcat fills a clear-cut hole in the picket fence of factory game loads—as for example in the .27-.30 calibre gap filled by the 7mm short Magnums, or the opening between .30 and .375 that a good .33 or .35 fills so well until the .338 appeared, or what used to be a hole between the .224 speedballs and the older cartridges until the 6mm wildcats and later their factory equivalents came along to fill it. There is no doubt in my mind but that the confirmed rifleman would have less fun, and in all probability do his job less well, without wildcats.

And the American offbeat cartridge is a source of amazement in the other corners of this world. The shooting gentry overseas are often a frustrated lot. Their local laws, or the practice of using primers not only Berdan but also mercuric or corrosive as all foreign loads were until very recently and still are in many areas, made reloading taboo legally or impractical mechanically. The spectacle of a New Zealander trying to poke sticks of cordite down into his .22/.303 is something, believe you me. He's *really* frustrated.

This envy of the American wildcatter can be a sweeping force sometimes, arousing all manner of cupidity. I recall a frosty evening in camp at the 9000 foot level in Baluchistan, in the craggy crease of mountains two days behind Quetta and not far from the Khyber Pass country. We were hunting *gad,* as the locals call the *urial* or *shapu* style of mountain sheep, and a cliff-hanging type of goat, the long-horned *markhor.* That had been a good day, with four fine *markhor* heads collected and plenty of meat in camp, and the Baluchis, who have been potting back and forth at the Afghan tribesmen since gunpowder was invented and so revere a deadly rifle, had been goggle-eyed with the performance of the wildcat I was shooting. They'd never before watched in hunting action, a scoped rifle, shooting a moderately heavy bullet at well over 3000 foot seconds and so shooting it flat to distances beyond their belief.

Rahmatullah, the hawk-eyed *shikari* who that morning had spotted the best of the *markhor,* had seen me shoot the trophy out of its crannied hide in the rock face over three hundred yards across the canyon, came over from the campfire and made *namasta,* the sign of respect. His speech had to be translated, but when I understood he wanted to look at that wildcat rifle I gave immediate assent because I know the Baluchi would handle it like a baby, tweak no scope knob and work no bolt.

He peered through the Kollmorgen 4X and examined the weapon's every inch. When he spoke I understood without translation. He wanted to buy the wildcat rifle. Nor did he need translation of my question, "OK, what'll you give me for it?"

The Baluchi went into deep thought for a moment, then replied through the interpreter. "For this remarkable rifle would I give thee fifty fat-tailed sheep (which is a veritable fortune in that hard country) and I would also give thee my second wife."

It would have been a bad deal from his point of view perhaps. There were less than thirty cartridges left, cartridges of a type never before seen beyond Quetta and not likely to be seen ever again. It might have been a good deal from my point of view, I had no use for fifty sheep, but I had been hunting for at least six weeks and who knew what his second wife looked like behind her veils? But from anybody's point of view, it proved that a wildcat rifle can be for you a good deal in the far places.

ALLYN H. TEDMON

As a boy, the writer was no different from the boys of today who have their "heroes" who write in shooting magazines. In the old days there was a group of writers similar to the ones who are active now and among these was Allyn H. Tedmon who is still active at 78. Being one of the very last of the old timers it is fitting to present a few of his ideas in this book.

In 1878 Allyn Tedmon's parents moved from the ancestral home in nothern New York State to Colorado, where he was born in late 1884. His life has been lived in Colorado and Wyoming with the exception of several years spent in New Jersey and New York attending Prep school. He is a graduate of the Colorado A & M College. The day following his graduation he took a job riding for the old S6 Ranch at $25.00 per month; dollars then were worth 100 cents, not 30 cents as of now.

Having been well trained by his favorite ranchman – uncle, Tedmon went through about all the hard and soft phases of cowboy life as given in the wonderful paintings of the late cowboy artist Charley Russel of Montana. Firearms always interested him, but during his years of boots, silver-mounted spurs, fine saddles and forking real cow-horses, guns were tools and shooting was a mere incidental sideline. However, the bug began to bite as while even a small child he hunted chipmunks and mice with a wooden Chicago air gun, followed a bit later with a Youth's Companion premium Columbia 1000 shot model. It once even killed a pigeon. His first real gun was a .32 R. F. Stevens, followed by a .32-40; Savage Mod. 99 .303 and others. In the spring of 1915 he sent to the factory for a Mod. 99 in the then wonder rifle of the day, the .250-3000 Savage. It has the honor of being one of the first real high velocity rifles ever to hit Wyoming. He makes no claim of being a mighty hunter nor a Camp Perry champion. Fact is, he is a born Conservationist, thus he was one of the first in Colorado to join the just-born Izaak Walton League of America back about 1923; he was awarded the diamond Service badge by the IWLA, being one of the few Conservation leaders still living. He is also a member of the National Wildlife Federation, holds membership in two very active Rifle and Pistol Clubs, and is a Life Member of NRA.

Meantime, he wrote many hunting stories and articles on Conservation and led many bitter battles in the State Legislature in opposition to the annual crop of anti-gun bills. He wrote a number of western fiction stories, also a few Junior outdoor stories. The late writer and firearms expert Chauncey Thomas was one of his best loved friends and advisors.

Tedmon is deeply interested in teaching children and teenagers the safe and effective use of the rifle. He has developed at least three courses of fire planned to produce combat and game shots; sort of post graduate rifle training to follow the regular NRA bullseye, high score program. These have been published in GUNS Magazine and were originally fired and tested out by Tedmon's sons, a skilled granddaughter and two little grandsons. Our terrible loss in Korea due to lack of such training inspired the development of the programs.

In spite of losing the use of his right eye, Tedmon and his devoted wife go deer hunting every fall. He has been having a difficult time training his left eye and hand to be useful for much but rest and/or sitting shots, which in no degree compares with his to-be-envied right hand skill with the rifle. He still prefers his Savage .250-3000 with hand loads because of its high accuracy, power-for deer and the like of course—and lack of recoil and muzzle blast. And he has tried them all; that is nearly all.

P. O. Ackley

REFLECTIONS OF A RIFLEMAN - HUNTER

by
Allyn H. Tedmon

My first rifle is just over 62 years old. A Stevens Ideal Model 44, caliber .32 Rim Fire, fitted with Lyman tang sight and an ivory bead front. My folks were living in New Jersey at that time thus I knew far more about saddle horses than boats. However, I knelt in the bow while my teen-age pal handled the oars as we floated silently along the water lanes hedged in by high, brown windswept cat-tails and rushes. We presently floated out into open water and beyond sat a fat muskrat out on a point feeding. Had it been a brown bear my heart could not have pounded harder. As Cliff gently backed the oars, I loaded my new rifle, and holding my best, pressed the trigger. The rat rolled over and I was one tickled boy as I lifted it into the boat. The rifle was now "blooded", a hunting rifle, and this minute it hangs above my head, one of my most prized possessions.

This .32 R. F. rifle was very satisfactory for some years; however, one day I managed to ruin the bore with an iron cleaning rod. But we sent it in to the factory and it was rebored and chambered for the .32-40 cartridge, also a new center fire breechblock. Total charge—$6.00. The American Dollar in those days was a DOLLAR. I now had a deer rifle so a school chum and I made a deer hunt in the Adirondacks, but I didn't see a deer. Soon after that hunt my folks moved back to Colorado. Here the rifle shot grouse, rabbits, prairie dogs, coyotes and the like, all with my "hand loads" of 40 grains of FFG black powder and a 165 grain factory bullet; for deer I used the 185 grain bullet.

That fall three of us set out more for the fun of the going than getting deer but the prospects weren't very bright in spite of the fact that a few of the buckskins still survived. The pioneers had proved beyond a doubt that the deer were not going to last forever. In most areas of Colorado deer were scarcer than hens teeth; most ranchers were at the time eating beef. Fact is deer were a curiosity, so much so that I knew of a roundup rider who rode a mile out of his way to tell his pardner, who in turn whipped and spurred to the spot where he too honestly saw a deer.

We left our saddlehorses and hunted on foot and later in the day darned if we didn't by dumb luck jump 4 or 5 of the vanishing specimens in an old burn. Of course we shot at them and by good or bad luck yours truly landed a 185 grain .32-40 bullet in the proper spot and to our surprise we had ourselves a deer. My first one, by the way. That was a long time ago and meantime that little handful of deer has over the years developed into one of the State's finest herds.

Since those long gone days I have hunted deer in many places and with different men. In addition I have spent considerable time and money preaching conservation of our national resources and what I consider good sportsmanship. As to hunting companions, aside from our own two sons, the man whom I enjoyed and admired most as a hunter and fine rifle shot was an honest-to-goodness sportsman. He always did more than his share in camp and went hunting because he loved the hills, not just to "fill his license." He hunted hard to get his game and his pet rifle was a single shot Hiwall Winchester with a short barrel fitted with Lyman aperture tang sight and bead front, caliber .30-40. With two cartridges between the fingers of his left hand, for an emergency, his first shot invariable brought home his meat, deer or elk. But if he by chance didn't get a shot you never heard him bellyache and cuss the Game and Fish Department because "he hadn't filled his license."

We disliked this unsportsman motto of our present day and age "sportsmen". We had our own private opinion of hunters, and would-be hunters who seem to think that their license guarantees them a deer. In their opinion the "filling of their license" is Guaranteed, by the purchase of a license. We shunned this breed. At various times we hunted from a party camp with known members; however, we preferred our own camp including usually a friend we had converted to "fill his own license."

My Amigo and I have made our last hunt together on earth. Too many months ago the Red Gods called and he left us for the Happy Hunting Ground that lies way over West beyond the Setting Sun. As I pecked these lines no doubt he is talking ballistics with Colonel Whelen, Chauncey Thomas, E. C. Crossman, C. W. Rowland, and hunting with Theodore Roosevelt, Ed Howard, Stewart Edward White, Paul Curtis and the rest of our finest

Riflemen-Hunters who have trailed over the Great Divide. His name is Lynne Chilcote; Rifleman, Hunter and finest of Sportsmen.

The Code we hunted by specified that each hunter shall kill his own game. We didn't approve of the too common practice of one hunter killing a second or third deer to be sure his partners "license was filled." Said partner, perhaps, is like too many of our "hunters" who annually go hunting with a rented or borrowed rifle, expecting someone else to shoot a deer for them. Or possibly he is one of these fellows who own a rifle but hasn't fired a shot in the past twelve months and who couldn't hit a 5 gallon oil can at 100 yards even from a rest. Or he may be one of the breed who laugh at the thought of sighting-in a rifle; considering himself one of these natural born American Riflemen that we hear about who really don't need sights! We just didn't choose to hunt with this class of natural born wonders.

While on the subject I might mention the "fill your license" first timers who know not that they know not, but they must go. Or the sports who make a mockery of their days in camp playing poker and soaking up booze while some one clear-headed and able hunts for the camp. One such fellow in talking to me bragged that their camp always "filled their licenses." What kind of a conscience must these people have who can look you in the eye and brag that he, I "filled my license", and then add insult to injury by relating what a long shot it was and all that sort of bunk. Don't think for a minute that the above hunting camp picture applies to all deer hunter camps, far from that, but there are just enough of this type to warrant much of the complaint and disgust that too often gives our cleanest sport a bad name.

A group deer camp made up of men who go on the trip as much or more for the opportunity to be close to Nature than to get a deer is something a fellow never forgets. Such a camp can be one of the finest experiences, especially for the novice on his first hunt, that can be imagined. The spirit of such a camp is in tune with the voice of Mother Nature. The motto should not be merely just "filling your license". Sure you'd like to kill a deer, your own deer, but if you do or don't, play the game fair. Maybe better luck next year. A true sportsman should enjoy his few days in the lap of the Red Gods whether he "fills his license" or don't.

The new and old friends you will meet, especially the older experienced men of the type of my lost friend. Then there is the clean air you will breathe and the clean water you can drink; the wonders of Nature on every hand, and the valuable hints on hunting that will dominate the stories told at the campfire. These are the worthwhile lasting values that a properly conducted deer-hunter's camp surely will give you.

Don't take the exciting stories of those 500 and 600 yard shots too seriously. Fact is that most deer, even elk are shot at ranges under 100 yards, the length of the average city block. They sound good but it is a horse of a different color when it comes to the average hunter with his average iron sighted .30-30, even if it has been carefully sighted in, to connect at a measured 200 yards the first and most important shot. One is reminded how much easier it would be to make that shot, not a mere 200 yards, but at least 500 yards with a typewriter.

We should also consider the fact that most deer rifles come from the factory with the poorest sights an experienced rifleman can imagine. One deer rifle I know well, a nice rifle, is fitted with a front sight with a gob of a bead so large that it isn't possible to line it in the notch of the rear sight, it would blank out a deer at 200 yards. Only 3 or 4 rifle models that I think of are issued with factory open sights fit for deer at much over 100 yards. This is the reason men who know but like iron sights promptly replace the issue stuff with an aperture rear sight with a large aperture. We should bear in mind that the U.S. M-1 rifle won the war; the new Armed Forces rifle the M-14 and the old 1917 bolt gun, as well as the sort of funny-looking rifle the British have lately adopted all are fitted with aperture rear sights.

There are many models of fine aperture rear sights by as many makers. For hunting select a simple, sturdy model, for instance something along the line of the Redfield Model 102 or some other similar make model. Such sights are simple, adjustable for elevation and windage. Almost fool proof and ideal for the average deer hunter. A word on the front sight—we find again many very desirable models, but I suggest that a 1/16th inch bead is a good size to select for deer, but nothing smaller. Harking back to the rear aperture sight, the aperture for hunting should be not less than 1/8th inch, yet I personally much prefer it be a

3/16th and if the hunting will be in thick, dense timber a full 1/4 inch aperture is none too big. Never handicap yourself with a tiny 1/32nd or less aperture—they are made for target shooting, not hunting. I strongly advise the novice hunter to start out with a first class set of iron sights. There is no bulk to them and there is no question but what they are better suited for the beginner to learn to handle his rifle as a deer hunter must do the trick if he is to be a successful deer hunter.

Telescope sights are becoming more and more popular; they are wonderful instruments. Their greatest virtue is the fact that it is easy for even the most excited nimrod to tell a man from a rabbit or a horse. I use scope sights because my eyes, not 18 years old any more, can use the brightness of my K3 Weaver when climbing the hills of the Mowitches. However, if my eyes were up to it, I would much prefer a set of top iron sights, they are so much handier, and a bit lighter. The 4X scope seems to be the best all around bet right now, but I still prefer K3 less magnification for the larger field. For open plains country there is the 6X, a grand sight but in the timber the field I find too small for anything but standing shots. Hunting scopes are nothing new. Many buffalo hunters used full-length scopes on their big Remingtons and Sharps .45 and .50 caliber rifles. The old J. Stevens Arms and Tool Co., also Malcolm made 3X hunting scopes at least 50 years ago. Stevens especially lists an internal adjustable hunting scope at around 50 years ago. Ed Howard the North Park, Colorado, noted rifleman used many of the long tube (as compared to our present day models) 4X and 6X Malcolms for hunting antelope, coyotes, wolves and deer. My first scope was a Stevens #438 that I got over 40 years ago on a Stevens 44 1/2 Model in the .25-20 Single Shot caliber. As Ed Howard would put it, that combination "killed a wagon load" of prairie dogs, jackrabbits and the like.

Any rifle is a deer rifle; that is to say that deer have been killed with most all calibers from the .22 R.F. up through the .25-20, .32-20, .38-40, .44-40 and so on. However, in this day and age in speaking of a deer rife, the rifle usually referred to is the .30-30, .32 Special, .300 Savage, .303 Savage and others. Marlin now makes their handy Model 336 for the fine .35 Remington, which for my money is one of the best and most reliable game cartridges we have. Its 200 grain bullet is a good killer, even on elk. While many elk are killed with the .30-30, it usually takes several hits to do the job; it doesn't compare with the .300 Savage. The original load of the .303 Savage killed a host of elk with its 195 grain bullet. Then there is the .33 Winchester, almost a duplicate of the .35 Remington, but Progress replaced it with the .348 Winchester. The old Model '95 Winchester in .30-40 caliber is a real deer or elk gun. With its 220 grain bullet and mild recoil it is a real hunting rifle in any man's language; so is the old Krag in same reliable .30-40 caliber. But today you must have a magnum!

Now all magnums have RECOIL, and hardly one hunter in ten has had proper training to handle it. A lot of these fellows are kidding themselves when they think they can handle a lightweight .30-06 Sporter without flinching and yanking the trigger. Could be but that ain't the way I heard it. On the average the .30-06 is too much gun for the untrained hunter; however, it can be hand-loaded down to about what the .30-40 is. As loaded with the 180 grain ball it too often spoils too much venison to suit me. I have two good Springfields but of late years I shoot the 06 so seldom that my unhardened left shoulder doesn't relish that non-magnum recoil. I prefer any of those mentioned above, or a .257 Roberts, .250 Savage, or .243 Winchester, for deer. The finest Springfield Sporter ever built, for use, not for beauty, is the Whelen model built at the Springfield Arsenal back in the '20s. I have a friend who inherited one of these fine rifles, weighs about 8 1/2 pounds, Lyman #48 rear sight, with the limited trigger training I have taught him, he doesn't flinch and yank the trigger with any loads. Learn trigger squeeze, that's the answer.

And now a line for you recoil flinchers, and I'm aiming at you one-box-per-annum deer hunters. The one box, if fired, is usually fired in the direction of the first game you see, rather than at a practice target a few days before season opens. The best investment you jerkers can make is a good .22 rim fire rifle with same type sights and model as your deer rifle, if possible. During the year shoot up at least one carton—500 rounds—of either .22 Short or Long Rifle ammo. Get a National Rifle Association booklet that will give you the low down on both trigger release; generally called trigger squeeze, and the proper positions used when firing a rifle. Prone position is about useless in the field, thus practice sitting, kneeling and standing. Use a rest of some kind until you can squeeze the trigger as you must learn to do. By now you may need another carton of ammo to sight in your rifle and do this at about 50 feet; use inch and a half bullseye. As season comes along replace the paper bullseyes with small juice cans filled with water. They are not so easy to hit as you may think and you will get a kick out of seeing the water and can go UP; especially if you use Long Rifle ammo. Now put a box of ammo through your deer rifle at 50 yards as explained, inch and a half above the tip of the front sight, and you are ready to go. Condensed milk cans filled with water at 50 yards—or even average tomato cans—will add a kick to this shooting, too.

Back to deer rifles, for you fellows who lose sleep dreading that '06 recoil, I suggest that you do some trading and get yourself one of the three following rifles, a .257 Roberts bolt action; a .250-3000 Savage in either bolt or lever action using 100 grain bullet or a Winchester .243 bolt or lever, also 100 grain bullet. And I'll add one more to the list, a .270 Winchester bolt. These are all fine deer rifles, all near 3000 feet velocity, fine accuracy and comfortable recoil.

In the East, especially, there are yet probably hundreds of Savage Mod. 99, Marlin Mod. 93 and Winchester Mod. 94 sticking around in the .32-40 and .38-55 calibers. These cartridges were also good deer rifles even in black powder days, and in their high-velocity loadings, also the Savage .303, they were the equal of the now popular .32 Special or the .30-30. Because the factories discontinued the high velocity loads in these calibers, there is no earthly reason why good hand loads can't be built and used in any of these old rifles that are yet in good sound condition. Especially check the old Winchester and Marlins carefully, also give the old model '99 Savage a good cleaning but if they have had any care they'll be perfectly safe. A friend, now gone beyond, had an *old* .32 Special model 94 Winchester that was so worn as to drop most of its primers, and yet he killed an elk with it, using 7 or 8 cartridges. When hunting with him, as I often did, I kept at a safe distance when he started firing. Fine fellow. T'was back in the 30s when pennies were scarce and he needed meat, but the rickety old .32 Special just couldn't hit them. Thus before the old wreck came apart I admit that I helped him out with my .45-70 HiVelocity. And by the way, if you want a real rifle and will limit your typewriter shots to 150 yards, just clamp onto a light-weight Winchester model 1886 in .45-70 caliber and use the Hi-Velocity load. A very satisfactory all around rifle—deer or elk.

The rifle you will use on your hunt should have its sights checked, especially if it has issue open sights. It may shoot 6 inches high and 3 or 4 inches to right or left. This test shooting must be done by you, because a rifle with iron sights set for one man almost without exception won't be set correct for your friend. No two humans see the sights the same; don't even hold the rifle the same. Be sure to use the identical ammunition that you will use on your hunt. In setting the sights use a rest of some kind—this is imperative. Also use a big bullseye, say 4 inches, so you are sure to see where and how you are holding. 50 yards is a good distance and remember that your bullets must hit above your aiming point to correct for trajectory. Hold the tip of the front sight just touching the bottom edge of the bullseye. To adjust the sights if you don't happen to know, move the rear sight in the direction you want the shot to go. If to right move sight right; if left, move left. Move the front sight opposite to the direction you want the bullet to go. Raise rear sight to shoot higher, lower it to hit lower. A too high front sight makes rifle hit low; if too low rifle will hit high.

Now rest the rifle over a rolled blanket and as suggested hold the front sight just touching bottom edge of bullseye. Fire 3 shots. They should be on the bull someplace. Now move your sights if necessary, and it probably will be—shooting at 50 yards remember and a .30-30 or similar caliber—then shoot 3 more shots. You should have a group and this group should be located approximately 1 1/2 inches *above* the edge of the bull where you held your front sight. The rifle will now be set for you to hit about on the button at 150 yards. So set you will be able to aim at a deer the same way (no sight changes) from 25 yards out to 150 yards and make a hit, provided you do your part and HOLD. Always take the shot from the steadiest position you can get into; rest rifle over log, arm against a tree. Always sit down if possible. Now the forgoing is for rifles with approximately 2000 fps (feet per second) velocity. If your rifle has a velocity of around 3000 fps, a 250 Savage for instance or .243 Winchester, your 50 yard group should land about one inch, or a bit more at your 50 yard range. So sighted these higher velocity rifles will "shoot flat" as we sometimes refer to the trajectory, out to 200 yards or maybe a little more. Is that all clear? With the 30-30 your "danger zone" is 25 to 150 yards; with the .257 Roberts this "danger zone" will be from 25 to 200 yards plus; this of course applies to the .243 Winchester, .250 Savage and other high velocity cartridges, and assumes that you will accept the fact that 150 yards and 200 yards are the approximate limits for shots on deer by the average hunter with the class of rifles as listed above.

Again to prove that highly trained riflemen do not make a practice of making "500 yard shots"; typewriter shots I call them; every shot they take, I am taking the liberty to give you here the record of my life-long ranchman friend Clarence Currie. A couple of years ago, don't have date here so it may not be, he kept a record of a succession of one shot kills he made preparatory to his entry in the annual One Shot Antelope Hunt so noted at Lander, Wyoming. The list runs—

With .30-06-180, Model 70 Winchester, 4X scope:
    One antelope, 200 yards.
    One elk, 200 yards.
    One deer, close to 400 yards (an exceptionally long shot)
With .218 Bee Winchester Model 43; 4X scope:
    One bobcat, running at 150 yards.
    One coyote, 217 yards.
    One coyote, 150 yards.
    One magpie, 100 yards.

The antelope really should have been listed last as it was the shot that won him honors at that year's One Shot Antelope Hunt. And how did he get that way? Well, as a member of the old Livermore Rifle Club he fired and qualified in all the National Rifle Association smallbore and .30 caliber programs. One year he and a friend won the Two-man team match, national event. He was determined to become a trained rifleman. He is also a widely experienced hunter in the USA, Africa and India. He is a 100% American-Hunter. The dream and untiring effort of our late Colonel Townsend Whelen; the Dean of all American Riflemen.

As regards to the necessity of having to make 400 or 500 shots at game—and I am not here including our scientific woodchuck hunters such as the late Ned Roberts, Harvey Donaldson and the few others to whom we owe so much for our present high velocity, super accurate rifles—when my friend returned from his first African Safari I asked him what his average shot was on all game from the little Dik-dik to buffalo. What is your guess after having probably read some of the bunk that has been written on the subject? You are wrong. After careful thought as we walked slowly past the contents of his trophy room he replied. "Why, I'd say my average shot was about 125 yards!" And this was in Africa where you shoot bumblebees at 600 yards or they aren't dead. His longest shot was 200 on his buffalo with a .470 English double rifle. His first shot did not finish the tough old buff, so he quickly dropped in a second, that did the business, using his knowledge of the trajectory of the big gun to estimate the necessary holdover. He and his White Hunter paced the distance; no guessing with a real Rifleman.

If you would like more on actual game ranges from men who do not guess, read Stewart Edward White's books covering his several African hunts; he used a specially stocked .30-06 Springfield, and a .405 Winchester, both fitted with Lyman's best rear aperture sights. Again read the late President Theodore Roosevelt's books starting way back in the black powder age with a .40-90 Sharps. This was followed with a beautiful .45-75 Winchester Model 1876; this one was followed with a .45-90 Winchester Model 1886 that he became very fond of; a great game rifle. On his last big hunt in Africa his battery consisted of a specially stocked and sighted .30-06 Springfield, a .405 Winchester and a beautiful English big bore double rifle, Rigby or Holland and Holland, doesn't matter, a gift of a number of prominent English gentlemen. Stewart Edward White has long been listed as perhaps the finest rifle shot ever to hunt in Africa. My friend Clarence Currie was a revelation to the White Hunters who ran his Safaris as a tip top rifleman; he used the .30-06 in both a Remington that was lost in a fire, and his Model 70 Winchester, with a .218 Bee Winchester as a light rifle; he rented the double rifle he used as such a weapon is useless for our game. Were my friend Chilcote only here, he could give you some figures to conjure with.

My favorite rifle for deer where we hunt is a Model 99 Savage fitted with a K3 Weaver scope, and in .250-3000 caliber. I now have two of these .250 rifles, one I got in 1915, and the other is a couple of years old. Got my first Model 99, a .303, nearly 60 years ago; meantime I had several others, two in .250, one a .38-55 and another in .303. I load most of my .250 ammo and the deer load I use gives a 100 grain bullet around 2900 fps. It is a killer from the headwaters and the outfit is accurate and it is very seldom that my bullet doesn't drive in where the crosshairs were held. Our younger son is far above average and he has killed numerous deer with his .250, iron sights; Lyman tang rear aperture. He shoots my handloads mostly but often he has only factory in his belt, but with few exceptions the first shot was the last, regardless which of us made the shot.

We have shot the Mowitches out to around 200 yards, but our average will run from 60 or 70 to 150 yards. Our elder son has a .257 Roberts in an action he liberated in Europe back in 1945. He has a 6X Weaver scope on his rifle and the outfit is accurate and about like our .250s, only a little more so. We try to select our shots and if the offering is too risky we pass it up. For instance last fall Mrs. Tedmon located a little herd of buckskins. We sat concealed from their view for quite some time—there were at least 15 or 20 in the bunch—when presently three headed in our direction, feeding as they came. Finally they had decided to just monkey around, nibble here and there, then started back to the bunch. They were between 300 and 400 yards of where we sat. The closest one looked big, in the scope, but I refused the shot and after they had returned to their starting place I told the chief observer that I was positive that they were well over 300 yards away. She didn't agree and thought I should have fired. When I paced the distance the closest animal was well over 300 *long* paces, and I made them long to be sure not to kid myself. The other two, beyond the one mentioned were over 400 *long* paces; clear out of range for my money; in other words off limits for our code of ethics. I could easily have hit that closest buckskin, I am sure, but there was a chance of my hold being off a few inches which would mean a wounded innocent, and nothing ruins a hunt and sickens me like the sight of a suffering Mowitch that can't be, or just isn't run down and must linger on, waiting for the coming of the Red Gods of the Rockies to end the flaming fever with a merciful death.

The next day, as I prowled silently along through the jumble of spruces, pines and buttresses of red granite, of a sudden I glimpsed the vanishing form of a delicately stepping deer as the alert animal vanished from view. Not long after this I walked onto the body of a beautiful doe, the victim, no doubt of some long-range obsessed thutty-thutty nimrod, or maybe a proud owner of a magnum something or other that he couldn't handle. The beautiful trophy was now mere coyote bait.

The following are a few thoughts that come to mind. Shoot your own rifle when sighting in. Be sure the ammunition you have to use fits your rifle; better run it all through the chamber and check before getting to camp. I repeat, don't rely on the safety alone. Bear this in mind. SAFETY spells YOU. Let the other guy load himself down with a .45 magnum belt gun. You have your rifle, what more do you need? Your hunting knife, to be safe, should hang on the back of your belt. A small belt ax can come in very handy if you are hunting in strange timber country. In your pants pocket carry a good sized jacknife, a folding screwdriver, a small sharpening stone, a filled waterproof match safe and above all a good best you can get thong pull-through to clear a snow-filled barrel.

For preseason practice use a .22 caliber rifle of the same type as your deer rifle if possible; at least the same kind of sights. Shoot up at least one carton (500 rounds) of ammunition, sitting, standing and also kneeling; range 50 yards using 100 yard size bullseye. Remember that the placement of the shot is more important than the caliber you use. Again your first shot must be good, don't expect the game to run into the wild second one. The best thing you can do is to join a National Rifle Association Small-bore rifle club. I'm sure there is one near your home area. The Club will teach you proper positions and more important proper trigger squeeze. Practice safe handling of your rifle, EMPTY of course—and be sure it is empty. Attend the Firearms Safety Programs, promoted by the NRA, that are being held in every state in the Union. Very likely there will be one or more in your community, check at the High School and also phone your area Conservation Officer. Don't miss this almost costless opportunity. For in-the-house-practice in firing nothing beats the BB Air Gun the kid son has been pestering you for. The range is 15 feet and at 15 feet these guns are plenty accurate. Stuff a carton full of newspaper to catch the little balls. The whole family can benefit from this sport. Write the Daisy or Benjamin Air Gun Companies for full information. You'll see their ads in all shooting magazines.

Never risk a shot at a deer unless you are dead sure it is a deer. Really you know that a cow, or rabbit, or man or horse doesn't look like a deer. Yet every year at least a couple of dozen humans are shot and sometimes killed, and the only alibi the shooter has is that: "I thought it was a deer!" If you do see a deer, and it is a deer, don't start shooting unless you know you have a good chance for a hit in the chest cavity. If you should hit a deer and just wound it make every possible effort, get help if necessary, to track it down and put it out of its misery. If you kill a deer and as now and then happens some stranger beats you to it and claims it, don't be bluffed. Stand your ground and if you are man enough, physically, beat the stuffing out of the stinker. In any event get his car license and report to your Conservation Officer as soon as possible so the crook can be grabbed at the checking station. Always get permission to hunt on privately owned land, and read carefully your game laws and abide by them because they have been written for your own good. The Public owns the game and as you are a part of the Public your license proves that you are cooperating in the protection of your own property. Be a good Sportsman and leave a clean camp. Play the game fair to all so that your hunt will be one that you will be proud to keep long in memory.

AFRICA SAFARI

There isn't anything particularly out of the ordinary in undertaking an African big game hunt these days. Several thousand well-heeled Americans make this turn-around every year. But when a man over seventy years of age makes a hunt it is something for all of us to admire, especially when this man is John Buhmiller, retired gunsmith and rifle barrel maker of Kalispel, Montana.

But Buhmiller played the hunt a bit differently than the average American big game hunter. When he went to Africa, he went to live with a white settler, an Englishman who was farming some miles outside Arusha. The elephant herds were raiding this man's crops. So bold had the giant pachyderms grown that it looked as if he would not harvest any crops at all that year. The only way you can dissuade an elephant band from nightly raids on the fields of maize is to shoot 'em up. The tuskers take the hint quickly after that and will move 50 miles before daybreak.

Buhmiller had paid the necessary license fees to shoot two bull tuskers. Safari hunters are permitted only two elephants per year. He shot both these bulls to help his farmer friend. Before he had completed his thirty day safari, however, other herds were trampling fences and destroying the remainder of the harvest.

"Won't the game department send someone in here to shoot up these scalawags and so give you some relief?" the Montanan asked his English host. "Yes," the settler explained, "but right now the bloody department has all its bloody hunters doing control against the tsetse over in the Lake Victoria country. My crops will be gone before they get back."

"I'll tell you what I'll do," Buhmiller offered. "You go see the game department people and tell them I'll shoot these raiding Tembo. I will stick around for the next three months and not only shoot up these elephant raiding you, but help out your neighbors, too."

Let it be explained that bashing in elephants is not only hard work, but it is also dirty, tiring labor and exceedingly dangerous. Elephants are shot at 60 feet and when you get up that close to the world's largest land animal, you can get into some exceedingly sticky situations. Beyond this, the successful spooring of the game involves miles and miles of slogging foot work. There is a saying that it costs a mile of foot marching for every pound of ivory. That is to say, that if you kill a bull with 75 pounds of ivory, you have put in 75 miles of tough spooring to come up with him.

In Tanganyika, where Buhmiller has hunted exclusively, the herds have been shot up for years in attempts to drive them out of the farming country. The game gets wise quickly that a hunting party is on its tail. When they are sure of this, every animal in the herd grows doubly alert and a vast anger surges through the mob. Most dangerous of all are the cows, especially those old matrons with calves at heel. These will charge on slightest provocation. Much of the information from Mr. Buhmiller has been sent to the author in personal visits and letters over the period of years since Mr. Buhmiller made his first trip to Africa. Excerpts of some of this material are as follows:

> In 1955 I met a farmer in East Africa who invited me to stay at his farm on my next trip over. He is in good game country, and would welcome some help in pest and varmint control.
>
> The last details of this trip were arranged by short wave radio since he is a "ham". He suggests that I arrive there the latter part of April, during the last of the rains to see and photograph a green Africa. The rains which come mostly during the night, would interfere but little with my activities during the day.
>
> I left Kalispell by plane April 20th; left New York the 22nd on the French Line, arriving at Nairobi the 24th, after making stops at Paris and Tripoli. No safaris are out during the rains, so I looked up some of the Hunters there, to get an ear

full of this and that. Saw Allan Tarleton and his snakes, Eric Rundgreen, the bow and arrow elephant guide, Tony Dyer, etc., arriving at the farm late the 26th. Roads were washed out and we went the last 100 miles by jeep, the last 10 miles accompanied by a tractor and a gang of natives in case we got stuck.

Normally the rains end about the first of May. This year they continued into June. We had up to six inches of rain in one night and at times I wondered if my room, made of sticks and mud, would wash entirely away. Mosquitoes came by the millions; also tsetse flies. These mosquitoes carry malaria, and everybody takes preventative medicine, and there is an occasional case of sleeping sickness—but the hunting was good.

Almost under the equator, the temperature was pleasant, mostly around 70-76, this being their "winter" time. August they say is their coolest month. Nearly every kind of farm crop and garden vegetable will grow at a fantastic rate during this wet season. I saw more flowers on one farm than is often seen outside of California. Here the main crops are maize (our common corn), beans, papayas, which are tapped, and dried juice being exported to the U.S. for making meat tenderizer; chili peppers, peanuts, etc. Most farmers are setting out coffee plants, which take 5 to 6 years to begin bearing.

Each farm employs about 40 to 50 natives, who perform all the labor. They are paid about 1 shilling a day (14c our money), for common labor and about 3 shillings for a caterpillar operator, plus a bonus at the end of the month if full time has been worked. They also get a daily portion of posho (corn meal) and meat, preferably buffalo but they will eat a few varieties of plains game, providing the throat has been properly cut before the animal was dead. These natives will not eat elephants or rhino, as they will in South Africa.

On my arrival, Fundi, a native guide was assigned to my service. He knew about a dozen words in English, I knew about that many in Swahili, but we would make out. He could not have a gun, but could carry mine, and any other items we might need. We always took off at daybreak without breakfast and would be gone until noon or later, when we would come in to eat and rest up for another jaunt in the evening. All hunting was done on foot. We sometimes used a truck to take us to the vicinity of our day's hunting to save so much walking. This area being largely made up of heavy bush and dense cover, it was deemed advisable to carry my own gun at all times, as a mad buffalo or a rhino, might charge unexpectedly at close range.

Fundi was good on elephants, and he loved to hunt them. He always found it difficult to pass by a fresh elephant trail. Many times we followed where we did not expect to shoot, just for the fun of it, and if the wind were favorable we might sneak around and through a herd for an hour or two, just watching them, and looking for a big bull. But the buffalo was my main interest, and we were expected to keep the farm boys supplied with meat. At times the buffalo would move out of the district for a few days, then we had to shoot zebras or something else.

The elephant is probably the worst varmint, from the standpoint of the farmer. They go in herds up to 50 or more, and what such a horde will do to a farmer's crops in one night is appalling. The farmers shoot them up, whenever they are caught too near the cultivated fields to give them a hint they are not wanted there. Tembo is an intelligent animal and will learn—the hard way.

The natives' pet dislike is the rhino. He has a habit of sleeping in the high grass, and during the rains we were continually running into them. They wake up in a bad mood, snort and mill around. If you stand still, he will finally run away. A couple of times I waved my cap and yelled "come and get it" but he didn't understand. On encountering one, the native always recoils—jumps backwards. You can always know he has either seen a rhino or almost stepped on a snake. (The sight of buffalo or an elephant will not do it.) When a sleeping rhino has been sighted he will want it shot immediately, or make a quiet detour. We would usually make a compromise by whistling it up, then stand still to watch its antics before taking off. Most natives will not walk through a rhino area without protection. It is seldom that a rhino has to be shot. He can nearly always be avoided. A shot fired at a buffalo would sometimes put a nearby rhino on a rampage. He might come tearing through the brush, straight towards the source of the sound. This happened to us two times. Once we dodged behind a thick clump of small trees which stopped him. The next time there was only brush. I drew a deadline at the edge of the brush about fifteen feet distant. If he came past that, he'd "get it" and he did. He crumpled and was dead within his length. There were four natives behind me that time and fifteen feet is too close for comfort. The rhino's nuisance value lies mostly in his propensity for scaring the daylights out of the natives, or he may charge your car if he happens along a farm road. Being a browser, he doesn't bother crops too much.

Probably the worst farm pest are the baboons. They travel in gangs of fity or more, have a great liking for corn when the grains are still soft, and have enough intelligence to make them difficult to deal with. He soon learns the minimum safe distance from a rifle. What is needed is a good 400 yard varmint rifle. We did some good work on them a few evenings, just before dark, with buckshot under their roosting trees. A baboon will eat his fill, then when leaving can carry a surprising number of ears with him in his mouth, hands and feet.

We were located about 30 miles from the post office and the roads are poor. It is customary for boys from different farms to take turns walking after the mail. It would then be passed along from one farm to the next until it would eventually arrive.

There are plenty of snakes in the area, including some of the world's most venomous, such as the cobra, black mamba and puff adder, also, the python. Several snakes were encountered, but nobody was bitten. They always seemed most interested in getting away.

The real purpose of this shooting trip was to test out the killing power of some rifles that I had made up. There is much controversy regarding the proper rifles for African use. I wanted actual first hand knowledge on the subject. I had made up and sent over by boat, a .378 Weatherby, .416 Rigby, .450 Magnum (using Norma cylindrical brass, 90 gr.

4320 powder and 500 gr. Barnes heavy jacketed bullets), 45-Weatherby (378 case opened up to .45 calibre, 100 gr. 4320, 500 gr. Barnes bullets), and a .505 Gibbs. There was a lot of difficulty and delay in getting these guns through the customs. The first five weeks I had to use a .458 rifle that I had sent over the year before. Then I received the .450 Magnum and the .45 Weatherby. The .378 had not been released by the customs at the time I left the country and the .505 ammunition was not released in time to use that gun, so these two calibres were not tried at all.

The .458 rifle proved to be very satisfactory, completely adequate for elephant and rhino. The buffalo is the tough one of the lot, in this area of heavy brush, one needs all the power possible for quick kills, and we found the .450 Magnum and the .45 Weatherby gave a large percentage of one shot kills. They were undoubtedly slightly better killers on buffalo than the .458. The Barnes soft points, with the heavy loads of 4320 powder at times would break up to some extent, but the penetration was good, and we also had .458 factory soft points break up in buffalo. Maybe too much has been said about bullets breaking up, as long as they kill satisfactorily, what does it matter?

The .416 saw little use. It was used on one each buffalo, rhino, and elephant, killing OK. It does not have the smashing power of the .45 Magnums, which may be needed in thick cover. For more open shooting many would prefer the .416.

Should there ever be occasion to make up another rifle for use in this same area, based on the experience gained on this trip, I would be inclined to favor the .450 Magnum using the full length Norma case. I saw little if any difference in the killing effects between this cartridge and the .45 Weatherby, and the Norma case is cheaper, easier to make up, and magazine capacity is greater. Also it will work nicely in a FN Mauser action, which will make up into a lighter gun than will a Brevex, and does not require a hand made stock. I would make the gun as light as practicable, with muzzle brake and would be tempted to make the barrel 22" length. All my guns on this trip were on Brevex actions, which are made at the factory with so little extractor clearance in the receiver ring that the bolt will not close on a cartridge loaded into chamber ahead of the bolt. I was fully aware of this, and considered it a serious affair, but thought that I would be very careful and avoid trouble. Two times it happened: once I had to go to the house from 6 miles out to poke a shell out the chamber as I had forgotten my little drop weight that belonged in my pocket. The other time I was dodging a wounded elephant in the brush with a similar jam.

I will never again go after dangerous game with a gun having this defect. Extractor clearance *can* be ground out in there with a hand Dumore grinder and pointed wheels mounted on long shanks. It takes a lot of awkward tedious grinding, but it can be done. The extractor can then best be modified for easy slipping over the shell rim, by building up a greater thickness on the claw portion, by brazing on a thin shim, about 1/32 inch thick on the forward end of the extractor, then a good long slope can be ground on this increased thickness, which will slip over the shell rim without effort, but a corresponding notch will have to be cut in the barrel breech to admit this additional length on the extractor. Do not cut into the chamber, but make a sloping cut from the edge of the chamber tapering to greater depth towards the outside.

The Pike instantly detachable scope mounts worked perfectly, and proved to be very useful for buffalo or elephant in dense brush or very close, where a scope would be too slow, the scope is carried in pocket. For other shots in brush farther distant where visibility is poor, the scope goes on instantly, and vision is clear and distinct. The .458 and the .450 Magnum were fitted with open V-type iron sights only. When sighting-in these rifles I was surprised that I could seem to make better targets with this type of sight than I could with a peep rear. For the quickest, close range shooting, there is no doubt in my mind that an open rear sight is quicker than any peep, and for the long shots that one often has to take, I found the open sights worked well enough. I wonder at times if we have been so loaded with propaganda on the peep sight that we have become prejudiced against the open sight and blinded to its virtues. Based on the killing of more than 50 head of big game—buffaloes and larger—the 45's make a very adequate and desirable arm for the largest game.

While the soft point bullets would at times break up to some extent on buffalo, these same heavy jacket bullets would barely open up at all on such game as wildbeast or zebra. I think this goes to show that the buffalo is really a tough animal. He is classed as "thick-skinned" animal, and I noted many times that the skin on his neck was fully an inch thick— as Fundi wielded his long knife. When shooting the lighter skinned animals for meat to feed the boys, two animals could be killed with one shot, by getting them properly lined up. We did it twice, and the bullet went completely through both animals each time.

As for close calls, which we read so much of in the magazines—to the disgust of those who know better, we didn't have any. When you are hunting alone with a native guide, you are on your own; there is no white hunter's gun to give protection. If some animal should attack you know that you must keep cool and shoot straight.

A rhino can nearly always be avoided. Allan Tarleton stated that in his 38 years of hunting he has had to shoot just one rhino. An elephant may let on that he is going to charge, and be only bluffing. We were charged by one unwounded buffalo, and he had to be killed. A wounded buffalo will usually charge a hunter if he gets careless, but one can avoid foolhardy risks. When a buffalo does come, he is not fooling, and somebody is going to get hurt unless he is shot down. Once two rhinos chased our Jeep for a quarter mile or more, most likely just curious. This area seems to have an unusual number of rhinos. At one time we had nine of them in sight. Our most upsetting experience was while hunting hippos in a native dug-out canoe. We knew one was very near the boat, when suddenly there was a snort, he ripped the boat with his teeth and spilled all five of us overboard. Later, after the comical aspect wore off, we were glad that no one had felt his teeth. We took the hint and quit for the day.

The following letter received from Mr. Buhmiller should also be of great interest to hunters contemplating a trip to Africa.

Dear Ackley:

A little low on ambition due to the hot weather. Am still playing with the big wildcats. The man who says wildcats are a waste of time, is partly right—at least for the man who spends the time and bullets to find out things, but experimenters learn things and eventually the factories feel compelled to make improvements. Just look at the English array of cartridges for big game; they remain today the same velocity and bullet weight as when designed many years ago; then scan some of the latest developments here, with the same calibres.

Since Africa is, and has been the greatest game field the world has ever known, one in my business might naturally turn to that direction seeking a market for guns, to offset the declining market here at home.

On my three months shooting trip last year, I had the opportunity to try out various .45 calibre rifles on game, and as a result of my experiences I naturally got ideas, and having complete facilities for making up experimental guns, and for testing them. I find myself continuing in the interesting game which I began nearly sixty years ago, when I made up my first gun, which was ignited with a match and firecracker fuse.

You will recall, that I sent various guns to Africa by ship, which I wanted to try out. A .450 Magnum, probably identical with the .450 Ackley Magnum, or nearly so, a .450 Magnum on the .378 Weatherby case, a .378 Weatherby, (which for some obscure reason was never passed through the customs, but was ordered returned to me on leaving Africa). I have now received it back badly rusted and pitted in the bore, from 14 months exposure to salt air. A .505 Gibbs which was never used due to delay in receiving the ammunition from England, and a .416 Rigby. For the first five or six weeks, I had to use a borrowed .458 rifle that I had made up and sent over the year before.

Now after using the three .45 calibre rifles and the .416, I was bound to get some impressions, and it would be strange indeed were I to make a return trip to the same area, and use any of the same guns without some changes.

The .458 was a very lucky gun for me. After carrying it for probably an average of ten miles a day for several weeks, I pondered that it could have been a bit lighter. After the .45 Weatherby was received, it was my constant companion, only slightly heavier than the .458 due to lighter weight wood in the stock. It gave a feeling of confidence, when hunting in dense brush. The load used was 100 gr. 4320 and Barnes 500 gr. bullet. It was a good killer but I wished many times that some one else could carry it for me, but I didn't dare due to the thick cover we so frequently encountered.

The calibre that one should use depends on so many things, that it might be most anything from a small American calibre, to the heaviest big bore obtainable. When shooting the smaller game, most any rifle suitable for deer will answer, and there is a lot of this shooting in Africa. Baboons and warthogs are pests, and are much detested. They become numerous, when the balance of nature has been upset by killing off too many leopards. They are wild and tough. A small calibre rifle will produce more bloody trails than carcasses. Then there are the larger varieties of common plains game. The .416 was effective and deadly on wildebeeste and zebra at long ranges when the natives needed meat and buffalo were not available. The real test of killing power on big game is quite generally conceded to be judged by the effect on the Cape Buffalo. Elephants topple quite easily from brain shots, Rhinos are not too hard to handle, but old Mbogo is tough. A brain shot will put him down in his tracks, of course, but his head is so well protected by the drooping horns on each side, the heavy armored boss on top, and his habit of holding his nose up in front, that a brain shot is very seldom possible. A shot in the spine may put him down, but most likely he will be up again instantly. Otherwise, I have never known one to go down when shot. The most deadly usual shot, from broadside, in the shoulder, slightly high, gets him down in 50 yards or less with a potent .450 calibre rifle. I doubt if the most powerful rifle would put him down in his tracks from shock alone, barring a hit in the spinal column.

Therefore, I wonder if there is any point in using anything heavier than a .458. This calibre will most certainly puncture his bones and lungs, with proper bullets, then it is only a question of minutes until he is finished. There is, however, the chance of a charge at an unexpected time, and *then* one would want all the power possible.

The .45's performed so well on the Big Stuff, that my .416 was completely neglected except for the smaller game, which was shot at the longer ranges. It was great for baboons, which were usually about 300 yards distant. If it could have been about 3 pounds lighter—it weighed about 11 pounds with scope—it would have been very popular. Before leaving for home, I felt compelled to give this gun a try, and it took one elephant, one rhino, each at about 125 yards, almost unheard of in Africa, and one buffalo. Very nice work. I cannot say that it was in any way inferior to a .450. Load used, 105 grains 4831, 400 gr. Barnes bullet, velocity on my chronograph, 2400 fs.

Since my return, I have taken the .300 Magnum Norma unformed cylindrical cases, necked to .423" (this is the so-called .404 Jeffrey calibre) and have chambered several barrels for this cartridge, with some variations, in length of body, degree of taper, and amount of belt in chamber, and have gotten velocities of 2600 and 2700 fs with the 400 gr. bullet. This is in a cartridge that can be used in the regular FN Magnum action. This outclasses the performance of the .416 Rigby cartridge by a considerable margin. Most persons making up a .416 rifle, use the Brevex Magnum action, which is expensive and heavy, and this makes necessary a special stock, since a regular Mauser will not fit by a mile. If one should want a cannon in this calibre I used the .378 Weatherby shell opened up to .423, most of the taper and belt removed for maximum powder capacity, getting with 125 grs. 4831 and 400 gr. bullet, and 120 grs. 4320 and 300 gr. bullets—just altogether too much velocity. 120 gr. 4831-500 gr. Barnes bullet, about 2700 fs. velocity. This figures eight thousand foot pounds energy, and this heavy jacket bullet, no doubt would stand up well under this velocity, on a broadside shot at buffalo. I wish I could try it, maybe next year. The 400 and 300 gr. bullets could be loaded down, and this would be no mean all around rifle for the man who wants to lug around only one gun. Regardless of what writers will tell you, an old woodchuck hunter, or 1000 yard Wimbledon shooter, will see many chances for long shots in Africa. Many times it is only sensible to take them. One of these .423's would be rather incomparable for this sort of thing. Ever notice how the velocity and energy drop off in the big bores out beyond 100 and 200 yards? This 500 gr. .423 is terrifically long, it would have killing power way out there.

The .45 Weatherby will soon cease to be a wildcat. It will be brought out as a regular factory calibre, to be known as the "460 Weatherby Magnum", and I can most heartily recommend it. It can be loaded with a case full of 4350 powder, and the 500 gr. Barnes or 480 Kynoch bullet, for a velocity of 2650 or 2700 fs and an energy beyond the 600 Nitro Express, but you can load it down some for less recoil and perfect killing power on the biggest game when shot under normal conditions. My working load was 100 grs. 4320, 500 gr. bullet. Outside of some special emergency, nothing more is needed, but you can carry a couple of blockbusters in your pocket just in case.

On a regular safari, one will be under the care and protection of a White Hunter. He can carry whatever calibre rifle he wishes, (but not under .375 calibre for large game in some countries). His every move will be watched, and if danger threatens will be protected. He can to a large extent choose the calibre rifle he wishes to use, but if he does use a .375 most likely his white hunter will do most of his big game killing—after he fires the first shot.

I find here in America, a terrific allergy to recoil in rifles. Before attempting to use the big bores, it is necessary to become used to the recoil of the heavier guns. Get something like a .458, load it down at first, get used to shooting, gradually load it heavier, until you can shoot it standing, and sitting without discomfort. Finally, use a few 600 gr. loads, when you can hit with it at 100 yards, you can tackle game with it. You will then realize that the alleged terrific recoil of a .30/06 and the .375 are purely comparative, and largely due to lack of familiarity and hardening of the shoulder. A muzzle brake reduces the thrust on the shoulder from 40 to 60%, due to the calibre, weight of bullet and velocity. Many shooters object to the muzzle blast, however, and you will have to make a try to decide which you prefer—less recoil with more noise, or, just plain heavy recoil. You don't notice it as a usual thing when firing at African game.

The question often comes up regarding a cheaper safari. There is no law, that I know of, requiring one to engage the services of a White Hunter in Africa. However, if one hunts with native guides alone—your White Hunter will have them as a matter of course, they cost only pennies a day and know the country—he will have to know at least a smattering of their language, or hire an interpreter, and will have to buy a car, or a light truck to get around in. It can be sold later. Then travel around and find a place to hunt. Shooting in this way, one's bag will usually be somewhat limited as to varieties, because the various animals have their own districts to a large extent.

Don't go to Africa with the idea that you will shoot varmints only, because, in general, you would do little shooting. Wildogs are seldom seen, and the game department biologists are not convinced that they are really harmful, they perform a useful service in weeding out the less fit and wounded animals, also in stirring the herds up, causing them to move around more. These dogs have little fear of man, and shooting them, is really very tame sport. You will find the baboons very shy in areas where they are being shot at, and shots will not come easy. The same applies to wart hogs. Crocodiles are so seldom seen, that they may be completely written off, unless you happen on to some unusual area—and I never happened to find one. In some areas, snakes are very numerous, and bear in mind, that some of the world's most lethal snakes are to be found in Africa—the spitting cobra, which can get your eyes at ten feet, the puff adder, and other vipers of similar type, and the black and green mambas and pythons. However, most times these snakes, if seen in time will show no aggression, but will glide out of your way, and bites are seldom experienced. During the rains, mosquitoes are common in some areas, they carry malaria, and anti-malaria medicine must be taken continually. Tsetse flies are an awful pest in some places, they seem to follow the buffaloes, so in good buffalo country you must expect to have them as an ever present pest.

There is no practical preventative against sleeping sickness but after it is once acquired, they have treatments for it. It is not common, and before entering an infected area, you will be warned or denied admission.

John Taylor gives some good hints in his book, "African Rifles" regarding how to find shooting, without going on a safari. Every prospective hunter should read this book as a matter of course. Go one better, and read Pondoro, also. Taylor tells you a lot of truths about Africa, which cannot be said of all the writers.

Africa is a wonderful country in many ways. During the rains, Africa is green and beautiful, but, that is not safari time. Swollen streams, and mud make travel impracticable in the hunting areas. When the rains quit, the land quickly dries up and soon it becomes unbelievably dry and parched. This, however, tends to concentrate the game herds near water, and is the best time for shooting.

J. R. Buhmiller, July 24, 1958

Since my writing my first notes for these pages, I have spent more time in Africa on the trail of marauders, and have some further comments to make. Things have changed in the little area where most of my time has been spent. For more than a year past, there have been game department hunters stationed there in an attempt to control these pests. This has resulted in educating the elephants, more than in reducing their numbers. Many still pass through in the night, sampling the crops as they go along, but are usually far away ere daylight. Or, if a small group happens to remain in the nearby dense forest during the day, there is no sound to give a hint of their presence; they have learned to forego the usual elephant noise, which ordinarily will be heard a half mile away or further. After the rainy season is over, and the ground is dry and as hard as concrete, tracking is very difficult. The old trails with tramped down grass, criss-cross and go every which way, and no sound to guide the trackers. One might pass near a small herd and have no inkling of their presence. The elephant fence that was erected on the northern boundary some three years ago is now useless, having been gone through, loosening the one inch steel cables, and the end of fence in the shallow water at the edge of the lake is being bypassed. This is an old natural runway, and most likely will see use for a long time to come. If a hunter does get up to a small group of these marauders, it takes a lot of luck to get more than one or two of them, as they don't stand around after the first shot is fired.

Buffaloes are scarce in this area since an epidemic of rinderpest about three years ago, which left dead animals scattered all over their natural range. Not many were shot, they just die of diesease, which often comes along when the animals become too numerous. The few remaining are very spooky and hard to hunt. There are still a number of rhinos around, which the game department wishes to preserve, but being considerably hemmed in by clearings, they no doubt feel persecuted, and often charge a man on foot. This happened to us (I always have two or more trackers with me) last year. On examination after his dispatch, there was a shotgun pattern of coarse shot on his shoulder! Out of the last five of these animals I have shot, four were charging, the other was doing crop damage. Most likely all will have to be eliminated, unless some of them move out, as the rhino does not adapt himself to living in a settled community.

The smaller game has mostly disappeared, except baboons, and these have suffered considerably from poisoned bait set out for their benefit. Last year being very dry all over East Africa, there was a migration of plains game into the area for water. The place was loaded with lions, as they had to follow their meal tickets. Some cattle and smaller livestock has recently been brought in by the farmers, and the presence of lions in the community caused no little concern, but the big cats caused no trouble, and we left them alone. It was not unusual to flush from six to eight in one day's hunting. Often lying around the carcass of a dead elephant, where they always chewed off the trunks, presumably being the only part of an elephant not protected by inch thick hide.

There is much outside interest as to the future of the game of Africa. What will happen to the game, depends on the political future of the country more than anything else. As it is now, and has always been, the native black looks on an animal only in terms of meat—today. He thinks not of the future. At the present time he is not allowed firearms, and can do little damage to wild game with his primitive spears and arrows. In some areas, there is a lot of illegal snaring of game. In wire snares, cunningly set in strategic places, any animal from impala to young buffalo may be caught, and once the loop is tight around his neck, nothing but the breaking of the wire will release the victim. In that event, the victim may live for years, but can never get rid of the wire which may become embedded in the neck or head. The main trouble with this snaring is that the natives who set the traps are too lazy to properly attend them, and most animals that are caught are lost to hyenas and vultures. If, in the future, the natives are not permitted to have firearms, under whatever governments may be in control, there would be hunting in Africa for a long time to come, in certain areas away from the beaten path.

Last year saw a severe drought in Kenya and Tanganyika, over an area perhaps twice the size of Texas. Cattle raising nomadic tribes like the Masai overgrazed, to the point of destruction, vast areas, which were further eroded by torrential rains in the month of November. These tribes have herds of the small humpbacked native cattle over large areas, as the pasture is grazed off, they move around to where the better grass is, and this year no doubt at least some of them will move into game reserves. These cattles can be the ruination of game areas, but nothing is ever done about it. They do not sell the cattle or butcher them, what good they are seems a mystery to a white man.

What guns to have on a safari, can range anywhere between two extremes, the one .375 rifle for everything, as was suggested by a man who fairly well knew what he wanted, to four rifles ranging from smallbore to large calibre, as was recently mentioned in a popular magazine. This latter could be an awful headache from start to finish. Two rifles, a .458 and .375 or .338 should fill the bill very nicely, and ammunition could be bought in Nairobi for both of them. On the .458 you should check the bedding before sending the gun, as well as to shoot it enough to get used to it, as well as to make sure of the sighting. Many of these have split their stocks through recoil, and it might be well to either glass bed the recoil lug on receiver, or add another lug to the barrel under the forearm, and make sure both lugs bear properly against the wood. If preferred, most any kind and calibre of rifle can be rented at a reasonable charge from Shaw and Hunter, the big gun store in Nairobi.

The rifle I will take on my sixth trip to Africa is a .450 Magnum, same thing as the .450 Ackley for all practical purposes. Weight 9 3/4 pounds, barrel length 23 inches, magazine capacity 5 shot with one cartridge in chamber gives six shots. Muzzle brake which gives about a 40% reduction in recoil, by actual test on my kick meter. This gun will handle factory .458 cartridges through the magazine, and groups them closely enough to the full loads for all practical purposes, in hunting big game. I had tried to accomplish this desirable feature previously, but was never able to come close to it, until I discarded the unnecessarily fast twist which seems to always be used with these loads. 24 inch and 25 inch twist certainly handles the 500 grain bullets, and closes up the grouping of the two loads at hunting ranges. I am going to use loads consisting of 405 grain soft points made for the .45/70 for use on medium size game, where the regular 500 grain soft point bullets are not satisfactory due to insufficient mushrooming on these smaller animals. A buffalo will open them up, but not the smaller animals. I have an idea I will use a load of about 80 grains of 3031 with the 500 grain bullet for some of my heavier duty work this year, as I'm sure this will give enough power for most every-day shooting. Then when needed, on wounded game in heavy brush I can use heavier loads.

One of the reasons why I return to Africa year after year is, that I have a never ending curiosity as to the killing power of various bullets on the tougher game such as buffalo. The elephant is not such a question mark; any bullet that will penetrate to the brain will bring him down in short order. The rhino is no great problem, ordinarily, to kill, but the buffalo is the tough one of the lot. As much as I have been interested in the buffalo, it seems that I have been destined to chase elephants instead.

This year I am going to try again for buffalo, and hope to get a little more first-hand information. There is a different bullet I want to try out, which I think will be more likely to leave a blood trail to follow up any wounded animal, and at the same time be more effective in putting him down.

The political situation is so gloomy in Kenya that one of my best friends there is sending his family to England, and he is leaving soon for Australia—says he is tired of trying to forecast what is going to happen, and does not want to be on the last bus out of there. He served as policeman in Nairobi, and saw plenty of Africa in the raw.

Another friend, who is a wheat farmer and also has cattle and sheep, bordering on the Aberdare mountains has just written me, "The feeling in Kenya today is very depressing. So many people have already gone, so many others want to go, others are going and so it goes on. We don't think we should go yet—things just might work out. We feel that if we left and all went well here, we could never come back to the same farm or life and one would feel so foolish living in another country with one's heart crying out for Kenya when there is no necessity to have gone. However, we are not being ostriches about it and are inquiring quite a bit about other possibilities, just in case."

J. R. Buhmiller, April 1962

KILLING POWER

Killing power is a subject which has been argued pro and con among hunters since rifles have been in existence, and one that will never be agreed upon.

There are some facts, however, which can be mentioned and some theories and formulae which can be presented so that the average shooter can draw his own conclusions. At least, it will give him some ammunition for argument.

There are several theories for which there are mathematical formulae and there are others for which there is no formula. There are three common theories which can be figured mathematically, each one of which has its exponents.

The first is the Kinetic energy theory, which measures the energy of the bullet in foot pounds. This is the theory used in compounding all of the ballistic tables furnished by the ammunition manufacturers to determine energy of bullets, and assuming we know the weight of the bullet and its velocity, and desire to know the striking energy in foot pounds, the following method can be used:

Square the velocity of the bullet in foot seconds, divide by 7000, to reduce it from grains to pounds. Divide the quotient by twice the acceleration of the gravity, or 64.32. This will give the striking energy in foot pounds of each grain of the bullet weight. Multiply this result by the weight of the bullet in grains and you have the striking energy of the bullet in foot pounds. The above described method is the one used by the late Charles Newton.

Another short cut for finding the energy of a bullet is to use the following formula:

Weight of bullet (in grains) x Velocity (in foot seconds) x Velocity (in foot seconds) x 0.000002218 = Energy in foot pounds.

Example: 100 grain bullet at 3000 foot seconds.
100 x 3000 x 3000 x 0.000002218 = 1996 foot pounds energy

Another method for the shooter who knows the approximate velocity of the handload and who wishes to figure the approximate energy of the bullet can use the following list of multipliers compiled by A. E. Ellinger, in 1949.

Energy Multipliers (Kinetic Energy) at various velocities for each grain weight of bullet.

Simply multiply the number shown opposite the stated velocity by bullet weight in grains.

Example: 150 grain bullet at 3000 foot seconds velocity, 150 x 20.00 = 3000 foot pounds.

Velocity	Multiplier
1500	5.00
1800	7.19
2000	8.88
2100	9.80
2200	10.74
2300	11.74
2400	12.78
2500	13.88
2600	15.01
2700	16.19
2800	17.41
2900	18.67
3000	20.00
3200	22.69
3300	24.14
3500	27.16
3750	31.23
3900	33.78
4050	36.43

The second theory is known as the momentum theory. The following explains Kinetic Energy versus Impact Energy or Momentum.

Momentum value = bullet weight in hundreds of grains times velocity in hundreds of feet.

Example:
Using a 300 Gr. bullet traveling at 2000 Feet per second
Weight of bullet in hundreds of grains = 3
Velocity in hundreds of feet = 20
3 x 20 = 60 Momentum value

	Bullet Weight Grains	Velocity Foot Seconds	Kinetic Energy Ft. Lb.	Momentum Value
No. 1	200	2000	1776	40
No. 2	200	2200	2148	44

Note that an increase of 10% in velocity of No. 2 over No. 1 boosts the K/energy 21%; however, the Momentum value increases only 10%.

	Bullet Weight Grains	Velocity Foot Seconds	Kinetic Energy Ft. Lb.	Momentum Value
No. 3	220	2200	1953	44

Here we add 10% in weight over No. 1; the K/energy rises 10% also. Note that the Momentum of No.'s 2 and 3 are equal (as we contend their killing powers are). However, see how the K/energy figures vary.

No. 4	300	1470	1400	44

Here we have added 100 grains to the bullet weight and have adjusted the Momentum value to 44 (to equal No.'s 2 and 3). The killing power, we feel, is equal to No. 2 and No. 3, note how the K/energy figure has dropped. This is all WRONG.

No. 5	300	2200	3150	66

Here we have added 50% to the velocity of No. 4. The K/energy figure has jumped about 125%—but the real killing power advanced exactly 50% to 66.

Now let us tackle the problem from another angle.

12 gauge rifled slug

No. 6	440	1400	1914	61.6
	(at 50 ft)			

The real killing power of this heavy slug is almost equal to No. 5 (at 66) although the K/energy rates it about as No. 3; sort of silly, isn't it?

Still another approach.

We shall now compare the great old Sharps cartridge of Buffalo fame with a 200 grain bullet at a velocity adjusted to the same K/energy figure as the Sharps:

Sharps .45 - 120 - 550 grain

No. 7	550	1450	2560	80
No. 8	200	2400	2560	48

This is perhaps the "payoff!" The Momentum figure favors the Sharps by a very wide margin, which *is certainly the case* insofar as killing power is concerned. It is as good an example as we can think of to toss overboard any ideas that Ballistic Table Energies are even useful, as a guide to killing potentials.

The third theory is known as pounds feet theory advocated by many big game hunters and printed in various publications many years ago. The computation of pound feet is made as follows:

> Multiply the muzzle velocity of the bullet by the bullet weight in grains. Divide this result by 7000 grains to reduce to pounds. The result will indicate pounds feet.

Keith uses the .405 Winchester for an example:

> The bullet weight is 300 grains. The velocity is 2200 foot seconds. Multiply 2200 by 300 which equals 660,000. Divide this by 7000, which equals 94.28 or roughly 94 pounds feet.

A common theory which is being expounded recently is the Shock theory, or Shock which is the result of high velocity of the bullet which blows up to create this Shock effect. Weatherby and other exponents of high velocity rifles feel that this is the logical requirement for killing power. This Shock theory of course applies to a comparatively light bullet at extremely high velocity, while the Momentum and Pounds Feet theories favor the heavier bullet at a lower velocity level.

Of course there are many holes in all of these theories or arguments, and the most serious one is the fact that they all disregard the design or construction of the bullet. There is no argument with the fact that the .450 Sharps is a good killer but the fact remains that present day hunting conditions are a great deal different than when this type of cartridge was in its heyday. Fifty years or more ago, when these cartridges were popular, the hunter could walk up or ride up to his game, place his shot about where he wished without considering problems such as lead, drop of bullet and other things which enter into the modern picture and it must be kept in mind that the velocities which were possible with such a cartridge were ideal for this old lead bullet.

The high velocity or shock theory presents an entirely different problem which can be solved only by the production of better bullets. There is nothing more deadly on any type of game than a bullet at extremely high velocity which blows up at exactly the right time and place, but these high velocity rifles give as many outstanding failures as they do outstanding kills and they do not work correctly over all ranges.

For example, the .220 Swift is one of our great one-shot killers of big game, but it also has produced some outstanding failures which the enemies of such cartridges play to the hilt.

These failures are being reflected in the laws which the various states are enacting everywhere to prohibit the use of small bore high velocity rifles. When using the Swift for deer, for example, if the animal is shot at extremely short range while the bullet is still traveling at high velocity, the bullet is apt to blow up on the surface and only make a painful flesh wound which will knock the animal down, only to promptly jump to its feet and run away. If the same animal is shot at a slightly longer range or at a point where the velocity at time of impact has reached the point for optimum results with the bullet construction available for this type of rifle, the results will be completely satisfactory.

There has been practically no progress made in the construction of bullets since the introduction of the present jacketed type which consists of a copper or copper alloy jacket and a lead core. This type of bullet seems to be well suited to velocities between 2000 and 3000 foot seconds, and give fairly reliable results within this velocity range, but at lower velocities such bullets do not open up reliably and at high velocity they have a tendency to blow up very badly and as the velocity increases still more, this tendency is geometrically magnified until a point is reached where the bullet will actually fly apart in the air before it reaches the target.

Bullet manufacturers insist on using the same old construction. They improved only their manufacturing methods and print pictures of a perfectly mushroomed bullet which has been recovered from a big game animal and try to convey the idea to the customer that such a bullet produces the perfect mushroom effect every time, while in reality, they probably fired many bullets to get the one ideal one for the picture and they do not mention the failures.

To utilize high velocity with its obvious advantages, some form of bullet with controlled expansion must be developed. Such a bullet must withstand velocities upwards of 5000 feet per second without any tendency to "blow up" either in the air or upon impact. It must be capable of opening up or expanding reliably at low velocity, even as low as 1500 feet. It must open up or expand at over 4000 feet without serious loss of weight or any tendency to disintegrate. It has been proven that easy and complete initial expansion causes "shock" without complete disintegration of the bullet. A bullet which opens quickly thus producing shock without losing more than 25% of its weight will also penetrate deeply, thus utilizing both shock and penetration. With some species of game, shock is all important. Other species may not be susceptible to shock and in order to make clean kills, deep or complete penetration is necessary. A bullet combining both characteristics is the only solution.

Some exponents of the high velocity or shock theory feel that any animal no matter how large can be killed with one shot, no matter where the shot is placed, if the velocity is high enough at the time of impact. This of course is ridiculous on the face of it, because no matter what type of bullet is used, how high its velocity or how heavy it is, there is still no substitute for a well placed shot.

It can be easily demonstrated that a bullet of controlled expanding type, that is, one which opens up or expands upon impact without losing an appreciable amount of weight produces just as great a shock effect as does the jacketed bullet which "blows up" or disentegrates, so long as the velocity at time of impact is the same. The controlled expansion bullet, however, retains at least 70% of its weight and continues on to completely penetrate the animal. Thus it combines shock with penetration. Even a 50 grain bullet fired from the .220 Swift at any reasonable range will expand perfectly and still completely penetrate game like deer or antelope.

In spite of the theories put forth by the various schools of thought, the only direction for improvement is in the way of velocity and we can look for higher and higher velocities. High velocity rifles in addition to producing the shock effect also reduce the guess work so important to the "once a year hunter." It has been conclusively demonstrated that relatively small calibre rifles such as the .25

using bullets in the neighborhood of 100 grain weight at velocities at 3600 to 3700 foot seconds are extremely deadly at all ranges that almost any hunter could expect to make a reliable hit so long as a properly designed bullet is used.

It can be concluded that high velocity rifles when used with properly designed bullets have completely outclassed the older types using slow, heavy bullets, and their effectiveness in the field have pushed cartridges meeting the requirements of the Momentum and Pounds Feet theories into almost complete obsolescence.

Paul Von Rosenberg has had wide experience hunting big game and is an accomplished ballistics engineer. Mr. Von Rosenberg has the following to say on the subject of killing power and bullet design:

> I started to write this article on "Killing Power." After outlining my thoughts I decided there are too many variables in assessing just what makes a game shot a killing one. So I decided against trying to express them to the end of analyzing killing power. An identical wound on two identical animals usually results in quite a variation in killing effect, even though they create approximately the same destruction of bone and tissue. Moreover the variables from shot to shot and from animal to animal are so great that it would take a lifetime of very scientific observation to cover all of them and base definite conclusions on inductive reasoning. In this article I shall try to set forth some beliefs that can be backed up by scientific fact which will show the items that are relative to creating an effective bullet wound. Once this wound is created the killing power of it will be a variable which I will not attempt to evaluate.
>
> My notes are the result of my experiences in killing, at this writing, just 50 head of big game, and witnessing about 30 more downed by hunting companions. In most cases the observations included the hit and game reaction as well as the autoptical ones to trace out the bullet path. To these observations are added a general knowledge of anatomy, physics, and mathematics, the latter helping in quantitative reasoning.
>
> My 50 head of big game include deer, elk, antelope, goat, and bear. I am extrapolating these experiences to our larger North American species, big bear and moose,

and believe they will apply equally well to African thin skinned game of similar size and anatomy. I am doubtful, however, if the observations will be relevant to thick skinned African animals, but the reader may consider those which might apply from his own experience.

First, let's examine just what a bullet wound accomplishes to kill a head of big game. The bullet causes one or more of the following: (1) damage to and disruption of a major nerve center such as the brain or spinal cord. (2) internal bleeding causing the malfunctioning of a major organ, usually heart or lungs. (3) external bleeding again affecting the heart and/or lungs. (4) breaking down and causing loss of use of one or more of the major bone and muscle parts which provide locomotion, and (5) hydraulic pressure transmitted to nerve centers which can cause (1) above.

Almost instant kills we sometimes observe are nearly always caused by (1) or (5). It is usually easy to determine if (1) is the cause if the bullet channel is traced out; however, there are occasions when the hydraulic pressure (5) is transmitted from some point quite remote from the disrupted nerve center.

The bullet's ability to cause a large and fatal wound is a function of (a) its striking energy, (b) its expansion and/or partial disentegration, and (c) its penetration. The energy is found from ballistic tables published by Winchester-Western, Remington-Peters or Weatherby for factory loads, or by Speer for hand loads, or can be calculated from the formula $E = V W/450,240$ where E is the energy in foot pounds, V is the striking velocity in foot seconds, and W is the bullet weight in grains. There are some who contend that energy should not be regarded as a relative function, and that some other factor should be considered in its place. One of these is pounds feet, obtained by multiplying bullet weight by velocity, WV (and then sometimes modified by multiplying by a constant.) Pounds feet is actually momentum, which is a physical consideration quite different from energy. The comparison is easy to make: energy is a function of the square of the velocity while momentum is a function of the velocity by simple multiplication. I reject the contention that momentum should be considered instead of energy for the simple reason that it is unscientific — not in keeping with the known and accepted laws of physics. Energy is the basic measurement of kinetic (moving) force and is the rate of doing work — in this case of creating a killing wound. I maintain, therefore, that other things being equal, the wounding capability of a bullet is in direct proportion to its striking energy at the range at which the bullet hits.

Another contention which has some vocal advocates is that the velocity is directly related to wounding capability. This contention is equally as wrong as the pounds feet consideration. In fact, I will go so far as to argue that velocity, per se, has absolutely nothing to do with wounding capability! To restate my position on velocity: if a bullet gives simultaneously adequate penetration, controlled expansion, and has given a striking energy, its velocity affects not one whit its wounding capability. True velocity has its effects on penetration, expansion and energy, but these latter three determine directly the bullet's wounding capability. Velocity is only an indirect consideration: too much velocity sometimes causes too much expansion and, conversely, not enough penetration—which is poor. High velocity for any given bullet weight causes high energy—which is for the better.

Velocity affects interestingly the consideration of penetration. A given bullet at 1800 fs may penetrate a certain distance through skin, bone muscle and fat; at 2400 fs it may penetrate 50% more than at 1800 fs — let's say this is maximum. At 3000 fs the penetration may have fallen off to even less than at 1800 fs because the bullet expanded too rapidly and disintegrated soon after entrance. The point I am trying to make is: a conventional jacketed expanding bullet fired into a given mass and consistency of skin, bone, muscle and fat has an optimum velocity for maximum penetration. Velocities either less or greater give less penetration.

Now to get back to my basic contention: that any bullet possesses killing power as direct functions of its energy, its expansion and its penetration. It is pretty obvious that of these three, energy is the factor that can be measured, evaluated, and controlled easiest. In fact we can get almost any striking energy we want by choosing a cartridge and load having enough powder capacity and bullet weight to achieve the figure desired. We are limited here, however, by acceptable recoil and gun weight. The reader may wish to refer to my previous article on Page 17 of the Ackley Handbook, where I discussed some of the aspects of obtaining adequate striking energy at game ranges by choosing bullets of high ballistic coefficient (efficiency). Considering that recoil limits the upper figures, I believe the following energies can be used to categorize favorite loads and plan what ones next calibre should have:

Game	Minimum	Adequate	Preferred
Deer, antelope, sheep, goat..........	900 ft lb	1200 ft lb	1500 ft lb
Elk, bear up to 600 lbs.................	1500 ft lb	2000 ft lb	2500 ft lb
Large bear, moose.	2100 ft lb	2800 ft lb	3500 ft lb

Remember, these are striking energies at game ranges—not at the muzzle.

Let's see how some factory loads compare with these figures: The 30/30 and the .250/3000 have always been regarded as average deer cartridges. Winchester's present loading of the 170 gr Silvertip is at a muzzle velocity of 2220 fs, giving 1350 fp at 100 yards and 1000 fp at 200 yards. Remington's .250/3000 load with the 100 gr Core-Lokt bullet is loaded to 2820 fs MV, giving 1390 fp at 100 yards, 1080 fp at 200 yards, and 835 fp at 300 yards. An accurate scope sighted 250/3000 can be a 300 yard deer and antelope rifle in the hands of a good rifleman. The .270 Winchester has made its reputation for clean one shot kills on deer and similar sized game, and has few superiors for long range work on these animals. The Remington Bronze point 130 gr loading starts at 3140 fs and has 1990 and 1660 fp respectively at 200 and 300 yards. These figures, according to the table above, make this a preferred deer category load up to 300 yards and an adequate elk category load up to 200 yards. Remember, these are considerations based on energy alone. We have not mentioned expansion or penetration, both of which must be right before any load can be considered adequate for the game in question.

Just a few more: The .30/06 Winchester Silvertip 220 gr has 2410 fs MV and 2320 and 1910 fp respectively at 100 and 200 yards. This load, on its energy, qualifies as an adequate elk load at 200 yards and a satisfactory large bear load at 100 yards. The .375 Magnum 270 gr Winchester load at 2740 fs MV is a real bone crusher and has 3620 fp at 100 yards and 2920 fp at 200 yards. This load, comparing figures with those in the table, is in the adequate or preferred class for elk, moose, and large bear at those ranges.

A short review of the above figures will show that the values in my table are pretty close to or slightly greater than commercial loadings of the various calibres recommended in the handbooks put out by Winchester and Remington. Handloading standards or "improved" cartridges to slightly more than factory velocities easily brings them up to the energy figures I list.

Energy seems to be pretty well covered by the above paragraphs. The handloader can refer to the data in my previous article "A Few Notes on Sectional Density and Related Items" which appeared in the first edition of the Ackley Handbook. From these data he can, with reasonable accuracy, calculate the remaining energy of his favorite loads at game ranges.

For energy, we turn back to the other two considerations which are relative to the wounding capabilities of the bullet—expansion and its counterpart, penetration. Bullet makers for many years have tried to design both of these features into a game bullet; that is to have adequate expansion for lower velocity shots in the rib cage of an antelope, and adequate penetration for a close range high velocity raking shot through the elk's hips—for example. Such performance is, indeed, difficult to attain. Most bullet designs take a step in this direction by exposing lead core, or a hollow point, or a thin cap over the forward end of the lead core. This makes the nose of the bullet easily deformed and expanded or disintegrated by contact with even low resistance tissue, skin, or thick bone. I believe any of the current nose designs—soft point, Silver tip, Core-Lokt, hollow point, Bronze point, or capped protected point—will expand satisfactorily at any reasonable velocity. My experience indicates that of these the hollow point and Bronze Point are occasionally erratic, giving noticeably more or less expansion than would be normal for the velocity and resistance.

The soft point is about as reliable as any and lends itself easily to manufacture. Its only disadvantage is that it is easily deformed by careless handling and by battering in the box magazine of the bolt action rifle. This latter can be corrected by having the magazine well sides fitted with stops at the cartridge shoulder. The stops can be metal strips welded or brazed to the magazine sides, or the shape of the magazine itself, if the rifle is custom stocked. These corrective measures for point battering have their limitation if the recoil is unusually severe or the cartridge case has sloping shoulders. Perhaps, here is one of the minor but apparent advantages of the so-called "improved" cartridge version with its steeper shoulder angle.

Most commercial rifles do not have this magazine protector and so the hollow point, Silver-Tip, Bronze-Point and capped protected point bullets resist this point deformation best.

From the above considerations, I believe we can conclude that the bullet manufacturer has only an average problem in designing his bullet so that it will have sufficient expansion and has in nearly all cases made his design so it is not lacking in this respect.

This leaves us penetration to consider. Penetration itself is easy to achieve by making the bullet with a full-jacketed nose, so called "solid" or full patch. If the nose, so constructed is round or blunt, the bullet will penetrate quite well in a nearly straight path. If the nose of the full jacketed bullet is sharp pointed "spitzer" —as M-1 service bullet, the bullet will frequently be deflected by bone or muscle and will tumble, creating a large wound channel, but reducing its penetration to about that of a conventional expanding bullet. We can conclude that, for a hunting bullet, we need the expansion of a soft point or other type than the full jacket. So we will have to turn to other bullet design consideration to obtain penetration. In other words, we want the expansion, so we cannot have the full jacket which will give us most penetration.

Let us digress from our analysis of bullet design for a moment to determine how much expansion and/or penetration we want. The simple answer on expansion is that we want as much as we can get without sacrificing adequate penetration. How much penetration do we want or need? The answer is not an easily determined one nor easily expressed by any unit of measurement. Two schools of thought have their protagonists. One school believes that the bullet should penetrate well to the opposite side of the game but remain inside, giving up all of its energy to the animal. The other school believes that the bullet should penetrate completely through the animal to cause external bleeding. External bleeding from the exit hole naturally is a contribution to the kill, but it is also valuable as it causes a blood trail from which the animal can be tracked. If the game is hard to stop and will normally travel some distance even when hit in a vital spot by a bullet of high energy, or if the cover is dense and even a short distance may take the game out of sight—or both—a large exit hole with external bleeding and a blood trail is an asset.

I subscribe to both schools of thought; my agreement with the "penetrate completely through the animal" school is in the case of dense timber and undergrowth as is found in our Pacific Northwest and coastal British

Columbia and Alaska. For open country, where the game is not too likely to be out of sight within 100 yards, I would be happy with thorough but not necessarily complete penetration.

So, how much penetration we want has the above consideration; even more, other factors make it difficult to determine or measure. Consider an expanding bullet which will normally penetrate through the lung cavity broadside of a bull elk; it hits a rib squarely on entrance and the remaining part lodges under the skin on the opposite side between two ribs. This bullet struck at a velocity of 2280 fs which was its remaining velocity at 200 yards. According to the first school of thought —to which I subscribed—this was ideal performance, and, if the energy was sufficient, a clean one-shot kill should result. Now let us try this load again: this time our elk is in heavy timber and as we see him he is quartering away from us at 50 yards. The down timber, tree trunks, and undergrowth obscure our field of view, but it is now or never because the bull is alerted and we decide that we can place the bullet high just forward of the hip—a raking shot, as my friend, Elmer Keith, calls it. The striking velocity of our bullet at 50 yards is 2590 fs and it so happens that 2280 fs was the approximate velocity for maximum penetration. The bullet went where we aimed from a carefully squeezed offhand shot, but our bull is gone in three jumps. We take out after him and after two miles of diligent tracking (you dear reader are a better tracker than I am), three and one-half hours later when the sun is setting we quietly come upon him lying down. He rises stiffly and we hit him again broadside, this time into the spine which drops him like a sack of potatoes. Boy, was that an ordeal! Even though it's late we want to dress him out and with scientific curiosity trace out those bullets. Our first shot clipped the last rib, went through the liver on a downward angle, leaving a lot of jacket fragments and then stopped under the diaphragm near the offside—plenty of expansion! Our second bullet went directly into the spinal column behind the shoulder blade and penetrated about ten inches of skin, muscle and tough bone structure. The first bullet had shed its core completely and the remaining back part of the jacket weighed 30% of the original bullet weight. If this bullet had held together better it might have gone forward into the chest cavity and done a more effective job. One could conclude that this performance was something less than ideal and more penetration was needed.

Analyzing the need for more penetration we find it could be accomplished in several ways or combinations thereof; they are: (1) reducing velocity to not less than that which gives maximum penetration with the existing weight and construction; (2) make the jacket thicker, either in its entirety or particularly at the base section: (3) reduce velocity by making the bullet heavier—this has the advantage over (1) above in that energy is not reduced: (4) design the bullet so that the rear approximate half would remain intact even though the front part expanded and disintegrated.

Considering the above modifications we reject (1) because it reduces energy, which we now believe to be as low as is adequate; (2) has its merits, but we must be sure, if we use heavier jacket thickness, that it is not so thick near the point that it restricts expansion of the nose section; here a tapered jacket from thick at the base to thin near the point is preferable. Some bullet makers do this quite nicely and examples are Hornady and DWM (German) "Strong-Jacket" design. Method (3) is one which has been used classically; the 180 gr. .30/06 has better penetration than the 150 gr provided they are of similar construction and loaded to approximately the same energy. Why? Simply because the heavier slug is moving at a lower velocity (provided said velocity is now lower than that for maximum penetration). The principal objection to (3) is that the heavier bullet at lower velocity has a more curved trajectory, making it less suitable for long range use. Again, as I pointed out in my previous article, flat trajectory is relative and for timber use the lower velocity loads will easily shoot flat enough for 100 yard use. However, there is no denying that big game is more and more taken at longer ranges in the open west, and that the demand for a flat shooting load is greater as times goes on.

Can we have our cake and eat it too? Perhaps, we can: Method (4) seems to have possibilities! If we had a bullet which on impact became, in effect, two separate bullets; one of which was designed for maximum expansion and the other for maximum penetration, we would have a much better solution than one of the other three methods. Bullets which are designed to do this "double take" are extant and have been for some time. They are the RWS "H" Jacket, the Ackley Controlled Expansion (not now in production), and the Nosler Partition Jacket bullets. Let us take a closer look at these.

The RWS-H Jacket made in Germany and now again available in this country through an importer and distributors has a folded section in its jacket which returns about 2/3 of the bullet diameter at about a midway fore and aft point of the cylindrical section of the bullet. The bullet parts, under impact, at this fold and we have an expanding front half and a penetrating rear section. This bullet is very effective, particularly in its 7mm 173 gr weight. My experience with it is limited and I believe it is comparatively little known because it has not, from about 1939 until just recently, been imported or advertised.

The Ackley Controlled Expansion bullet is not a conventional core and enclosing jacket construction as is the RWS. Instead, a solid copper base half is machined and/or drawn to form an extension forward with a partial cavity. The core, inserted, projects about 1/4 its length to form the soft point. The core is shaped almost symmetrical from front to rear having a spitzer front, and a spitzer tail which fits the shape of the base cavity. Upon impact, the front half, mostly core, expands violently, while the solid copper rear half penetrates well, holding its shape and direction. Unfortunately, due to the high cost of manufacture, this bullet is only a future possibility rather than a present day reality. It is hoped Ackley can make arrangements in the near future to again produce this bullet.

The Nosler Partition Jacket bullet, available in a limited number of diameters, has apparently a bar stock automatic screw machine produced jacket which is open at its front and rear, both of which portions have lead core wedged in. The front half is die shaped to a good spitzer, and the base is flat. The center of the jacket, which forms a partition about .100" thick is machine relieved for about .200" along the parallel sides to bore diameter to prevent displacement of the core bearing on the partition. The Nosler bullet has a good reputation in the game fields and does what its maker claims for it—expands well at the forward portion and penetrates through heavy bone and muscle with the rear half. This bullet sells for about twice as much as a conventional jacketed bullet due to the higher cost of manufacture which, undoubtedly, has restricted its general use.

Perhaps some enterprising manufacturer will design and prove a bullet which can be made with existing bullet forming machinery, and which will possess the characteristics of these controlled expanding designs and still sell for a popular price. I am sure if the demand by hunters is strongly enough voiced the responsive action by bullet manufacturers will produce some better game bullets than are now available. Perhaps, the reader may wonder if our present types of more conventional bullets are not quite satisfactory. In general, with an intelligent selection of bullet weight, diameter, construction and velocity of loading, I believe the answer is in the affirmative. I must say from my own experience, though, that there is considerable room for improvement. I must say, in all fairness, that I have never lost a head of game hit because of what I reckoned to be inadequate performance. On the other hand I have trailed game or had them move off much too far and fast after a good hit to believe that I was shooting the best bullet for the conditions at that time.

Among the custom bullet makers Fred Barnes has for many years made his bullets of copper tubing which permits heavier jackets for any given diameter than the more popular method of drawing a jacket cup from sheet stock. As a result, Barnes bullets usually give more penetration than most other jacketed bullets of the same diameter, weight and striking velocity. I mention this in passing because some may be interested in the bullets of conventional construction which are noted for maximum penetration. This consideration is an important one to the handloader who has a wildcat capable of giving considerably higher velocities for its calibre than any factory loads. If a commercial arms manufacturer makes 150 gr .308 bullets intended to be loaded to about 3000 fs MV and a wildcat can easily step them up to 3500 fs, the added velocity may be too much for the bullet in question. Barnes, knowing this, tries to make his bullets hold together better to stand the higher impact velocity of the faster loading. Other custom bullet manufacturers tend to do likewise, but with nearly all bullets Barnes construction makes the jacket 25% to 40% heavier than others.

Field experience, and lots of it, I am sure, can contribute to the contentions I have made in this article. I would welcome reader's experiences and reactions. Their results may prompt bullet manufacturers to make design and construction improvements which will make tomorrow's game bullet a better performer than today's.

KILLING POWER

Les Bowman of Cody, Wyoming, big game outfitter and widely experienced big game hunter has a few views about killing power. For the past ten years or more, Les has been in on more big game kills than almost any other man in the United States and has had an opportunity to observe the effectiveness of all sizes of cartridges in the hands of both experienced and inexperienced hunters. Les believes as most of us, that an experienced big game hunter can do well with most any cartridge of reasonable size, but he also has some ideas concerning inexperienced hunters who are recoil conscious and who are handicapped in many other ways. Les Bowman has the following to say:

Born before the turn of the century, in Northern California, I grew up with a gun in my hand and never have gotten to a point where a gun is not interesting.

Way back when, it was slow speed bullets and a leaning toward large bores, but gradually this changed, because of the development of better metals for gun actions and barrels, better bullets and far better powders. What we used to think took a 25-20 to do, we suddenly found a 22 long rifle doing better. I've personally hunted a large variety of game on this North American continent, from cotton tails to moose and bear, with sheep, elk and deer thrown in for good measure. Probably 150 deer and over 75 elk have fallen to my rifles in my hunting time. Altogether, I have done quite a bit of hunting, here and there and so have naturally formed my own opinion as to how big a rifle I need.

However the most deciding factor in these opinions is quite a few years experience in the big game out-fitting business. Our hunters kill somewhere between one hundred and two hundred big game animals every year. Last fall we packed out ninety pack horse loads of elk, alone. This gives us a pretty good insight into what makes a good gun and bullet, and what doesn't. We are interested in getting one shot kills as often as we can. First—it's humane, second—the meat is better than badly shot up game, and third—it pleases the hunter.

For these reasons we have made a study of guns and ammunition here and have found several factors that can be tied together. So, to get at the facts let's take the basic factors of shooting.

No. 1—First a hunter must hit what he shoots at, and next he should put any bullet he uses in a spot that will be fatal to the animal. This still gives him quite a bit of latitude in making a one shot knock down or real quick internal bleeding kill.

In breaking down this number one thing, we find many variables, such as gun fit, experience, sights, judgment of distance, trajectory of bullets and flinching, becoming definite factors.

No. 2—The bullet, on reaching its destination, must be so constructed that it causes a *deep* wound of great shock. To do this it must expand immediately, to approximately two or three times its original diameter, but it must also hold together its mass weight. A bullet which blows up immediately on contact, makes a bloody shallow wound that too often causes a blood trail but results in a lost animal. Even if it kills it spoils far too much meat.

Let me define what I believe would be the perfect bullet, although I know it's impossible to have this. A bullet, which at *any speed* its propelled, or at *any distance* it travels, would open up immediately on impact yet maintain its total weight, would penetrate the animal completely, dropping to the ground on the other side. This bullet would have expended its total energy inside the animal. It is highly inconceivable that any animal would not be knocked down by it and the resulting shock be fatal. In the case of a lung area shot, internal bleeding would cause death in seconds.

However, since we know this can only be achieved by a bullet where velocity, distance, animal resistance, etc., are just right, the next best thing is a bullet that will open immediately on impact, hold together most of its mass weight and leave it to the gun and distance to furnish sufficient maintained energy to penetrate either deeply or clear through.

Now, we will go back to the number one factor. There are fine guns, built by standard gun companies and custom gun makers, to fit all types of hunters. There are good sights, open and telescope, for all purposes. But there is nothing yet, that tells the shooter the distance, how many inches or feet to compensate for accuracy, how much to allow for winddrift, etc. The only sure method for this is to get a gun that shoots as flat as possible throughout regular hunting ranges.

To do this with a big bore rifle means running up the foot pounds recoil, and when that happens the average hunter flinches, and when once flinch develops it is really hard to get rid of.

With medium caliber, low recoil, flat shooting guns and proper bullets, we get maintained velocity giving foot pounds energy at bullet impact. And by proper expansion we have the size wound normally made by the big bore, which so often does not expand. It is true you could kill game with a bowling ball, *if* you threw it hard enough. But, as in fighting in the ring, the fast sharp blows of a light fighter do more damage than the roundhouse swings of the giant.

When one of our hunters comes out here equipped with a medium caliber flat shooting rifle, using good bullets of fair sectional density and we see him shoot it reasonably accurately and without flinch, we are quite sure he will get his game. And he usually does.

Last fall we had more wounded game and more misses, by what we call "over-gunned" hunters than by hunters using lighter caliber guns. With recoil being so high, most big bores are usually of medium or slow speed, with resultant high trajectory. Even if you do hit a light animal at some distance, the bullet, made to expand in heavy game, doesn't have enough velocity to expand properly in light game. Consequently it goes in without expansion and although wounded, the animal escapes, to die later or recover slowly, as the case may be.

Now we will go back to number two. We may have a fine flat shooting, well scoped rifle, capable of laying them right in at up to 300 yards or more, without compensation for trajectory, in close enough groups to stay in the sure killing area, *but* the bullets blow up or they shed cores and lose weight and do not penetrate enough to be fatal. Here the solution is the *proper* bullet.

Last fall two new guns made their debut, just prior to hunting season up here. The .244 Remington and the .243 Winchester. Both are 6mm. Both are different cases but are approximately the same in ballistics. In my opinion both these guns are tops for deer and antelope, in open range country. But both these calibers used on game, with 1955 factory bullets, were from good to poor as to killing power, where with proper bullets, they would have been good to exceptional. When the factory bullets did kill, we noticed they blew up and spoiled way too much meat.

We had one each of these guns here, last fall, which we used. We hand loaded our own ammunition, using *good* bullets, meant for *game*, not varmints, and both guns made wonderful kills at all ranges, in the hands of our hunters. Altogether, they accounted for forty head of game. For the past five years I have owned, used and frequently loaned to others, a 6 M.M. It has accounted for 47 kills, so far. These have been mostly one shot kills, due I believe to the use of proper bullets.

While it is possible to use only one gun for all mountain hunting, it's highly preferable to have at least two guns. On a straight deer or antelope hunt we feel far more confident of a hunter doing a good job with a gun of .243 caliber up to .270, with correct bullets, than with a .300 magnum. But when elk are involved with maybe moose and bear thrown in for good measure, a gun from .270 up is highly preferable. But you must use the proper bullets. And we are always more concerned with the hunter's choice of bullets than with the caliber of his gun.

We are asked many times to state what gun we've found that can be used for deer, antelope and on up to real heavy game, that we would recommend, if a hunter could only buy one gun. Our answer is always the .270. Remember that with this gun too, you must use the proper bullets.

If I were asked to pick three guns for use on varmints, light game and heavy game I would pick a .222, a 6 M.M. and a 7 M.M. or .300 of the high velocity type, respectively. With the right bullets I would be ready for any type varmint or big game on the North American continent.

Of our fifty-five hunters last fall, nine carried straight .300 Magnums. Seven of them were hunting antelope as well as bigger game. Six of the seven flinched in various degrees after each shot. Evidently they had heard and read that any smaller caliber wouldn't even kill deer, let alone elk. Also, they had with them a few boxes of shells, bought with no regard to the bullet and what it would be used for. All of these loads were okay for elk and big game. They were really designed by the makers for use on big game, only. One hunter fired fifty rounds in two days at antelope and never got one down. I am sure he hit some but I'm also sure the bullets never opened up on that small game. Also the shooters were flinching, with so big a gun and not much shooting experience, so most of the shots were probably misses. With one of my hunters I finally gave up and stopped to talk things over for awhile. After suggesting he try my .243 and having him make a dozen dry shots, then fire three live rounds at a target, we went hunting again. This time he connected with a fine big buck antelope, for a one shot kill at over 300 yards. I had a happy hunter and a convert to a smaller calibre, with *good* bullets for light game.

I do know there are some people who can shoot real big caliber, high velocity guns consistently and not flinch. But the biggest majority of us cannot. I have a .35 Newton, used for Kodiak bear and when I target this gun in, I do so on the sandbags, with lots of padding between me and the gun. Then I do my shooting practice with a smaller caliber, using light bullets and use the big gun for actual game shooting only.

My advice to old and new hunters alike, is for them to shoot any gun they like and have confidence in and can shoot consistently without flinching. *But* to pay more attention to the bullets they use than to the caliber. And no type gun or caliber is any better than its bullets. We have found from experience that high velocity *with* proper bullets, is far better killing insurance than big bore slow stuff.

There is of course a number of big bore enthusiasts who are against high velocity guns, but the majority of guns made by reliable manufacturers, who do a lot of research, are medium caliber type guns. These are used by a big percentage of the successful hunters today.

When the time comes that hunters think more about the proper type bullet and its killing power and less about the size and bore of the gun they shoot, I believe we will have more sure kills and less wounded and lost game.

The preceding was written five years ago. Mr. Bowman has the following to say at this time after the development and introduction of some of the new magnum cartridges including the .264 Winchester Magnum, 7mm Remington Magnum and the .338 Winchester Magnum.

The past five years or so have witnessed some major changes in the requirements of the shooting public in general, that is reflected in the products offered by our major gun companies, in rifles, calibres and cases. In much the same way as our citizens have become two, three or more car owners so have the shooters become a two, three or even a multiple gun owner. More emphasis is now placed on a gun for a special purpose and most shooters have given up the "one gun that will do everything" idea.

Calibres on short magnum cases of the type and size generally known as the belted Newton is one of the new items widely accepted by the shooting public. Two of the major arms companies have brought out calibres on this type case and more are coming. In the lighter straight cases, the .280 Remington immediately became very popular and is giving the old standby, the .270 a lot of competition. In the shorter straight case of 7mm Mauser capacity, the 6mm's have completely upset the applecart and have almost killed the demand for the reliable old .257 Roberts. In the smaller cases the .22 Remington and the .222 Remington Magnum have outmoded such cases as the .22 Hornet and others. There has been considerable experimental work done in necking up the .222 Magnum cases to 6mm. This is known as the 6x47. By length and calibre it is a legal big game cartridge in most states and though of less velocity and energy than the larger 6mm's, it is adequate for deer, antelope, etc. Its low recoil and muzzle blast allows accurate bullet placement and for many shooters this contributes greatly to more certain kills.

In the heavier brackets, such as those used in Africa or on Polar bear in Alaska, several new calibres are now available. The .338 Winchester being at the light end and on up through the .458 Winchester and the .460 Weatherby to the top side. In Africa probably no other cartridge has had the immediate and full acceptance that the .458 Winchester has had. Here we have a short magnum case and it is about the very maximum in recoil that can be accurately handled by the average man. The .338 Winchester is also on the same short case and was especially designed for Alaskan brown, polar bear and large moose. The big bore addicts have adopted it for use on such game as elk and black bear.

These short magnums can be and are built on actions generally shorter than normally used in standard H&H magnum cases and are the same general length as the '06 or the .270 case. Many owners of these rifles have had them rebuilt to take one of the short Magnum calibres.

Another new short magnum calibre is the .264 Winchester that has given new life to the 6.5 bore-groove diameter. This calibre was specifically designed by Winchester for modern day short action rifles and for long range western type shooting, where very flat trajectory is wanted.

The most recent addition to the short case calibres is Remington's new 7mm Magnum. This calibre is becoming very popular as many like the added weight choice in bullets which the .264 Winchester lacks.

None of these short magnums are new or original. Charles Newton made a nearly identical case, except for the belt, and chambered rifles for several calibres using it in 1912 to 1920.

It is modern steels for better barrels and actions, better case shape and capacity, combined with modern powders and modern bullets of far better design, that makes these various calibres so useful in this old case size. Also, the belt has helped simplify and take care of head spacing, etc. New interior case design, especially at the head, has added tremendously to strength and safety. It is my belief that these new short magnum cases are the best and strongest ever made.

In spite of a great deal of adverse criticism by the big bore, heavy bullet enthusiast, the lighter calibre rifles still sell to a large majority of hunters, in greater numbers than any other types and increased demand makes other type light calibres a certainty for the future. Lighter calibre rifles, because they can be shot more accurately by the average shooter, due to better handling qualities, lighter recoil and less apparent "kick", still account for as many or more one-shot kills on game as do big bore heavy bullet rifles. For several years the trend has been toward higher velocities in all these lighter calibres. This, combined with the near perfect bullet designs in use today, give better shocking power and "shock" is a prime factor in instantaneous one-shot kills.

Years ago the average hunter owned and usually could afford to own one rifle, but in the past decade or so he has moved up to the two gun status and in many cases to many more than two. Hunters who used to consider the bagging of a deer with their .30/30 once a year, as tops in hunting, now take off for Africa, Alaska and big game hunts in the West almost yearly. And in spite of the constant reminders by some of the old-time hunters that "only big bullets at slow speeds" will kill game, the hunter who hunts the world over has almost universally adopted rifles that are flat shooting, accurate, easy to handle and of a calibre commensurate with the game being hunted.

In the old days when round lead balls, and later on, when cast lead bullets were used, the size of the ball or bullet governed the size of the wound channel and unless a certain limited area or nerve center or bone structure, such as the spine was hit, bleeding was the cause of death. Now the wound channel made is much larger than any bullet diameter, even by bullets of .224 diameter, by controlled expansion built in modern bullets. Modern rifles push them with velocities that cause hydrostatic shock waves that travel outward from the wound channel and kill by shock as well as bleeding. Penetration is more controlled and more of the total energy of the bullet is expended inside the animal. Energy expended on the hillside on the other side of an animal by bullets that go right through with small wound channels, does no good. What many call "knockdown power" is really not that at all, but should be called "shockdown power."

During the years we have been in the hunting business we have done a great deal of experimenting with all makes, types and weights of bullets. Hundreds of autopsies have been done on killed animals, bullets recovered and their action carefully noted. These checks were made on animals from antelope and deer size to elk, moose and grizzly bear. The results of our investigation on game animals of something over 2000 head killed has firmly convinced us that calibre or bore size is secondary to other factors in making good game kills.

Calibre Sizes for North American Game

I am most definitely not a one rifle owner, having some fifty big game rifles in nearly all modern type calibres plus a few wildcats in my gun cabinets. While it is certainly not necessary for a hunter to own as many rifles as this for taking North American game, it is my considered opinion that at least three different calibres should be used and four would be better, if a hunter is going to hunt a wide variety of game.

While this article deals primarily with guns for North American game, it may be well to mention also, that regarding calibre sizes for African game, 85% of the game in Africa can be taken without medium and heavy calibres.

First on the list would be the .22 long rifle size, used for rabbits and other similar type game. The usual bullets used for this are of lead, such as the .22 long rifle hollow point.

Jacketed bullets should be used for the killing of varmints and predators, and these in the low calibre range center fire case size as used in the .222 Remington and the .222 Remington Magnum heads the list. While a few states allow the use of such guns on deer size animals, I do not feel they are adequate, as the weight and quantity of material in such bullets does not allow enough for properly expanded size or weight for penetration.

Most states limit big game rifles to a bore size of .23 calibre. While no factory rifle or cartridge is made for a true .23 calibre rifle, P. O. Ackley of Salt Lake City has custom made many of them for his own use and for his customers. The one in my gun rack I consider a top long range antelope and deer gun and I do not own a rifle that makes any longer and cleaner kills on antelope size game. Bullets are made by Fred Barnes of Grand Junction, Colorado and R. B. Sisk of Iowa Park, Texas. These can be had in jacket thickness for varmints or heavier type for game use. Although this calibre has been used successfully by experts for game up to Kodiak bear size, it is essentially a fine flat shooting deer and antelope rifle of low recoil, for the handloader and gun nut.

Deer and antelope class rifles really start with the very excellent .243 Winchester and .244 Remington. These are also calibres we do not consider adequate for killing elk or other such size game, although they have been used quite successfully on hundreds of them. I regard them as two of the top rifles for open range deer and antelope hunting, when used with proper bullets of 100 grain or higher weight. At the small end of the calibre scale for general North American big game use I would name the 6.5 calibre and this is best exemplified today, by the very flat long range .264 Winchester. This is followed by the .270 calibre in its various forms and then by the 7mm and the .280, also in various case forms. To get the best results, strict attention must be given to bullet choice in all these calibres, as they all accommodate bullets of light varmint weight and construction, up to bullet weights adequate for polar and brown bear size, in most cases. Big bore advocates are always warning hunters that no calibre under .30 and some insist under .338 is adequate for even big deer size animals. This is of course, sheer nonsense and a rather ridiculous statement. Far more game is killed quickly and surely with calibres of .30 and lower than with the out-size big bores.

The .30 calibre rifle is one of the most popular calibres anywhere in the shooting world today, and is used by hunters for all types of game, except a few of the large size African game animals. It is made in many case sizes and this governs velocity and power. They range from the .300 Savage, the newer .308 Winchester up to the .30/06, .300 Magnum and to the ultimate in the .30 calibres the .300 Ackley "improved" and the .300 Weatherby Magnum, that are used on animals of all sizes the world over.

A rifle selected for the larger North American game only, such as the Polar bear, Brown bear and large Alaskan moose could be the new .338 Winchester and the new .358 Norma. These are entirely adequate in calibres above .30 calibre. However, many shooters prefer calibres of less recoil and find the 7mm Magnums exactly what they want, with the 7mm Weatherby probably being the one most often selected.

This radical change from the use of the slow big bore calibre, that was once necessary, to smaller, faster flatter shooting rifles was made possible mostly through bullet improvement in the past decade or so, plus modern powders to propel them more efficiently.

Bullet Placement

I consider bullet placement the most important point in the killing of any type of game anywhere. How big the bullet is or how powerful the load in back of it is, the proper placement of that bullet is necessary to make a good kill. Accuracy of bullet placement is governed by many things. The physical and mental makeup and the experience of the individual are most important. The less recoil, on the average, the better one shoots. The use of flat shooting calibres eliminates the necessity of being a good judge of trajectory to a great extent and also lessens wind drift. Practiced use of telescope sights are a help to everyone.

Proper Bullets

The second most important point of good game kills is the proper bullet for the game you are after. While a .300 Weatherby, for instance, will shoot varmint weight and structure type bullets excessively fast and very accurately, it takes heavy jacketed, properly constructed bullets of reasonably heavy weight for penetration, expansion and shock, on heavy animals like Polar and Brown bear, to attain a quick and sure kill. The same principle applies to the lighter rifles such as the .243

Winchester and the .244 Remington that use bullets from 60 grain to 90 grain for varmints and predators and 100 grain and 105 grain thicker jacketed bullets for game.

As to the future of the calibres we have been discussing, I am of the opinion that one or probably two more calibres will be brought out on the short Magnum case, in the near future. Also that a new cartridge capable of going through the short actions such as the Remington 722, the Winchester 88 and others will be brought out in a case similar to the .244 Remington or the .308 Winchester. In as much as there are already a couple of 6mm's on such a case and the 7mm is still with us, with a .308 and .358 in the heavy class, it is indicated that the .270 would be the choice of most hunters, particularly those who like a rifle of low recoil and good velocity using proven game bullets already developed. Modern powders have also made such a case-calibre combination possible, one that will nearly approach that of the standard long case, longer action .270 Winchester. With the heavier round nose bullets this would also be a useful eastern deer rifle of low recoil.

Most all western game is killed at under 200 yards. If a hunter is experienced and a top shot used to recoil and is hunting in country where he may be required to make shots of up to 500 yards, he can do his shooting with any of the new short Magnums, at most all North American game very successfully. On the other hand, if he will pass up shots over 250 to 300 yards and stalk his game closer, he may enjoy shooting one of the new, modern standard and short standard case calibres much more and be just as deadly in killing his game and probably a great deal more accurate in bullet placement. Any one who has a .22 long rifle, a standard case center fire, such as the .243 Winchester up to the .30/06 and a short Magnum like the .264 Winchester, 7mm Remington Magnum, 7mm Weatherby or a custom rifle on the .30 Belted Newton case has all the rifles necessary for North American game. If he has money to spend, then the addition of a .300 Weatherby, a .338 Winchester or similar rifle for Alaska Browns, Polar Bear and Alaskan moose is a nice addition to his battery.

As far as I am concerned I do not think there is such a thing as an all around rifle. All around for what kind of hunter? A calibre that might suit one hunter wouldn't please the next one at all, being neither adequate for the game he wanted or pleasant for him to shoot.

The area in which a hunter plans to hunt should also be considered in choosing a calibre. For instance, in states or areas where grizzly or moose may be taken, a calibre on the short magnum case, such as any 7mm would be best to have allowing ample bullet size and plenty of power for the biggest game and still small enough to be equally good on other types of game like elk, caribou, sheep or goats. While many small case calibres have been used on the big bear, moose and grizzly, the new short case magnums have more power for penetration and shock. Of all the standard case calibres, the .30/06 comes closer to being an "all around" rifle than any other.

In black bear, elk, deer and caribou and antelope, sheep and goat country any one of the standard case jobs is entirely adequate, used with the proper bullets. These can be used in most any legal calibre size to suit the shooter.

Hunters may be divided mostly into two classes. The group of hunters who firmly believe that a big bore, heavy bullet placed just anywhere and at any angle in a game animal is the only way to get him. They use so-called "raking shots" and in fact usually just throw lead until a hit is made. This type frequently use the auto-loaders and pump guns with the same idea in mind. Sheer fire power and/or bullet size is depended upon in these cases to get their game.

The other type hunter is the marksman type of hunter who depends on properly placed bullets, of usually one shot to do his killing. This type hunter is a true sportsman. He picks each shot carefully, places the bullet correctly for a near instantaneous and one-shot kill, and gets a thrilling satisfaction from his ability to do this.

The custom gunmaker and stocker have given the big gun factories added incentive in designing and marketing better products. Remington's new 700 series line of rifles is a case in point. Handloading of ammunition by the shooters of both shotguns and rifles has a multiple appeal in money saved, better loads worked up for individual guns and the self satisfaction gained from actually creating ones own loads. Both custom gun business and the manufacturers of handloading equipment and their components, such as bullets, primers etc., have become big business. They have been a factor in increasing gun and component demands by the public to a point where big factories now widely advertise and sell components and some even market actions and barrelled actions to the trade.

Altogether the gun business is now big time, with calibres, models and refinements to fit all shooters' desires and requirements and for all members of the family from the youngsters and wives to the man of the house.

The author has made the statement from time to time that the .220 Swift is the greatest one-shot killer on deer and similar game ever produced. Many letters have been received to the effect that such a statement is proof that anyone making such a statement just proves his ignorance, that he just doesn't know what he is talking about. His opinion remains the same, which is that if 100 head of deer, for example, were to be shot with the .220 Swift (with good bullets) under average conditions and an equal number killed with a .30/06 under average conditions, that the .220 Swift would produce the most clean kills.

It is the author's studied opinion that anyone who states the .220 Swift is not a great one-shot killer, is in effect saying he never fired a .220 Swift. Some years ago the Chief of the Fish and Game Department of one of our mountain west states decided to get a regulation to outlaw the .220 Swift. Users of Swift rifles were incensed and asked the author to intercede. One, whom we must concede did not do everything legally, had killed 49 deer with 49 shots, a feat he had never even approached with other cartridges. The matter was taken up with the Fish and Game Department Chief who stated that the .220 Swift was a .22 calibre rifle so consequently was just not a deer gun. He further stated that he had killed 600 head of big game and consequently knew that the Swift couldn't kill a porcupine. Under some questioning as to his actual experience with the Swift, it soon came to light that he had never fired a Swift rifle. Now this man was obviously an experienced hunter, but how could he be qualified to say anything, either pro or con, about a cartridge he had never fired? The regulation went through. Now this same state has a new crop of law breakers. Regulations of this kind, and there are a multitude of them through the fifty states, have made it almost safer to poach a deer than it is to attempt to kill one legally.

A regulation stating that it is illegal to hunt deer with a rimfire rifle may be in order, but the hair splitting regulations now being enforced make little sense. We read in the papers daily about highway deaths and the safety councils would have us believe that every driver is out to commit suicide. In reality, the accident rate per million miles travelled is smaller each year and continues to go down. This must mean that the great preponderance of drivers drive carefully. The same can be said of hunters. There are very few who would go afield in quest of big game who would take an inadequate rifle. Regulations of this kind may bring in revenue, but great disrespect for the law at the same time.

Mr. Lester Womack, now a ranger at the Grand Canyon National Park, is an experienced hunter who has had wide hunting experience both as a big game hunter and in control work. He has used the .220 Swift almost since its introduction and has had wide experience hunting in the company of hunters using much larger cartridges. He has had greater opportunity to observe the effectiveness of the Swift in comparison with other cartridges than almost anyone. Mr. Womack has the following to say about the .220 Swift:

An average adult jack burro. A lucky shot behind the ear at fifty yards dropped him in a dead run.

That great ivory hunter, the late W. D. M. Bell, killed more than eight hundred head of the biggest bull elephants in Africa. For this task did he use the .416 Rigby? The .450/500? The .600 Nitro Express? Certainly not. He used the 7mm Mauser. In those days, as now, in Africa as in America, the argument of the big bore versus the small bore raged. Mr. Bell found that the 7mm rifle killed elephants dead—and nothing will kill deader than dead. He was an exceptionally cool shot and had an excellent knowledge of the anatomy of the elephant. Even the .600 Nitro will not kill elephants with poorly placed shots and there are many recorded instances where elephants simply vanished—carrying with them a number of these massive 900 grain slugs! Now, in this land of ours, there are hunters who will tell you with a straight face that the 7mm Mauser cartridge is barely adequate for deer and should never be used on the elk or brown bear. The fine .270 Winchester, some will tell you, is a passable deer cartridge and that is about all. For any of the smaller calibers they have nothing but contempt.

Just why these cannon worshipers should hold such animosity toward the small bore rifle is not too obvious. Perhaps it is just a hang-over from the big lead bullets of black powder days. Perhaps it is just because, in this country anyway, most people like everything big. Big houses, big autos, big hats, the bigger the better.

Each year these big bore enthusiasts take to the field with their particular rifle, be it .35 Newton, .375 H&H, or .458 Winchester, and announce to the world that they have the only suitable rifle for taking the thin skinned game of America. They go to great lengths to denounce the smaller calibers and their users and extoll the virtues of the big, heavy, bullet. To the heavy bullet clan's way of thinking, the big bores kill like the wrath of God, and the little ones are mere toys. On the other hand, the small bore rifleman goes his way, gets his share of game, and it never enters his head to deride the big bore. If anything, he feels a bit sorry for the chap who must shoot a rifle with a punishing recoil and fearsome muzzle blast.

In the early days of game laws, some attempt was made to determine what rifle was legal and what rifle was not legal to shoot big game. At that time the Game and Fish Department of my native state of Arizona came up with the magic number of 87. A rifle propelling a bullet of 87 grains was legal, but the 86 grain .25/20 was left out in the cold. Then again, the

.32/20 with its 100 grain bullet had the blessings of the Game and Fish, as did a whole array of pistol type cartridges with bullets over 86 grains in weight. Later on some attempt was made to rectify this sad situation by getting out the ballistic tables and selecting cartridges that had a certain bullet weight AND a certain number of foot pounds of energy at 100 yards. Recently, they have modernized the regulations by announcing that the legal rifle will be .23 caliber, or larger. Then they go on to state that *handguns* of .357 Magnum and .44 Magnum caliber will also be legal. Hot Dogs! It is now about time to gaze in the crystal ball and "revise" these laws again. It would seem that the only way out of the dilemma of this monumental mess would be to legalize any gun that goes "BANG."

From these "Weapon Regulations," it is more than noticeable that the Game and Fish Department has discriminated against the very small bore cartridges, i.e.: the .220 Swift, .22/250, and .228 Ackley Magnum. Do they have valid reasons? Has the Department conducted exhaustive research and found that these cartridges with their light weight bullets and ultra high velocities do not produce clean kills? Has the deparmtnet discovered some mysterious fact that the merest six thousandths of an inch will make one rifle suitable for taking big game and the other not? To the best of this author's knowledge, no game department in this country has made any effort whatsoever to conduct any serious studies on the comparative efficiency of various cartridges.

For the past twenty years this writer has made an effort to find out why the small bore, ultra velocity rifle has been outlawed by the majority of the big game states. To this end I must confess utter failure. From the non-user the answers are always the same: "It's too small." "They won't penetrate." "They only wound and won't leave a blood trail," etc.

A few years ago I was going through the question and answer section of a national outdoor publication and came upon a statement that stopped me cold. A chap had written asking what loads they recommended in the .22/250 for deer. To this innocent question one of the "experts" curtly answered: "The .22/250 Varmiter is not suitable under any circumstances for deer, nor is any other .22 caliber rifle." Period, finish, et all.....
I sat down at once and got a letter off to the editor of the magazine, taking strong exception to this statement. I asked what experience this statement was based on;

the kind and number of deer shot by this party, and the loads used. A very courteous letter came back from the editor to the effect that the "expert" was not alone in his opinion and that "this is one of those answers that can only reflect opinion and can never be proven one way or the other." As a life member of the organization that published the magazine I felt I was entitled to somewhat more satisfaction, so a second letter went out. I stressed the point that all I was interested in were the facts which prompted this party to make such a statement. To this the editor replied that "Quite frankly, I hesitate to impose upon Mr. -------- to supply the information that you request in your letter of March 31st." He ended this letter by very acidly announcing the fact that this was "not a ground for continuing debate upon a very debateable point." My third letter was never answered, so I must assume that neither the editor nor his "expert" had ever killed a single head of deer with the .22/250.

As an old small bore buff, this writer was electrified late in 1935 with the news that Winchester had developed an ultra-velocity cartridge. First reports were a bit sketchy, but the fact that a factory rifle, the Model 54 Winchester, was available with a cartridge of factory loading that gave an instrumental muzzle velocity of 4,140 feet per second with the 48 grain bullet was enough to stir the imagination.

For some time I had been shooting the relatively new .22 Hornet. With its greater velocity and flatter trajectory, it was decidedly more effective than the .22 Long Rifle I had used for years on the prairie dogs, jack rabbits, and coyotes, of the southwestern desert. If the Hornet was efficient at a muzzle velocity of 2,600 feet per second, what could be expected of the Swift with 4,140?

My first Swift was acquired in 1942, somewhat by accident. It was purchased from a disillusioned turkey hunter that had found it was anything but a turkey rifle. Right off I mounted a 330 Weaver scope on the new acquisition and obtained a set of loading dies. World War II was on, but I had a good supply of powder and primers and R. B. Sisk was able to supply a quantity of his very fine 49 grain Express bullets. I was in business.

The first day in the field with the new Swift was most revealing. We were hunting the desert West of Wickenburg, Arizona. This is an area of vast, flat valleys, hemmed in by barren desert mountains. The valleys are cut by deep arroyos running into wide stream beds, always dry except in the rainy season when the violent desert rains send muddy torrents of water rushing to the Hassayampa River. For such a seemingly barren country there is an abundance of wildlife. Jack rabbits, coyotes, bob cats, and badgers provide the rifleman with plenty of sport. Sitting on the bank of an arroyo and glassing the wide stream beds, one can shoot jack rabbits at ranges from 50 to 300 yards. Here the flat trajectory of the Swift was uncanny, and the effect of such velocity on these big rabbits was something to behold! Never had I seen jack rabbits disintegrate like this; the occasional coyote was killed in his tracks, looking as if someone had yanked a rug from under him. Here, I decided, was the last word in a varmint rifle.

After several months of this desert shooting I began to wonder what the effects would be of this tiny, high speed bullet on big game. Of course it had been arbitrarily outlawed for use on big game by the Game Departments of most states.

Then my work took me to an area where a large number of deer are struck by highway traffic each year. The animals that aren't killed outright must be hunted down and destroyed. Here no restrictions were placed on the weapon used and I had free reign. These were some of the largest of the Rocky Mountain mule deer and an excellent experiment for the Swift. Many deer were broken down and posed no problem except to walk up and shoot them. Others took a great deal of search to find and were quite wary. Though badly injured, many with broken legs, they could still get around rather well and proved quite able at eluding the hunter. I soon found that the Swift was the most efficient rifle I had ever used on deer. With any solid hit a deer went down and never got up. It was a very rare occasion when a second shot was required. Upon autopsy it was found that the bullet disintegrated in the body cavity. It was noted that the lung-liver area shot was extremely effective. Here the bullet seemed to disintegrate into infinitesimal fragments and spread through a wide area. Even the "gut shot" put them down, but they didn't appear to die on their feet as with the liver shot. The standard 48 grain factory load and the 49 grain Sisk Express handload seemed to perform about the same.

In 1949 I came into a supply of 50 grain Ackley Controlled Expansion bullets. These bullets are virtually solid copper, pierced at the tip in the punch press, and ten grains of lead inserted. This is then folded into place by the next operation of the press which produces the ogive of the point. In practice, this bit of lead starts the expansion of the copper. These bullets, unfortunately, are no longer available.

The first deer I shot with the Ackley bullet was a bit over 100 yards away. A large barren doe, she faced me at an angle, and I aimed low in the midsection. As the rifle fired, she fell, and a puff of smoke went up from the limestone ledge behind her! She was dead when I arrived; the bullet passing completely through the lower part of the shoulder, lungs, and out the rib cage on the far side. Here was truly deep penetration. It has been my experience that this bullet will generally pass completely through on a broadside shot. However, the broadside shot is still very deadly. Another memorable shot with the Ackley bullet concerned a large three point buck. Three points on one side, that is, because the other had been shot off by a hunter. He had also been shot through the knee of the right front leg, rendering it useless. This leg was carried curled up under his chest and the hoof had grown out several inches longer than the other from non-use. Needless to say, he was very spooky, and it took several days to get the cross wires on him. This was finally accomplished late one afternoon as he was running up a hill, as best he could, for a stand of timber. It was a poor shot but I had to take it. The bullet struck him in the right hip-pocket, through the intestines, grazed the heart, and a fragment came to rest in the left shoulder. On the impact of the bullet he fell, slid back down the hill a few feet, and all was quiet. A bullet hole was noted in one ear. When opened up it was found that he had been shot through the lungs twice some time before, breaking two ribs, and the wounds had completely healed over. On each side the lungs had grown to the broken ribs, with no apparent harmful effects. So ended the life of a spunky old patriarch—with one 50 grain Swift bullet.

In the summer of 1948 an opportunity presented itself for testing the Swift on animals larger than deer. In the wild, desolate canyon and plateau country of northern Arizona roam scattered bands of feral burros. These are the descendants of the faithful beast of burden used so extensively by the prospectors of the old West.

They are a far cry from the diminutive donkey of the amusement park variety. The ancestors of today's burros either escaped from their owners or were simply released to make their own way when the "pay dirt" of the mines gave out and they were no longer needed. Through selective breeding the early miners had developed an animal as large as a small Missouri mule. They were not only used for packing ore but were ridden by husky miners. They had to be tough and were preferred to any horse or mule by the people who lived in this harsh country. Even on their poor range of today these animals are generally in good shape and a large jack in his prime will tip the scales at 600 pounds, or more.

Tough and highly adaptable to the arid conditions of their environment they began to prosper. In fact, they prospered to such an extent that they began to literally eat themselves out of house and home. They had no natural enemies to speak of. The native wildlife was no match for this aggressive newcomer. The wild burro successfuly drove the big horn sheep and deer from the limited number of available springs and took over large areas of wildlife range that the cattleman had not invaded. I was assigned the job of helping to bring the number of these animals down to the safe carrying capacity of their range.

My companions in this reduction program were armed with a variety of weapons: .30/40, .30/06, 8mm Mauser, and other acceptable big game rifles. At first they were very skeptical that I would use a .22 caliber rifle on anything as heavy as burros. Past experience had shown that these animals took a lot of killing. I agreed to abandon the Swift if it did not prove as effective as any other rifle used. After the first day in the field they agreed that this was indeed a good burro rifle; either I had made some very lucky shots or the tiny bullet was effective after all. A few more days and they were wanting to shoot the Swift themselves.

The burros, gregarious by nature, run in bands of a dozen or so. At the first shot the band will stampede in all directions and the shooting is fast and furious. Here the Swift proved itself time and again as each solid shot would put the animal down. It was soon obvious to all that the Swift made more clean, one shot kills, than any other caliber used. Range seemed to make little difference in the performance of the Swift, and these animals were killed up to 600 yards.

Feral burro in typical environment. These animals thrive in this harsh country.

Possibly there are a couple of reasons for the Swift's phenomenal success as a big game rifle that are not apparent to the non-user. First, let us consider bullet construction. From experience this writer has found that any bullet of heavy enough construction to stand the 4,140 foot seconds muzzle velocity will perform well on big game. This means that the bullet must have a fairly heavy jacket, or it will simply disintegrate in mid-air before reaching the target. A light jacketed bullet will disintegrate every time, and I have even had some of the so-called "Hi-Velocity" bullets do the same. In addition to using a heavy jacket on Swift bullets, Winchester copper-plates the core in an attempt to insulate it from the vicious friction heat created by passage through the bore. Custom bullet makers are content to use an extra heavy jacket, and these bullets give deep penetration in large animals. Fred Barnes, the bullet man of Grand Junction, Colorado, uses copper tubing to make the heaviest jacketed bullets available for the Swift. The Sisk 49 grain Express bullets with their tiny soft point give excellent accuracy and performance on all animals from jack rabbit to jack-ass. A number of Swift addicts I know are jealously hoarding a supply of Ackley Controlled Expansion bullets for use on elk and larger game.

Another factor overlooked almost entirely in the performance of the Swift, is rotational spin. At 4,140 feet per second the Swift bullet leaves the muzzle spinning at the fantastic rate of 212,916 revolutions per minute! Time and again I have heard some arm-chair ballistic engineer announce that the poorly shaped Swift bullet has lost so much velocity at 500 yards that it hasn't the speed of the .22 Long Rifle. Perhaps this is true, although I know of no one that has chronographed one at 500 yards, but we know from experience that they kill at ranges beyond this very effectively. So, there must be something besides velocity to make a killer of this tiny bullet at extreme ranges and rotational spin is the only thing left. Velocity falls off rapidly due to air resistance, BUT, the bullet loses very little of its rotational spin during its entire flight. Autopsy on animals killed at extreme ranges show damaged tissue some distance from the entry point of the bullet—the same as animals shot at close range. As the bullet enters an animal, at any range, and begins to upset, the centrifugal force causes it to go to pieces—with devastating effect.

As a big game cartridge then, this author has weighed the Swift in the balance, so to speak, and it has not been found wanting. Still, this is only one hunter's experience. The test is incomplete. In all fairness, many men would have to duplicate my study to find all the answers. One thing is definite: If I were forced to choose only one rifle from my rack and forsake all others, the choice would be simple—I would reach for the .220 Swift!

1/2" armor-plate from frontal area on U.S. half-track. In this penetration test, the 48 grain .220 Swift factory load penetrated completely, leaving holes approximately 3/8" diameter. 100 grain .270 Winchester; no penetration. G.I., so-called armor piercing round, made shallow craters, .070" and .098" deep respectively. All shots fired from a distance of 30 feet.

The .17 Calibre

To go still further in proving that game animals do not take so much killing as some would have us believe, some research work was done to uncover a few facts about the diminutive .17 calibre. The most popular .17 calibre bullet is the 25 grain and its effectiveness on large animals is quite astounding, especially to big bore (Magnum) addicts who have had the opportunity (or have been forced) to observe the effect of these small high velocity bullets on fairly large animals. This is not to advocate the use of a 25 grain bullet on big game, but to simply point out that there is something wrong with some of the theories on killing power. Lou Williamson, a young gunsmith of Fort Worth, Texas, has used .17 calibre rifles quite extensively in order to find out just what they can and will do. Lou writes the following:

The various .17 calibre cartridges have excited my imagination almost as far back as I can remember, starting with boyhood and my trusty Daisy Red Ryder Special, which did not have a very high velocity and shot projectiles that I found out much later were very poorly shaped ballistically. Nevertheless, I managed to consistently hit what I was aiming at, as long as the range did not exceed 15 to 20 feet. Shooting flies off of the garage walls was easy, and one time I even accomplished the difficult feat of hitting a live shotgun shell primer while it was still in the case. However, I did remove the shot and powder, although, looking back, I'm surprised at my foresight. Upon being hit by the steel BB the primer blew out of its pocket and turned into a pretty classy projectile in its own right, flying straight at my head and plowing a neat furrow fore and aft along my scalp. I also had the dubious honor of being the only kid around who would shoot small pistol primers out of my Daisy, and incidentally they made a very satisfying "pop" when they hit a hard object. Such memories sorta frighten me now, though, since I'm trying to raise two boys of my own. Hope they make it!

The first three .17 calibre cartridges I became familiar with were the .17 Hornet, .17 Bee and .17 Lovell, with no exotic names, and despite the exotic names nothing has really changed very much, except accuracy. We now have the .17 Woodsman, .17 Pee Wee, .17 Javelina, .17 A&M, .17/.222, and others I'm sure, but I don't feel that all these case designs have really accomplished very much. Velocity is still pretty much the same, however, accuracy lately has improved considerably, although I'm sure this is not due to case design. Velocity wise, the .17 Bee practically equals the .17/222, which has considerably greater powder capacity. The betterment of accuracy has come about as a result of more uniform bullets and much better barrels.

Barrels and bullets have always been the big problems in accuracy attainment. Demand for the .17's has never been as great as, for instance, the .224's; consequently, money and time, for research and improvement has been sadly lacking. Lately, however, the situation seems to be changing. With the population rapidly expanding, and rural areas becoming more and more settled, the demand for a calibre that has a comparatively mild report, and yet will not produce many dangerous ricochets, is steadily increasing. I believe the various .17's fill the bill perfectly.

My personal experience with the .17 calibre cartridge has been limited to two: the .17 Javelina, which is a shortened, necked down, blown out .222 case, and the .17 Ackley Bee, simply a necked down, blown out .218 Bee case.

I have heard a lot of talk and controversy concerning accuracy, wind drift, and killing powder. I shall try to cover these in turn.

The first .17 I built for myself was a .17 Javelina with a 22-inch Ackley barrel, muzzle diameter of .565, using a Sako L-46 action, and a piece of highly figured Texas Mesquite for the stock. The rifle is equipped with a Weaver J2.5 scope and a Litschert 8X attachment, in a Buehler Mount, and complete—it weighed under seven pounds.

My first attempts at working up a load were very disappointing. I could not get my groups under approximately 1-1/2 inches. I reworked the bedding of the barrel in the stock at least three times, but this made very little difference in accuracy. I tried any number of loads using 3031, 4198, and even 2400, with both 20 and 25 grain bullets. The results were still the same, the groups just would not tighten. That left two things, the barrel and/or the bullets. I was confident that the fault did not lie with the barrel, as it just looked too "purty" inside, and it turned out I was right. The bullets! I ordered some Holmes 25 grain bench rest bullets, and they did the trick. My groups immediately started to tighten. I finally settled on 17.0 grains of 4198 with the Holmes bullet and my best group so far measures 5/16". I believe that this pretty well shoots the story that the .17's are inaccurate.

One more thing concerning accuracy. I recently built a .17 Ackley Bee on a .310 Martini action just to have a car gun. The barrel is 20 inches long and measures .565 at the muzzle. The military stock and fore-end were left on (with some altering of the latter) and the rifle is equipped with a J4 Weaver scope, and it weighs a mere 5 3/8 pounds complete. I whipped up some cases, fire-formed them, and literally threw together some loads for preliminary testing (making sure they were safe, of course). These loads consisted of approximately 13 grains of 4198, measured not weighed and a 20 grain Sisk bullet. To my surprise I obtained groups of less than an inch with this haphazard combination. I am anxious to see just what this rifle is capable of and I'm sure that finding the proper combination it will beat the heck out of what it's doing now.

Therein lies the crux of the matter, as they say. If the accuracy critics of the .17's would take the time to find the proper powder, primer and bullet combinations for their rifles without trying to burn up the barrel with speed, I'm sure they would reach the same conclusions I have, and that is, that the .17 calibre cartridges are as basically accurate, as any other purely varmint cartridge.

And now to wind-drift. I cannot quote you a bunch of unintelligible mathematical formulas to confuse you (and me). I can only relate to you my opinions and observations for what they're worth. The 25 grain .17 calibre bullet has the same sectional density as the 55 grain .224 bullet, and while it has less than half the weight, it also has less than half the cross-sectional area for the wind to work on. I cannot see why it would be more susceptible to wind-drift than any other bullet with the same sectional density at the same velocity. Maybe I'm wrong, but my range experience bears out these thoughts. With a gusty cross-wind (and a Texas gust is a pretty good sized gust) my groups show approximately twice as much lateral dispersement as normal. I do not consider this excessive since my groups are still approximately an inch across, (I said my best group was 5/16 inch, not my average group.)

As for killing power. This I can find absolutely no complaint with. Of course I don't use the rifles on elk but I have shot deer with some rather dramatic results as I'll tell you about later. The first kills with the Javelina was a buzzard, "jest a sitting in the trees." Instantaneous kills, but no spectacular explosive effect as is sometimes seen with the larger varmint calibres. I believe though, that this can be attributed to the fact that I was using the Holmes bench rest bullets, which are tremendously accurate but a little thick jacketed for much explosive effect on small varmints, although all kills were instantaneous. The Sisk bullets are much more explosive but, in my Javelina, are not nearly so accurate. I have also killed porcupines out of pine trees (the porcupines were in the pine trees, not me) at anywhere from 150 to 200 yards. Same story, instantaneous kills. Last summer, while we were driving up Sarcillo Canyon on my father-in-law's ranch in southern Colorado, my wife spotted a coyote in the upper end of a long draw. .I stopped the car and fumbled around to get my rifle, which was locked up in the rear of my Morris station wagon, but by the time I got the rifle, the coyote was running up the hill at the far end of the draw. I put the cross-hairs on an opening ahead of him and as his nose crossed them I touched off. The coyote folded and slid about fifteen feet back down the hill, stone dead. I started walking and it took 304 long paces to get to him. A lucky shot you say—sure, I agree, but it does speak well for the killing power of the .17 calibre rifle don't you think?

Every year I make my annual South Texas deer hunt sort of an experimental hunt. The first deer I shoot with my .257 Roberts Improved, and believe me, it never fails, no matter it seems, where I place the shot. The second deer I usually try out something new on. This past season I decided to try the .17 Javelina. Before some of you start yelling; Texas allows any center fire cartridge to be used on deer. Some counties prohibit rimfires but this is the only calibre restriction in the game regulations. I won't go into the details of the hunt because it is not the purpose of this report, and mind you, I am not unequivocably recommending the .17's for big game, but in this particular instance the results were rather startling, at least to me.

I shot a running deer at a range of 125 to 150 yards, the shot entering the left side high, just ahead of the pelvis. Upon being hit the deer's front quarters collapsed completely with the rear end still up in the air and rear legs stiff. The deer bleated two or three times and rolled over stone dead. Another practically instantaneous kill! My brother and I searched the hide thoroughly for evidence of a wound, and we finally found a minute drop of blood where the bullet had entered, but there was no exit hole. I then cut the throat but no blood flowed. Hanging the deer in a tree I proceeded to dress it out, and upon coming to the wound area the blood fell out as if it were another organ. In the time it had taken us to approach the deer, all the blood in the body had converged on the wound area and had already coagulated. Maybe this is nothing spectacular to some, but it is the first time I have ever experienced these results from a rifle shot. The shock must have been terrific.

I am convinced that I have found an eminently satisfying purely varmint calibre, both for short and medium ranges. I would not recommend it for consistent performance at ranges exceeding 250 yards, however, even though, as I have related, good kills are obtainable at longer ranges.

I feel sure that anyone desiring this type rifle would do well to give one of the .17's a fair trial, without relying on a lot of hearsay. I'm confident that they'll wind up feeling about them as I do. I believe there is a tremendous future for them.

Another small bore addict who wishes to remain anonymous tried a .17 calibre on wild burros of the Southwest. His report is as follows:

I don't have much to offer, as the -------- Game Department takes a dim view of people shooting burros at all, as the bird watchers and horse lovers want to protect the burro, even though they are taking over the desert sheep country, driving off the sheep and ruining the water holes. Had been wanting to shoot a burro with the .17 ever since I made up the little rifle I have, but never wanted to carry it on a burro hunt, and perhaps after a day or two of rough hunting to find burros at perhaps 250 or 300 yards. Would be like using a pea shooter. Hadn't hunted them for several years, as I probably have killed my share already. However, this opportunity came up to hunt from a Jeep, and both my buddy and I wanted to see if the .17 would do more than just tickle them.

We hit the burro country about one week after the water dried up there, so did not find the burros until nearly sunset. Finally found a canyon with three of them, one old big jenny, one young nearly grown one, and one about half grown. After the usual stalking came out of the canyon rim about 100 yards above them, and ------ had told me to go ahead and shoot when ready, and take the first shot, as he would back me up with the .25/06 if necessary. The first shot with the .17 took the old gal in the neck, below the vertebrae. She got sick and could just barely take a step or two. Hit her again in the shoulder and just back of the shoulder, and she finally went down, and could not get back up. ------ hit the nearly grown one in the shoulder, and it travelled about 10 or 15 yards, and collapsed. I handed him the .17 and he took the small one in the neck and it dropped and never got up. The 25 grain bullet went through the jugular vein and out the other side, blood all over the place over an area of 20 feet in all directions. It looked ridiculous, the tiny pin holes in this big burro, yet getting the job done. By this time it was just about sunset and we had several miles of roadless desert and canyon country to get over before dark, so we did not take time to probe for bullet depth, etc., etc. I kidded ------ about the performance of the .17, as in this instance it was a better killer than the .25/06, which goes to prove that it takes a lot more than three kills to prove anything. I might try to kill 50 more burros and never again get the job done with the 25 grain bullet.

As I remember, I have gotten 4 turkeys and 5 javelina with the .17 calibre, never lost a one of them that was hit. I don't believe that any turkey hit, and I shoot them in the big middle, ever spoiled any more meat than a chunk about the size of my thumb. I believe that the bullet passed through every turkey that I have shot, and the javelina shot this year was hit right behind the shoulder at about 185 yards, bullet passed all the way through, and the pig went down in about a minute, within 100 feet of where he was hit.

REDUCED LOADS

In this author's opinion there is sufficient evidence that reduced charges of slow burning powders cause detonating effects which warrant concern on the part of the handloader. Such reactions or detonations are extremely hard to reproduce in the laboratory, but so many blown up rifles have been brought to the writer during the past twenty years that had been fired with reduced, or slightly reduced charges of slow burning powder that the problem can hardly be ignored.

This phenomenon occurs mostly in badly over-bore capacity cases—a good example being the "improved" .25/06. At least a dozen rifles chambered for this cartridge have been brought to this writer in wrecked or severely damaged condition, and no other cause could be found, but in each instance the load had been a reduced charge of slow burning powder such as 4350, 4831 or H450.

One Model 70 Winchester rifle chambered for the .240 Page Super Pooper was practically demolished with a half charge of 4350. The owner had developed a satisfactory load consisting of 50 grains of 4350. He later decided that the load was too powerful for some of his hunting, so the powder charge was cut to 25 grains. The first shot blew the primer. The second seemed normal so the shooter decided that perhaps the first cartridge had a double charge. The third shot just about demolished the rifle.

It is often written that slow powders in reduced charges with excessive airspace in an oversize case causes high pressures. This may be the wrong term since obviously 25 grains of powder is not going to produce the pressure that 50 grains does. This might make one believe that other factors contribute to the devastating effect. For example, the light charge of powder may assume some special position within the case, such as becoming compacted in the forward portion of the case body and neck directly in contact with the bullet. This would place the powder some distance from the primer. When the primer is detonated,

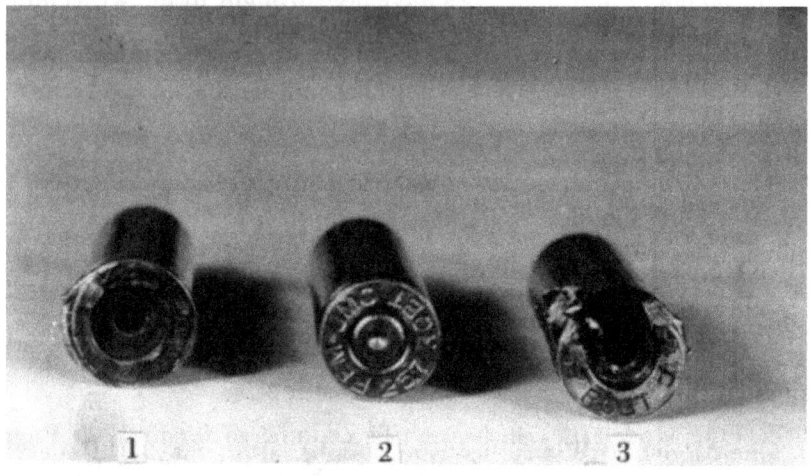

Figure 1. Cartridge #1 fired with a 50% reduced charge. Case in the middle, #2 appeared to be normal. Case #3, is one which caused all the damage.

REDUCED LOADS

Figure 2. This photograph shows the damage done inside the receiver.

Figure 3. Case #3 shown in the end of the barrel after the barrel was removed from the receiver but before the case was taken out of the barrel.

the flash has to travel a comparatively long distance through the airspace before igniting the powder. This flash could build pressure enough to further compact the powder charge into a tightly packed or almost solid mass against the base of the bullet and against the sharp shoulder of the cartridge case. After this has taken place, the rear surface of the charge ignites and as it builds pressure, a further compacting of the unburned portion of the powder occurs until a point is reached where the "fire goes out", or the charge detonates causing the brass case to flow back into the action because the compact mass of powder and bullet is obstructing its passage down the barrel. We believe this sometimes occurs because in numerous instances when test firing guns in a vertical position with the muzzle down, the guns appeared to misfire, but when the cartridges were broken down it was found that the powder charge was packed so tightly behind the bullet that it could be removed with a small screwdriver only with great difficulty, and when the portion of the charge nearest the primer was removed, it was found to be partially burned. It can easily be imagined what could happen if the primer had been enough stronger to ignite the powder charge more completely.

Another example is a .220 Swift which was being loaded with 70 grain .22 High Power bullets. Knowing the bullets were .004 oversize, the owner started with 25 grains of 4831 powder and worked up. Pressures seemed high. At about 30 grains the primers started to loosen. Finally he decided that perhaps the pressure indications were due to something besides the oversize bullet and tried 40 grains of powder and this heavy charge showed no excessive pressure, and the lot of bullets were used up with no further trouble. On the surface of things it would appear that the main difference between these two charges OTHER THAN THE WEIGHT of powder was the airspace which was quite great with the light charge as compared to no air space at all with the heavy charge.

A bad accident happened with a Rolling Block action which was barrelled for the very badly over-bore capacity .244 H&H. Loads were worked up using .50 calibre machine gun powder and a 100 grain bullet. Results were quite satisfactory with upwards of 70 grains of this powder. The charge was later reduced 20 grains. The gun literally disintegrated with the first shot. Parts of the gun and scope were picked up a hundred yards around. These parts of the action and barrel were sent to a metallurgical laboratory and no flaws of any kind were found. Another action was barrelled to make an identical gun and further tests were made. It was finally concluded that the reduced powder charge caused the trouble.

The Ordnance Department has observed the phenomenon, and the DuPont Company has observed it in tests made in their laboratories.

Suppliers of components have in some instances tried to hush up accidents of this type because they feel it will hurt the sale of components if they are brought to the attention of the shooting public. Actually one would think that the truth would be far better than to keep handloaders in the dark. All suppliers of reloading components stock a wide variety of powders. Within the lists are powders adapted to specific applications, so the correct powder could just as easily be sold, as to try to push some number which may result in an accident. Certainly one accident hurts the game more than the simple truth.

Claims are made by manufacturers of primers that their Magnum types help to nullify the detonating effects of reduced loads of slow burning powders and this can very well be true. Magnum primers produce a flash of longer duration which could help penetrate airspace and still satisfactorily ignite the powder. The following is a copy of "Technical Bulletin No. 100" issued by the Cascade Cartridge, Inc. in April 1961. This report has to do with the development and performance of special Magnum primers which should be of great interest to users of over-bore capacity cartridges with slow burning powder and with both full and reduced charges.

In response to the many requests received by us, the following is a report on the development and performance of the CCI Magnum Primers.

The amount of brisance of the priming mixture was one of the chief problems in the development of the magnum mixture. The term 'brisance' can be defined as the rate of explosion or the shattering effect shown by the explosives. If a primer is violent or very brisant in character it will ignite the large or difficult to ignite powder charges. However, the manner in which this ignition takes place is neither uniform nor desirable. In fact, in some cases we find it highly undesirable because of the 'frangibility' of some powders. A frangible powder is one in which the individual powder grain can be broken into many smaller granulations by the explosive blast of a violent primer, thus increasing the burning rate of the powder many times, which in turn results in extremely dangerous pressures.

To avoid the above condition, it was found that the proper primer fuel in the mixture could give a very excellent answer to our difficult ignition problem. All propellent powders must first be raised in temperature to a point where they will burn. This temperature is known as the 'kindling temperature' or, as in the field of ballistics, as the 'temperature of ignition'.

This temperature of ignition is different for each type of powder. For example, a pistol powder would require a much lower temperature for ignition than a slow burning rifle powder. The primer fuel which was found to be successful has the ability to produce a maximum heat level and to maintain this heat level inside the case for a much longer period of time. The advantages of this can be shown very easily to your own satisfaction with the use of a 'home barbecue'. If we pour gasoline on the charcoal fuel in the barbecue and ignite it with a match the resulting fire is of a short duration and 'brisant' in character. Also, it is doubtful that the charcoal fuel started to burn. Now, if we pour 'coal oil' or something similar on the charcoal fuel and ignite it with a match, the fire is of a much milder nature and of longer duration, resulting in the ignition of the charcoal fuel. Because of the 'longer heat duration', produced by the No. 250 Large Rifle Magnum Primer, we were able to ignite large powder charges in the manner desired and achieved a much more uniform ignition. It should be noted here that the longer heat duration is not something which can be detected without the use of special equipment. The No. 250 will produce all its heat and energy in the matter of a few thousandths of a second, and will in all visible and audible appearances be the same as any other primer.

In order that we might prove our margin of uniformity many types of tests were made. However, the cold tests should be considered as of major significance. As previously stated, we must raise the temperature of the powder charge to the ignition temperature before it will burn. Therefore, if we drop the powder temperature down to -70°F., we have in effect made the powder charge many times more difficult to ignite. Please realize that we do not expect primers to be used at these extremely low temperatures in the field and our object here is to exaggerate the condition. Results were most pleasing. For example, a typical test using 74 grains of 4831 powder in a .300 H&H Magnum show an average velocity loss from 72°F. to -70°F. as follows:

	Maximum	Minimum	*Extreme Variation*
Average competitive brands	3157 fs	2801 fs	356 fs
CCI No. 250	3190 fs	3065 fs	135 fs

As can be seen from the above, the percentage of velocity loss of the No. 250 is considerably less than our competition. A fact that was found to exist in every different type of powder tested.

A mathematical application known as 'standard deviation' can be used to find the degree of uniformity which exists in a given string of test shots. With this standard deviation, we are able to predict to a very fine degree, the amount of uniformity which will exist in literally thousands of unfired rounds of any given load. The importance of the predicted uniformity should not be overlooked even though explanation of the mathematics used in its computation is far beyond the scope of this report. Standard deviation indicates the uniformity of a primer at any temperature, and this was a great help in the development of of the No. 250 mixture. Normally, when cold tests are shot, we find the standard deviation will show a much larger foot seconds spread. This is not desirable. It was most gratifying to this department when we found that the mixture now used in the No. 250 primer gave excellent standard deviation at all temperature ranges.

Many examples could be given, however the following are typical. Test temperature minus 70°F. figures shown in foot seconds.

Standard Deviation:
    Average competitive brands   125.4 fs
    CCI No. 250   17.4 fs

When the temperature is raised to 72°F. the excellent standard deviation qualities still exist.

    Average competitive brands   53.0 fs
    CCI No. 250   13.0 fs

In conclusion this department feels that the magnum primers can be used in any size case with any type of powder. Even though the first intent of this primer was to provide the large capacity case shooter with a better primer for his particular needs, we find the shooter using reduced loads can also benefit in many ways.

Briefly, the advantages of the magnum primers can be summarized as follows:

1. Reduced charges will be more uniformly ignited because of the maximum heat duration and the fact that the shape and placement of the powder charge in the case is not a critical item since the available heat is sustained for a period long enough to ignite the powder charge properly even though it has had an excessive air space to heat. This is one of the problems encountered with regular primers in reduced loads.

2. Another advantage is the fact that the magnum primer will light powders which are heavily coated with deterrent. Maximum heat is present long enough for all powder grains to ignite and burn at their intended intensity. This is a great advantage to large case capacity shooters.

3. Also, we feel this primer will be of major importance to anyone hunting or living in an area of extreme cold. Not only

will he have a greater degree of velocity uniformity, but he will enjoy an increase in velocity over current primers.

4. The increase in uniformity of pressure and velocity and the excellent standard deviation qualities achieved with the magnum primer is aimed at an end product of even greater dependability and accuracy. Cascade Cartridge, Inc., Elmer R. Imthurn, Ballistician

Jack O'Connor, the famous arms authority has had extensive handloading experience and has often observed the detonating tendencies of slow burning powders. He has quite extensively researched the subject and herewith are presented some of his thoughts on the problem.

Blow-ups with Slow Burning Powder, by Jack O'Connor

Several years ago I took a pet .270 out to do some casual practice shooting. I had fired several shots. Then I let one off. The report sounded like that of a cannon. Smoke curled up out of the action, and when I tried to open the bolt, it would not budge. The barrel had to be taken off the rifle in order to get the cartridge case out, and we found one of the locking lugs cracked. The primer pocket was egg-shaped and twice the normal size, and the head of the case was plastered all over the face of the bolt. Getting ahead of the story, Al Biesen, the Spokane, Washington custom rifle maker, put in a new barrel and a new bolt and the rifle was OK.

When I had time, I pulled all the bullets in the unfired cartridges in that particular box of ammunition. I had loaded with 130 gr bullets and 60 grains of 4831. I threw the charge with two yanks on the lever of an Ideal powder measure. All the powder charges were O.K. except one. One cartridge contained only 30 grains of powder. What caused the blow-up I couldn't dope out, but this half charge stuck in my mind.

Not long after this, Bill Steiger, a technician who works for Speer Products, the bullet makers, was working up loading data for some cartridge. He had decided on a recommended maximum load with 4350 and was going down to minimum. Then the Model 70 Winchester he was using blew up. Every charge he had fired was carefully weighed and loaded right there. There was no doubt about the kind and amount of powder used.

Then reports of blow-ups began to trickle in to the Speer office. Vernon and Raymond Speer kept me informed and we began to notice that a great many reports of blown-up rifles had one thing in common—the cartridge that did it was loaded with a reduced charge of slow burning powder.

About this time I got a letter from a puzzled chap in Salt Lake City. He had been loading a .270 with 4831. I had recommended 60-62 grains with the 130 grain bullet—in both cases, slightly compressed loads. He wanted to hear the powder rattle when he shook the case, so just to be safe he started with 50 grains. Now and then he got what were high and unpredictable pressures. "How come?" he asked me.

I suggested that he stuff some cartridges with 60 grains and touch a few off. He was sure that if 50 grains gave him apparently high pressure, 60 grains would kill him. He tied old Betsy to a tree, yanked the trigger with a string, and got not a single sign of high pressure.

Then these reports started coming in to P. O. Ackley. Again the blow-ups were with REDUCED loads of slow burning powder. One cartridge that gave a lot of trouble was the "improved" .25/06. Full of slow burning powder, it worked fine, but when some of the boys tried half charges of 4831 and 4350, things began to happen.

Then I wrote a few modest paragraphs in my department in "Outdoor Life", stating what had happened and saying that something funny was going on. One of my original theories was that there was a possibility that the large grained powders with airspace between the grains were being over-ignited when loosely loaded. I had discussed this theory with Vernon Speer and General Julian S. Hatcher of the N.R.A. when General Hatcher was on a visit at Lewiston, Idaho. The general said that the same phenomenon had been noticed from time to time at the government arsenals, but he had no explanation for it. Dick Speer, of Cascade Cartridge Company, was at that time in close touch with the government arsenals, as he was making millions of primers for the government. He told me that the phenomenon of high and erratic pressures with reduced loads of slow burning powders had been observed on a good many occasions.

When my few paragraphs appeared in "Outdoor Life" the handloaders of the nation went into a dither. Hundreds of them wrote me and other hundreds wrote the "American Rifleman." I answered that I had observed the phenomenon and so had others but I did not know why it happened. Not the boys on the "American Rifleman!"

They ran pressure tests of various charges of 4831 in a .270 and found that the relationship between the amount of powder and the recorded pressure was consistent. Therefore, they said, in the inimitable and somewhat pompous way adopted by the savants on the staff of the "American Rifleman,"—" there was nothing to it." I was not mentioned by name, but the inference was that whoever started the story didn't know what he was talking about.

All of this struck me as being a little like driving through Idaho on a main highway, seeing no elk, and then reporting that there were no elk in Idaho because someone had driven through Idaho and had not seen any. These blow-ups don't happen every time, but they happen!

The last one I heard of happened right in the range house at Speer Products. A wildcatter was there with what he called a Super .300 Weatherby—a .300 Weatherby case blown out with a shorter neck and more powder capacity. He had worked up to a maximum load and it had been chronographed. He decided to try *half* of a maximum load of .50 calibre machine gun powder. The rifle was a rechambered Model 721 Remington, a rifle with a very strong action.

Then, BLOWIE! He simply blew the hell out of his Model 721. The wildcatter, a physician, came out of it with minor cuts, contusions and abrasions, but he was pretty shaken—and so were those who witnessed it. Now this was not a case of the wrong powder, the bullet or anything else, as the charges were weighed before witnesses.

This has been a mysterious business and people have not wanted to stick their necks out about it. I talked to one chap who works for one of the major loading companies. He said the phenomenon had been observed and was common. The next time I saw him he denied having said any such thing. Either he is nuts or I am.

Then I got another outfit interested in what was happening—an interest stimulated by the fact that they had run into some unpredictable blow-ups and were as interested in how it happened as P. O. Ackley and I were.

Here is a report:

"These reports show that for certain priming mixes pressure increases were obtained as priming charge weights were decreased (all variables being held constant). This increase in pressure is, of course, unexpected, since pressure normally decreased with decreases in priming charge weights.

"This phenomenon of higher than expected pressures has been observed in ballistic work by different experimenters. It is mentioned in Section 357 "Wave Pressure" of the 1959 edition of "Naval Ordnance." This is the textbook prepared for use at the U. S. Naval Academy. Section 357 reads as follows:

"During the small interval of time when the charge is being ignited, there may be produced in the gun, under certain conditions of loading, abnormally high pressures known as wave pressures. These pressures appear to result from hurling back and forth of the gas mass between the breech block and the base of the projectile, and seems to be of the nature of the best phenomenon, in which two such pressure waves come into phase with each other to create a pressure abnormally high. If wave pressures continue after the projectile has begun to move, they may act on portions of the bore not strong enough to withstand them.

"Unsymmetrical charges are one cause of wave pressures. With such charges, ignition is not uniform and the charge fails to fill the powder chamber simultaneously in all its parts with a pressure that is uniform and uniformly increasing. Instead, the portion of the charge first ignited may propagate a pressure wave which may be supplemented an instant later by a similar wave propagated by the portion of the charge next ignited, and so on. Abnormally high pressures may result. Certain French experiments made to determine the effect of unsymmetrical charges showed that when the charge was placed loose in the chamber, the maximum pressure attained was 34 tons per square inch as compared to 14 tons produced by a symmetrical charge of the same weight. The wave pressures may be avoided by filling the entire powder chamber instantaneously with a burst of flame that will ignite all portions of the charge at the same time.

"Wave pressures may also be produced if the charge occupies a comparatively small portion of the chamber length and is concentrated at the breech end of the chamber."

In other words, you are apt to get this pressure wave effect with a small powder charge in a relatively large chamber.

Experiments by one of the leading ballistic laboratories of the country resulted in these conclusions:

The blow-ups occur under the following conditions:

1. The use of slow burning nitrocellulose type of propellants.
2. Low loading densities.
3. Poor or incomplete initial ignition of the propellant.
4. Reflecting surfaces in the system which are normal to the pressure waves generated during ignition.
5. A rate of pressure wave generation such that the waves are "in phase" as they are reflected back and forth through the system.

So, after all this scientific chatter, let's sum it up for the handloader.

What causes these unpredictable pressure and occasional blow ups is the use of heavily coated slow burning powders in reduced charges that leave a lot of air space in the case. When this is coupled with under-ignition from a weak or faulty primer, the whole charge does not start burning at once. Instead, gas is apparently formed. This ignites, causes a violent wave. More powder ignites, and all hell breaks loose.

The handloader can avoid trouble by using enough slow powder so that the charge is lightly compressed, by using a hot primer. Those who do this won't get into trouble.

It turns out that Parker Ackley, the Speers, and I weren't seeing the boogey men under the bed. When things are just right these blow ups CAN happen! *Jack O'Connor.*

On the bottom of page 8 of "The NORMA Gunbug's Guide" which was edited by Nils Kvale of the Norma factory there is a short discussion concerning slow burning powders and we quote:

Finally, is there any danger in loading too low? Powder experts claim there is. If a load is reduced so much that the case is filled to, say one-third of its volume, there is a possibility that the primer flash will rush along the surface of the powder, igniting part of it, creating enough pressure to push the bullet into the forcing cone where it comes to a halt—and then, when the ignition has spread to the entire powder charge a few thousandths of a second later, the lodged bullet cannot again accelerate fast enough to keep a dangerous pressure from arising. As a matter of fact, guns have blown up under conditions for which no other explanation could be found.

Incidentally, this small book which was put out by the Norma factory is available from Norma Precision, South Lansing, New York for $.25, or direct from A. B. Norma Projektilfabrik, Amotfors, Sweden, is a very valuable pulbication and every shooter should have a copy. The Norma factory produces some very fine powders which will be shortly available to American shooters and will be distributed by all Norma dealers in the United States. Of course, Norma powders are quite familiar to shooters of other countries, and the "Norma Gunbug's Guide" contains a good list of loading data for the more popular cartridges covering the various Norma powders.

On the other side of the question we have experienced experimenters, powder suppliers, writers and handloaders who feel there is nothing to this problem, and that the phenomenon does not occur at all and that all of the blow ups attributed to it can be explained in other ways. Mr. Bruce E. Hodgdon who supplies more powder to handloaders and dealers than almost anyone in the country, other than the manufacturers themselves, very heartily disagrees and has the following to say:

It has been pointed out in several publications that reduced charges of slow burning powder cause pressures greater than maximum charges.

Every load so quoted, in calibres we have test barrels for, has been checked. None has produced the high pressures the writers claimed.

As evidence of said high pressure, one writer submitted "insipient and complete case separations." I deliberately loaded up to 90,000 lbs. P.S.I. The case did not separate. The point is, case head separation is not caused by excessive pressure.

I fired 300 rounds in the .270 alone, with every reduced load of 4831 and 4350 I could think of. 200 rounds each in a .30/06 and .257 Weatherby, and added H570 and 5010 to the powder roster. 150 rounds in the .264 Winchester Magnum. Incidentally, this case is less than full of powder as loaded by the factory. Why doesn't it show excessive pressure? The slow burning powder is supposed to do that—and this powder is slower than 4831.

The laboratory data shown below is typical of similar tests in various calibres.

Here is laboratory test in .30/06 using 180 grain Speer bullets, Winchester case, Winchester Primer, I.M.R. 4831 powder:

Grains 4831	Pressure
60 gr.	41,800
58 gr.	40,300
56 gr.	35,600
54 gr.	31,600
52 gr.	30,000
50 gr.	28,400
48 gr.	24,100
44 gr.	22,100
40 gr.	19,100
36 gr.	13,700
32 gr.	10,800
28 gr.	3,600

Here is a laboratory test in .30/06, using I.M.R. 4350, 170 grain Hornady bullet, Winchester Case, Winchester Primer. Reloaders have been warned not to use this load. It is a good, safe, dependable load.

Grains 4350	Pressure
55 gr.	38,600
55.5 gr.	41,800

Mr. Hodgdon has complete pressure equipment as does the author, and like Mr. Hodgdon, the author had not yet been able to produce detonation experimentally. However, the author fully expects to prove the theory in the laboratory in the not too distant future.

WIND DRIFT

The accepted theory explaining the effect the wind has on a bullet in flight is called the DELAY theory.

"Delay" is the difference in the time of flight over a fixed range between the actual time it takes the bullet to cover the distance and the time that it would require if it could make its flight in a perfect vacuum. Delay is governed by the muzzle velocity and the ballistic coefficient. This theory says that a bullet starting out at low velocity has a smaller "delay" factor than the same bullet starting out at a considerably higher velocity. For example, a low speed .22 L.R. starts out at about 1050 foot seconds. The same bullet has a muzzle velocity of 1375 foot seconds when fired from a .22 LR HiSpeed cartridge. The slower bullet loses less velocity over the 100 yard range than does the high speed bullet. The time of flight at 100 yards is .287 second. The HiSpeed does the 100 yards in .259 second. Should these two bullets be fired in a vacuum, the time of flight would be .262 and .225 respectively. The delay for the low speed is .025 second and the delay for the high speed is .034 second. If these "delay" times are multiplied by the rate of a cross wind, it will be seen that the faster bullet is blown off course farther than the slower one.

There are those, and there are many, who violently disagree with this theory. They believe that if two identical bullets are fired over a given course, the one with the shortest time of flight will drift less, simply because the wind had less time to act upon it. Whichever theory is correct, the fact remains that even the "delay" adherents strive for higher velocities as frantically as the others.

Mr. Homer S. Powley, currently one of our most active ballisticians, believes in the "delay" theory and has the following to say in an attempt to simplify the theory so that the average reader may have a better understanding of the problem. Mr. Powley is the originator of the Powley Computer for Handloaders.

SHOOTING IN THE WIND
by
Homer S. Powley

We are all submerged at the bottom of an ocean of air surrounding our world. This air is like a very thin fluid. It is in almost constant movement across the surface of the earth. As it moves it produces pressure on everything. The movement is called wind and shooters are very much concerned because it changes the course of bullets.

As we watch the wind move tree branches, smoke, flags, etc., we see that the movement is highly erratic. It seems to change direction and speed almost continually or may even seem to stop entirely. In general, you might think that wind movement is so much at random that there is not much which can be told about it. However, the wind has been studied and there are lots of things we know about it.

The air is grouped in large masses of high and low pressure, each covering an area which is ordinarily about 1,000 miles in diameter. Air is piled up in long ridges of high pressure in some places. In other areas there are long troughs of low pressure air. High pressure air is continually spilling down off the ridges and headed towards filling up these troughs which may be 1,000 or more miles away.

Due to daily heating by the sun and forces from rotation of the earth, these masses are in constant, slow rotation. Rotation from a high pressure ridge is clockwise and rotation into a trough is counter-clockwise. Air masses are usually spaced alternately as to highs and lows.

Between the air masses there is the situation of cool air from highs mixing with warm, moist air from lows so that storms occur. These are formed in long, narrow lines, called "fronts", with extreme turbulence.

In the United States east of the Rocky Mountains the general pattern is that all of the air masses are moving together like a set of rotating gears in pretty much an easterly direction all of the time. The whole movement is about from 10 to 30 mph.

West of the Rockies the air masses in general are moving generally in a northerly or southerly direction.

At any place, therefore, we are always having an air movement and the wind necessarily is blowing most of the time. Since the air is rotating and even though the general movement might be easterly at our particular spot, the wind may be coming from almost any direction. As a matter of fact, if you watch the change in wind direction from day to day, it comes in, say, first from the north, then northeast, then from the east, and southeast, etc., just as though it were swinging like the hands of a clock with you at the center.

This is the general picture and does not hold true during brief times when storms are passing over your area.

No matter what your local wind indications may be, the big effect is that there is a large air mass moving past you practically all of the time. These air masses drag on buildings, hills, trees, etc., and the movement is turbulent, especially close to the ground.

All of this has been mentioned to indicate the extreme importance for you as a shooter to find all the indications you can as to what the general direction and speed of this air movement is across your area. Very frequently the wind seems to be coming from one direction at the firing points and from another direction at the targets. This is due only to local turbulence.

Many shooters who have a good string of alibis have been missing out on a chance to blame the wind for poor shooting. The effect of wind is much greater than ordinarily supposed. It was Fred Ness who was talking about high velocity, flat shooting rifles and first published the remark that a 10 mph crosswind had as much effect on the bullet as does gravity. This is news to many and considered a secret by other experienced shooters.

If, which is not true, the air were standing still and completely turbulent, or "boiling", shots would only scatter at random and there would not be much to be done about it. Since, however, there actually is an air mass movement between you and the target, the situation is something like crossing a river in a boat where there is always a current flowing. In crossing a river in a power boat the amount that you are carried down stream before reaching the other side depends only on how fast the boat is moving. It does not depend on the size, weight, or shape of the boat. As soon as you enter the water the entire boat moves downstream. Obviously the faster the boat is moving, the less you are carried downstream before reaching the other side.

If you started across the river in a powerboat and immediately cut the motor so that you would coast as far as the other bank, it would be very nearly like a bullet fired from a gun. How long you would coast and, therefore, how far you would be carried downstream would then depend upon the initial speed, size, weight, and shape of the boat. That is to say, the time it took to coast across the river would depend upon the resistance to forward motion only of the boat.

The loss in forward speed of a bullet depends upon its initial velocity, size, shape, and weight. The size, shape, and weight of the bullet can be expressed by one number, the ballistic coefficient. Therefore, if you know only the muzzle velocity and ballistic coefficient of a bullet, it is possible to determine the time of flight across a rifle range. If, in addition, you know the average speed of the air through which the bullet is moving, you can then calculate how much the bullet will be deflected on the target due to the average wind.

Engineers and ballisticians routinely use what is known as the "delay formula" for making this calculation. It is a problem in vectors and has had much experimental verification so we will not worry about the details here. It should be remarked, however, that accurate long range artillery fire would be quite impossible unless it were definitely known how to perform such calculations.

But, we have just reached the big difficulty in practical shooting in the wind. We just stated that *if* the average wind velocity were known, it is easy to calculate the wind deflection. It is by no means easy to know what the average wind speed is. On a target range, if we fired some shots to see how much the bullet was deflected, it is easy to use a reverse calculation to find out what the average wind speed *was*. A hunter, however, cannot fire sighting shots to determine the average wind speed before he shoots at his game. Even if he could, he could not be certain of a hit because of the likelihood of the speed of the wind having changed during the time between the time of his sighting shots and firing at his target.

We now have the problem of finding out a little more about the behavior of the wind and especially its variation. How do we find out about this?

An experienced hunter or a seasoned target shooter will try to find out from observation just as much as possible about what the over-all air movement is between himself and the target. He will also look behind him and beyond the target. He will watch high trees and low grass. He will watch how birds are flying. (If he is a very experienced crow shooter he will have noticed that crows always sit facing directly into the wind whereas hawks and other birds do not.) He will watch the direction of cloud movement. If he has a Dwyer pocket anemometer or a pith ball on a string, he will watch its indications to see what the average indication is. He will take into account the time of day. He will watch for mirage between himself and the target.

What is mirage? Whenever the surface of the ground is warmer than the covering air, heat will be transmitted upwards. This is frequently the situation at night but we do not do much shooting at night. Sunlight, as everyone knows, carries a lot of heat. It passes readily through the air without doing very much heating of the air. However, it does heat the ground so that very frequently when the sun is shining the ground is warmer than the air. The ground then transmits this heat to exhibit mirage. The air very close to the ground receives some of this heat, and since warm air rises, it starts upwards in gobs or streaks. It is something like heating the bottom of a kettleful of water; you can see streaks of schlieren due to the warm water rising through the cooler water. Looking across the surface of the ground, these streaks or schlieren are most readily seen through a telescope. They are more readily seen through a higher power telescope; in fact, sometimes the "boiling" effect is so great as to make the target shimmer or blur out completely.

The schlieren from mirage would be vertical if the air were not moving. Since the air is usually moving, these streaks are slanted and produce a different kind of shimmer on the target with the result that it seems as if you can see the air itself moving. For a practiced, experienced shooter, this indication of mirage is the most valuable thing available for estimating average wind velocity across the range. Unfortunately, even when the sun is shining, and the wind velocity exceeds 12 to 15 mph the mirage effect seems to disappear to the point where it is no longer useful. Mirage can seldom be noticed when the sun is not shining.

Going back to studies which have been made of the general character of air moving over the earth, the smoothest air movement is above 1000 feet of altitude. The closer to the ground the more the air movement is retarded so that, theoretically at least, air in actual contact with the ground is not moving at all. Let us assume that at a point exactly 1 foot above the ground the wind velocity is 10 mph. At 2 feet it is moving 11 mph. At 5 feet it is moving 12.5 mph. Likewise, at 10 and 20 feet above the ground the velocities are 14 and 15.5 mph. At 100 feet it doubles, becoming 20 mph. At 1000 feet it is 28 mph.

Due to rotation of the earth the wind at higher altitudes is in a different direction than wind on the surface. As you go up from the ground the wind direction rotates to the right. There is a greater rotation of wind direction in the summertime than in the wintertime. Most of the rotation occurs within 1000 feet of the ground. The rotation amounts to about 45° or 50°. That is to say, if the surface wind was from 12 o'clock the wind at an altitude of 1,000 feet or more would be coming from between 1:30 and 2 o'clock. Remember this when watching the movement of clouds.

Wind turbulence has been measured near the ground. Let us say that in the wintertime there is a certain small amount of turbulence at sunrise. After 10 A.M. this will noticeably increase and reach a maximum at about 3 o'clock in the afternoon and then decline to a sunset value the same as the sunrise value. The amount of turbulence will have doubled by mid-afternoon. In the summertime it will have tripled, making for difficult shooting.

The wind velocity goes through changes during the course of a 24 hour day which have also been studied. Let us say that the average wind velocity during a 24 hour peiod is 10 mph. This average will be realized during about 2 hours at sunrise and sunset. It increases from sunrise to about 14 mph, reaching this peak at about 2 P.M. and declining to 10 mph at sunset. After sunset and during the nighttime it declines still further, reaching a minimum value of about 6 mph at 2:30 A.M. By sunrise it has increased again to 10 mph. All of this during the cold half year. During the warm half year and assuming the same 10 mph average the picture is the same except that by 10 A.M. the average speed has increased from 10 to 15 mph, increasing to a maximum of 16 or 17 mph at 2 P. M. It will still be running about 15 mph at 5 P. M. and return to average at sunset. During the night it decreases to its minimum of about 4 mph at 1 A. M. Of course, 10 mph is not always your average daily wind speed but all other average figures are in direct proportion.

The indications we get from watching flags, windsocks and anemometers are that the wind at shooting distances above the ground is rather bumping along with lots of twisting and turning. These are indications of turbulence. The flag or windsock is always whipping and pith balls are always jumping around. If you can watch an anemometer for a period of 10 or more minutes you can get a very good idea of the average wind speed across your area. The wind direction at a given point usually is constantly shifting within a 60° range. That is to say, a 9 o'clock average wind direction will continuously show fluctuations between 8 and 10 o'clock.

You might imagine from watching an anemometer reading jump around that the average wind is behaving this way all across the range. This is not the case. The reason it jumps around is local turbulence at one point only. The way to prove this to yourself is to start shooting at regularly spaced intervals on the same range and watching the bullet deflections. They are by no means absolutely uniform but on the other hand you will find that actual bullet deflections are much more uniform and less than the extremes of the anemometer would indicate.

The illustration shows some data taken this way in northern Ohio in fairly flat country. Curves A and E were made on a 600 yard range; the others were made at Camp Perry on the 1000 yard range. Curve C is the average of anemometer readings taken inside the range at exactly the same time Curve D was

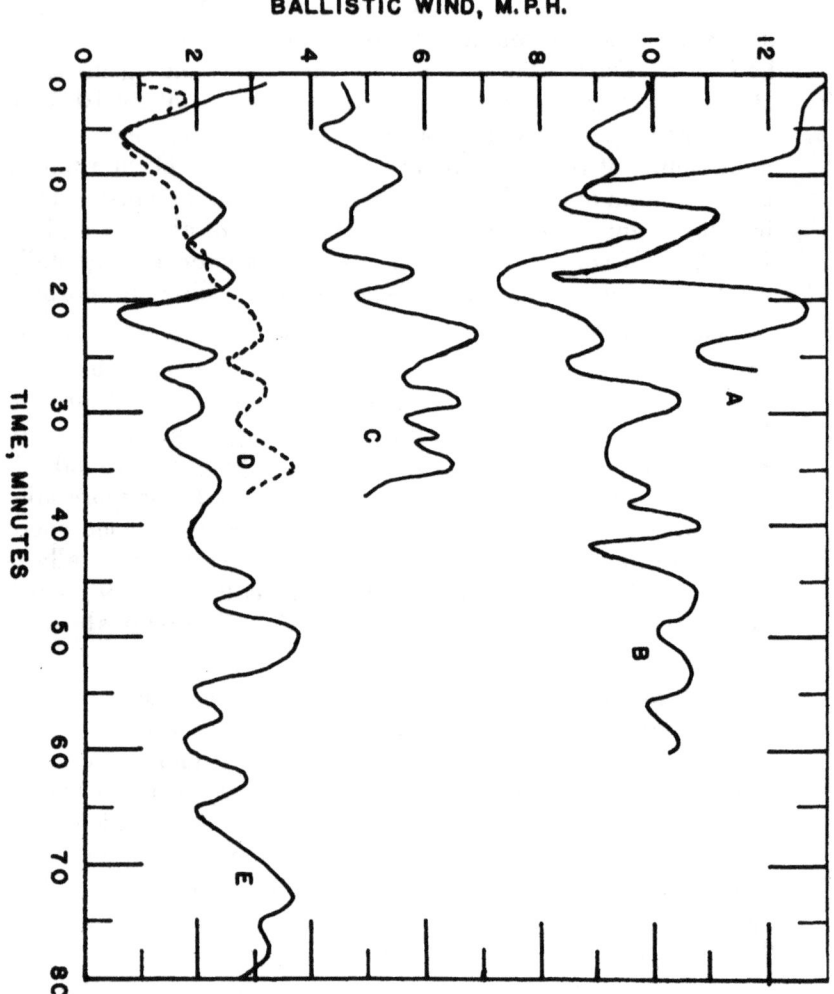

being fired. From a knowledge of muzzle velocity and ballistic coefficients, all of the bullet deflections were converted to the average constant crosswind which caused them. This is indicated in the illustration as the ballistic wind.

The wind during the taking of Curves C and D was not a direct 9 o'clock crosswind but rather came in at 11 o'clock so that only one-half its effect was shown by the bullets. This is exactly in line with other information. For example, for a wind of given velocity coming from 8 o'clock or 10 o'clock the effect on a bullet is 3/4 to 7/8 that of a 9 o'clock crosswind. A 7 o'clock or 11 o'clock wind will have 1/2 the effect of a 9 o'clock wind.

Notice the fact that the wind goes into peaks or valleys about every 6-1/2 or 7 minutes. Some recording anemometer readings which were made in Maryland over a period of 4 hours indicate the same thing with a period of about 8-1/2 minutes.

In New Jersey recently some measurements were made with a 300 ft. *vertical* wire whose deflections were converted into mph of wind. These readings indicated a period of 7 to 8 minutes for times between velocity surges. This is interesting because it shows that using bullets as an anemometer rather close to the surface records the same pulsating effect as at least 150 ft. above the ground.

This, then is evidently the way air masses are moving across the surface of the earth.

Let us now look at the amount by which various particular bullets are deflected by a 10 mph crosswind at 1000 yards. We will compare 180 grain .30 caliber bullets with a muzzle velocity of 2800. A slug, square at both ends, is deflected 300 inches which is 25 feet or 30 minutes. An ordinary blunt hunting bullet will be deflected 200 inches which is about 17 ft. or 20 minutes. A Spitzer flat-base is deflected 110 inches which is 9 ft. or 11 minutes. Finally, a Spitzer with boat-tail is deflected only 80 inches which is about 7 ft. or 8 minutes. The ballistic coefficient for the slug is 0.18 and for the Spitzer boat-tail 0.48. Shooters who participate in the 1000 yard Wimbledon Match almost always use Spitzer boat-tails which quite deservedly have the reputation of being good "wind-buckers." The basic reason, of course, is because they suffer less forward retardation due to air resistance and, therefore, have a better ballistic coefficient, getting over a range faster.

In the .30-06 a good Wimbledon load is 57 grains of 4350 behind the Sierra 180 grain Match King which gives a velocity of about 2850. The wind allowance for a 10 mph crosswind is 8 minutes. The same bullet in a .300 H & H ahead of 67 grains of 4350 has a velocity of about 3150 and the 10 mph crosswind allowance is 7 minutes. When shooting a 1000 yard match, sighting shots are allowed so that the shooter can adjust for the wind and get on the target before shooting for record.

Now look again at the illustration to see what can be expected from here on. It will take the shooter the better part of one-half hour to complete his shots for record. Obviously he will have to change from his initial sight allowance all during the course of shooting. This is where he has to become expert in watching for *changes* in the wind. It should now be obvious that the higher the muzzle velocity and the higher the ballistic coefficient of his bullet the less his *change* in wind allowance has to be and, therefore, the better his chances of winning. The V-ring at 1000 yards is 2 minutes in diameter. It goes without saying that the shooter and his gun should be otherwise capable of keeping all of his shots within this 2 minutes entirely aside from the effect of wind variations.

We have been discussing shooting at very long ranges. What about shorter ranges? At 200 yards a small bore shooter will have just as much trouble with the wind as the big bore shooter does at 1000 yards. With the .22 long rifle standard velocity cartridge a 10 mph crosswind will deflect the bullet 16 inches which requires a wind allowance of 8 minutes. It is a peculiarity of the muzzle velocity and ballistic coefficient combination that muzzle velocities higher or lower than the standard 1145 velocity will require more wind allowance. For example, with the same .22 caliber bullet at a velocity of 1335, the 10 mph crosswind allowance at 200 yards is 10 minutes.

A 180 grain Match King in .30-06 at 200 yards requires a wind allowance of only 1 minute meaning that the same 10 mph crosswind has moved this bullet only 2 inches.

For those who would like to know more about the methods of calculation we can recommend reading Chapter 10 of Dr.

Cummings' book "Everyday Ballistics." The times of flight used are obtained from knowing the ballistic coefficients.

A 10 mph crosswind has been frequently mentioned. This is because it is an ordinary amount and also because it makes for easy figuring mentally. We would like to make it absolutely clear that a 20 mph crosswind will have exactly twice the deflection effect of a 10 mph wind and also a 5 mph wind will have exactly 1/2 as much effect.

For a constant or ballistic wind, the effect on the bullet over the far one-half of the range is substantially greater than over the near half. This is the reason many experienced target shooters find it better to watch through their spotting telescopes focused at three-quarters range.

10 MPH WIND AT 3 O'CLOCK OR 9 O'CLOCK

Ballistic Coefficient	Muzzle Velocity	Wind Deflection, inches		
		200 yds.	300 yds.	400 yds.
0.15	2700	11.8	29.3	55.0
0.15	3100	9.4	23.3	47.0
0.15	3500	7.6	20.0	40.0
0.15	4000	6.2	16.0	32.3
0.15	4600	5.2	13.0	26.0
0.20	2700	7.9	20.0	36.7
0.20	3100	6.6	16.3	32.0
0.20	3500	5.3	13.3	27.0
0.20	4000	4.4	11.0	21.3
0.20	4600	3.6	9.5	17.5
0.27	2700	5.9	13.8	25.5
0.27	3100	4.8	11.0	21.5
0.27	3500	3.8	9.5	18.0
0.27	4000	3.1	7.7	14.5
0.27	4600	2.6	6.0	11.5
0.37	2700	4.0	9.6	17.3
0.37	3100	3.3	8.0	14.3
0.37	3500	2.5	6.0	12.4
0.37	4000	2.1	5.0	10.0
0.37	4600	1.9	3.7	8.0

10 MPH WIND AT 3 O'CLOCK OR 9 O'CLOCK *continued*

Ballistic Coefficient	Muzzle Velocity	Wind Deflection, inches		
		200 yds.	300 yds.	400 yds.
0.50	2700	2.9	6.8	12.0
0.50	3100	2.4	5.7	10.0
0.50	3500	1.9	4.7	8.7
0.50	4000	1.7	3.8	7.2
0.50	4600	1.4	3.0	5.5

The table shows the wind deflections to be expected for practically the entire range of high velocity rifles for ranges between 200 and 400 yards. A ballistic coefficient of 0.15 corresponds to medium weight .22 caliber bullets and light weight .25 caliber; 0.20 covers medium weights in .27 and .30 caliber; 0.27 covers light weight bullets in .25 to .30; 0.37 is representative of medium to heavy bullets in .27 to .35 caliber. Finally, 0.50 is representative of most spitzer boat-tail bullets. For specific bullets refer to the Speer Loading Manuals.

Here is a rule-of-thumb which is useful to know when hunting. If you have made a kill at some range with a known wind allowance and another shot comes up in the same wind at twice the distance, allow for a deflection four times as great; if at one-half the range, the deflection will be one-fourth as much. Look at the table.

According to the Western Ammunition Handbook, the .220 Swift will shoot 11.3 inches low at 300 yards from a 100 yard zero. The 10 mph wind deflection at 300 yards is 11.6 inches; this is the sort of thing Fred Ness was talking about. In a 10 mph wind a 250 grain bullet in the .348 Winchester will be deflected two feet at 400 yards, a serious problem for an Elk hunter.

For a perfectly straight wind at 6 o'clock or 12 o'clock, no wind allowance is necessary. Furthermore no elevation allowance is necessary for most rifles as far as 1000 yards. For any rifle likely to be useful in competition at 1000 yards this is true. You have possibly heard a lot of gossip contrary to this around the 1000 yard ranges. If you happen to be using the M-2 Ball Cartridge, then it would be proper to add one minute of elevation to allow for a 10 mph 12 o'clock wind or take off one minute for a

6 o'clock wind. Other guns using lower ballistic coefficients and muzzle velocities would require more allowance but you probably won't be using them. For the M-1 Ball and better cartridges you will not have to worry about it.

In practice a 12 o'clock wind will be continually changing direction between about 11 o'clock and 1 o'clock; similarly a 6 o'clock wind will be switching between 7 and 5 o'clock. These are known as fish-tail winds and are very difficult for good shooting. 11 o'clock and 7 o'clock 10 mph winds have the same effect as a 5 mph 9 o'clock wind; similarly a 1 or 5 o'clock 10 mph wind will have the same effect as a 5 mph 3 o'clock wind. It is easy to see why the fish-tail winds have their reputation for causing trouble. You can only keep your fingers crossed unless a useful mirage happens to develop. Then you can tell which way the bullet will be deflected. You have to shoot just as soon as you can after you have observed the indication.

You may have been wondering whether there is a difference in allowances according as to whether the wind is coming from your right or your left. Be assured that there is no difference required for either windage or elevation.

There is a complication developed by mirage which is sometimes erroneously ascribed to the wind. When there is mirage and you are shooting close to the ground there is a curvature of the line of sight. The effect of this is to make you shoot lower, by perhaps as much as a minute at the most, than when there is no visible mirage. This is important in bench or target competition. The effect is entirely independent of the wind but, of course, is still there when shooting in both wind and mirage.

It seems to be well known that with right-hand rifling twists there is an effect called "drift" which causes the bullet to go to the right, more so at very long ranges. Also, of course, with left-hand twist rifling, the drift is to the left. Again, contrary to the magnifying effect of gossip, it need cause you no particular concern. As far as 500 yards it can scarcely be measured and at 1000 yards it amounts to 1-1/2 minutes for M-2 Ball and about one-half this for the M-1 Ball cartridge. Differences of more than this you hear about are probably the result of unconscious cant, or sight mounts which are not absolutely square. Wind deflection effects are usually so large that the small drift effect is almost completely covered up.

Now that we have developed a considerable amount of information concerning the behavior of the wind and its effect on shooting, what can be done about it? All that can be done is to apply our knowledge to improve our observations and thereby improve our judgment of what allowances to make when shooting in the wind. It is a big help to know what to expect from the wind. Our shooting should improve. In any event, we now have additional facts before us which should make our alibis sound more convincing.

There are some mechanical devices in very early stages of development which may make it possible to accurately measure the effect of the wind before shooting. If we get these, there are still many other interesting shooting problems to investigate. Meanwhile, we have to wait.

The following was submitted for further clarification of mirage, by Donald D. Barr, of Solon, Ohio.

"Mirage" is a range term for the heat waves or air currents which shooters use to determine the speed and direction of the wind. Although the experienced shot notes the motion of the trees, bushes, grass or flags for information of the wind velocity, he depends *mainly* on the mirage. Not only is it the *most reliable guide,* but it can be seen drifting when everything else is motionless.

"Mirage" is best seen against a white background—top or bottom of the targets, top of butts, or the white parts of the target's number board. If it is a hot and sunny day, there will be no difficulty seeing the mirage. If it is a dark cool day, it will take an excellent spotting 'scope to clarify the atmosphere so it can be seen.

Due to the great controversy among the "experts," and the shots that are truly experienced and also cannot definitely agree, as to what visual effect mirage apparently causes when the shooter looks at the target, this discussion will be primarily concerned with "a" method for estimating the wind speed from the apparent visual motion of any existing mirage.

To "read" mirage, the spotting 'scope should be focused for a point approximately two-thirds of the distance from the firing line to the targets. The greatest effect in the bullet's travel will occur in the final one-third of its flight to the target; therefore, we are primarily concerned with the conditions in that area.

Also, with the telescope focused at the approximate two-thirds range, we are able to read the cumulative effect of the wind that will exert a force of any significant magnitude on the bullet.

The observable mirage we see when we peer through the scope will have the appearance of clear moving water, and if there is no breeze, a plain "boiling" or straight up flow will be the predominant effect. If the wind comes from 12 or 6 o'clock, the boiling effect will be faster than usual, and if from 3 or 9 o'clock, the mirage has a flowing effect like a stream of water.

Any wind coming from an angle, depending upon its velocity, may combine with the boiling and give a diagonal drift to the boil, or may cause an apparent horizontal flow across the field of view. The exact effect these lateral winds may have on the flight of your bullet can be predicted fairly closely by correctly reading the cumulative effect observed through your scope.

If the mirage is easily seen, the wind is actually slow. The flowing water will appear to move slowly across the target and have high and easily discernible peaks, according to some sources. Actually, we should be concerned mostly by the apparent speed of the whole body of mirage at the points we are watching. A fair *guess* at the speed of the "slow" mirage would be three to five miles per hour.

Mirage flowing much faster across the targets and number boards, but still easily seen, probably has an average speed in the seven or eight miles per hour range. If it is barely visible, the speed of the wind in reality is fast, for wind dispels mirage. We can *guess* this speed to be from ten to twelve miles per hour when the faint watery lines appear as streaks across the discernible places.

Occasionally, mirage can be seen at higher wind velocities, but the "authorities" contend that mirage flattens out and disappears after the wind has reached a speed of fourteen to sixteen miles per hour.

Don't worry, for if you *know* and zero your rifle, you can miscalculate the wind almost three miles per hour and still get a hit in the 5 ring at 1,000 yards.

Experience is truly the best teacher where mirage is concerned. Wind doping is the prime factor in determining the ability of a long range shooter or coach, all other things being equal.

Mr. John G. O'Hara has no use for the "delay" theory of wind drift and has made intensive tests and studies on the subject. Mr. O'Hara submits the following to explain his ideas and theories.

> 5504 Oakmont Circle
> Nashville 9, Tennessee
> January 4, 1962

Mr. P. O. Ackley
2235 Arbor Lane
Salt Lake City 17, Utah

Dear Mr. Ackley:

The enclosed article, "The Wind and the Curve Bullet," is a treatise on bullet deflection, that to the best of my knowledge, has not been published before. It contradicts the old and accepted "delay" theory of bullet deflection. This article is not just some wild idea of mine, but it is based on known and proven aerodynamic principles. Even though aerodynamics is more concerned with wind velocities of maybe 75 MPH and up, rather than winds of 5 to 30 MPH and with large cylinders rather than a small bullet, we have seen that the equation for lift coefficient $q = 2\pi \frac{V_s}{V_w}$ does not contain any terms depending on cylinder cross-section and thus applies to a cylinder regardless of size, even a small pointed cylinder as a bullet.

It is high time the riflemen of America learned the facts about bullet deflection by wind regardless of the prestige of some of our high and mighty ballistic experts. The two formulæ, $D = D_1 (\frac{R}{R_1})^2$ and $\frac{V_o d}{T} = W$ are original, with me at least, and I believe that they have not been published before. The formula $\frac{V_o d}{T} = W$ indicates that for a given bullet diameter d = inches, Vo = foot seconds Muzzle Velocity, T = twist inches per turn, that there is a critical wind velocity W, M.P.H. that will cause deflection to be primarily in the vertical direction. This condition will seldom exist with modern high velocity rifles, as an example, consider the .30/06. $V_o = 3000$ feet per second, $T = 10''$, $d + .308''$ and by the formula we have $\dfrac{3000 \times .308}{10}$ = 92½ to indicate that a cross wind of 92½ m.p.h. will produce a deflection primarily in a vertical direction. Now consider the .22 L.R. $V = 1145$ feet per second, $d = .222''$, and $T = 16''$ and we have $\dfrac{1145 \times .222}{16} = 16$ to indicate that a wind of 16 m.p.h. will produce a deflection primarily in the vertical direction. There are other slow speed, slow twist rifles that may in a moderate wind show a vertical deflection, as .44/40 Winchester, .44 Special and .45/70 and the like.

While I have witnessed this lift effect of a wind on a large rotating cylinder I have not made conclusive test with a bullet. I would suggest the .22 LR regular at 1145 foot seconds, 16" r.h. twist, and a wind of 16 m.p.h. should give a deflection primarily in the vertical direction, if the wind is from 9 o'clock it should shoot high. Now turn and shoot in the opposite direction so as the wind is from 3 o'clock and it should shoot low.

Concerning the formula $D = W(T - \dfrac{R}{V})$, I can find no direct relation between the deflection and "delay," $(T - \dfrac{R}{V})$ of course I am not a mathematician. This formula does not consider whether a projectile is stabilized by spin or stabilizing fins, certainly does not consider a projectile having a uniform velocity or a positive acceleration. If range $R = V_o t + \tfrac{1}{2} J t^2$ then dividing through by V_o gives $\dfrac{R}{V_o} = t + \dfrac{\tfrac{1}{2} J t^2}{V_o}$ and substituting this value of $\dfrac{R}{V_o}$ in the "delay" formula we have $D = W(t - t - \dfrac{\tfrac{1}{2} J t^2}{V_o})$ or $D = -W(\dfrac{\tfrac{1}{2} J t^2}{V_o})$. Now if J depends solely on bullet weight, bullet shape and bullet velocity than "delay" does depend on some of the factors that we have seen have an effect on deflection and so in specific cases the relation of twist, density of air, shape of bullet, weight of bullet and bullet velocity may be such that an approximate value for deflection can be found from the formula. Actually I do not condemn the formula, only the interpretation of the formula by our ballistic experts, that deflection is caused by "delay" and that deflection is a function of delay.

Very truly yours,

(*Signed*) JOHN G. O'HARA

"THE WIND AND THE CURVE BULLET"
By JOHN G. O'HARA

Most all riflemen are more or less concerned about bullet deflection by the wind and the cause of this deflection should be of interest to all riflemen. The purpose of this article is not to stop deflection but to explain the cause of this peculiar wind effect and at the same time discredit the old and accepted superstition that claims deflection is caused by some mad old witch, "Delay." See "Bullets and the Wind" by William C. Davis, *American Rifleman*, January 1956. After explaining the cause of deflection I will give my "Rule of Thumb" method of estimating deflection, useful to the hunter-rifleman.

The cause of deflection has remained something of a mystery to both riflemen and ballistic engineers. They are aware that this deflection is something other than, and many times greater than a simple wind drift. The great experimenter, the late Dr. Mann, did not understand this wind effect, see "Bullet's Flight" by Franklin W. Mann. In the past twenty years we have seen more than a dozen articles by the ballistic experts, attempting to explain the cause of bullet deflection by the wind. Most of these experts gave the old and accepted formula for estimating deflection $D = W (T - \frac{R}{V})$, where $D =$ deflection in feet, $W =$ wind velocity in feet per second, $T =$ time of flight in seconds, $R =$ Range in feet and $V =$ muzzle velocity in feet per second and based their explanation, as to the cause of deflection, on this formula. The formula does have merit, it is simple and in some cases gives deflection values with a degree of accuracy. However, to accept this formula at face value and interpret it to mean that deflection depends on delay, $(T - \frac{R}{V})$, and that deflection is a function of delay, is entirely erroneous.

If the trajectory of a bullet, in a cross wind, could be divided into its component velocities it would have (1) velocity in direction of fire, (2) velocity of drop, due to the pull of gravity (3) velocity of drift, caused by the spinning bullet falling through the air, (4) velocity of deflection, caused by the effect of a cross wind on a spinning bullet. The cause of the first two are well understood by most riflemen but the cause of drift and deflection is not so well understood. Are drift and deflection caused by some mysterious witch, as the experts would have us believe, or by some tangible force, the magnitude of which can be calculated?

Consider the formula $D = W(T - \frac{R}{V})$. If we apply the "dimensional theory" we have $L = \frac{L}{t}(t - \frac{L}{L/t})$ and find $L = 0$ to indicate $D = 0$, naturally this is not always true. Now if range $R = V_0 t + \frac{1}{2} Jt^2$, when $J = 0$ we find $t = \frac{R}{V}$ and substituting in the delay formula we have $D = W(\frac{R}{V} - \frac{R}{V})$ and find $D = 0$ to indicate that a projectile having a uniform velocity is not deflected by the wind, again, this is not true. Now if a projectile has a positive acceleration, then $\frac{R}{V} > t$ so D would be negative to indicate that the projectile would be deflected into the wind, this is also not true. However the above is not to deny that under certain conditions it can be shown that delay, $(T - \frac{R}{V})$, depends on certain factors that also have an effect on deflection.

Consider a baseball thrown by a ball pitcher, assume he throws the ball three times, each with the same velocity, and there is no wind, (No. 1) straight ball, (No. 2) curve ball to the right, (No. 3) curve ball to the left. Since the velocity and delay were the same for all three balls, what caused one to go straight, one curve right and one curve left? The curves were certainly not caused by delay, nor is a curve bullet, the only difference between the three balls was rate and direction of spin. Now consider the magnitude of the force necessary to deflect the ball so abruptly to right or left as if it had glanced off some invisible obstacle. I will show that this force, that causes a baseball to execute such abrupt curves, may reach a magnitude of 12.5 times the force of the air resistance causing the ball to lose velocity.

Consider a steel ball balanced in mid air on a jet of air. Probably few boys have completed their apprenticeship in a machine shop without going through the stage of playing with the air hose that is used to clean machinery. The favorite trick is to keep a steel ball, or other object, balanced on the jet of air from the air hose. What force supports the ball and what force keeps the ball in the air stream? The supporting force results, in part, from the partial vacuum above the ball created by the high velocity flow of air around the ball and also from the impact pressure of the air impinging on the lower portion of the ball. This impact pressure is $q = \dfrac{PV^2}{2}$. If the ball swerves toward the edge of the air stream the velocity of the air flowing by the side of the ball nearer the edge of the flow is considerably less than the velocity by the side of the ball toward the center of the flow and by Bernoulli's equation $P + \dfrac{PV^2}{2} = H =$ CONSTANT, the pressure is increased on the side near the edge of the flow and decreasd on th side nearer the center of the flow, resulting in a transverse force on the ball toward the center of the flow tending to keep the ball in the center of the flow where the air velocity is highest.

You may reason that a steel ball balanced on a jet of air or a curve ball is not deflection, true a curve ball is in fact drift, however the basic principle is the same whether it be a curve ball, drift or deflection. The curves in all three cases are caused by a transverse force acting on the projectile and this force is caused by the aerodynamic effect of a cross flow of air, a flow perpendicular to the axis of rotation, superimposed on the circulation of air about a rotating body. I might add that the flight of a plane also depends on this aerodynamic effect.

To discover the nature of the force that causes a curve ball deflection and drift, let us leave the ballistic experts with delay while we consider the principles of aerodynamics.

From "Principles of Flight"* we have:

"In 1852 Magnus called attention to the transverse force on shells which he attributed to their rotation. Later, Rayleigh utilized the conception in explaining the curves executed by a cut tennis ball, while still later Lanchester based his explanation of lift and drag of wings on this idea."

Consider a cylinder of radius r, length S, rotating clock wise with a surface speed of V_s, so as to create a circulation of air about it of strength Γ, where $\Gamma = 2\pi r V_s$. Now if a rectilinear flow of air, flowing from left to right, of velocity V_w, is superimposed on the circulation it follows from Bernoulli's equation, $P + \frac{PV^2}{2} = H = \text{CONSTANT}$, that the pressure is decreased above and increased below, resulting in a transverse force upward. Kutta and Joukowsky have shown that this transverse force is $L = \rho \Gamma V_w S$, where $\rho =$ mass density of the air, and $\rho_0 = .00237$ lb./ft./sec.

If a flow of air is brought to rest by impinging on a plate of area A, the impact pressure on the plate is $q = \frac{PV^2}{2}$, and the force on the plate is qA. If lift coefficient C_L is the ratio of lift to impact force qA, then $C_L = \frac{L}{qA}$. And for our cylinder $C_L = 2\pi \frac{V_s}{V_w}$, and when V_w is less than

*Edward Archibald Stalker—PRINCIPLES OF FLIGHT. The Ronald Press Company, 1931.

some 300 feet per sec. maximum lift is obtained when $\frac{V_s}{V_w} = 2$, so $C_{L\ MAX} = 4\pi$. If the transverse force acting on a nonrotating cylinder in a cross flow of air is $F_1 = f(\frac{PV_w^2 A}{2})$ then the force acting on the same cylinder rotating in the same flow of air, when $\frac{V_s}{V_w} = 2$, is $F_2 = 4\pi F_1$ or $12.5 \times F_1$. So we see that the effect of a cross wind on a rotating cylinder may be as much as 12.5 times as great as the effect on the same cylinder when not rotating.

Returning to our curve ball we see that if the spin is such that $\frac{V_s}{V} = 2$, where V_s = surface speed of the ball and V = velocity of the ball, J = acceleration in direction of throw and a = acceleration perpendicular to direction of throw, then $a = 4\pi J$, or simply put, the force causing the ball to curve is 12.5 times as great as the force of the air resistance causing the ball to lose velocity. We may consider the magnitude of this force in another way, assuming the ball to be thrown with a velocity V = 75 M.P.H., then the force causing the ball to curve would be equal to the force of a wind of $4\pi \times 75$ or 937.5 M.P.H. acting on a nonspinning ball. In principle this is also true of a spinning bullet in a cross wind, even though $\frac{V_s}{V_w}$ is usually much greater than 2 for a rifle bullet, and the lift is in the drag direction. So we see that the effect of a cross wind of velocity V_w = 20 M.P.H. on a spinning bullet may be equal to the effect of a wind of velocity $V_w = 4\pi \times 20$ or 250 M.P.H. acting on the same bullet without spin.

For a spinning bullet in a cross wind the force causing deflection is $F = P\Gamma V_w S$, where V_w = wind velocity, for a spinning bullet dropping through the air the force causing drift is $F = P\Gamma V_D S$, where V_D = velocity of drop, and for a spinning baseball the force causing the ball to curve is $F = P\Gamma VS$, where V = velocity of the ball.

Now we have discovered the cause and magnitude of the force acting on a spinning baseball, a spinning bullet in a cross wind and a spinning bullet dropping through the air. This transverse force will cause the bullet or ball to move "off course" with an acceleration a and if the distance the bullet is displaced is deflection D then $D = \frac{1}{2} at^2$, and $a = \frac{F}{m}$, $m = \frac{W}{g}$ so the general equation for deflection is $D = \frac{Fg}{2W} t^2$ where $F = \rho \Gamma V_w S$.

At the high velocity of a rifle bullet the air at the point of the bullet is compressed, the air becomes thicker and heavier, thus we can not use a value of $\rho = .00237$ but must find a corrected value of ρ by the following relation $P = P_0 (\frac{P}{P_0})^K$, $K \simeq 1.41$ and $P - P_0 = \frac{PV_0^2}{2} (1 + \frac{V_0^2}{4a_1})$ where a_1 = velocity of sound = 1080 ft. per sec. So it is seen from the above equations that deflection for a given bullet depends on wind velocity V_w, muzzle velocity V_0, twist of rifling T, time of flight t, and range R in such relation that a mathematical equation for calculating this deflection is of little value to the rifleman. Thus we use ballistic tables and "rule of thumb" methods to estimate deflection and leave the equations to the mathematicians.

Considering range $R = V_0 t + \frac{1}{2} Jt^2$ in relation to the above equations for deflection and force F, it appears that an approximate value could be found for D in terms of R, such as $D = D_1 (\frac{R}{R_1})^n$, where D_1 is the deflection at range R_1. I have found a value of $n = 2$ gives deflection values with sufficient accuracy for all practical purposes, so we have a "rule of thumb" method for estimating deflection, for all hunting ranges, from some actual deflection value at some known range. As an example, assume you find, by test firing, that the deflection at 100 Yds. is $1\frac{1}{2}"$ in a 15 M.P.H. wind at 9 o'clock. By formula $D = D_1 (\frac{R}{R_1})^2$ find deflection values for all hunting ranges as shown below.

Range	Deflection	Windage
100 Yds.	1½"	1½ minutes
200 Yds.	4 x 1½" or 6"	2 x 1½ or 3 "
300 Yds.	9 x 1½" or 13½"	3 x 1½ or 4½"
400 Yds.	16 x 1½" or 24"	4 x 1½ or 6 "
500 Yds.	25 x 1½" or 37½"	5 x 1½ or 7½"
600 Yds.	36 x 1½" or 54"	6 x 1½ or 9 "

Both ballistic experts and riflemen have noticed that certain bullets showed little horizontal deflection in certain cross winds when the velocity was near the velocity of sound, and not understanding the nature of this wind effect, concluded that such bullets were deflected very little by a cross wind. This is not necessarily true, as we have seen that if the relation of wind velocity to bullet spin is such that $\frac{V_s}{V_w} = 2$ we will get a maximum vertical force, either up or down, while the drag or horizontal force is at a minimum. This wind effect is deflection whether vertical or horizontal. To the best of my knowledge the ballistic experts have never suspected that deflection could be other than in a horizontal direction, even though it has been verified in wind tunnel test that if a rectilinear flow of air is superimposed on the circulation about a rotating cylinder and $\frac{V_s}{V_w} = 2$ lift will be at maximum and vertical and lift coefficient C_L will be $= 4\pi$, while drag or horizontal force will be near 0. Now a bullet in a cross wind is in fact a small pointed cylinder rotating in a transverse flow of air.

With modern high velocity, fast twist rifles, we do not have the relation $\frac{V_s}{V_w} = 2$ but $\frac{V_s}{V_w}$ may be nearer 4 — 8 thus the deflection is almost entirely in the horizontal direction. However some of the older, slow twist, rifles as .22 L.R. Reg., .44-40W., .44 Special and .45-70 and the like may in a cross wind of certain velocity show deflection mostly in the vertical direction. If Vo = muzzle velocity in feet per Sec., d = bullet diameter in In., T = twist of rifling in inches per turn, and W = wind velocity in M.P.H. then when we have a cross wind of such velocity that $\frac{V_{od}}{T} = W$ we can expect deflection to be primarily in a vertical direction and expect a very small horizontal deflection. As an example consider the .22 L.R. V = 1145, T = 16″, R.H. and $\frac{V_{od}}{T} = \frac{1145 \times .22}{16} = 16$ to indicate that in a cross wind of 16 M.P.H. the deflection will be mostly in a vertical direction. If the wind is from 9 o'clock deflection is up and if the wind is from 3 o'clock the deflection will be down.

We have discovered the cause of a curve ball deflection and drift; also discovered that deflection may, for certain critical wind velocities, be up or down and we have a simple formula for estimating deflection from some known deflection.

Whoever is wrong or whoever is right, all ballisticians agree that wind drift is a subject for a great amount of research and study in order to arrive at a more complete understanding. Fine discussions of wind drift can be found in Chapter 10 of "Everyday Ballistics" by Charles S. Cummings, II and "Volume 2 SMALL ARMS DESIGN AND BALLISTICS" by Townsend Whelen.

The following table showing actual deflection due to wind can be seen at a glance for a number of representative calibres.

Load	Representative Calibres	Diam.	Wt.	Type	Representative Manufacturer	Sectional Density	Coeff. Form	Ballistic Coeff.	Muzzle Veloc. Ft. Sec.	Drift in 10 MPH wind* Yards			
										100	200	300	400
1.	.264 Winchester 7mm Rem. Magnum .284 Jet Magnum	.263	140	Spitzer SP	Winchester Hornady Nosler	.290	.566	.512	3100	0.5"	1.9"	4.6"	8.6"
2.	7mm Weatherby 7mm Mashburn .284 BJ Express	.284	160	Spitzer SP	Nosler Remington Barnes	.284	.566	.501	3250	0.5"	2.1"	4.9"	9.0"
3.	.308 Norma .300 Ackley 30/.338	.308	180	Spitzer SP	Barnes Remington Nosler	.271	.587	.462	3150	0.6"	2.5"	5.6"	10.4"
4.	.308 BJ Express .270 Winchester	.277	150	Spitzer SP	Barnes Nosler	.280	.566	.493	2950	0.6"	2.5"	5.8"	10.6"
5.	.270 Winchester	.277	130	Spitzer SP	Sierra Nosler	.242	.566	.428	3150	0.7"	2.6"	6.0"	11.1"
6.	Same as No. 2	.284	175	Semi-Spitzer SP	Nosler Remington	.310	.683	.454	3050	0.7"	2.7"	6.1"	11.2"
7.	.257 Jet .257 Robert Imp.	.257	115	Spitzer SP	Nosler Sierra	.249	.608	.410	3150	0.7"	2.7"	6.3"	11.4"
8.	.224 Jet .220 Swift Imp.	.224	63	Spitzer SP	Sisk	.180	.566	.318	3700	0.7"	2.8"	6.5"	12.0"
9.	.243 Winchester .244 Remington	.243	100	Spitzer SP	Hornady Remington Sierra	.242	.608	.398	3100	0.8"	2.9"	6.7"	12.2"
10.	.30/06	.308	180	Spitzer SP	Speer Nosler	.271	.587	.462	2700	0.8"	3.1"	7.0"	12.7"
11.	.30/06	.308	150	Spitzer SP	Remington Hornady	.226	.587	.385	3000	0.8"	3.2"	7.2"	13.2"
12.	.338 Winchester	.338	200	Semi-Spitzer SP	Speer Winchester Barnes Hornady	.250	.710	.352	3000	0.9"	3.3"	7.6"	14.1"
13.	6mm International .243 Winchester .244 Remington	.243	85	Spitzer SP	Sierra	.206	.632	.326	3250	0.9"	3.5"	7.9"	14.4"
14.	.22/250 .220 Swift	.224	55	Spitzer SP	Sierra Speer Sisk	.157	.608	.258	3700	0.9"	3.6"	8.3"	15.1"
15.	6mm International 6mm-.222 Magnum	.243	75	Spitzer SP	Sierra	.182	.656	.277	3400	0.9"	3.7"	8.6"	15.8"
16.	.222 Rem. Magnum .219 Wasp .219 Improved Zip.	.224	53	Spitzer HP	Sierra	.151	.632	.239	3300	1.1"	4.6"	10.6"	19.5"

*Drift is proportionate to Wind Velocity; Double values for 20 MPH wind, etc.
For a factual discussion of drift see "Bullets and the Wind," by William C. Davis, American Rifleman, Jan. '56, page 45.

PRESSURE

We have always heard statements to the effect that certain actions were designed for certain pressures. For example, a Krag action is supposedly good for not over 41,000 PSI. The Swedish Mauser for 43,000 or some such figure and so on. Where these figures come from seems to be a mystery. Perhaps it is because the military ammunition was loaded to these pressures and automatically assumed to be maximum for the rifles for which it was made.

Usually pressure figures are misleading. They do not take into consideration the design of the cartridge nor the method by which the pressure figures are obtained. The usual method for measuring pressure is by means of crusher cylinders, so as to measure the pressure at right angles to the axis of the bore about midway along the body of the chamber. This method gives a fair idea of the actual chamber pressure exerted upon the walls of the chamber in all directions, but bears little relationship to the amount of this pressure actually transmitted to the bolt or breech block in the form of thrust. The English method actually measures actual thrust against the bolt by inserting a crusher disc into a specially designed bolt in such a manner that the disc receives and measures the actual thrust which in turn is converted to breech pressure.

It would seem that the thrust figure is the one in which a handloader is most interested. It is important to him whether the bolt stays in his action or not, probably more important than chamber pressure which is, or can be contained by using high tensile strength steel.

Wildcatters feel that minimum body taper design reduces bolt thrust. This theory tends to be substantiated by results. A large number of wildcat cartridges have been submitted to the writer to be included in this book and almost every one utilizes to some degree the general principle of minimum body taper and sharp shoulder idea. Almost all factory cartridges introduced during the last few years incorporate these ideas although extremely sharp shoulder angles are avoided by American factories because of production difficulties. There could be some question about this since the European factories seem to have little difficulty producing extremely sharp shoulders or even completely venturified shoulders.

We often hear that the Winchester Model 1894 action was designed for low pressures and is an action which could be described as "weak". The writer's experience has been that almost any modern action in good condition will withstand pressures which result in blown primers with properly designed cartridges. Another claim which is always aired is that the brass case is the weak link. This may be true, but the brass case is a lot stronger than some would have us believe.

Many experiments and tests have been performed to find the real truth. From experience we know certain things. For example, it is a simple matter for any owner of a Model 99 Savage .250/3000 rifle to load his cartridges to a point where the extraction becomes impossible. For example, 34.5 grains of HiVel #2 is supposed to drive the 100 grain bullet 2900 foot seconds with a chamber pressure of 52,000 psi. Any increase is likely to freeze the mechanism so that a rod must be used to knock the case out while pulling on the operating lever. This tendency seems to be intensified in old (limbered up) actions. Once this point has been reached in the load, the barrel can then be rechambered for the "improved" .250/3000. A good way to do this is to simply rechamber with the original shoulder angle but using a reamer which will increase the diameter at the shoulder to about .455 instead of the original .416 amounting to a reduction in body taper of .039 for a slight increase in case capacity.

Once the rechamber job has been accomplished, cases can be formed by simply firing factory loads. Starting with the load of HiVel #2 which previously froze the action (around 36 grains and a 100 grain bullet) it will be found that extraction has become extremely easy. Since the case capacity has been increased, the velocity will show about a 2% reduction. To continue the test, the powder charge can be increased a grain at a time until trouble develops. This time, extraction trouble seldom shows up before something else gives, which is usually a swollen chamber indicating that the bolt thrust which caused extraction troubles with the original chamber has virtually disappeared while the chamber pressure has been increasing. By rebarrelling the action with a high strength barrel and again chambered for the minimum body taper case, the loads can once again be increased to a point of loose primers before any extraction trouble shows up. This requires around 42

PRESSURE

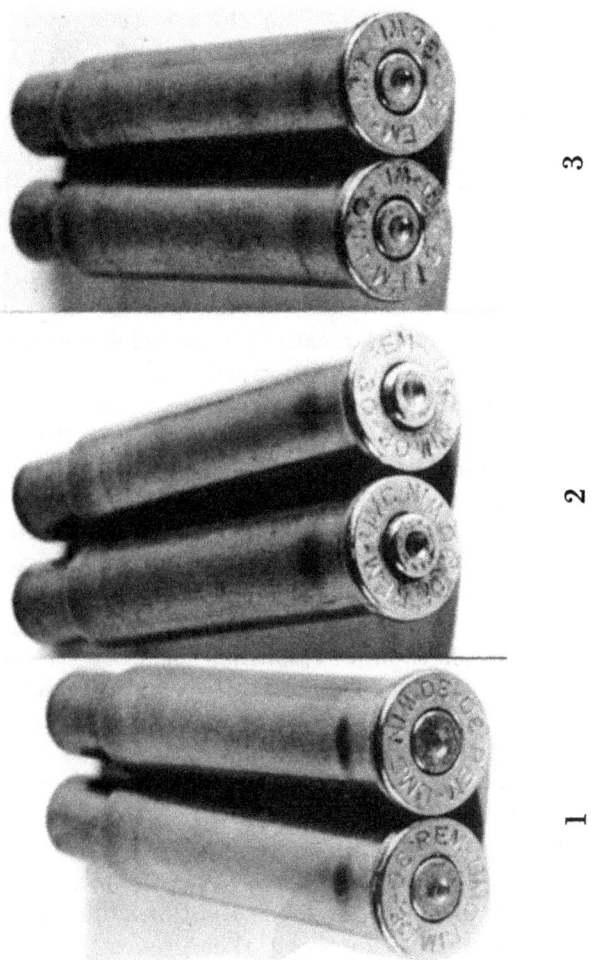

Figure 1.

grains of HiVel #2 and the 100 grain bullet for a velocity of approximately 3400 foot seconds. (This load used for illustration purposes only and not recommended for general use.) Now, the only change that has been made was to lessen the body taper.

To further illustrate this principle, an old, discarded, beat up Winchester Model 94 rifle was resurrected from the junk pile. The barrel was rechambered for the "improved" .30/30 with a 40° shoulder and minimum body taper. The rifle was fired with two factory loads shown as No. 1 in the illustration. The headspace was minimized when the barrel was chambered and when these two cartridges were fired, they formed perfectly with no primer protrusion. The barrel was then unscrewed one turn and two more factory cartridges fired. These two cases are marked No. 2. Primers protruded an amount equal to one barrel thread, but the cases did not back up against the bolt which means that the brass withstood the pressure. Two more factory cartridges were lightly oiled and fired with the barrel still turned out one turn. These are shown as No. 3. Note that the primers show no protrusion but that the shoulders are blown forward a distance equal to one barrel thread. Thus the oiled cases did not adhere to the chamber, but backed up against the bolt, which prevented primer protrusion. It also illustrated how case separation can be prevented while fireforming cases in a rifle with headspace. Next, the barrel was unscrewed two full turns and another factory cartridge fired. This was accomplished by lengthening the firing pin enough to reach the primer. The first one was fired in a dry chamber. The case stayed in the chamber but the primer fell out since the barrel was out a distance more than equal to the thickness of the primer. The second was lightly oiled and separated when fired, also dropping the primer. These two cases are marked No. 4. Note that the dry case is perfectly formed with normal neck showing the case did not back up and that the brass showed no weakness. The barrel was then turned back in one-half turn to make it one and one-half turns loose, and two more cartridges fired (dry chamber). The primers just stuck in the pockets but the brass cases still did not back up to contact the bolt, nor did they separate. No. 5. By studying these pictures it can easily be seen that the brass cartridge case WILL withstand at least SOME pressure, that the minimum body taper takes the "load" off the bolt or locking system, that oily chambers increase the bolt thrust, and that the action was designed for a certain pressure, is a fallacy.

PRESSURE

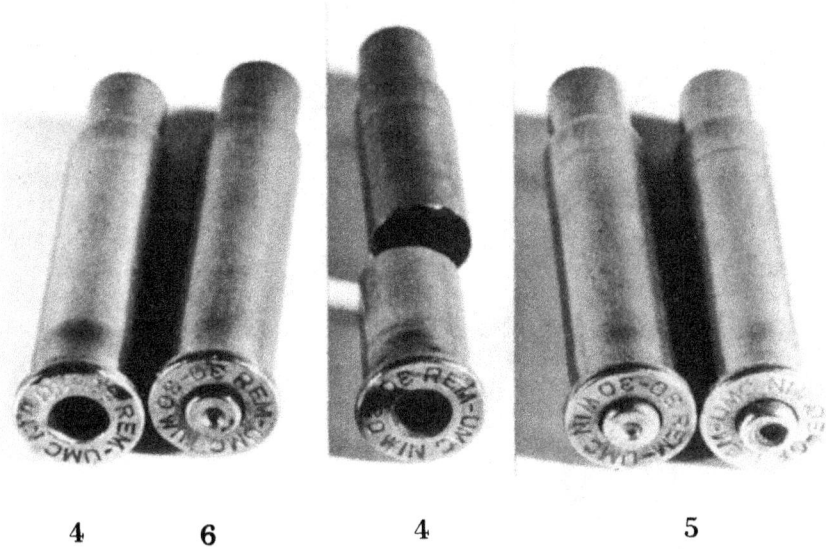

| 4 | 6 | 4 | 5 |

Figure 2.

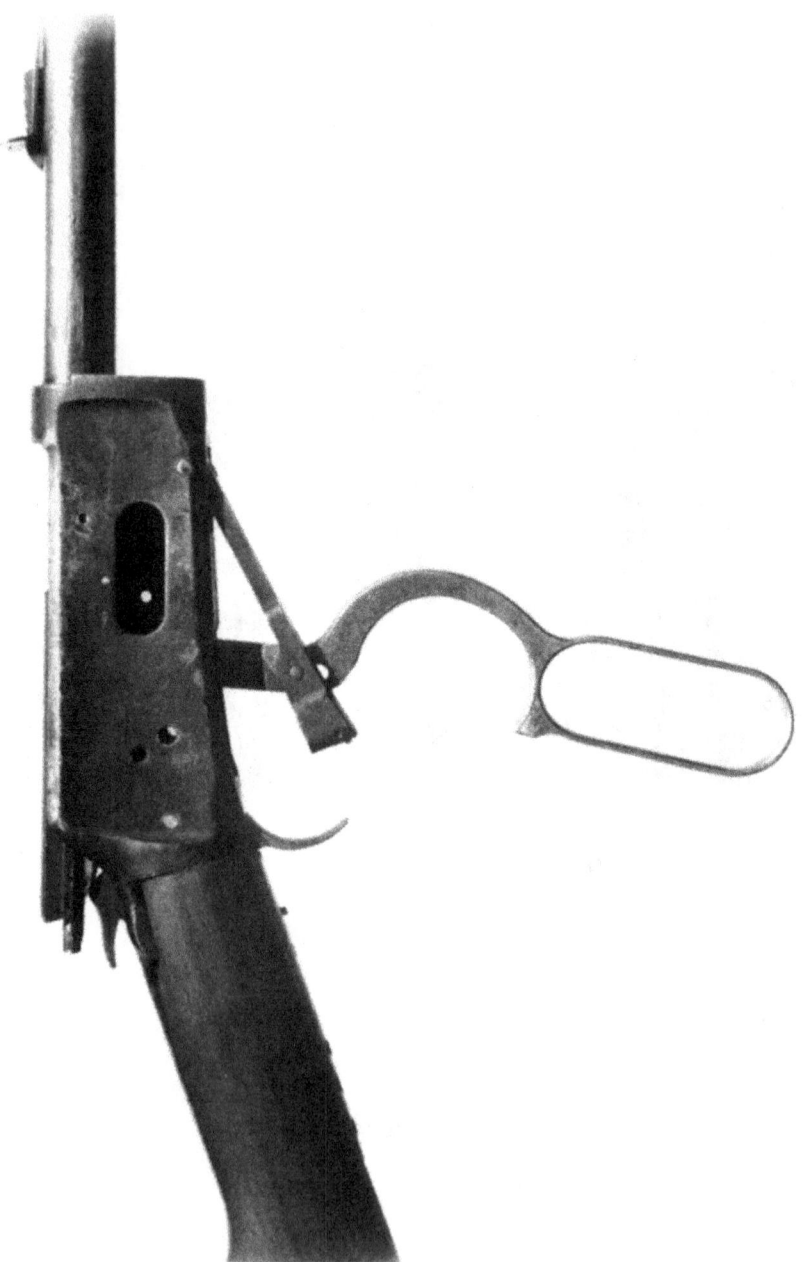

Figure 3.

Figure 4.

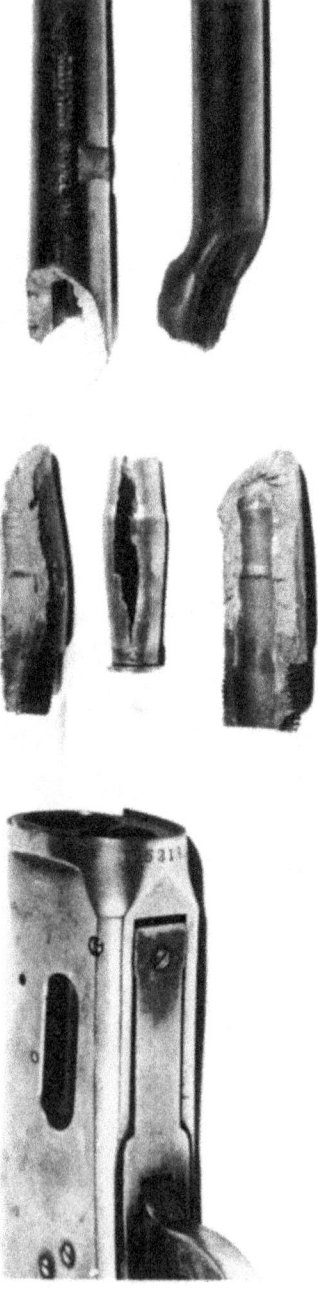

Figure 5.

Figure 6.

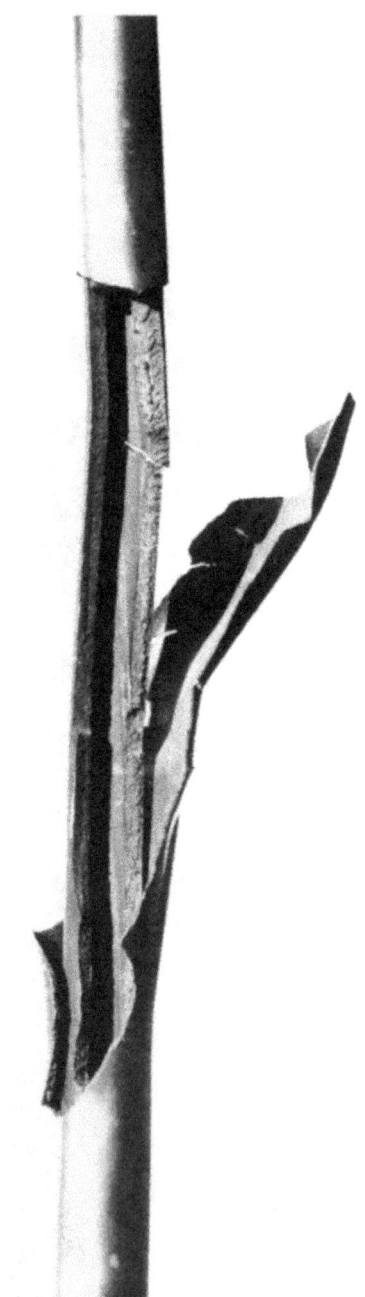

Figure 7.

To further prove the point, the locking lug was removed from the action entirely leaving the breech block or bolt with no means of support other than the finger lever. See illustrations. The rifle was fired several times with the barrel tight. All cases appeared to be normal except for excessive primer protrusion. One of these cases is shown as No. 6.

Now to state that this action will handle only certain pressures, or that the brass case will not support any amount of pressure seems to be out of order. There is plenty of room for further testing along these lines but the tests described seem to indicate that a very small percentage of the CHAMBER pressure was transferred to the breech bolt in the form of thrust. In this test the barrel absorbed the pressure while the action merely furnished the means for detonating the cartridge except when the chamber was oily.

The other illustrations show a Model 94 which was accidentally blown up. The load was supposedly 16 grains of Unique behind a 150 grain cast bullet. A double charge was inadvertantly thrown with the results shown. The action was not damaged except for the threads being expanded when the chamber section of the barrel split. The barrel separated completely just forward of the chamber, the bullet passing downward severing the magazine tube and blowing the forearm to pieces. The shooter was not injured. This shows how the high pressure could not be contained by the barrel but that the relatively straight standard .30/30 case did not back up against the breech bolt enough to harm any of the action parts. The receiver has since been replaced and the rifle works perfectly.

While on the subject of blow ups, pressure, etc., a blown up RELINED barrel is shown which "exploded" with a normal load. The tube was too light to contain the pressure and cracked. The gas rushed through the crack and shattered the very thin remaining portion of the original barrel. This illustrates the reason why it is never recommended to reline for high power cartridges.

Pressure is measured in two ways. The American method is by means of a copper crusher so arranged as to measure the chamber pressure at right angles to the axis of the bore. The English system is accomplished by means of a crusher disc so arranged that the bolt thrust is measured which is then translated into breech pressure.

These two methods are beyond the reach of the average handloader because of the cost of the equipment and the cost for having pressure tests made by laboratories possessing suitable equipment is almost prohibitive. This means the handloader must relay upon other means to estimate the pressures of his handloads. Homer S. Powley is now marketing a computer by means of which the handloader can figure pressures within practical limits, but most handloaders still rely upon the various manifestations of pressure such as the appearance of the primer, ease of extraction, etc.

Shooters working with wildcat cartridges are apt to indulge in pressures as high as possible, and still keep things together. Naturally, this applies equally to handloaders who load commercial cartridges as well. It is hard to describe pressure by simply quoting frightening figures, such as 50,000 psi or 70,000 psi, or by quoting the old sayings having to do with certain actions being built to withstand 25,000 psi, 50,000 psi, etc. Such figures disregard the cartridge design; and other considerations, which have marked effects on the problem.

Vernon Speer, author of the fine Speer series of loading manuals has worked out a method of observing pressures which seems best adapted for use by handloaders who load their ammunition at home far removed from scientifically equipped laboratories. Mr. Speer has the following to say:

"There is a tremendous difference in the way different rifles handle pressure and it is entirely possible that a rifle used in one test was different in this respect than another one we used. We do not have a pressure gun in our laboratory, because it is my opinion, backed up by quite a few years experience, as well as firing data from various laboratories using pressure guns, that data received from them is exceedingly unreliable. For a company such as Remington or Winchester having the same gun and operator comparable results to check on production problems are no doubt sufficiently accurate for the purpose for which they are used.

"We use the head expansion method in determining the pressure at which a cartridge case was fired. It is our belief that the cartridge case is the weakest link in the modern bolt action rifle. If the pressures at which these cartridge cases are fired do not exceed the elastic limit of the unsupported rim of the cartridge case, then we consider that the pressures are entirely usable, regardless of what they might be. We fire increased loads, increasing the charge by about a grain at a time, checking the rim diameter of the cartridge case with sensitive measuring instruments, both before and after firing. If any measurable increase in diameter of the rim of the case is noted, we consider that pressure excessive and reduce the charge about 6% and list it as a maximum load in our loading table. There is no reason why the handloader cannot use this same procedure himself and determine whether or not the loads he is using are safe and practical for use in his rifle.

"In our laboratory, we look for all of the signs of pressure such as sticky cases, tough extraction, flattened or cratered primers, as well as the rim expansion method noted above. Some cartridge cases are softer than others, notably Norma cases, and will not stand the higher pressure loadings possible in Remington and Winchester cases. This tends to bear out our contention that as long as the brass cartridge case is worked within the elastic range of the brass, then the pressure in the pounds per square inch, regardless of what it might be, is safe and practical for use in that particular cartridge. I hope I have been able to explain this pressure problem to your satisfaction."
Vernon D. Speer, February 6, 1958

There is now an inexpensive gauge on the market which simplifies measuring rim or head expansion for pressure indications made by St. Louis Spring and Brake Supply Compnay. This gauge is very simple to set and easy to use. The same company also is marketing a very useful and simple adjustable case length gauge.

HEADSPACE

A subject of greatest importance to the gunmaker or gunsmith who does any amount of barrel fitting or chambering or any amount of rechambering work is headspace. The gunsmith must have a complete understanding of this subject so that he is able to instruct his customers in the proper use of hand loading tools, especially for those who are interested in Wildcat cartridges which they themselves will make from some other type of brass.

There are many definitions of headspace, but no attempt will be made here to define headspace because it will simply add to the confusion already existing concerning this important subject. Therefore, instead of attempting to define headspace, it will be dealt with by describing each method by which headspace is measured.

There are four common methods of determining headspace, and these four methods are closely related to the four general types of brass cartridge cases. The four ways are: 1. From the bolt face to some point on the shoulder of rimless cases. This point on the shoulder is known as the datum line. The datum line is usually indicated on official data sheets or drawings. For example, the datum line on a .30-06 or .270 cartridge case is the point on the shoulder which measures exactly .375 diameter. This measurement varies with the size of the case. For example, a .25 Remington has a datum line of .392. 2. Rimmed cases on which the headspace is the thickness of the rim or the distance from the face of the fully locked bolt to the forward edge of the rim of the cartridge case which contacts the end of the barrel. The rim thickness varies with some rimmed cartridges, but normally it runs from .063 to .067. One notable example of a case which is different is the R2 Lovell and the old .25-20 single shot, both of which have considerably thinner rims. The .25-20 is an obsolete cartridge, but the R2 is currently being produced and sold by Griffin and Howe, Inc. 3. Belted cases in which the headspace is the distance from the face of the fully locked bolt to the forward edge of the belt which is .220 on the H & H Magnum cartridge. 4. Rimless pistol cartridges are usually straight and have no shoulder or rim to provide a stop and the headspace on these cartridges is measured from the face of the fully locked bolt to the end or mouth of the cartridge case. For example, the 45 ACP is a short, straight, rimless cartridge. When this cartridge enters a chamber its forward travel is stopped by the end of the cartridge case coming in contact with the end of the chamber.

Wildcat cartridges were mentioned as being a problem to the gunsmith in conjunction with headspace. Wildcat cartridges are not usually standardized to any degree and headspace gauges are not always available for them and even reliable chamber data is not available. Usually reputable tool makers can furnish tools for any well known wildcat cartridge, but very seldom do they furnish headspace gauges. Therefore, the gunsmith will find it necessary to determine the headspace himself as nearly as possible. This means that there will be considerable variation in the headspace of some wildcat cartridges as they are chambered for by different gunsmiths, and it will be up to the owner of the rifle to make his own brass to fit his own individual chamber. It is often advisable for the gunsmith to provide a set of forming dies which have been adjusted and tested with the gun before it is delivered. Such dies can be of the plain hand type and of extremely simple design, but they can be designed in such a way to absolutely preclude any possibility of the owner of the rifle to produce cartridge cases for his gun with dangerous headspace. If such forming and loading dies are furnished with the rifle to fit ordinary commercial loading tools such as Pacific, Echo and others, it will be necessary to instruct the customer in the proper use of it and adjustment of the dies. Many wildcat rifles are sold to customers who should never own such a gun because it seems to be impossible for some shooters to ever completely understand the problems of headspace. This results in a dangerous condition for the shooter himself and endless headaches for the gunsmith who built the rifle because invariably such shooters will blame the gunsmith for building a gun with excessive headspace. This difficulty also occurs with some owners of standard calibre rifles, for example some of the loading tool manufacturers make their sizing dies slightly short so that the headspace of the cartridge can be adjusted to fit the individual rifle. Other manufacturers furnish their full length sizing dies on the long side so that it is impossible to set the shoulder back on the cartridge to a dangerous extent. For the gunsmith, either method will result in headaches because the owner of the long die will find it impossible to size old cases which he may have picked up on the shooting range so that they will enter his rifle which may have minimum headspace. The owner of the short die on the other hand will pick up such odd cases or use the fired cases from his own rifle and proceed to size them in his short sizing die which he will insist on setting down tightly against the shell holder of the tool. This will result in setting the shoulder back to a point where headspace may be increased to a dangerous degree. Some commercial dies can shorten the headspace of a rimless case as much as .020 or .025. It should be noted here that headspace is considered excessive if there is more than .006 space between the head of the fully chambered cartridge and the fully locked bolt. Thus, a cartridge .025 short on the headspace is apt to separate or rupture near the solid head and can result in a blown up gun and injury to the shooter.

There are also a great many problems which arise with the so called improved cartridge. The word "improved" is a bad selection and does not accurately describe such cartridges but this word has stuck with us and so we are stuck with it. There are three general classes of cartridges which the gunmaker will be required to be familiar with and to work with. These are standard, improved and wildcat. A standard cartridge can be defined as a cartridge which is available commercially and can be bought in any sporting goods store or other stores selling ammunition and is commonly manufactured by the various manufacturers of ammunition. An improved cartridge is a factory cartridge which has been fired in an improved chamber and thus has its form changed during the process of firing the first time. In other words, a rifle made to handle an improved cartridge, for example the improved .257, will still handle factory ammunition but the fire formed cases can be reloaded or hand loaded to considerably higher velocities without danger to the shooter. A wildcat cartridge is one which cannot be obtained commercially or one which will not handle factory ammunition in any form. Wildcat cartridges must be made from some easily procured cartridge case such as a .30-06, .30-30 and similar ones. Some wildcat cartridges justify their existence. A few of them fill a gap which exists between certain commercial cartridges. Some do not justify their existence at all and have no advantage of any kind over corresponding factory cartridges. This is also true of so-called "improved" cartridges. More will be said concerning the various possible improvements and merits of some of the various types of wildcat cartridges.

In rimmed cases, theoretically there is no contact between the shoulder by the rimmed cartridge and the shoulder of the chamber. In fact, there is considerable space at this point and when the cartridge is fired in the chamber the shoulder blows forward or "fills out" and forms a solid contact. But this occurs only upon firing or when the pressure inside the case rises to a point sufficient to expand the brass cartridge case into all parts of the chamber.

The shoulder of belted cases does not contact the shoulder of the chamber. They fit into the chamber exactly as described for the rimmed case.

As described previously, the headspace of rimless cartridges is normally measured from the face of a locked bolt to some point on the shoulder called the datum line and this datum line on the .30-06 and some others is the point which measures exactly .375 in diameter. The old method, however, was to measure the headspace from the face of the fully locked bolt to the top of the shoulder or the sharp corner at the junction of the body where the slant of the shoulder begins. The .30-06 is the only cartridge measured by the old method. The length of the .30-06 case from the face of the bolt or the cartridge head to the point of the shoulder is 1.94" and the headspace is kept within the limits of 1.94" and 1.946". It must be kept in mind that that particular measurement which is not common to any other cartridge at the present time is from the head to the top of the shoulder. While on the .257 for example, the headspace is measured to the datum line which for the .257 is also .375 and the measurement from the face of the fully locked bolt to the datum line or the point measuring .375 diameter on the shoulder is 1.7937. This measurement is considered to be the minimum headspace measurement permissible. The maximum headspace permissible would be .005 to .006" in excess of this minimum measurement. Measuring the headspace of a .30-06 by the same method, namely from the face of the bolt to the datum line which is the .375 point on the shoulder, the actual measurement for the minimum length of the chamber is 2.0479 in contrast to the figure commonly used of 1.940. When considering improved cartridges and the chambering for the same it must be pointed out that the headspace must be considerably less than what we think of as minimum. For example, when chambering for the .30-06 we normally use a 1.940 gauge and get the bolt so that it will easily close with only a slight "feel" or close without any "feel" at all, but at the same time will absolutely refuse to close on a 1.946 gauge which means that the headspace of the chamber comes within the limits and somewhere between these two figures. Therefore, the 1.946 gauge becomes our "No Go" gauge since the bolt refuses to close at all on this maximum gauge. For the improved cartridge it is necessary to use the 1.940 gauge, as the "No Go" gauge, and our "Go" gauge must be approximately .004 shorter. There our "Go" gauge will become 1.936. When considering the .257 as a further example the standard minimum headspace for this cartridge is 1.794 with a maximum headspace or "No Go" gauge measuring in the neighborhood of 1.800 or if the bolt will close on the 1.8 gauge the chamber is considered to have maximum headspace and should be corrected. The improved chamber then will require a gauge of 1.790 as the "Go" gauge and the standard gauge of 1.794 will become the "No Go" gauge. It must be remembered that all of this applies to rimless cartridges only and must be closely observed. The reason for all this is the fact that when headspacing for improved cartridges the practice will be to fire factory ammunition in this improved chamber and thus form the cases in that manner, a process which is known as fire forming. Since factory cartridges will be fired in a chamber radically different from the standard chamber which is relatively like the cartridge itself the only point of contact is going to be exactly at the junction of the neck and shoulder. (No. 1 in illustration).

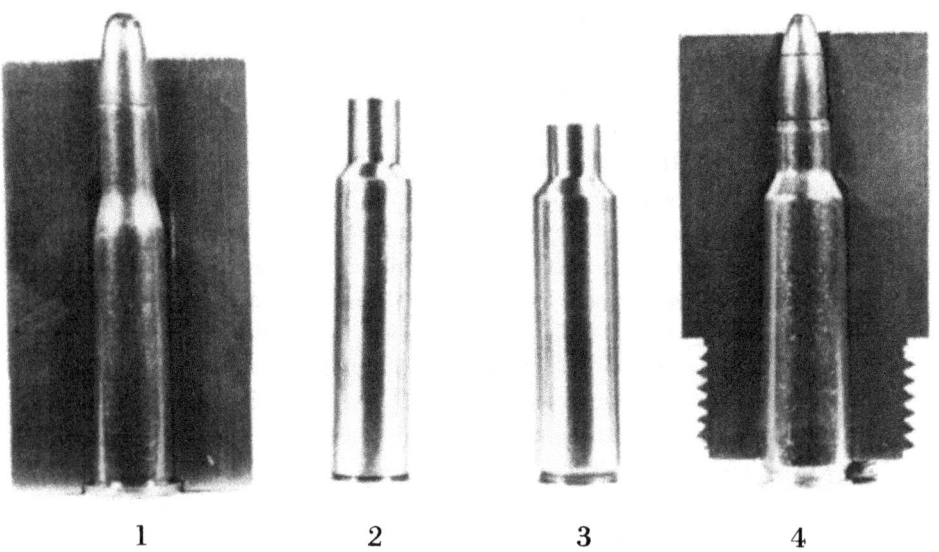

1   2   3   4

By observing this illustration it will be noted that the point of contact is necessarily only at this point. Once the cartridge has been fired the whole case will then take the form of the improved chamber, as shown as No. 3 in the illustration, and from then on the whole thing can be considered as the standard cartridge is going to appear as shown in the illustration No. 4 when it is fully chambered. The reason that the headspace must be somewhat less than popularly considered as minimum is that there is sometimes considerable variation in the length of individual cartridges when measured from the head to the junction of the neck and shoulder. When cartridges are inserted in chambers having relatively the same shoulder angle they are bound to contact at some point on the shoulder, but this is impossible when the factory cartridge is used in an improved chamber. Therefore extreme caution must be exercised to insure an intimate contact at the only point possible. If this precaution is not observed and a standard factory cartridge is fired in an improved chamber which is slightly over the recommended minimum there is good chance that the cartridge case will separate near the solid head when the charge explodes. This can easily result in a dangerous condition which can completely wreck the action to say nothing of the possible injury of the shooter.

The question of headspace for improved cartridges of rimmed design is not as complex as for rimless since the rim of the case is the only point which has to be seriously considered and of course the rim thickness remains the same whether the chamber is standard or improved. Therefore, if the headspace is minimum for one, it will be minimum for the other although slightly greater care must be exercised to make sure that the tolerances for the improved chamber are held minimum. The contact at the shoulder is of no importance with the rimmed cases since there is full support at the rim and it happens to be a fact that many wildcat cartridges being made from rimmed brass can be blown out considerably in length. In other words, the shoulders are moved ahead materially (No. 1 illustration) which shows a standard 25/35 case in the improved 25/35 chamber. It will be noted that there is no contact at all anywhere between the chamber and case except at the head. When this cartridge is fired in the improved chamber it will be expanded in all directions except to the rear where the head is tightly supported by the bolt or breech block. With rimmed or belted cases the shoulder can sometimes be moved ahead as much as 1/8" without rupturing the brass. The amount of fire forming possible depends on the quality and condition of the brass in the cases. It is sometimes possible to fire a cartridge such as the Zipper in a perfectly straight chamber like a 32/40 and the case when removed will be perfectly straight without any indication of a shoulder or neck. All of this means that rimmed and belted cases are slightly easier to deal with when designing or fire forming improved cartridges. On the other hand, if an attempt to fire a rimmed cartridge in an improved chamber which does have excessive headspace to a degree, they have a tendency to separate just ahead of the solid head of the case exactly the same as the rimless cases do.

The purpose of the improved chambers is to increase the capacity of any given cartridge through the process of fire forming, and to perhaps change its shape to what would be considered a more efficient one. Unfortunately, there are conflicting schools of what the design of the cartridges will or should be. Many shooters and students of the subject feel that a very sharp angle is desired on the shoulder of the cartridge. Some feel that this angle, combined with sharp corners, is the right type of design. Others feel that there should be a venturified effect which produces a chamber and cartridge case which will have an extremely sharp shoulder angle and have a larger radius at the top of the shoulder and the junction of the neck resulting in a rounded form of shoulder sometimes called venturified or semi-venturified or some other term which may serve to describe the design. Still others feel that a long sloping shoulder is the right idea, stating that there will be less resistance to the powder gases finding it harder to make their way forward around the sharp shoulder design. Exponents of the sharp shoulder ideas feel that the sharp shoulder creates greater resistance to the burning powder thus holding more of it in the case during the burning process which prevents such a high percentage of unburned powder being blown out into the throat of the barrel to create a sand blasting effect at which point erosion quickly destroys accuracy. Some feel that the sharp shoulder is especially adapted for the light bullets which do not offer a great deal of resistance through inertia to create higher burning pressures or with the medium weight bullets which combine a greater amount of inertia along with the extra resistance of the sharp shoulder. Modern design tends to be toward the sharp shoulder angle with comparatively sharp corners although most designers prefer a small radius of something like 1/32" at the corners. It is doubtful that these small radii help one way or the other but some feel that the life of the brass will be somewhat prolonged if sharp corners are avoided. There seems to be little evidence to support any of these theories.

Normally, sharp shoulder design of Wildcat and Improved cartridges is accompanied by minimum body taper or at least an approach to this condition. It can easily be demonstrated that comparatively straight cases without much taper combined with the sharp shoulder arrests the forward flow of brass thus preventing the necessity of trimming the cases to length frequently. It appears that a body taper of not more than .0075 per inch allows the case to grip the walls of the chamber sufficiently to prevent the brass from creeping or flowing and this is helped a great deal by the extra resistance of a sharp shoulder with sharp corners all of which creates greater resistance to the forward flow of the cartridge case metal. This continuous lengthening of cases occurs mostly in cases with sharply tapered bodies and relatively long or slanting shoulder such as the .220 Swift, 250/3000, .280 Ross and others of similar design. It has always been necessary to trim these cases to length after a few firings and loadings. This forward flow of brass occurs mostly at one point; that is, in order to lengthen materially it must be taken away from one point and transferred to another. And this borrowing of material occurs at the point of junction between the solid head and the body of the case. As this action proceeds, the excess brass flows forward and takes the form of excessive neck thickness and length and is trimmed or reamed away by some means. Thus the robbing of brass at this one point, creates a weak point where it ultimately separates. Two of the worst offenders are the .220 Swift and the .300 Magnum, the latter having a belt which solidly supports the head, will sometimes separate after 6 or 7 reloadings. If cartridges of this type are fired in an improved chamber which changes their form to what is known as improved and which actually consists of a sharp shoulder and minimum body taper, the case life will be increased many times because this design inhibits the forward flow of brass, thus doing away with the necessity of trimming the cases to length often and the loss of cases through head separation.

Since this fire forming method of making improved cartridges increases the capacity of the case at the same time that it changes its form, this increase in capacity must be given consideration by the designer. Experience has shown that there are certain case capacities which are maximum for given bore diameters. For example, a cartridge using bullet .224 in diameter can have a case capacity of no more than 40 grs and still give good over all results and efficiency. The maximum capacity for a .25 calibre is somewhere between 50 and 55 grs and the .30 calibre case must be kept under 70 gr. This all means that cartridges such as a .300 H & H Magnum already having a case capacity of over 65 gr have maximum or greater than maximum case capacity, and when fired in a so-called improved chamber or chambers of similar design which may be described by other names, the case capacity is increased to a point where the ratio between the capacity of the case and bore is not optimum. This means that when a .300 Magnum, .220 Swift and other similar calibres are blown out, which in their original form already have a maximum capacity for their bore diameter, they will show no improvement in ballistics and in some ways the characteristics will not be as good as those of the original case and about the only improvement that can be observed is the better case life, the lack of necessity of trimming to length and better extraction.

Such over bore capacity cases are bound to result in a reduction of barrel life which for some greatly offsets any advantage gained. Thus it is necessary to shorten such cases before they are fire formed to some improved form which automatically takes them out of the class of improved cartridge and places them in the class of pure Wildcat. There is one other point of advantage that must be described in conjunction with the minimum body taper and sharp shoulder design and that is the greater ease of extraction. It can easily be demonstrated that such a design results in much easier and more positive extraction and at the same time allows heavier loads and higher pressures to be used without detrimental effects, thus enabling the shooter to reach considerably higher velocities without endangering himself or his rifle. Take for example the .257 Roberts cartridge. When this factory cartridge is fired in one of the better versions of the improved chamber, its capacity will be increased some 10% and at the same time the body taper will be greatly reduced with the shoulder angle being sharply increased. All of these changes result in greater case capacity which in turn lowers the loading density which means that there will be less velocity per grain of powder than with the original case before it was fire formed. This tendency is offset some what by the sharper shoulder, but it can be easily demonstrated that this increase in case capacity does reduce the velocity per grain of powder to a measureable degree and consequently it is necessary to use slightly heavier charges in the improved case to get the same velocities that a slightly lighter charge would achieve in the original case. However, the design of the improved case is such that after fire forming has occurred the loads can be increased considerably over and above the original to achieve a considerably higher total velocity. In the case of the Improved .257 the velocities are approximatey 10% higher than for the standard cartridge in the average rifle. And such velocities can be reached without dangerous pressures.

Pressures must be considered when working with such cartridges, but here again it can be demonstrated that the Improved designed cases can safely handle higher pressures as they are normally measured than could be safely used in the original case. There seems to be no accepted explanation for this because pressures which would be considered abnormally high for cases of rather tapered design seem to show no detrimental effects in a case of similar capacity with the improved design. This may be because the straighter sides of the improved case grasp the sides of the chamber to an extent which is sufficient to reduce the back thrust against the bolt to a measureable degree, thus more or less doing away with the tendency of the bolt to spring back from the thrust of the cartridge as it is fired and then spring back into place after the pressure of the exploding charge is expanded, allowing the bolt to sort of straighten out, forcing the rather tapered case back into the chamber, something on the order of driving a lathe center into the tail stock of a lathe making it rather difficult to remove. It can be demonstrated that relatively straight sided cases or cases with a minimum body taper can be loaded heavy enough to blow the primer out of the case and actually melt or vaporize some of the brass and still be extracted without aid of a rod.

Cartridge design is something in which many gunsmiths will sooner or later become interested in and each gunsmith will have his own ideas as to how a case should look and perform and no matter what his ideas are and what the final form of his cases turns out to be he will probably find a following among shooters who will provide him with a considerable amount of business if he consistently performs his work and takes pains to put out only truthful ballistics figures which can be depended upon by his customers to be safe in all of the rifles that he will ultimately produce. He should always make sure that his figures are enough on the conservative side so that owners of his rifles will not become disappointed if they have occasion to have their loads chronographed by some disinterested party. Many gunsmiths have found it possible to build up a substantial business by developing their own cartridges and once they are developed, promoting the business by means of proper advertising. The cartridge designer should also keep in mind that it may prove to be hard to demonstrate that one design of a cartridge is more accurate than another. Many designers or so called designers of Wildcat cartridges are prone to claim that their designs are more accurate than similar designs or even totally different designs. This is probably completely wishful thinking on their part. Certainly, it is a claim which is extremely hard to prove or demonstrate. It is much easier to prove the statement made by the other school of thought. Members of this school feel that accuracy is an inherent characteristic of the barrel itself and so long as cartridges of comparable capacity or cartridges which are not badly over bore capacity and have semblance of a reasonable ratio between bore and case capacity will all shoot equally well in barrels of equal accuracy or better still, they feel that a barrel can be chambered for one version of a cartridge and thoroughly tested and rechambered for some other vesion which is claimed to be better and thoroughly retested without any appreciable change in accuracy. This experiment has been performed numerous times with the same result each time. For example, a .224 barrel can be chambered for something like the .219 Wasp which is a relatively short, high velocity .224 cartridge developing something like a maximum of 3600 fs with a 50 or 55 gr bullet. The same barrel can then be rechambered for an Improved .219 Zipper which has for all practical purposes the same design except the length of the case which is substantially longer resulting in two or three grains more powder capacity but still will be inside the maximum 40 gr limit, the Improved Zipper holding not much over 34 or 35 grains. A thorough test of accuracy with the rechambered job will not reveal any increase or decrease in accuracy except for one possibility that there can be some flaw just forward of a short chamber which conceivably could be affecting accuracy and which would be removed when the barrel is rechambered for a longer cartridge. But assuming the barrel is already a perfect one there would be no measureable change in accuracy between the two chambers. Carrying the experiment still further, the same barrel can be rechambered for a cartridge such as the .22/250 or .22 Varminter which is made by necking the .250/3000 case down to .22. When the same barrel is rechambered for this slightly larger case which is still within the case capacity limits there will still be no measureable change in accuracy so long as the psychological reaction of the experimenter remains the same during all phases of the experiment. Of course when reading accounts of such tests one of the greatest factors is the mental reaction of the experimenter. If he has a preconceived notion that some particular cartridge is better than another one he may be prone to manipulate conditions so as to influence the results. It is absolutely necessary to perform each phase of such experiments with an open mind and with the same care and technique.

BORE CAPACITY

The ratio between bore and cartridge case capacity is a subject about which more is heard these days than ever before. The term "over bore capacity" is applied to many cartridges which is to say that an extremely large cartridge holds more powder than the bore can possibly handle efficiently. .Powley ties up bore capacity with expansion ratio. Expansion ratio is ratio between the total volume of the bore and the volume of the case. It is the number of times the gas will expand by the time the bullet reaches the muzzle. High expansion ratios mean good barrel life. Low ratios mean short barrel life. Low ratios may result in the highest velocity but in many instances this slightly higher velocity is more than offset by greatly reduced barrel life, critical loading and general inflexibility.

There is no set rule or way to determine the proper or maximum case capacity, at least as yet. We can't say we should have a capacity equal to one third the weight of the bullet—that is, three grains of bullet weight to one grain powder weight, or 50 grains of powder for a 150 grain bullet—but by long experience and observation we have been able to ascertain approximately the maximum case capacity for the common bores. For example, we know by trial that a 35 grain .22 calibre case is about the most efficient, giving relatively high velocity, fair barrel life and good flexibility. By increasing the case size to a little over 40 grains we get slightly higher velocity but barrel life suffers badly and flexibility suffers to the extent that it is sometimes hard to find a suitable load. By increasing the case capacity to a point where the powder charge exceeds the weight of the bullet, barrel life drops to very few rounds with no appreciable gain in velocity. Examples of the first category might be the .219 Donaldson Wasp and Improved Zipper. The second class could be the .220 Swift or the .22/.250 and the third class might be the .300 Weatherby necked to .22. The tests described elsewhere in this book involving rimmed, rimless and belted cases in .25 calibre also illustrated this point. Warren Page, Gun Editor of "Field and Stream," tested three 6.5

cartridges and his results served to illustrate the importance of case capacity in relation to bore capacity. .The three cartridges were the .260 AAR, a blown out .270 Winchester case necked to 6.5 and the .264 Winchester Magnum. All tests were made at the Remington Ballistics Laboratory. The following figures were accumulated during the tests.

Instrumental Velocity at 15 feet. Add 20-25 feet for Muzzle Vel.

A. .260 AAR–FN, 22" barrel, chambered by Ackley, Davis stock
   CCI #200 Primers, Remington brass FF
   Capacity 55.5 grains

100 gr bullet	a. 3373	140 gr bullet	a. 2865	140 gr bullet	a. 2954
54 gr 4350	b. 3345	48 gr 4350	b. 2882	51 gr 4831	b. 2903
	c. 3333		c. 2899		c. 2920
	d. 3367		d. 2865		d. 2941
	e. 3384		e. 2894		e. 2915
	f. 3373		f. 2878		f. 2907
	g. 3367		g. 2869		g. 2924
	h. 3378		h. 2907		h. 2937
	i. 3361		i. 2903		i. 2954
	j. 3378		j. 2911		j. 2894
Aver. Inst.	3366	Aver. Inst.	2887	Aver. Inst.	2925
EMV	3390	EMV	2910	EMV	2950
Dev.	51	Dev.	56	Dev.	60

B. 6.5/.270 Improved Stegall–FN, 22" barrel chambered by Stegall
   W120 primers, SuperSpeed brass FF
   Capacity 67.5 grains

100 gr bullet	a. 3425	140 gr bullet	a. 3101
61 gr 4350	b. 3484	60 gr 4831	b. -
	c. 3454		c. 3091
	d. 3426		d. 3145
	e. 3472		e. -
	f. 3367		f. 3091
	g. 3503		g. 3086
	h. 3425		h. -

		i. 3413			i. 3086
		j. 3478			j. 3077
Aver. Inst.		3446	Aver. Inst.		3113
EMV		3470	EMV		3095
Dev.		136	Dev.		68

C. .264 Winchester Magnum—Model 70, 26" barrel shortened to 22"
CCI #350 primer
SuperSpeed brass
Capacity 79.5 grains

100 gr bullet		a. 3503	100 gr bullet		a. 3472
Win./		b. -	66 gr 4350		b. 3503
factory		c. 3534			c. 3478
		d. -			d. 3527
		e. -			e. 3454
		f. 3509			f. 3503
		g. 3490			g. 3503
		h. -			h. 3431
		i. 3534			i. 3454
		j. 3521			j. 3466
Aver. Inst.		3515	Aver. Inst.		3479
EMV		3540	EMV		3500
Dev.		44	Dev.		96
140 gr bullet		a. 3096	140 gr bullet		a. 3165
Win./		b. 3086	65 gr 4831		b. 3140
factory		c. 3063			c. 3180
		d. 3063			d. 3160
		e. 3044			e. 3185
		f. 3096			f. 3170
		g. 2976			g. 3170
		h. 3040			h. 3195
		i. 3053			i. 3190
		j. 2990			j. -
Aver. Inst.		3051	Aver. Inst.		3173
EMV		3075	EMV		3200
Dev.		120	Dev.		55

It will be noted that the .260 AAR took a maximum safe load of 54 grains of 4350 powder behind a 100 grain bullet for an average muzzle velocity of 3366 foot seconds.

The larger blown out 6.5/.270 gave an average velocity of 3470 foot seconds using 61 grains of 4350 powder behind a 100 grain bullet and 60 grains of 4831 powder drove the 140 grain bullet 3135 foot seconds average.

The still larger .264 Winchester required 66 grains of 4350 powder to get the 100 grain bullet up to 3500 foot seconds and 65 grains of 4831 powder to get 3200 foot seconds muzzle velocity with 140 gr. bullet.

A short study of these velocities reveals that the blown out .270 case with a volume of 67.5 grains took 7 grains more powder to increase the velocity of the 100 grain bullet 80 foot seconds faster and that the .264 required 5 grains more powder to get only 30 foot seconds over the .270 case. The .264 required 12 grains more powder to get 110 foot seconds over the .260 AAR which has a case capacity of 55.5 grains. The 100 feet extra velocity requiring 12 grains more powder cuts the barrel life to one-third or one-half that of the .260 AAR, and it is much more critical to load for. The muzzle blast is much more unpleasant and for most shooters that extra 110 feet is just not worth the cost. It might be added that it would be pretty hard to see much difference in the trajectory under average hunting conditions and further, it would make little difference to the animal being hit. Of course, even a few extra feet of velocity is worth the price to a few shooters who are interested in velocity at any cost.

Al Ellinger has the following to say on the subject of bore capacity:

A short discussion on this interesting subject may be of interest to both students and experimenters in Ballistics. There is little understanding of what the term "bore-capacity" means except in the laboratories of the ammunition makers. Even there, while the designers may know all about it, some of their products fall far short of following the lesson that bore-capacity teaches.

To define it briefly: Bore-capacity is a measure of efficient powder burning in a restricted space. This burning is affected by six different factors as follows:

1. Type of powder
2. Bore-groove diameter
3. Pitch of rifling
4. Sectional density of bullet
5. Allowable pressure
6. Case shape

Each point will be taken up in turn during the course of this paper. First let's talk over this "powder burning" more fully.

The *amount* of powder consumed is only one factor in favor of designing cartridge cases of proper bore-capacity. Accuracy, uniform pressures, and ease of mechanical functioning are a few of the other reasons.

It is generally understood that, if we increase the "boiler-room" behind a certain caliber of bullet and use it, that the resulting velocity and energy will keep step with the powder used. This is true only up to a certain point, beyond which if more powder is added, very little increase in velocity is attained; in some cases it is actually reduced. Pressures under these circumstances are very likely to be enormous.

We can increase a certain load, grain by grain. . When the inertia factor begins to take over, the pressure curve goes UP, and fast—but the velocity curve begins to lag badly. At this point or DELTA, where the two curves of pressure and velocity begin to separate, we have the bore-capacity of that particular combination of components.

To be specific: Several qualified experimenters have concentrated on developing the .25 caiber. They have employed the .30-06 case necked to .25; also the .30 Newton, the .348 Winchester and the belted H. and H. Case. All of these are above bore-capacity for the small area of the .25 caliber bullet, except the very heaviest. Because of this small area or cross-section they cannot be accelerated beyond our present high velocities unless we are prepared to accept higher chamber pressures than currently considered safe. (The Germans made a barrel that was about .32 Cal. at the breech and tapered to a .25 Cal. at the muzzle which accomplished some wonderful velocity-pressure balances, though it was utterly impractical from a general use standpoint.)

Now there is a very concrete and mathematical reason for our inability to exceed certain velocities at a given pressure. The equation for Pressure is: P equals F, divided by A; in which P is pressure; F is Force and A is area. It will be seen that if we increase A (area) then P will fall off instantly, provided F is constant. All of this is unchangeable. No amount of nice design or super-finishing will affect it, materially; but, to return to the 25 caliber:

It has been found that the .257 Remington case somewhat increased in capacity, is the ideal in every way for this popular caliber. If we insist on a belted case, for some reason, it should be shortened to a point where its cubic contents will equal that of the improved .257 case. Being larger in head-diameter, it will cause more "back-thrust" than the .257 case, but it does have certain advantages to the handloader, in more accurate head-spacing, and the like.

1. *Powder*

All powders have their own distinctive "burning characteristic." Snappy or fast burners are best for low-inertia (light) bullets. They get up to good pressures *fast*—and have to, because the lighter bullet *starts easier* and accelerates far too rapidly for "slow" powders.

Progressive or "slow" powders give to high-inertia (heavy) bullets a more moderate starting push. They also have a steeply-rising pressure curve once they do get under way. When this phase occurs the bullet has reached some acceleration in the bore; the "burning chamber" is extended to include the breech end of the bore also; as a result, the danger of extreme pressures is reduced. Highest pressures are probably reached in well-designed cases using No. 3031 powder at from 3 to 5 inches from this breech; with No. 4350 powder it is highest at from 8 to 12 inches. This is not to say that the highest velocities are attained at these points in the barrel. Acceleration is still at work overcoming inertia. As the Gas-Velocities themselves are in the nature of 4,000 to 7,000 ft. per sec., there is a constant "push" all the way to the muzzle; perhaps about enough to overcome bore-friction in the last few inches of the bore.

In Charles Newton's time, bore-capacity was from 10% to 15% below the point it occupies today simply because of the improvement in "progressiveness" in modern powders. The pressure-wave of No. 4350, for instance, is altogether less steep than in No. 10 or No. 15 old-style powders. While it is true that we can slightly reduce bore-friction by using bullets of shorter bearing surface and lubricating alloys, the chief factor is INERTIA or weight of the bullet. Once the slug is moving it is far easier to accelerate it; at the same time we have the added space of the bore as an expansion chamber—in short—a lesser pressure for a greater length of TIME.

2. *Bore-groove diameter.*

This is simply a matter of measurement. For accuracy in comparing different cases, the depth and width of the grooves should be measured so that the *area* of the "slugged" bullet is exactly known.

3. *Pitch of rifling.*

Aside from the stabilizing effect of this factor (Twist), little attention has been given to the *consumption* of *power* which occurs in the spinning of modern bullets at their truly terrific velocities. One of the latest textbooks on Internal Balistics shows that the energy consumed in *turning* the *projectile* is as high as 35% of which is available to *move it forward.*

It will be interesting to note here that all experimenters in velocities of 5,000 foot seconds and over, including Sedgley and Jim Howe, used smooth-bores. They wanted 100% of the energy available to move the bullet *forward*—not the 65% remaining in the case of a rifled bore! Therefore, when we consider bore-capacity we must give thought to the pitch and depth of rifling.

4. *Sectional density of the bullet.*

This has to do with the weight and caliber of the bullet. However, as it varies as to the square of the caliber, we can eliminate weight and length just as long as we consider a given Mass over Area (sect-density). . As it works out: The *same pressure* applied for the same *length of time* to two bullets of the *same sectional density,* regardless of caliber, will result in the same acceleration and *must* attain the *same* velocity. A thorough understanding of this fact is of the greatest importance. You are respectfully referred to a paper on this subject by the same author.

5. *Allowable pressure*

This is the touchstone of the entire subject! It is the limiting factor in the attainment of today's super velocities. As we view the components used today in assembled ammunition, the brass case with its low tensile strength and the removable primer, it can be assumed that the pressure given by the Experts, of from 50,000 to 55,000 P/sq. inch, are right at the safe limit. . The modern bolt-rifle will withstand far more of a blow than these pressures will strike; we do have to consider the weakest part of the "chain"—the case and the primer. It is, of course, true that if we could safely boost chamber pressures to 65,000 or more P per sq. inch, in velocities, bore-capacity, etc., would mount accordingly and some of the late "super-duper" wildcat shells do just that; we can well temper our "valor with discretion" as a wise man would. Then also, powder chemists may come through with still more progressive powders that will permit better performance at safe pressures. Steel cases have not worked out well; even then the weak point of the primer is still to be considered.

6. *Case shape*

To a modified extent, case shape has an effect on working pressures. A short case of a given capacity reacts differently than a very long one of the like capacity. This seems to be because of the difference in time required to ignite all of the powder. In a short stubby case, all of the powder grains are nearer to all others than in a long tubular form of case. A long case probably has the effect of lengthening the ignition period of all powders. This cannot be held as an advantage, however, as the matter of burning most of the powder in the bore, instead of the case, must be taken into account here.

The very-tapered brass case, with long tapered shoulder, causes high pressures long before their potential bore-capacity is reached. Evidently this is due to the powder grains being broken up, compressed and "funneled" trying to get out of the case ahead of the gas spreading ahead of the primer. Incidentally, this same funneling and compression causes stretching of certain case-necks, notably the .220 Swift and the .275 and .276 Magnums.

The modern greatly improved and fairly straight-sided case, with a shoulder slope of from 30 to 35 degrees, also moves the powder forward; but, it *compresses only* from the *rear — not from* the *sides,* of the chamber. Evidently, in this form of case, the powder blown into the "throat" of the barrel is of bore-diameter, a sort of "plug." The powder in the outer parts of the case has time to *burn in* the *case,* while the compressed center portion is on its way behind the bullet.

Considerable light will be thrown on the matter of "erosion" if an enlargement of certain cases be made. If the lines of the shoulder are continued to a point within the bore and if these lines do not converge within the neck of the case, we almost certainly will have a case of erosion, especially in the higher intensity loadings. The ultra Gas-Velocities blow the unburned grains of powder against the sides of the bore with such force that they serve as a thousand little cutting edges. Where the neck of the case takes this beating, as in shoulder of a good angle, much less of the powder in grain form will reach the steel of the barrel with the result that "accuracy life" is greatly extended.

Speaking of bore-capacity, one of our best-known experimenters who is also a hunter of all types of American game, in a book recently published, says that in his opinion, the properly designed cartridge case can be filled with powder to a point where a bit of compression of the powder is permissable. In theory this could work out satisfactorily, if temperatures could be uniform, bullets correct in size, weight and otherwise exactly uniform; also if the case capacity were absolutely uniform in quality and quantity. Lacking any of these, one would be flirting with disaster to attempt to use ammunition, so loaded. There is another matter to think of. What about changes in bullet weight and the use of different powders; both modifications are reasonable for hand loaders especially. Many shooters use the same rifle for many types of shooting such as targets, vermin and in the hunting of game from small deer to elk and large bears. It does not seem reasonable to assume that one weight of bullet would be ideal for all of these purposes, now does it? The best we can do is to work out a size of case that is a slight compromise, especially at one extreme of the list of bullet weights.

We can design the case for the heaviest weight of bullet liable to be used and with the slowest powder at a high density of loading. When normal and safe pressures are reached, this case will be very nearly the best proportions for lighter and faster bullets when propelled with faster powders.

Taking the .30-06 as an example. This case as is just about balances a 200 gr. bullet with very little airspace, using No. 4350 powder. With No. 4320 it gets the maximum out of 180 gr. flat-based bullets; No. 3031 is the top performer with 150 gr. sizes. But—to get the greatest energy from 110 to 120 gr. bullets (of low inertia) we need very fast powders such as Hi-Vel No. 2 or equivalent. In only one of these combinations will the "ideal"' be reached. By intelligently fitting the powder to the bullet, we find a compromise point where a whole series of different weight projectiles can be made to perform at, near to maximum velocities—and at—NORMAL PRESSURES.

This book contains a good number of rather radical cartridges for which rather optimistic claims are made, both in the loading data furnished by the originators, and the advertising appearing in a number of the national sporting publications.

To further check some of the theories presented earlier in this article, the author selected a 6mm barrel at random, and fitted it to an Enfield action. First it was chambered for the .240 Super Varminter, which is simply the '06 or .270 Winchester case necked

BORE CAPACITY

down to accept standard 6mm bullets. New GI brass was necked down and prepared for the test. The following loads and velocities were checked:

75 gr. bullet	55 gr.	4831 powder	3442 fs
	56	4831	3549
	57	4831	3601
	58	4831	3655
90	54	4831	3223
	55	4831	3312
	56	4831	3355

The last loads for each bullet weight are maximum. One more grain blew the primer with each bullet weight. From experience, we know this cartridge is over bore capacity, which sometimes results in short barrel life and erratic accuracy. These velocities can be duplicated with the Improved .244 Remington, or the Page Super Pooper, with measureably less powder.

The barrel was next chambered for one of the highly advertised .240 cartridges based on the 06 case blown out with extremely sharp shoulder and short neck, to produce maximum powder capacity. The following loads and velocities were recorded. The last loads for each bullet are maximum, and one more grain blew the primers with each bullet weight.

75 gr. bullet	60 gr.	4831 powder	3549 fs
	61	4831	3580
	62	4831	3667
	63	4831	3670
90	57	4831	3223
	58	4831	3312
	59	4831	3360

By comparing the results with both cases in the SAME barrel it will be seen that there is no significant increase in velocity for the extra five grains of powder.

The barrel was again re-chambered for the .244 H & H Magnum and the test repeated with the following results:

176 HANDBOOK FOR SHOOTERS AND RELOADERS

75 gr. bullet	68 gr.	4831 powder	3644 fs
	69	4831	3644
	70	4831	3650
90	66	4831	3399
	67	4831	3420
	68	4831	3444

Here again, we were not able to realize significantly higher velocity in spite of the extra powder consumed. The slightly higher velocity could well have been due to the different make brass which was necessarily commercial Magnum brass, while for the two cartridges previously tested, the same lot of GI brass was used. Certainly, it seems after conducting these tests, that there is a definite limit to case capacity for any given bore. The relatively small Improved .243 Winchester case, produces the same velocity as these three much larger cases, with from fifteen to twenty-eight grains less powder.

It must be kept in mind, that the SAME barrel was used for testing all three cartridges. .Everyone knows that certain barrels will accept heavier loads, and sometimes produce higher velocities than other barrels, but any barrel, whether it accepts maximum or minimum charges, will show the same relative results when successively chambered for increasingly larger cases. Many guns are blown up by shooters trying to use charges in their rifles which supposedly have produced the spectacular velocities advertised by gunmakers who doubtless obtained the highly advertised velocities in a selected rifle.

To further check the case and bore capacity problem, another barrel was selected from stock at random. This one was a .270, and was fitted to a Model 98 Mauser action. It was first chambered for the .308 Winchester case necked to accept the standard .270 bullets. It has been thought by many experimenters for some time, that the .308 case might prove to be the ideal .270, to produce results similar to the Improved .257/.270. The barrel was cut to 26", and the following results were produced by the .308/.270.

Only maximum loads are shown. In each instance, one more grain blew the primer

150 gr. bullet 47 gr. 4831 powder 2886 fs

The barrel was rechambered for the Ackley Improved .270 Winchester. The maximum load was

150 gr. bullet 55 gr. 4831 powder 2968 fs

The barrel was rechambered for the third cartridge, one of the widely advertised blown out short neck versions, and the maximum load was

150 gr. bullet 60 gr. 4831 powder 2972 fs

These figures would seem to prove that the STANDARD 270 Winchester is surely top, and probably a little over bore capacity, because normally it will duplicate these velocities with about 56 gr. of 4831. Further study shows that smaller cases, like the Improved .257/.270 and the .308/.270 almost reach this velocity level with still less powder.

A FEW NOTES ON SECTIONAL DENSITY AND RELATED ITEMS

by *Paul Von Rosenburg*

Some of the following notes are data from the laws of physics stated in such a way to be easily related to the subject at hand; others are opinions of the writer based on the laws of physics and approximately 20 years observation and experience with the rifle and its projectile.

First, let us discuss some of the terms used in arriving at sectional density so that a clear understanding of them can lead to correct conclusions. Density: this is the weight (mass) of a substance per unit of volume. In the case of bullets it is the number of pounds per cubic foot of the material or materials of which the bullet is constructed. Jacketed bullets are heterogeneous; that is they are made of several dissimilar metals, usually copper and lead. Some jackets have the copper alloyed with nickel, tin or zinc. Some cores have the lead alloyed with antimony or tin. These metals all have different densities, but for the sake of this discussion, as is common practice, we will assume that all jacketed bullets have the same density. This is technically not so because some bullets have as high a percentage of their total weight as 90% in the lead core, while others have copper jackets which represent 50% of the total bullet weight. Perhaps a mean, should the reader be interested, is about 32% jacket and 68% core (this is an average of 10 popular 150 gr. 30 cal. bullets.)

Next is Sectional: this term is merely an expression for the cross-sectional area of a bullet. The main thing to remember here is that the cross-sectional area increases with the square of the diameter.

Now we come to Sectional Density itself: here we have the weight of a bullet for its cross-sectional area. Sometimes sectional density is defined as weight per diameter, which is incorrect. The formula expressing sectional density is:

$$SD = \frac{W}{7000 \, D^2}$$

where SD is sectional density
W is weight in grains
D is diameter in inches
7000 is number of grains per pound

Thus it can be seen that sectional density is weight per *cross-sectional area,* not diameter.

Since we are concerned with relative values of sectional density our formula is valid, but not completely accurate because we do not actually calculate the cross-sectional area. We merely relate the area to the square of the diameter (DSq.) Because areas of different diameter bullets are proportional to their diameters squared, our comparison is a valid one.

A second look at sectional density shows that it is another way of relating lengths of bullets, provided their shapes are about the same. Or, putting it another way: bullets of the same point shape substantially the same proportion of jacket and core weight, and the same length, have the same sectional density. If this fact seems elementary and commonplace, you have not been misled by a popular misconception. This erroneous belief is that a bullet which is long for its diameter has high sectional density. Picture a 200 gr. round nose .308" bullet about 1.20" long. It is almost 4 times as long as its diameter and looks like it has high sectional density. As a matter of fact, it has. From our formula we calculate SD equivalent to .302. Now look at a 500 gr. .475" bullet also 1.20" long. It is only 2-1/4 times as long as its diameter, and looks a little dumpy—not too long for its fatness. Yet it has a sectional density, from our formula, of .315, which is more than the 200 gr. .308"! So we can see that the long slim round nose pencil of a bullet exemplified by the 160 gr. 6.5 mm, the 175 gr. 7mm, the 220 gr. 30 calibre., the 250 gr. .318", and the 300 gr. .333 looks like it has high sectional density—and it does. But so does the same length bullet of greater diameter, whose greater diameter makes it appear squat. Examples would be the round nosed versions of the 400 gr. .411", the 500 gr. .457", the 500 and 600 gr. .475", and the 410 gr. 416", and 480 gr. .465".

As we examine smaller diameter bullets we find even greater lengths for diameters but sectional densities seldom reach a value greater than .300. A few examples are:

weight	diameter	SD
100	.243"	.242
117	.257"	.254
129	.264"	.265
130	.277"	.243
150	.277"	.279
139	.284"	.246

Some of these bullets are spitzer (pointed) shaped rather than round nose and so are even longer than the previous examples. Remember, if the shape and length are about the same, sectional densities will also be about the same.

Now, what does our knowledge of the sectional density values of various diameter and weight bullets mean? The principal useful fact is that sectional density, along with nose shape, is the determining factor of ballistic coefficient, usually shown as C. And ballistic coefficient is the factor that determines how efficient a bullet is in overcoming air resistance in flight. That is, how well it retains the muzzle velocity and energy imparted to it by the rifle. But more of this later.

Next we have shape: we have used this term before and it is a common term. In the case of a bullet we are referring to point shape, ranging from a blunt semi-round nose to a long slim pencil point or spitzer. We shall see that the shape of the bullet affects ballistic coefficient as well as other properties to the successful design of a game bullet.

We now come upon a new term, similarity: this is literally a geometric definition, explained as follows; bullets which are similar have the same shape and the same length for their diameter. They do not, however, have the same sectional density. If bullets are similar, their sectional densities are proportional to their lengths. Also to their diameters, since similarity, by definition, means constant ratio between length and diameter. An example of almost similar bullets would be the 55 gr. .224" spitzer and the 150 gr. .308" spitzer. The former has an SD value of .157 while the larger and heavier one has an SD value of .227. The principal application of similarity of bullets is that bullets which are similar—which have the same length for diameter and the same shape—will require the same twist of rifling if they are projected at the same muzzle velocity.

Let us examine another interesting and valuable term: trajectory. This is the curved path (in a vertical plane—viewed from the side, that is) followed by a bullet in flight. Usually we are concerned with the degree or curvature, and a flat trajectory is one which curves but little. No bullet can possibly have a truly flat trajectory, but some are relatively flat. A flat trajectory—with little curvature—is desirable because it requires less accurate range estimation and holdover on long shots to successfully place the bullet in a vital spot on game. This is a relative virtue. Generally, a flat trajectory is of increasing value if (1) the ranges are often long, (2) the ranges are hard to estimate, and/or (3) the target—vital area on game—is small. Naturally a combination of these factors makes flat trajectory even more desirable. How do we obtain a flat trajectory. First we project our bullet at high muzzle velocity, and second, we select a bullet which is efficient in retaining this velocity. Over game ranges up to 500 yards the muzzle velocity is much more important in obtaining a flat trajectory than retaining the initial velocity. Generally speaking, bullets of the same muzzle velocity will have substantially the same trajectory over game ranges.

The particular numerical factor about trajectory in which we are first interested is drop. This is the drop from a straight line projection of the rifle bore. It is measured in inches and varies with the square of the time of flight. If a bullet has a muzzle velocity of 3200 fs and a velocity of 2540 fs at 300 yards it average velocity over this range is 2870 fs and the time of flight is .314 seconds. The drop, by calculation using the acceleration of gravity, is 18.9". Another bullet, of lower ballistic coefficient, also has a muzzle velocity of 3200 fs but a velocity of only 1980 fs at 300 yards. Its average velocity is 2590 fs and time of flight .348 seconds. Its drop is 23.2". If each of these rifles were sighted in to hit the point of aim at 225 yards with scopes 1.4" above the bore centers, the first example would hit 7.6" below the point of aim at 300 yards and the second 10.9" low. The difference between the two is small and of little importance in shooting at game the size of a deer. Therefore, these two bullets with the same muzzle velocity have almost the same trajectory from a practical consideration.

We mentioned that trajectory is a relative virtue, which is to say that high muzzle velocity necessary to produce flat trajectory is also a relative thing. To the Maine or New Brunswick deer or moose hunter, most of whose shots are 50 to 100 yds. and to whom 150 yards is a long shot in the woods, 2000 f.s. muzzle velocity will provide an adequately flat trajectory. To him a bullet that is round nosed (or at least bluntly pointed), long for its diameter and with high sectional density is preferable to other bullets lighter in weight and with high velocity. The deer and antelope hunter of Wyoming, or the sheep hunter of British Columbia has need for the high velocity which produces flat trajectories. Somewhere in the neighborhood of 3000 f.s. is required for regular success. There are loads that give as high as 3600 f.s. that can be used to advantage, but one must be careful to select a bullet type and construction that will not blow up upon impact if a meaty or bony part of game is struck at a striking velocity of 3000 f.s. or more.

Now let us return to ballistic coefficient. As we said a bullet with high ballistic coefficient is desirable because it retains well the muzzle velocity and energy imparted to it. Digressing for a moment let us remember that the energy of a bullet is a function of its weight and the velocity at which it is traveling at the moment of impact. A point to emphasize is that while energy is directly proportional to bullet weight, it is a function of the *square* of the velocity. That is to say: double the weight and the energy is doubled; double the velocity and the energy is *four* times as great!

When the bullet is at its maximum velocity, immediately after leaving the barrel, it is traveling at "muzzle velocity." From there out to game ranges the bullet is on its own, so to speak. When some bullets are on their own they do quite well, while others fare not so good. This is a way of expressing velocity and energy loss from the maximum which was obtained at the muzzle. Thus, we see that some bullets lose their velocity rapidly, while others lose velocity but little for each 100 yards of travel. Remember, while a bullet is losing its velocity, it is losing its energy much faster because energy is a function of the square of the velocity, as we said. Why are we so concerned with the loss in velocity and energy? Very simple; game is shot away from the muzzle and we are interested in how well our bullet is doing at 50, 100, 200, 300 or even 400 yards away. Let us look at a graphic example. We have two 160 gr. bullets. One has a representative spitzer point, with head radius about 6 bullet diameters. The other has a round nose. We will start them off at the same muzzle velocity, and then they are on their own:

Bullet	Weight	100 yard Velocity	100 yard Energy	200 yard Velocity	200 yard Energy	300 yard Velocity	300 yard Energy	400 yard Velocity	400 yard Energy
A	160 gr.	3200	3640	2960	3110	2740	2650	2540	2290
B	160 gr.	3200	3640	2730	2640	2320	1920	1980	1400

We can easily see that bullet A retains its velocity better than B and delivers, in this case, 63% more energy at 300 yards than B. The importance of this example is that if we wish to deliver high striking energy at anything like long range we must give first consideration to selecting a bullet which is efficient in retaining its velocity. This property can well be thought of as ballistical efficiency. Of course we can make up for lower ballistical efficiency by starting our bullet at a higher muzzle velocity or by using a heavier bullet, or both. These have their drawbacks. Very high velocity is usually obtained at a sacrifice in barrel life and moreover we are soon limited by how large a cartridge case can be employed with a given rifle action. I do not imply that a velocity higher than 3200 f.s. is a poor compromise, but the law of diminishing returns starts to be felt if we go much above 3200 f.s., and practically puts a barrier at 3750 f.s. for a big game bullet. Heavy bullet weight can partially make up for what would otherwise be poor ballistical efficiency (certainly increasing weight raises ballistic coefficient and efficiency) but here we run into increasing recoil, especially if a light rifle is desired. In our example above, increasing the bullet weight of B by 38% to 220 grs. would partially offset the lower efficiency value imposed by the blunt nose, but would also increase recoil to a point where it would probably be quite unpleasant to most shooters when fired from an 8 lb. rifle from bench rest as when targeting in the rifle. This matter of recoil will be touched on later, but I am referring to recoil particularly as it seems when target shooting the rifle slowly and deliberately from a bench or prone with rest and/or sling.

Now we know that low velocity loss is important in a big game bullet where the game range is regularly 100 to 150 yards or more. So let's look at some of the characteristics which make for high ballistical efficiency.

The first of these is sectional density, which we have discussed. Ballistical efficiency is directly proportional to sectional density. Here are a few sectional density figures:

SECTIONAL DENSITY

Weight In Grains

Diameter	55	70	90	100	110	120	130	150	160	180	200	220	250	300	350	400
.224"	.157															
.243		.170	.218	.242	.267											
.257		.152	.195	.217	.238	.260	.282									
.264				.206	.226	.247	.267	.308	.329							
.277				.187	.205	.224	.243	.279	.299	.336						
.284					.194	.211	.229	.264	.282	.317	.352					
.308						.181	.196	.227	.242	.272	.302	.332	.378			
.333										.232	.258	.284	.323	.387		
.358											.201	.223	.246	.279	.335	
.375													.254	.305	.345	
.411														.262	.305	.339

The second characteristic which makes for high ballistical efficiency is form. By form we mean "streamline point shape" and generally speaking a long slim sharp point is the most streamlined and helps our bullet travel through the air with a minimum of velocity loss. We might note that the boattail form of the base of the bullet also makes it more streamlined. However, the benefit of boattail on a bullet traveling at a velocity greater than sound (about 1130 f.s.) is quite small, probably affecting ballistic coefficient less than 1%. Moreover, at game ranges, our bullet is always traveling faster than sound.

The form of the bullet is expressed as the coefficient of form, I, which is a value given for each point shape. Usually the spitzer point is expressed as having a radius equivalent to a certain number of bullet diameters. About the least number of bullet diameters that will make spitzer is 3, and this would be called commercially a semi-spitzer. Other sporting bullets are available by custom bulletmakers and the various commercial makers having 5, 6, and as high as 8 calibers radius. A normagraph is usually matched to the bullet in question to determine its head radius. One custom bullet maker, Speer, catalogues his bullets by their head radius, and these may be used for comparison with those by other makers to determine the approximate head radius.

We can take our figures for sectional density and divide them by the figures for coefficient of form and arrive at ballistic coefficient; the formula is as follows:

$$C = \frac{SD}{I}$$

where
- SD is sectional density
- I is coefficient of form
- C is ballistic coefficient

Some values for I are given herewith: Round nose 1.00
3 caliber head .72
4 " " .66
5 " " .60
6 " " .56
8 " " .49

Thus we can see that a bullet with an 8 caliber head radius has twice the ballistic coefficient that a round nosed one has of the same weight and diameter. The range of values coefficient for sporting bullets runs from about a low of .150 to a high of .630, with most modern big game bullets falling within the range of .230 to .500.

We now have our figure for ballistic coefficient; let's see how we can use it. The mathematics necessary to compute remaining velocities when the muzzle velocity and ballistic coefficient are known are beyond the scope of this paper and too complicated for the layman to become familiar with. Therefore, we will take some representative figures which will apply with not more than 10% error, and in many cases will be within 5%. This simplified procedure will relate the ballistic coefficient with the percent of velocity loss for each 100 yards of flight. Naturally the velocity range in which bullet is traveling will affect the results, as will the increasing range wherein the bullet slows down appreciably. However, for ranges up to about 600 yards and for velocities from approximately 3750 f.s. to as low as 1750 f.s. these values will have a practical application for the shooter. They are as follows:

Ballistic Coefficient (C)	Vel. loss, Percent per 100 yds.
.223	16%
.238	15%
.252	14%
.270	13%
.290	12%
.314	11%
.340	10%
.373	9%
.410	8%
.461	7%
.536	6%

As an example let us consider a 25 cal. bullet, diameter .257" with a weight of 90 grs. and a point having a head radius of 5 calibers. We calculate our ballistic coefficient as follows: .195/.60 equals .325. We interpolate from our velocity loss chart above and find that our bullet loses about 10.5% of its velocity per hundred yards. If our bullet starts out with a muzzle velocity of 3000 f.s. the remaining velocities are: 2685 at 100 yds., 2415 at 200 yds., and 2160 at 300 yds. Thus our bullet, on its own for 300 yds., has lost 28% of its muzzle velocity. Its energy at the muzzle is 1800 f.p. and at 300 yds. is 935 f.p., a loss of 49%. So we show clearly the much larger loss in energy than in velocity. The example we have used is that of the light spitzer at rather high muzzle velocity akin to original loadings of the .250/3000 and .22 Savage HiPower. Another example might be a 27 cal. bullet, diameter .277" with a weight of 150 grs. and a point with a 6 cal. head radius. We calculate the ballistic coefficient as .496 with a loss per 100 yds., of 6.5%. With a muzzle velocity of 3000 fs (obtainable with 4350 or 4831 powder in the .270 Win.) the remaining velocities are: 2805 at 100 yds., 2625 at 200 yds., and 2450 at 300 yds. This bullet has lost only about 18.5% of its muzzle velocity over the 300 yds. Its energy at 300 yds. is 1920 fp, a loss of 36% from the muzzle energy of 3000 fp. These figures represent one of our more efficient bullets and by comparison with the first example the striking energy at 300 yds. is more than twice as much, and as much as the 90 gr. .257" bullet at the muzzle. Generally if the bullet construction gives adequate penetration and expansion its killing power is pretty much in direct ratio to its energy. It is not within the scope of this article to discuss killing power, which is a very controversial subject, and to the discussion of which many factors must be considered; however, there will be little disagreement with the above contention that if the bullet in question gives, simultaneously, adequate penetration and expansion—regardless of how the adequacy of these two essentials is attained—its killing power on game will be a function of its striking energy at the range at which the bullet hits.

Summing up, ballistic coefficient tells us how efficient our bullet retains its velocity and energy, and if we want good killing power at long range this is an important factor. Much better to start off with 3640 fp muzzle energy and have 2290 fp left at 300 yards than to start off with 4000 fp and have only 2000 fp left at 300 yds. Especially so when we consider the variation in expansion and penetration of a given bullet when it has twice as much energy to give up under one condition (a close offhand shot) as another (a 300 yd. or over only shot of the hunt). Certainly a bullet that varies little in velocity over the game ranges will perform more uniformly than one which starts off like a whirlwind and peters out to a whisper! Velocity is our best bet to obtain a relatively flat trajectory. So if we want to kill big game at long range our medicine is high velocity and high ballistic coefficient.

One of the best recent achievements in this direction is Barnes' wildcat the .288 Supreme. A 200 gr. spitzer is loaded in a full length blown out magnum case ahead of 90 gr. of 5010 (machine gun) powder to give about 3025 fs. Some might feel such a load goes to the extreme, but there is no denying that it represents an achievement in delivering striking energy at long range. Some of the other .270, 7mm, and .30 cal. magnums are also in this category. To take advantage of the long range capabilities of these loads one must be an accomplished rifleman and, of course, must have the opportunity to require long range shots. Again, these virtues are relative, and the hunter-rifleman is wise to graduate to more "gun" as the occasion demands it. Perhaps, some would say, rightfully, that loads such as these are for the experienced and expert shot. But, that is a category many of us aspire to, and the cartridge should not limit the man.

The concluding subject of recoil is relevant to the selection of a load that will do a good job on game—particularly a long range load. When a modern cartridge is loaded to deliver killing power at long range on game as large as elk or our bigger bear, the energy level at the muzzle is in the neighborhood of 3300 fp. or more. Now such loads rarely give recoil which is noticeable when shooting at game. However, when shooting them at target from bench or prone, or when they are used on varmints for off season practice there may be some objectional recoil depending on the tolerance of the shooter. Regardless of the recoil sensitiveness of the individual, the values are relative, and one can tell just about how much push he can take without discomfort. Therefore, it would be of value to have some comparative figures. The formulae and calculations involved are perhaps too complicated to justify the results to the lay reader. Suffice to say that we must relate bullet weight, powder weight, muzzle velocity and gun weight to obtain the values. Listed herewith are some representative figures:

Bullet Wt.	Powder Wt.	Muzzle Vel.	Gun Wt.	Recoil Ft. Lb.
90	35	3000	7.0 lb.	8.0
100	40	3000	7.0 "	10.0
100	55	3300	7.5 "	14.9
120	52	3000	7.5 "	14.5
100	53	3550	8.0 "	15.8
130	56	3150	8.0 "	17.4
150	56	3000	8.0 "	18.6
150	67	3250	8.0 "	25.5
180	57	2750	8.0 "	18.5
180	70	3000	8.5 "	26.1
180	80	3350	8.5 "	36.5
200	90	3025	8.5 "	37.3
250	64	2700	9.0 "	28.6
250	80	2950	9.0 "	39.8
275	68	2550	9.0 "	30.2
285	86	2750	9.5 "	40.8
300	90	2800	9.5 "	46.7

The facets of sporting rifle ballistics are interesting to contemplate, and to some add a measure of pleasant understanding to the use of the rifle. Others may be less interested and feel that common sense and judgment are sufficient to evaluate what it takes to make a successful hunting load. With these I have no quarrel; but for those just a little inquisitive, this article hopes to bring a few facts and figures which may be both interesting and of value to a better understanding of the mechanical device which serves as a big game rifle. In any case successfully placing the shot on game is at least 50% of the task of making a clean one shot kill. May the reader always have the satisfaction of this accomplishment. See page 544 for TIME OF FLIGHT CHART.

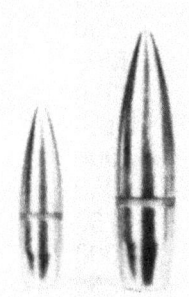

This illustration shows two bullets which are similar. Left is a 68 gr. .22. The right is an 172 gr. .30 calibre.

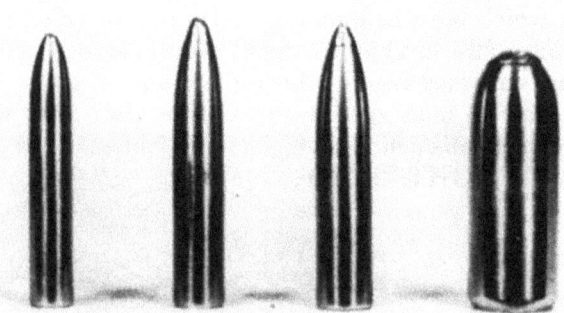

This illustration shows four bullets which have approximately the same sectional density. From left to right is shown a .22, .349; 6.5 .349; 7mm, .345 and the .450, .342, respectively.

A SIMPLE CHRONOGRAPH WHICH CAN BE MADE BY THE INDIVIDUAL SHOOTER FOR HIS OWN USE

The ballistics pendulum or "bob" can be made from a piece of iron pipe or any other metal pipe or tubing of suitable diameter. The diameter of the pipe depends on the weight of the finished "bob." For heavier calibres, such as .375 or .450 Magnum a pendulum weighing 150 pounds would be about right. For calibres beginning with the super .22's such as the .222 Remington going up through 30.06 or .35 Whelen a 90 pound "bob" is about right. For extremely light cartridges such as the .22 rim fire up to the .22 Hornet a 50 pound "bob" would be correct.

To construct the medium size pendulum, a piece of steel tubing about 6" in diameter and 30" in length can be used. A plate should be fitted to one end and welded in place, and two brackets, one on each end, must be attached to one side of the pipe by welding or bolting to act as hangers for the bearings.

For those who do not want to go through with the mathematics of the ballistics pendulum, the supporting rods or chains can be made 66-1/4" from the center of the bearings or each knife edge bearing, and usually this distance should be 66-1/4" from knife to knife edge. Small ball bearings are quite inexpensive and although not being quite as friction free as a straight edge, they are much easier to use and the added amount of friction would be negligable. Each supporting chain or rod should have a turnbuckle installed about midway so that the rods can be exactly adjusted to 66-1/4" center to center after the pendulum has been installed.

The steel tube or pipe is filled with perfectly dry sand which is held in place by a circular disc of plywood sawed to fit inside of the tube. Some cover this disc with a piece of old inner tube to help prevent too much loss of sand through the bullet holes.

The pendulum is suspended and the lengths of the supporting rods are carefully adjusted to 66-1/4". A frame will have to be made to accept the sliding rod to measure the swing of the pendulum.

The "bob" or pendulum should be carefully weighed so that it weighs a predetermined amount, for example, 90 pounds including half of the weight of the supporting rods. After the rods, chains or wires used for supporting the "bob" are fitted with a turnbuckle midway of bearing to bearing, the supports can be separated by unscrewing the turnbuckles and the lower half, including the turnbuckles themselves can be weighed. Once the parts are all completed and the pendulum has been suspended from its supports, the following formula can be used.

Divide the weight of the chronograph in grains by the weight of the bullet in grains and multiply this figure by .2018.

For example, the 90 pound chronograph weighs 630,000 grains (7000 grains to a pound). The standard military .30 calibre bullet is 150 grains. Divide 150 into 630,000 which gives us 42,000, then multiply this figure by .2018 which gives us 847.5. This means that every 1" of swing of the pendulum or chronograph is equal to 847.5 feet per second. If the swing of the pendulum is 3-1/4", multiply 847.5 by 3-1/4 which gives us an instrumental velocity of 2754 fs.

Usually the firing is done at 20 to 30 feet and the normal practice is to add 50 fs to the muzzle velocity. 2754 fs plus 50 fs equals 2804 fs.

For anyone who wishes to be more scientific in the operation of the pendulum chronograph, the following procedure can be used.

The pendulum should be hung in a draft-free room, the shooting point not less than 15 feet from it. Special regard should be given to provide accurate reading of the swing, on the movable rod or slide used. This latter of course measures the movement of the pendulum on the bullet impact.

To set up the pendulum, first weigh the "bob" on as fine a scale as you can find. This is most important. To this add one half the weight of the supporting wires, bearings, etc. Provide also a means of attaching a box suitable for holding one or two hundred bullets of assorted weights. Thus, when a bullet is fired into the pendulum, one of equal weight may be removed from the box thereby maintaining a constant weight.

We may now determine the "Time of Swing" of the pendulum. Be sure the "bob" swings freely with no binding of the knife edges. Now give the pendulum a good push. A swing is counted for each direction of travel. A complete to and fro movement is an oscillation, counting as two swings. With a stop watch in hand, start counting and continue over a period of five or ten minutes. Be accurate in your count. Now divide the number of swings you have counted into the number of seconds elapsed. This figure will be Tn the constant of

$$\frac{Pi}{T\,12}$$

Multiply T by 12 (to convert to inches) and divide into 3.1416. The answer is the "constant" for the basic formula to follow. It will not vary unless the weight of the "bob" is changed or the length of hanging wires varied. It will be used in all velocity calculations.

The basic formula to measure velocity is:

$$V = \frac{M}{m} \times \text{Constant} \times H$$

Where:
V—velocity of bullet
M—weight of pendulum in grains
m—weight of bullet in grains
C—Constant (above)
H—horizontal swing of pendulum

For an example:

We have counted 250 swings in 5 minutes or, 300 seconds, and find that T=1.2. Multiply by 12=14.4. This divided into 3.1416= .2108
or C.
M is say=500,000 grains   5,000
m (bullet)=100 grains   100)500,000
$\frac{M \times T \times 3}{m} = V$ or:

5000 X .2108 X 3 = 3162 feet per second.

We have now measured the velocity of our bullet. To convert to energy in foot pounds, we will follow the following formula

$$\frac{V2 \times m}{450240}$$

So: V2 = 9998244 X 100 = 999824400 divided by 450240 = 2220
Answer: Energy of 100 gr. bullet at 3162 fs velocity = 2220 f.p.

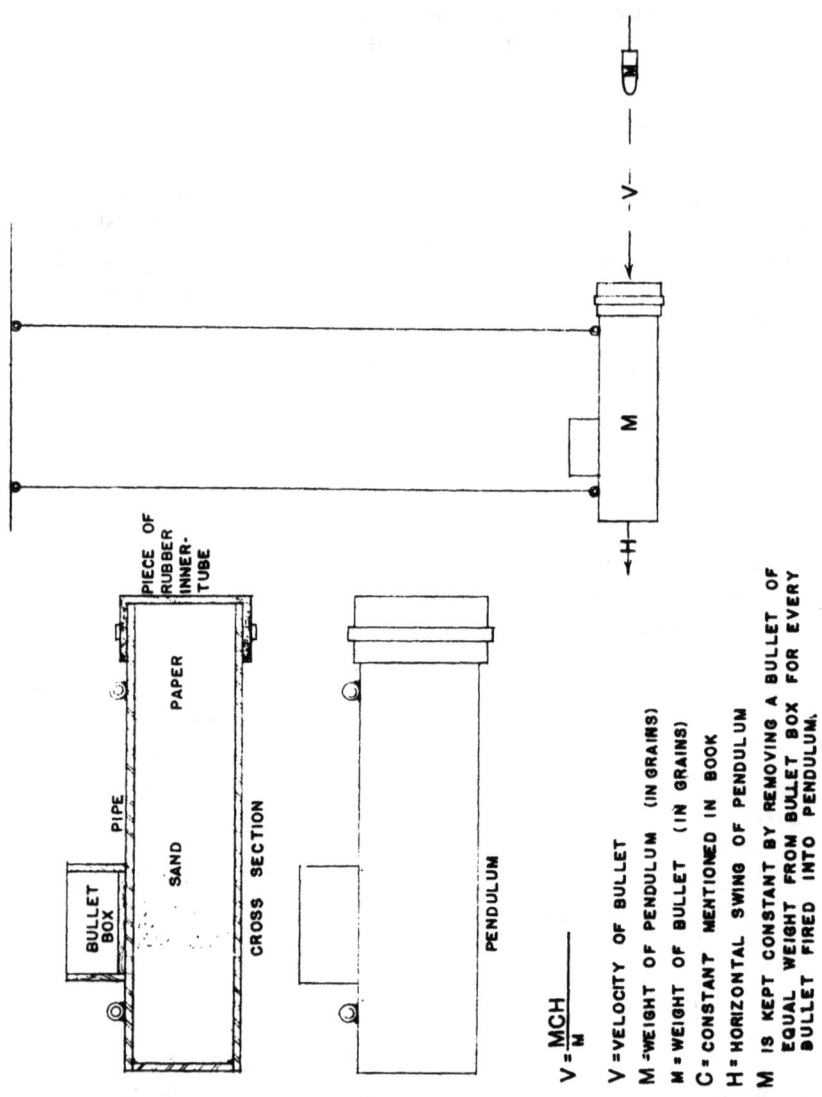

A SIMPLE CHRONOGRAPH

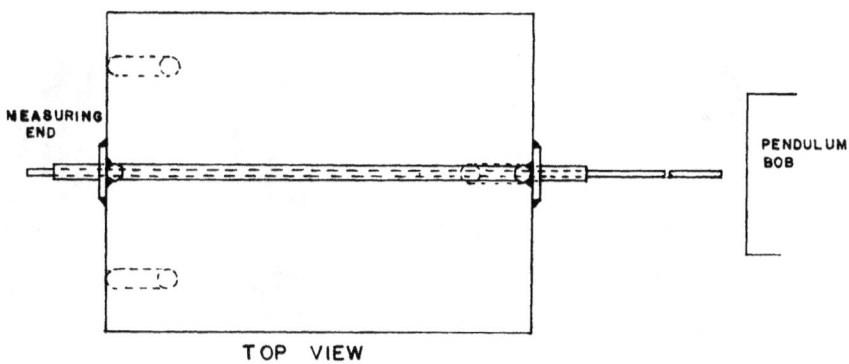

TOP VIEW

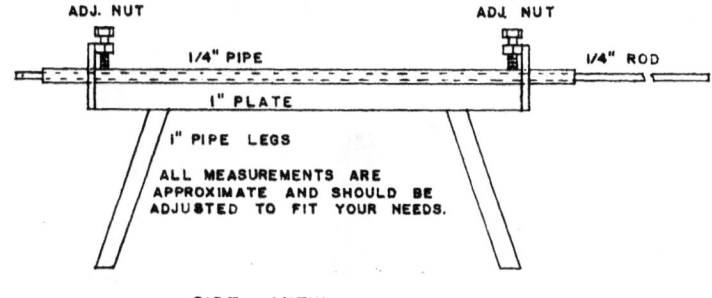

SIDE VIEW

MEASURING STOOL IS SET SO THAT THE 1/4" PIPE AND 1/4" ROD ARE FLUSH AT THE MEASURING END WHILE THE ROD IS IN CONTACT WITH THE END OF THE PENDULUM AND THE ROD IS DIRECTLY IN LINE WITH THE SWING OF THE PENDULUM. THE ADJUSTING NUTS ARE TIGHTENED TO HOLD THE PIPE IN PLACE. THE ROD CAN THEN BE MOVED TO ABOUT THE EXPECTED LENGTH OF SWING TO REDUCE THE DRAG. AFTER THE SHOT, THE EXPOSED ROD IS MEASURED VERY ACCURATELY.

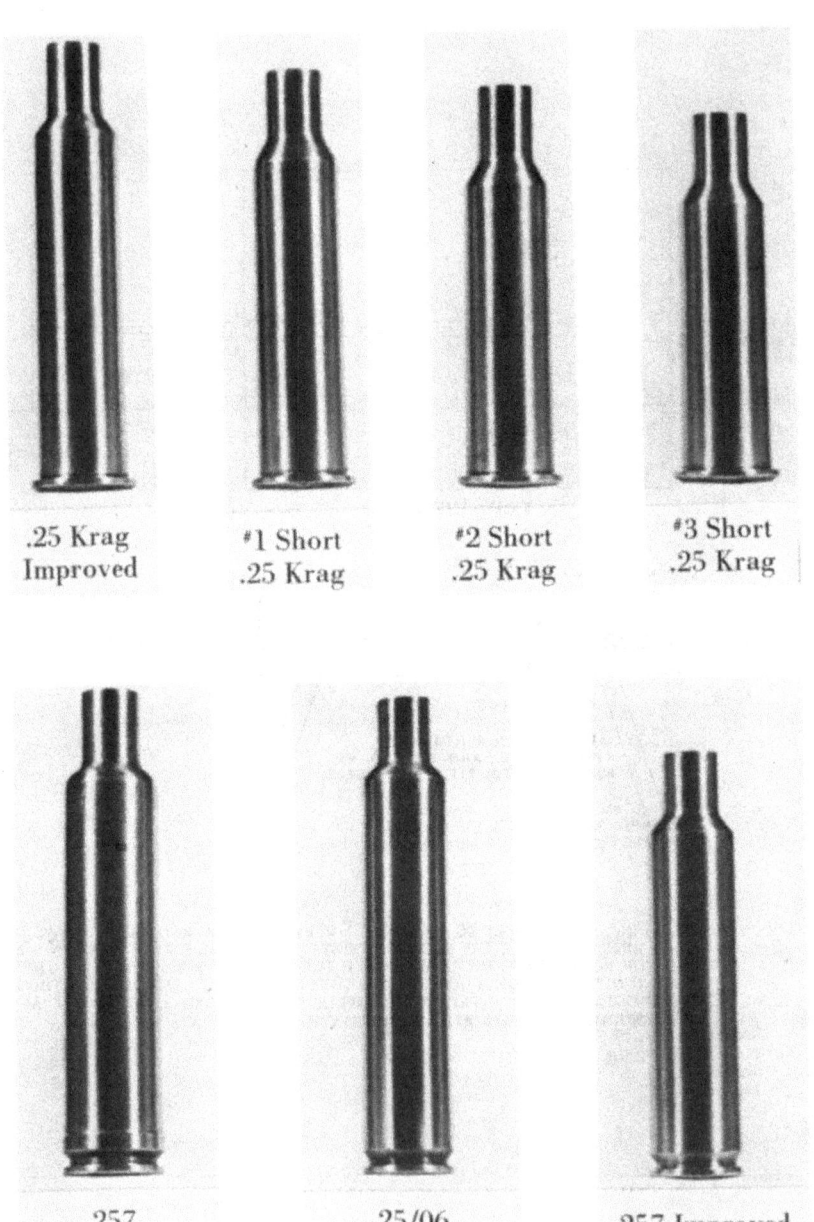

Cartridges Used in Rimmed vs. Rimless Experiments.

RIMMED VS. RIMLESS CARTRIDGES

There is an opinion that rimmed cartridge cases will withstand higher pressure than rimless, simply because the diameter of the rimmed case is considerably smaller in relation to the head diameter than is true of the rimless style. Another way of saying it is that the rimmed or flanged case has sort of a reinforcement consisting of a rim or flange around the primer pocket which theoretically does not allow the primer pocket to expand as readily as the narrower rimless style. This argument was carried to somewhat of an extreme at times, so it was decided to run detailed experiments to try to determine whether there is actually anything to this theory or not.

A P14 Enfield action was selected and a long .25 calibre barrel blank was fitted to it and chambered first for the so-called short .25 Krag case with a 30° shoulder. This case has approximate capacity of 40-41 grains, depending on the type of powder used. The following loads were tested and velocities were checked on a Potter Electric Chronograph.. The same make of 100 grain bullets were used throughout the tests.

100 gr. bullet	40 gr.	Ball C powder	3194 fs.	
	41		3300	max. load
	36	4198	3344	max. load
	36	3031	3134	
	38	3031	3300	
	40	4320	3210	
	36	HiVel #2	3134	
	38		3300	
	39		3412	
	40		3460	max. load (did not loosen primer.)

The barrel was then rechambered for a slightly longer Krag case holding 45 grains and the following results were obtained.

100 gr. bullet	43 gr.	HiVel #2 powder	3534 fs.	
	44		3574	blew primer
	44	4895	3424	blew primer

Next the barrel was chambered for the regular .25 short Krag described in this book as Ackley .25 Short Krag. This is an Ackley cartridge developed especially for single shot actions. This case holds from 50 to 53 grains depending on the type of powder used. It is normally described as about a 51-52 grain case and has the same 30° shoulder as used on the first two experimental cartridges. The following results were obtained with this 50-53 grain case.

100 gr. bullet	42 gr.	HiVel #2 powder	3344 fs.	
	44		3508	absolute top
	42	3031	3224	
	43	4064	3236	
	44		3278	
	46		3424	
	47		3508	primer leaked
	53	H450	3278	
	48	4320	3438	
	49		3558	maximum
	49	H380	3412	
	50	H380	3460	
	51		3508	
	52		3546	
	53		3610	primer leaked
	49	4350	3300	
	50		3338	
	51		3410	safe (compressed charge)

The fourth case was an experimental sharp shouldered short Krag with minimum body taper design. This cartridge has the same length as the previous less radical number three above, but being a blown out version the capacity was increased to 56-58 grains. The following results were obtained with this short "improved" cartridge.

100 gr. bullet	57 gr.	H450 powder	3472 fs.	
	58		3521	maximum
	53	4350	3502	compressed charge
	45	HiVel #2	3508	
	48	4064	3546	

The fifth chamber used was the old time .25 Improved Krag which is a full length Krag case blown out for minimum body taper design with a 40° shoulder to create a case which will hold up to 60 grains of some types of powders. The following results were obtained with this largest capacity of the series of Krag cartridges.

100 gr. bullet	58 gr.	H450 powder	3412 fs.	
	59		3496	
	60		3344	
	55	4350	3289	
	56		3546	O.K.-case full
	47	HiVel #2	3012	
	48		3289	
	55	H380	3496	Blown primer
	56		3623	Blown primer

After completing all possible tests with different length and design of the Krag rimmed case, the same barrel was then rechambered for the "improved" .257 Roberts. It was impossible to start with the standard .257 Roberts because the previous "improved" Krag chamber is slightly larger at the shoulder which precluded chambering for the standard .257 Roberts, therefore the "improved" .257 Roberts was used. The "improved" .257 Roberts is considered to be a 53-54 grain case since it holds 54 grains of 4350 powder when tightly compressed. The following results were obtained with the "improved" .257 Roberts described elsewhere in this book.

100 gr. bullet 48 gr. H380 powder 3246 fs. top load
                47   4320   3322
                52   4350   3389
                53   3472
                54   3546 highly compressed

The seventh chamber used was the "improved" .25/06 which could be considered a 60-61 grain capacity case although some users of this cartridge get more powder in it by compressing the charges very tightly. The following results were obtained with this somewhat larger case based on the blown out full length '06 brass.

100 gr. bullet 55 gr. 4350 powder 3322 fs.
                56   3389
                57   3521 primer leaked
                58   4831   3448
                60   3546
                61   3613 primer leaked

Finally the same barrel was rechambered for the .257 Weatherby Magnum which holds 75 grains.

100 gr. bullet 67 gr. 4350 powder 3571 fs.
                65   4831   3205
                67   3322
                69   3424
                71   3521
                72   3584 loosened primer

It will be noticed by studying the figures that when we started with the rimmed case holding 40-41 grains we were able to get up to something over 3400 fs with the 100 grain bullet without loosening the primer with normal powders like 3031 and HiVel #2. Of course it would be possible to loosen primers with powders like 4198. By increasing the capacity of the case five grains we were able to increase the velocity less than 100 foot seconds before primers started loosening. By increasing the capacity still more by rechambering for the original .25 short Krag, which holds 50-53 grains we were able to increase the velocity only very slightly, or around 50 foot seconds. However, by studying the loads which were used it will be noticed that different powders began to show better results. For example, we were able to increase the velocity considerably by turning to H380 powder.

The fourth chamber, or the "improved" short Krag case showed that we were able to increase the velocity measureably, but it will be noticed that we got exactly the same velocity with top loads of HiVel #2 which in the 51-53 grain case required 44 grains. But in the larger volume "improved" short case it required one more grain of powder to get the same velocity which led us to believe that we had reached the maximum case volume for the .25 bore when normal powders are used in the 51-53 grain case.

As a further check in the full length "improved" case which holds a little over 60 grains we found that we got an actual reduction in velocity with powders such as HiVel #2 and that the best results were obtained by using slower burning powders such as H450 or 4350. It will be noticed that none of the powders used would produce velocities in this larger rimmed case tested equal the lesser volume case. So this fifth check about convinced us that the optimum case capacity for the .25 calibre cartridge of the rimmed variety has to be somewhere between 50 and 53 grains.

After the barrel was rechambered for the "improved" .257 Roberts which was the first rimless case used and which has a case capacity quite similar to the standard short Krag used in the third test, we were able to practically duplicate the results obtained in the rimmed cartridge. For example, we were able to get a velocity of 3410 foot seconds with 51 grains of 4350 powder in the rimmed case and 3389 foot seconds with 52 grains of 4350 powder in the rimless case, and 3472 foot seconds with 53 grains of 4350 rimless case. This would indicate that the slightly larger rimless case requires a grain or two more powder, but obviously just as high velocity was possible with the rimless case as with the rimmed case before primers loosened.

The seventh test using the large over capacity "improved" .25/06 showed that practically no increase in velocity was possible by increasing the volume of the case. For example, a compressed charge of 54 grains of 4350 gave a velocity of 3546 foot seconds in the "improved" .257 as compared to 56 grains of 4350 powder for a velocity of 3389 foot seconds in the "improved" .25/06.

Before we could reach the top velocity that we got out of the "improved" .257 Roberts the primers leaked in the "improved" .25/06. By using slower burning powder, namely 4831, we were able to duplicate the velocity of the "improved" .257 Roberts but only by using six more grains of powder.

When the barrel was chambered for the still larger case, the .257 Weatherby, it will be noticed that still no increase in velocity was possible before primers leaked. For example, we were able to get 3546 foot seconds with the "improved" .25/06 before primers started leaking, and only able to get 3521 foot seconds in the large Magnum case before primers started to leak and this required approximately eleven more grains of powder in the Magnum over the .25/06 "improved" which in turn required six more grains of powder than the "improved" .257 Roberts to get approximately the same velocity.

It must be pointed out that the loads used in this experiment are entirely too hot for regular use, and that these loads used in these tests were purely experimental and are not in any way recommended for normal use. It must also be kept in mind that this experiment was controlled as nearly as possible by using the same action and the same barrel without changing the length. The same Chronograph was used and a number of men conducted the experiment so as to insure its absolute fairness.

Some of the proponents of the rimmed case tried to alibi the good showing of the rimless case by saying the breeching system of the P14 which can be described as closely approximating "safety breeching" was responsible. Why this claim was made has never been made quite plain since obviously the breeching system was set up and was the same for all tests. A further test of breeching methods was made by using a Model 98 Mauser bolt and fitting the barrel so that the bolt contacted the end of the barrel very tightly with only a very narrow extractor cut just barely deep enough so that the fired case could be engaged by the narrowed and thinned down extractor. It was found that the primer loosened at a certain pressure level which was not determined because of the lack of pressure equipment, and as the loads were increased after the primer pocket started expanding, the complete enclosure of the rimmed cartridge head prevented the primer pocket from expanding any more and there was no appreciable escaping of gas around the bolt. The barrel was then cut back so that the rim exposure was the same as in the P14, or about .063 and by carefully working up it was found that the primers leaked with exactly the same loads as with complete inclosure. As the loads were increased after these leaks started, the primer pockets would continue to expand more than was possible with the completely enclosed case. However, quite obviously there was no advantage in the complete enclosure because no one is interested in using loads which expand the primer pockets each shot.

The barrel was then cut back to produce the normal head exposure, or exactly the same as found in the standard 98 Mauser action, with exactly the same results. That is, the primer leaked on the same load as in the two previous tests and not until the head exposure of over .125 was any difference in results noticed. With this excessive exposure, or exposure to a point where the solid head was entirely outside of the barrel, it was found that cases could be ruptured between the solid head and the end of the barrel which of course is a completely logical thing.

Previous to this experiment another test of safety breeching was conducted. This time a 1917 Enfield action was used with a normal breeching system. As with the Mauser action, the action was wrapped in tissue paper. Loads were increased to a point where primers started to leak. Then it was observed that powder burns had appeared along the rails of the action indicating escaping gas which would have gone down into the magazine had the magazine parts been attached to the action. The loads were increased to a point where large holes were blown or burned through the paper. After this part of the experiment had been completed the barrel was then removed and the barrel was faced off smooth so as to eliminate the recess in the head of the bolt, and the forward end of the bolt was turned back so that there was about an 1/8 inch extension which was then fitted into the breech end of the barrel in such a manner that the flat bolt face contacted the bottom of the barrel recess very tightly, and also so that the head of the bolt was completely enclosed in the end of the barrel. Only a very small extractor cut was made. This resulted in a breeching sytem which is as nearly gas tight as it is possible to make.

Then the whole experiment was repeated and it was found that the escaping gas occurred in exactly the same manner as with the normal systems but in this instance even larger holes were blown or burned in the paper which forced us to come to the conclusion that there is very little value in the various safety breeching systems except for the advertising standpoint.

BARREL STEEL

A lot is said, and a great deal is claimed for certain analyses of steel which have been, or are being used, for the manufacture of rifle barrels. Custom barrel makers often select some quite ordinary steel with a trade name or create a name themselves which they feel is descriptive of the steel itself and at the same time which they feel will introduce a certain element of mystery. Claims are made, which would fit any number of other steels just as accurately, which strive to convey the idea to the reader that no other material can equal it. This may go on for a couple of years when suddenly the whole theme is dropped in favor of some other kind of steel and a whole set of new claims are formulated. This kind of advertising should be considered as purely sales propaganda.

Often barrels are advertised as being made of "Crome-Moly", "Carbon Manganese" or some other term to roughly describe the type of steel. Some advertise by using the makers name like, Timken, Ryerson, Crucible, etc. These terms mean very little, if anything. All steel mills produce a large number of analyses, and types of steel, and it would be hard to say that one mill produces a better steel than some other equally famous mill. To simply state that Timken or Ryerson barrel steel is used exclusively means absolutely nothing, because all major suppliers can supply any analysis from wrought iron to Tungsten High Speed steel. To state a steel is chrome-moly, chrome-nickel, or similar descriptive term, is no more illuminating, because a trace of the alloying elements in infinisestimal amounts can "justify" using the terms. Such terms are "blown up", without actually saying anything, but simply leave the reader to draw his own conclusions, after his train of thought has been sort of headed in the right direction.

Steels are classified or designated by number. There are three common numbering systems, all of which use identical numbers with different prefixes. Steel is made to the specifications laid down by the Society of Automotive Engineers (SAE), American

Society of Mechanical Engineers (ASME), and the American Iron and Steel Institute (AISI).

These numbering systems utilize four numbers for the alloy steels most commonly used for the manufacture of rifle barrels. Each figure designates a certain alloying element, as well as the quantity of the element. When steel is sold under a number prefixed by one of the above abbreviations, the buyer is assured that the steel will meet the specifications laid down by the society in every respect. He is further assured that once he has determined the best steel for the purpose that he intends to use it for, he can re-order by number, and know he will be getting the same thing.

When ordering "cold rolled" for example, nothing shows what the analysis is. The term can be applied to almost any cold finished analysis. On the other hand, if AISI 1040 cold drawn (or cold finished, or cold rolled) is specified, the analysis is fully shown at a glance. The first figure in the number proclaims the steel to be "carbon steel". The second figure being a zero, means it is not an alloy steel. The third and fourth figures show the average amount of carbon in the steel. 40 in this analysis, means 40 points of carbon, or .4 of 1%, since each point is .1 of 1%.

Another example is SAE 2340. The SAE indicates it is made to SAE Specifications. The first figure, 2, shows it belongs to the family of nickel steels, since the figure 2 designates Nickel. The second figure, 3, shows the average amount of the alloying element (Nickel) as 3%. The third and fourth figures show the average amount of carbon, just as in the first example. Thus, if a rifle barrel is described as being made of SAE 2340, it immediately shows the barrel is a 3% Nickel alloy, containing 40 points carbon.

The following table shows the numbers used for commonly used alloy steels.

Type of Steel	Numerals (and Digits)
Carbon Steels	1xxx
Plain Carbon	10xx
Free Cutting, (Screw Stock)	11xx
Manganese Steels	13xx
Nickel Steels	2xxx
3.50% Nickel	23xx
5.00% Nickel	25xx
Nickel-Chromium Steels	3xxx
1.25% Nickel, 0.60% Chromium	31xx
1.75% Nickel, 1.00% Chromium	32xx
3.50% Nickel, 1.50% Chromium	33xx
Corrosion-and Heat-Resisting Steels	30xxx
Molybdenum Steels	4xxx
Carbon-Molybdenum	40xx
Chromium-Molybdenum	41xx
Chromium-Nickel-Molybdenum	43xx
Nickel-Molybdenum	46xx and 48xx
Chromium Steels	5xxx
Low Chromium	51xx
Medium Chromium	52xxx
Corrosion-and Heat-Resisting	51xxx
Chromium-Vanadium Steels	6xxx
1% Chromium	61xx
Silicon-Manganese Steels	9xxx
2% Silicon	92xx

Most chrome moly barrels are made from SAE or AISI 4140 and 4150, but sometimes 4130, but the buyer knows very little about the actual analysis, unless the number is shown. Some barrels are made from SAE 3140, 2340, 4340 or 6140, and of course there are many other grades that could be used in any of these categories.

Enfield barrels made during World War I, were made from SAE 2340, as were the receivers and bolts. Most of the World War II Enfield, Springfield and other barrels were made from 4140 or the equivalent. Original Springfield barrels were 1340 or 1350. Most .22 LR barrels are made from steels like 1113 or

1117. Many highpower rifle barrels are now being manufactured from steels similar to AISI 1141, and often described as carbon manganese.

At present, there seems to be little indication that one analysis is better than another, so long as the required physicals are present, and the steel is free from stresses. The Ordnance Department records indicate that there is little difference between carbon manganese, and the alloys for resistance to erosion. Actually, some alloy steels have seemingly shown shorter life than regular steel. At this time, the primary values of "name Steels" or special alloys, lies in the advertising value, and nothing else. The reader of present day advertising should not be led into drawing conclusions, without first ascertaining the SAE or equivalent number, and even so, he will be little better off, because of the lack of evidence to prove one number better than another.

Also, there seems too little, or no evidence to prove stainless steel wears any longer than other steels. Some feel it must be better, because it costs more, which means nothing. Most stainless steel barrels are made from type 416. This is a low carbon, high chromium type, without other important alloying elements. There are other closely related numbers, but all are about the same. The more complicated stainless alloys are impractical because of the poor machining characteristics. Probably the one advantage of stainless is its resistance to rust or corrosion. Corrosion must not be confused with erosion. Sometimes it even seems that stainless is even more prone to erode than ordinary steels. The big drawback of stainless steel is the difficulty of bluing, which more than offsets its rust resistance. Actually, rust is no longer much of a problem, since the advent of non-corrosive primers.

Some of our largest arms manufacturers are using stainless steel in their barrels for one or two of their most erosive cartridges. For example .220 Swift, .264 and 7mm Magnum barrels are made of stainless steel. These makers claim that the stainless steel shows measurably longer life. However, the author has had long and extensive experience reboring rifle barrels and stainless barrels and alloy steel barrels wear out and are sent in to be rebored after approximately the same number of shots. If there is an advantage in favor of stainless steel it would seem that it is mostly offset by the higher cost and other disadvantages. Certainly stainless steel is not too attractive to custom barrel makers who do not have the facilities found in the large factories.

Neither should the mistake of judging a steel by its price be made. For example, a steel designated as AISI 4140, is of just about the same quality from all sources, because it has been produced according to the standard set by AISI. It is a legitimately priced steel, meaning it is supposed to be sold for about the same price by all the mills, and that is the way it is, unless the material is purchased from some jobber, or small supplier who purchases the steel from the most economical source, and then renames the steel with a fancy name which effectively covers up the analysis. Many times very ordinary steel is advertised as special barrel steel, and the price upped several hundred percent.

There has been an epidemic of this kind of selling during the past few years, resulting in some rather erroneous conclusions on the part of shooters. Many good steels are sold under some trade name examples of which are RYCUT 40 (or 50), MAXELL 3 1/2, HyTen (at least two grades), RYAX, STRESSPROOF, and many others. Usually such steels are modifications of the regular AISI or SAE grades. RYCUT is a modified 4140 or 4150, as is HyTen or MAX-ell 3-1/2. The modifications consist of the addition of extra manganese. These modifications increase the machineability ratings without detracting from the physicals. Other mills use re-sulfurization to help the machineability. The addition of sulfur detracts from the overall quality of the steel, but does noticeably improve the machineability. The addition of lead seems to have little effect other than to help the machineability. All alloy steels have .5% manganese, but in this amount, it is not considered an alloy.

To be considered an alloying element, about 1% manganese is required. Modified 4150 usually contains about 1.65% manganese. This amount of manganese definitely increases the machineability and contributes to heat treatability. It imparts the characteristic of deep hardenability, which means that a properly heat treated bar will show about the same hardness all the way through in contrast to some grades being noticeably harder on the outside than in the center.

Steels like RYAX or STRESSPROOF are commonly designated as CARBON MANGANESE by the barrelmakers. They are very free machining, but at the same time possess the required physicals needed for rifle barrels. Because of the free machining characteristics better interior finish is the rule, especially in barrels that are rifled with some form of standard rifling cutter, or broach. As stated before, this class of steel appears to wear just about as well as the more complex alloys.

This class of steel is also often designated as ORDNANCE steel by barrel makers because the analysis is very similar to the original Springfield barrels which carried that designation. Even though there is little evidence to show alloy steels wear longer than CARBON or CARBON MANGANESE steels, if there is such a thing, it would probably show up in the nickel alloys. Nickel alloys have been practically discarded because of their poor machining qualities. Barrel makers are forced, for obvious reasons, to use steels which possess relatively good machining qualities.

Many times gunsmiths who purchase barrels from the various barrelmakers, find barrels from one source machine much easier than barrels from some other source, and conclude that the one make is much harder than the other. Such a conclusion can be erroneous. This is not necessarily the case. The more easily machining barrel may show a much greater hardness when put on the Rockwell or Brinnell machine, and might also have much better physicals. This means that it is not safe to conclude that a steel which all but ruins expensive chamber reamers, and literally eats up lathe bits, is harder or stronger than another grade which is a lot easier on tools.

Recent trends in advertising have been in the direction of making statements, which in themselves say nothing, but which direct the readers thoughts into channels which will ultimately lead him to believe certain steels produce greatly increased accuracy life, are a great deal more accurate than the barrels made from some other material, or some other equally fallacious conclusion.

It would be hard to truthfully say that barrels from one maker would show greater accuracy life than from another maker who perhaps uses an entirely different material. Actual variations in average accuracy among the different makes of barrels are most likely due to the manufacturing methods, inspection, and numerous other things, rather than to the type of steel used, so long as the steel used is properly heat treated, to produce the required minimum physical requirements and freedom from internal stress.

Testimonials are used extensively to advertise certain makes of barrel steels. Obviously, testimonials are not a source of reliable information, and although they may or may not be actual stories of the results obtained by certain individuals, they cannot be regarded as being an accurate indication of what the average buyer could expect. This applies equally well to guns, rifle barrels, patent medicines, or any other product being promoted for sale to the public.

Some years ago, J. R. Buhmiller did extensive research on barrel steels. He asked the research editors of the American Peoples Encyclopedia to make a study of the problem. The following is their report:

STEEL FOR RIFLE BARRELS

In considering barrels we had best start with the steel they are made of. In the old days of black powder almost any bar of iron and steel would do for a rifle barrel just so long as it was easily machinable, and was made of homogeneous material. Black powder loads gave a breech pressure of never to exceed 25,000 pounds per square inch, and the lead bullets gave little frictional wear, and no great tensile strength, elastic limit, or resistance to erosion was needed. But today with smokeless powders giving pressures up to 55,000 pounds, extremely hot powder gases, and bullets jacketed with much harder metal, the character of the steel used has become of increasing importance, and nothing but a modern alloy steel, properly heat treated, will give the desired performance and endurance demanded by present day conditions.

Springfield Armory makes its rifle barrels from hot rolled manganese steel known to the steel trade as S.A.E. No. 1350, and also as W.D. 1350. Its composition is:

```
Carbon . . . . . . . . . . . . . . . . . . . .  .45 to .55
Manganese . . . . . . . . . . . . . . . . . 1.00 to 1.30
Phosphorus and sulphur . . . . . . . .  .05 maximum
```

This steel is obtained in bars. Before being used it is annealed for three quarters to one hour at 1600 F., than air cooled. It is then heated to 1550 F and quenched in Houghton No. 2 quenching oil. It is then drawn at from 1050 to 1150 F so as to obtain a Brinnell reading of from 228 to 256, and is then air cooled. The final physical properties are:

```
Yield point . . . . . . . . . . . . . . . . .   75,000
Tensile strength . . . . . . . . . . . . . .  110,000
Elongation . . . . . . . . . . . . . . . . .      20%
Contraction in area . . . . . . . . . . . .      50%
```

In this condition it is then drilled, reamed, and rifled. All of the above treatment of the steel from the original bar obtained from the steel company, is done at Springfield Armory under laboratory control. It is understood that the Remington Arms Company and the Savage Arms Corporation use the same or very similar steel, with similar treatment.

From about 1897 to about 1931 the Winchester Repeating Arms Company used a 3% nickel steel, heat treated to obtain the desired physical properties, for their barrel on their high power rifles. Such barrels are stamped 'Nickel Steel' on the outside, usually close to the breech. About 1931 Winchester changed its barrel steel, and also changed its policy as to steel. It now calls the steel it uses 'Winchester Proofsteel,' this being a trade term to designate 'the best steel that the Winchester laboratory can find or develop for the purpose intended.' At the present time it is understood that the steel which Winchester is using in their high power rifle barrels is a chrome-molybdenum steel, heat treated to give the desired physical properties and machinability. It is further understood that the physical properties and the resistance to erosion of this present steel is very slightly higher than that of S.A.E. No. 1350 steel.

It hardly pays the rifleman to worry much about steel used in his barrel, because he can do nothing about it, and if he gets his barrel from one of the above companies he knows that the steel is excellent, and is up to every requirement.

I know of no failure of any barrel made by these four plants due to the steel except only where the steel was made during war time where speed was a prime requirement.

The small custom rifle makers are entirely at the mercy of the steel companies as to their steel. They must take it for granted that they obtain the steel they contract for, and that it is properly heat treated, as they do not have a laboratory to inspect it. Among our most prominent custom rifle makers I have never heard of a failure of their barrel steel due to weakness. I have heard some complaints as to resistance to erosion, but how well founded these were I do not know.

Source: Townsend Whelen. *The Hunting Rifle.* Stackpole and Heck, Harrisburg, 1950. Pages 76-77.

Chrome-molybdenum steel. Any alloy steel containing chromium and molybdenum as the predominating alloying elements. Chromium gives hardness and toughness to the steel, while molybdenum improves the forging and machining properties and increases the strength. Chrome-molybdenum steels are noted for high strength and toughness. Only small amounts of alloying elements are used in the standard steels. A chrome-molybdenum steel used in the form of airplane tubing, Army-Navy steel AN-T-69, contains 0.80 to 1.10% chromium, 0.15 to 0.25 molybdenum, 0.40 to 0.60 manganese, and 0.25 to 0.35 carbon. It has a tensile strength of 95,000 psi min, with elongation 10%, and is slightly air-hardening. It draws well, and tubes with a wall thickness of only 0.035 in. are made. Molybdenum adds real hardness to steel to a greater degree than tungsten, and the amounts used in these steels is sufficient to make them slightly redhard and air-hardening. SAE steel 4140, which has the same composition as the airplane tubing but with 0.40% carbon, has a tensile strength up to 260,000 psi, elongation 8%, and Brinnell hardness 490 when oil-quenched and drawn. This type of steel, with 0.30% carbon, AISI steel 4130, is used for structural parts where welding is to be done. The chrome-molybdenum steels marketed by the Crucible Steel Co. under the name of Almo steel for airplane, automotive, and ordnance work, have tensile strengths up to 167,000 psi, with elongation 18%. A steel used for superheater tubes at 900 lb pressure and 925° F, contains 5% chromium and 0.50 molybdenum. Chrome-molybdenum steels, with high carbon, have great resistance to wear at high heat, and are used for die blocks for forging. Cromo steel, of the Michigan Steel Casting Co., is a cast steel with a tensile strength of 100,000 psi and elongation 15 to 25%, used for large die blocks. Albor die steel, of Wm. Jessop & Sons, Inc., used for dies for stamping hard metals, contains 0.90% chromium, 0.30 molybdenum, and 0.90 carbon. It is tough and deep hardening. Atlas No. 93, of the Allegheny Ludlum Steel Co., is a shock-resistant steel with 0.65% chromium, 0.35 molybdenum, and 0.55 carbon. Chrome-molybdenum steels with carbon to 1% are used for castings for bucket lips, crusher parts, and other heavy-duty parts. They have tensile strengths up to 150,000 psi, with elongation 12 to 14%...

Manganese steel. All commercial steels contain some manganese which has been introduced in the process of deoxidizing and desulphurizing with ferromanganese, but the name was originally applied only to steels containing from 10 to 15% manganese. Steels with from 1.0 to 1.5% manganese are known as Carbon-manganese steel, Pearlitic manganese steel, or Imtermediate manganese steel. Medium manganese steels, with manganese from 2 to 9%, are brittle and are not ordinarily used. The original Hadfield manganese steel made in 1883 contained 10 to 14.5% manganese and 1 carbon.

Manganese increases the hardness and tensile strength of steel. In the absence of carbon, manganese up to 1.5% has only slight influence on iron; as the carbon content increases, the effect intensifies. Air hardening becomes apparent in a 0.20 carbon steel with 1.5% manganese, and in a 0.35 carbon steel with 1.4% manganese. The manganese steels used for dipper teeth, tractor shoes, and wear-resistant castings, contain 10 to 14% manganese, 1 to 1.4 carbon, and 0.30 to 1 silicon. The tensile strength is up to 125,000 psi, elongation 44 to 55%, weight 0.286 lb per cu in., and Brinell hardness, when heat-treated, of 185 to 200. Cold working hardens this steel, and dipper teeth in service will work-harden to a hardness up to 550 Brinell.

High-manganese steels are not commercially machinable with ordinary tools, but can be cut and drilled with tungsten carbide and super high-speed tools. The Austenitic steels, with about 12% manganese, are exceedingly abrasion-resistant and harden under the action of tools. They are nonmagnetic. The coefficient of expansion is about twice that of ordinary steel. Various trade names are used to designate the high-manganese steels. Rol-man steel, marketed by the Manganese Steel Forge Co., contains 11 to 14% manganese and 1 to 1.4 carbon, and has a tensile strength of 160,000 psi and elongation up to 50%. Amsco steel, of the American Manganese Steel Co., contains 12 to 13% manganese and 1.2 carbon. The tensile strength is 125,000 psi, and it will work-harden to 500 Brinell. Tisco steel, of the Taylor-Wharton Iron & Steel Co., has up to 15% manganese, and is used for rails and crossovers where high resistance to abrasion is needed. Timang, of this company, is a high manganese steel made in the form of wire for rock screens. A German stainless type of steel, made without nickel, has 12% manganese. It is called Roneusil steel. High-manganese steels are brittle when cast and must be heat-treated. For castings of thin sections or irregular shapes where the drastic water quenching might cause distortion, nickel up to 5% may be added. The Manganese-nickel steels have approximately the same characteristics as the straight manganese steels. Nickel is also used in high-manganese steel wire, and the hard-drawn wire has strengths up to 300,000 psi. Manganal is a hot-rolled plate steel of high strength and wear resistance marketed by Joseph T. Ryerson & Son, Inc. It contains 11 to 13% manganese, 2.5 to 3.5 nickel, and 0.60 to 0.90 carbon. The tensile strength is 150,000 psi.

Structural steels with 0.50% carbon and from 1 to 2 manganese have tensile strength above 90,000 psi. Martinel steel, or Martin elastic limit steel, of Alfred Holt & Co., was an early English steel of this type. D-steel, developed by the British Admiralty for warship construction, contains 1.1 to 1.4% manganese, 0.33 carbon, and 0.12 silicon. The tensile strength is 96,000 psi and elongation 17%. N. Y. Central rails have 1.30 to 1.60% magnganese and 0.65 carbon. Man-Ten steel, of the U.S. Steel Corp., is a medium-carbon, medium-manganese structural steel. Steels containing 1.30 to 1.90% mangaese are now being used in automobile manufacture to replace more expensive alloy steels. Most mills now list these steels as Special alloy machinery steels; those containing about 0.10% sulphur are designated as Manganese screw stock. The SAE steels X1330 and X1340 are of this type. E.Z. Cut plate steel of Joseph T. Ryerson & Son, Inc., is a free-machining steel for molds, gears, and machine parts. It has 0.14 to 0.21% carbon, 1.15 to 1.4 manganese, and 0.17 to 0.23 sulphur. The tensile strength is 65,000 psi and elongation 30%, but when carbonized and water-quenched the tensile strength is 100,-000 psi. The sulphur is in the form of manganese sulphides. Stressproof steel, of the LaSalle Steel Co., is a high-tensile steel which has machinability equal to 76% of an SAE 1112 besemer screw stock, and, because of its resistance to warpage, is used for such parts as long lead screws and worm gears. It contains 1.35 to 1.65% manganese, 0.24 to 0.33 sulphur, 0.15 to 0.30 silicon, and 0.40 to 0.48 carbon. The minimum yield point is 100,000 psi. When heat-treated to 285 Brinell, it has a tensile strength of 135,000 psi and elongation 13%. The manganese steels with about 1.5% manganese and low carbon are much used for railway castings, and when deoxidized with titanium have tensile strengths close to 100,000 psi and elongation 30%.

Intermediate manganese steels are also sold under trade names such as Hylastic, of the American Steel Foundries. Max-El No. 4, of the Crucible Steel Co., is a pearlitic manganese steel with a small amount of chromium and 0.75% carbon, used for spring collets and called Collet steel. Slight amounts of chromium will increase the strength and hardness of the intermediate manganese steels. A forging steel for shafts and crankpins, designated as Manganese-vanadium steel, contains 1.5 to 1.75% manganese,

0.15 vanadium, and 0.25 carbon. The strength is 90,000 psi and elongation 30%. Moloie is the nam of a Manganese-molybdenum steel of W. T. Flather, Ltd. Pearlitic Nickel-manganese steel contains 1.25% manganese and 1.25 nickel. It has high yield point and ductility. A steel used by the Union Pacific Railway for draft yokes has 1.4% nickel and 1.5% manganese. The strength is 95,000 psi.

Source: George S. Brady. *Materials Handbook.* McGraw-Hill, New York, 1951. Pages 173-174; 448-450.

Additional References:

Jack O'Connor. *The Rifle Book.* Knopf, New York, 1949. See especially pages 72-73.
Townsend Whelen. *The American Rifle.* Century, New York, 1918. See especially pages 129-131.
R. S. Archer, J. Z. Briggs, and C. M. Loeb, Jr. *Molybdenum Steels, Irons, Alloys.* Climax Molybdenum Co., New York, 1948.

The late Phil Sharpe wrote:

Dear Mr. Buhmiller:

I do not personally know of erosion tests such as you contemplate, and wonder if it will be worthwhile. To make a reasonable test would be expensive. You should have ten barrels of each type of steel, and each should be group tested, assuming that they make a minute of angle groups at the start, until accuracy consistently runs to two minutes. Each barrel should then be slit open and examined under 15X to 20X magnification. With the .300 Weatherby you will get the fastest erosion—I have seen some of these barrels go in 300 rounds, but even then the tests will be expensive and very time-consuming. A complete record would have to be kept. A single barrel in each type of steel would not prove a thing—you will find variation in individual barrels of the same stock, but the average would give the picture. Fast firing will not answer—uniform firing must be the order. One shot every 30 seconds or so will heat the barrels too hot to handle in 10 shots.

Another angle. Chrome Moly is harder to work, as you say. Have you ever sectioned a new barrel? The next time you get an order for a 26 inch blank in this and in Carbon Manganese, use 30 inch stock. Cut off the rifled scrap and split that section for examination under about 20X. You will probably find that the hard-to-work stock is not cut as clean, and rifling cutters tear the metal. This roughness leaves open pores which accelerate erosion.

Thus, while the tougher stock MIGHT give longer life if as smoothly cut as the softer stock, its poor machinability discounts its advantage. But as to actual resistance to erosion, the only way to determine this would be actual firing tests plus final examination.

Cordially,

Signed: Phil Sharpe

In 1954 Gen. Julian S. Hatcher, Director of the NRA Technical Service said:

I have taken time to look up Ordnance Department research on this. It can be briefly summed up in the statement that excluding machine guns in very rapid fire, there is very little difference in relative erosion resistance between the ordinary carbon manganese steel and any alloy steel, including chrome moly.

Some of these alloy steels gave much less barrel life than the regular steel. The chances are that these were the ones that had just the right amount of carbon in so as to cause them to have a lower melting point.

On June 1, 1962, General Hatcher said:

Dear Mr. Ackley:

I read your letter of May 24 with interest.

I have learned nothing that changes what I wrote in 1954 that you mentioned.

My impression is that its the heat of a very hot charge that erodes the gun barrel and that in the very large charge cartridges the heat of the gases is considerably above the melting point of any steel that you can use. It is when you get a very large charge and consequently a very hot powder gas that erosion gets bad ---"

Very sincerely,

Signed: J. S. Hatcher
Technical Editor

Most authorities blame rapid barrel erosion to heat and pressure. It would seem, however, that the sand blasting effect of the unburned portion of slow burning powders being blown out into the barrel at terrific velocity would have an even more marked effect than heat alone. For example, heat and pressure is probably about the same in an Improved Zipper as it would be in the so-called .22/60 which requires approximately twice as much powder to get equal velocity. The barrel life of the Improved Zipper is excellent while that of the badly over bore capacity case is less than 300 rounds. The burning temperature of the faster powder used in the Improved Zipper could be higher than the slower powder required for the larger case. The actual pressure could also be as great in the smaller case which means that there are probably at least three factors contributing to barrel erosion—Heat, pressure and "sand blasting".

THE LOWDOWN ON LOADING DIES

One of the most common pieces of equipment found on the handloader's bench is one or more sets of loading dies to fit his pet reloading tool. The different types and makes of tools will not be discussed, only dies will be the subject dealt with here.

In the past, manufacturers of reloading tools and dies have used different styles of threads, but this practice is rapidly becoming a thing of the past. Today, the majority of manufacturers have standardized on tools and dies with 7/8" x 14 threads or, if the tool is arranged to take larger dies for shotshell loading and other purposes, a bushing is furnished which adapts the tool for use with dies with this thread.

In spite of being simple in design and simple to use, reloading dies are the least understood and produce more headaches for the user and manufacturer than anything else used to reload rifle and pistol cartridges.

Loading tool manufacturers maintain relatively close tolerances when manufacturing tools and dies. But necessarily there is some variation among tools and dies of any manufacturer and, especially when dies from one maker are used in another maker's tool, these variations show up. Some manufacturers furnish only dies and make no tools. Others specialize in tools only, and make no dies. This means that the individual handloader must learn how to adjust his dies for his own individual rifle in the tool he uses. To further complicate things, seldom do two rifles of the same calibre have the same headspace. Simply screwing a sizing die down against the shell holder of the tool is no guarantee that things are rosy. Actually, it would be more or less a miracle if such a "setting" resulted in ammunition correct for the rifle in which it is to be used.

Die manufacturers use different materials for dies, but most of them use some form of free machining screw stock. They have found that this type of steel, when properly carburized or case hardened, will last long enough for all practical purposes. They know that properly made and hardened dies made of B1113 steel or the equivalent, will load enough ammunition to wear out a score of ordinary rifles if the dies are properly cared for.

Since dies can be made much more economically from this type of material, and sold for a price in keeping with this ease of manufacture, it is also more economical for the handloader, because he is able to buy dies at a much lower cost with a good chance that they will never wear out.

Sometimes dies are made of some type of tool steel such as Graph-Mo. A sizing die made from Graph-Mo might size a quarter of a million cases as compared to half that many in a die made of screw stock, but it is seldom that an individual handloader would ever wear out dies made of screw stock or of cold rolled steel. The fancy die might appeal to the custom loader who makes a business of handloading for others.

Dies are sometimes made of solid tungsten carbide. Such dies, of course, will last a lifetime no matter how many cartridges are loaded. They are also free from scratching or scarring troubles which can be experienced with case hardened or tool steel dies. However, under ordinary circumstances, the handloader has little use for an expensive carbide die.

Dies are a relatively simple piece of equipment. *Figure 1* shows a cross section of a pair of dies.

The illustration shows a cross section of C & H dies. The different parts are common to other makes of dies, although some may vary in design. The difference between the two different makes of dies can be seen by comparing the cross section illustration of the C & H dies to the cross section illustration of RCBS dies in *Figure 2.*

It can readily be noticed that the design of the sizing die is quite similar for each make. The big difference in design is found in the seating die. The C & H seating die is quite typical of other

LOADING DIES 221

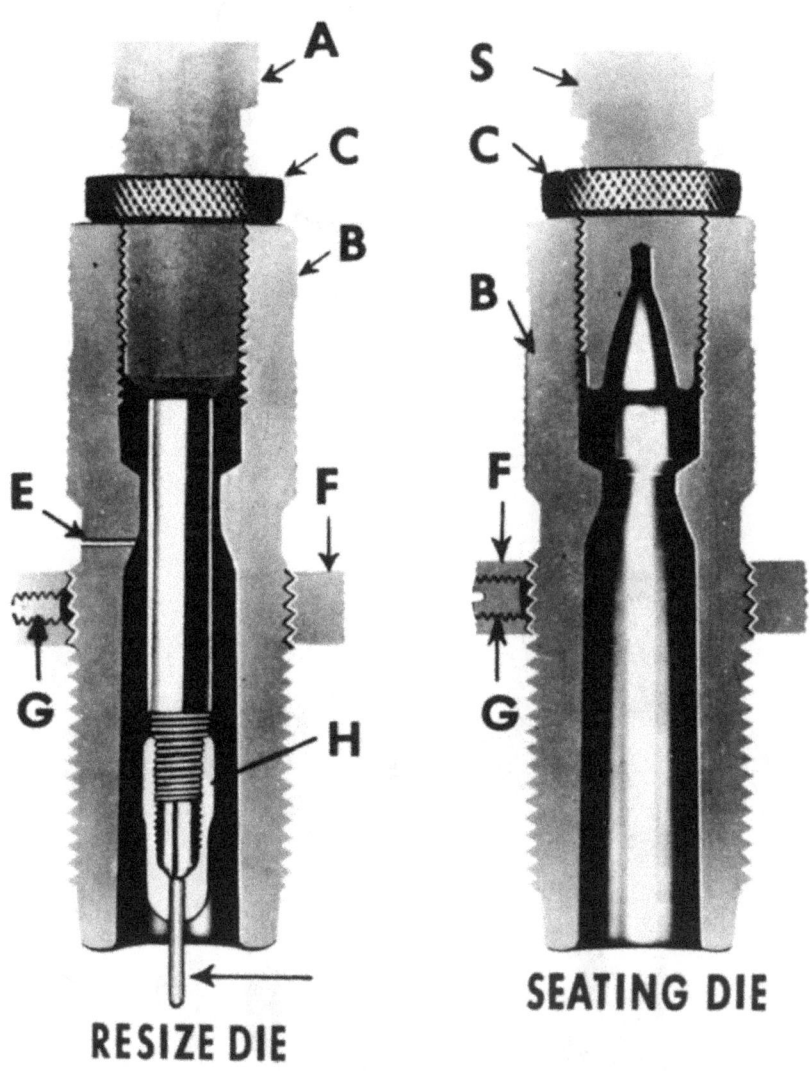

Figure 1.

A - Decapping Unit
B - Die Body
C - Concentric Locking Ring
D - Vent Hole
E - Locking Ring
F - Locking Ring Set Screw
G - Inside Neck Expander
H - Decapping Pin
S - Bullet Seating Stem

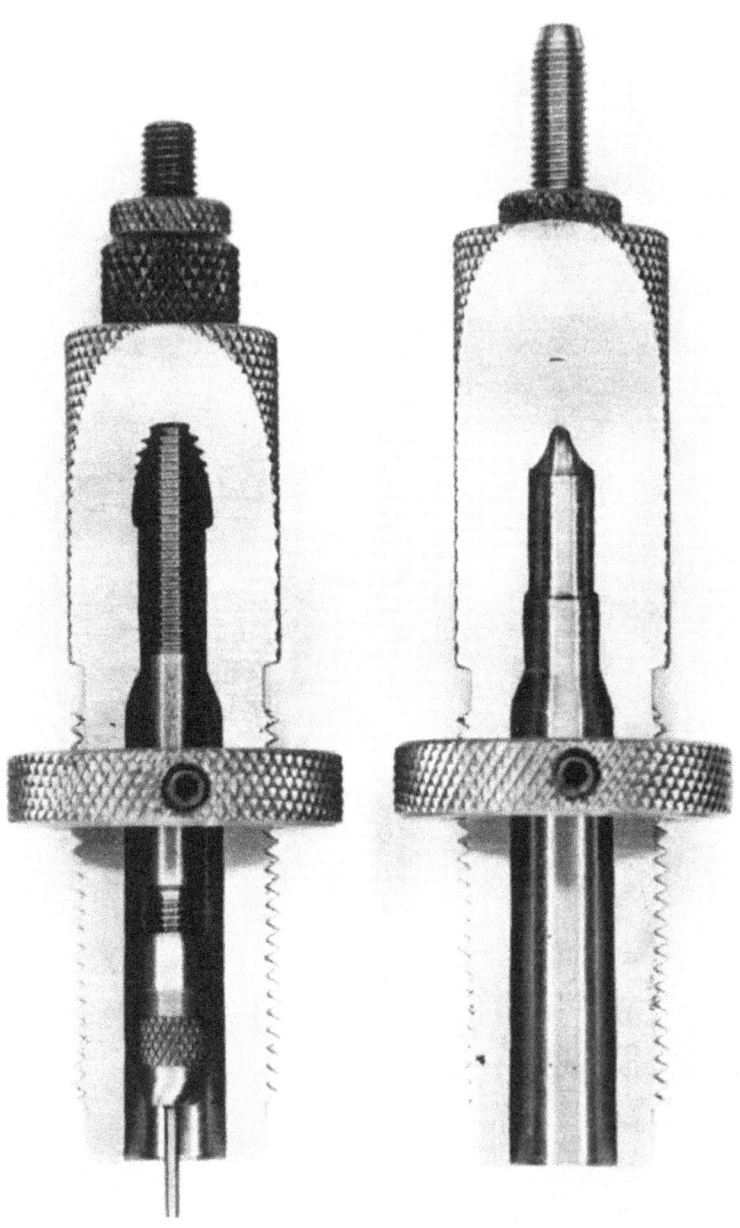

Figure 2.

makes including Pacific, Easton, Herter, Lyman and others, while the design of the RCBS seating die is common only to RCBS brand and GHS dies made by Tom Harper.

The main feature of the RCBS die is the straight line principle incorporated in the design as compared to the other makes. By comparing the illustrations, it will be seen that directly above the neck of the chamber in the seating die made by C & H and others mentioned, that there is a large cavity with no guiding part for the bullet except the ogive which is cut into the adjustable seating stem. The RCBS and GHS designs feature a reamed portion just above the chamber which is reamed to the bullet diameter. For example, if it is a .30 calibre die, this reamed portion would be approximately .308 to .309, which lines up the bullet with the axis of the case before the bullet comes in contact with the seating stem.

The seating stem of the C & H and similar dies is more easily manufactured because it can be the same size for all calibres with the exception of the ogive cavity, while the RCBS and GHS designs require the portion of the seating stem containing this ogive capacity to be of the particular bullet size for which the die is made. Since both designs of dies produce satisfactory ammunition, the advantage of one design over another must be left up to the individual himself.

Although dies with standard threads are the main topic of discussion, there is one exception which will be discussed. It is the straight line hand-type of die, including a hand-type full length sizing die which is equipped with an inside neck reamer. This type of die can easily be made by any gunsmith. The seating die can even be made out of a chamber section of an old barrel. Many handloaders prefer to use this type of seating die in conjunction with their regular bench type tool, simply because it insures perfectly concentric bullet seating as compared to the possibility of the bullet being seated cock-eyed with the standard die which screws into the tool. An exception is the Vickerman seating die.

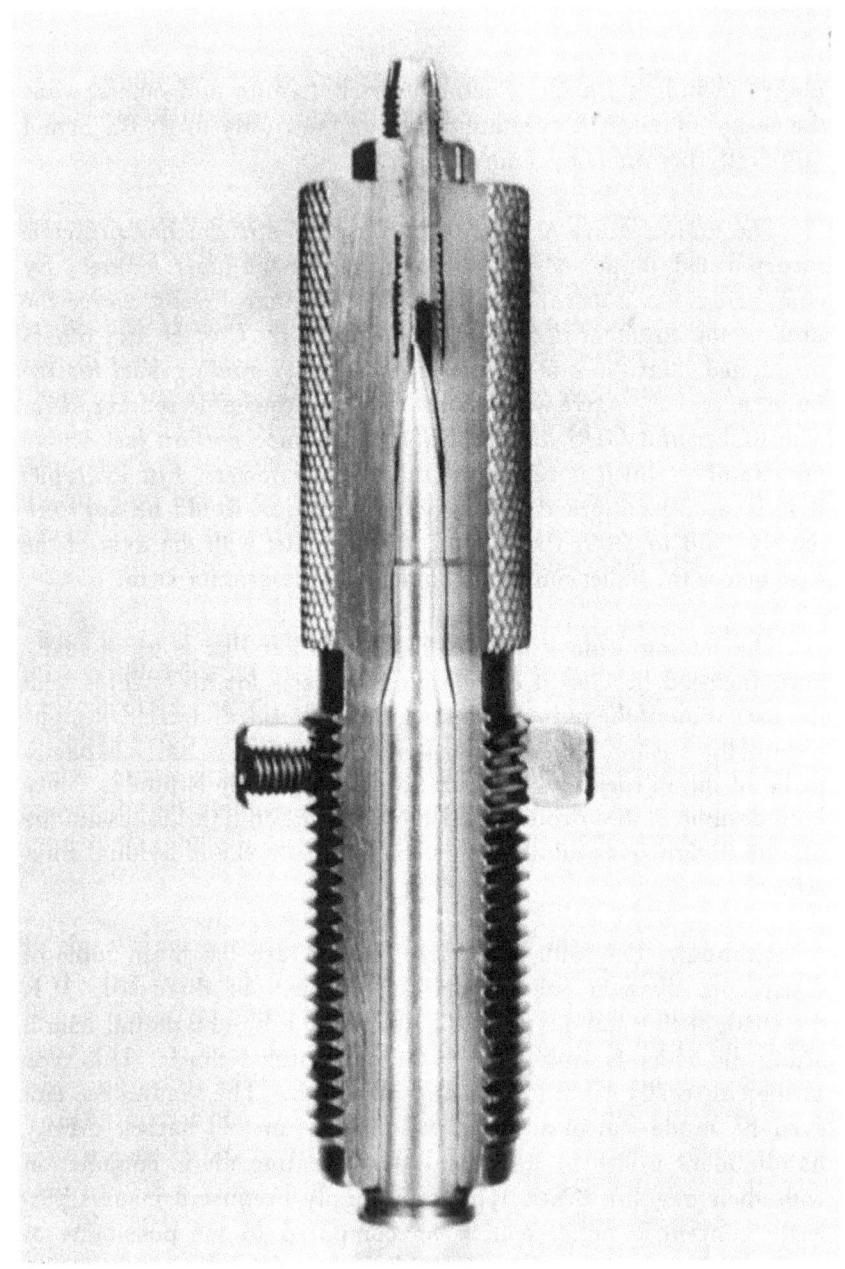

Figure 3.

LOADING DIES

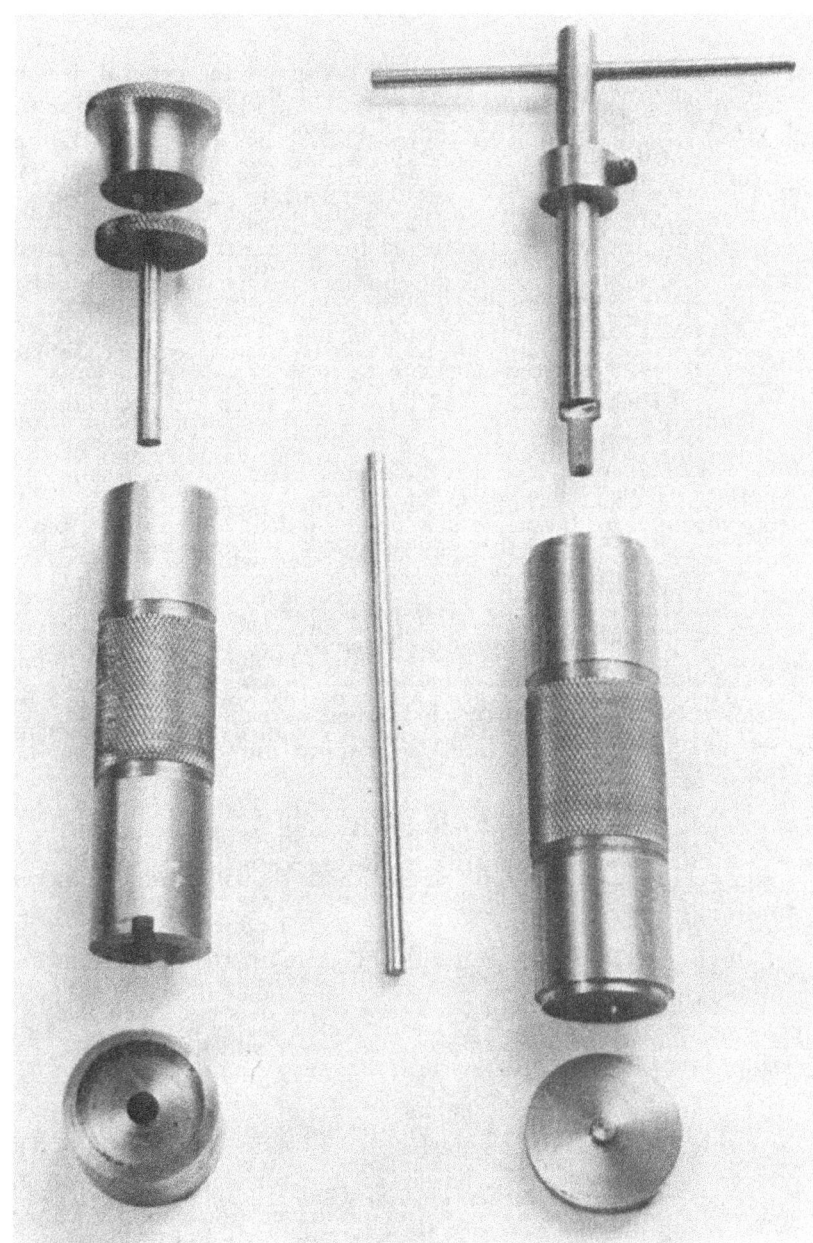

Figure 4.

Figure 4 shows parts of these dies and the general design. These dies are made of the same type of material described for the threaded type of die, but as a general rule, the dies should be approximately twice as long as the overall length of the cartridge. On the left of *figure 4* is shown the seating die which consists of the main die body which is chambered for the cartridge to be loaded. This die is usually made with the chamber reamer used to chamber the rifle. A notch is cut across the bottom of the die so that a small screwdriver or other suitable tool can be used to extract the cartridge in case it sticks slightly. The base is cut so that it fits both the loading and sizing die. The base is shown with about a half inch hole drilled through it so that the primer cannot come in contact with anything when the bullet is seated. This prevents accidental firing of the cartridge while it is being loaded. The seating pin is shown with an adjusting lock nut and cap which is threaded for seating depth adjustment. The ogive cut is made in the lower end of this seating pin the same as for the threaded type. The portion above the chamber of the die is reamed to the exact bullet diameter. The primed and charged case is inserted into the die, then the die is set into the base. The bullet is dropped into the top of the die as shown in *Figure 5*.

The seating pin is inserted into the die and the bullet pushed down against the case. The top of the adjusting knob is then struck a sharp blow with the palm of the hand, or with a soft mallet as shown in *Figure 6*.

Obviously the bullet can only be seated perfectly straight and concentric with the axis of the case as few other dies can, with the possible exception of the Vickerman bullet seater which will be described later.

As mentioned before, the base for this die is also made to fit the sizing die. The base as illustrated, shows the seating side. The reverse side is bored out larger so that when it is placed on the end of the sizing die, the case can be driven down into it without injury. The sizing die is illustrated with the inside neck reamer and trimer.

LOADING DIES 227

Figure 5.

Figure 6.

The fired case after being decapped, which is usually accomplished by a simple punch, is forced into the sizing die by use of a bench vise or press.

In *Figure 7*, the base has been put in place. The small cap with the projection in the center is placed on the head of the case with the projection in the primer pocket. This small cap is crowned so as to prevent cocking which might result in bending of the head of the case.

This is an extremely quick and easy setup to make, and it can be done much quicker than it can be told. The whole thing is squeezed together in the vise until the cap comes up firmly against the end of the die. This automatically makes each case with identical headspace. The headspace should be adjusted in the die to match the headspace in the rifle when the rifle and dies are being made. Once the case has been fully pressed into the die, the cap and base are removed and the reamer inserted into the die as shown in *Figure 8*.

The stop shown on the reamer is set so that when the reamer is all the way down against the stop, it trims the cases to length as well as reaming the inside of the neck for perfect concentricity. The reamer shown is an easily made "half" type. If preferred, it can be made with three or four flutes, but this requires the use of a milling machine and will work no better.

The upper portion of the sizing die has been reamed to considerably larger size than the neck of the case. For example, the set of dies shown in *Figure 9* is for the popular .22/250, and the upper portion of the sizing die has been reamed to 3/8", and the reamer is made from a piece of 3/8" drill rod.

For larger calibres, this portion of the die necessarily has to be larger so that the trimming portion of the reamer will be large enough to trim the mouth of the case for perfect squareness and the correct length. The obvious advantage of this type of die which should be made for each individual rifle, can readily be seen especially if used in conjunction with the regular bench type

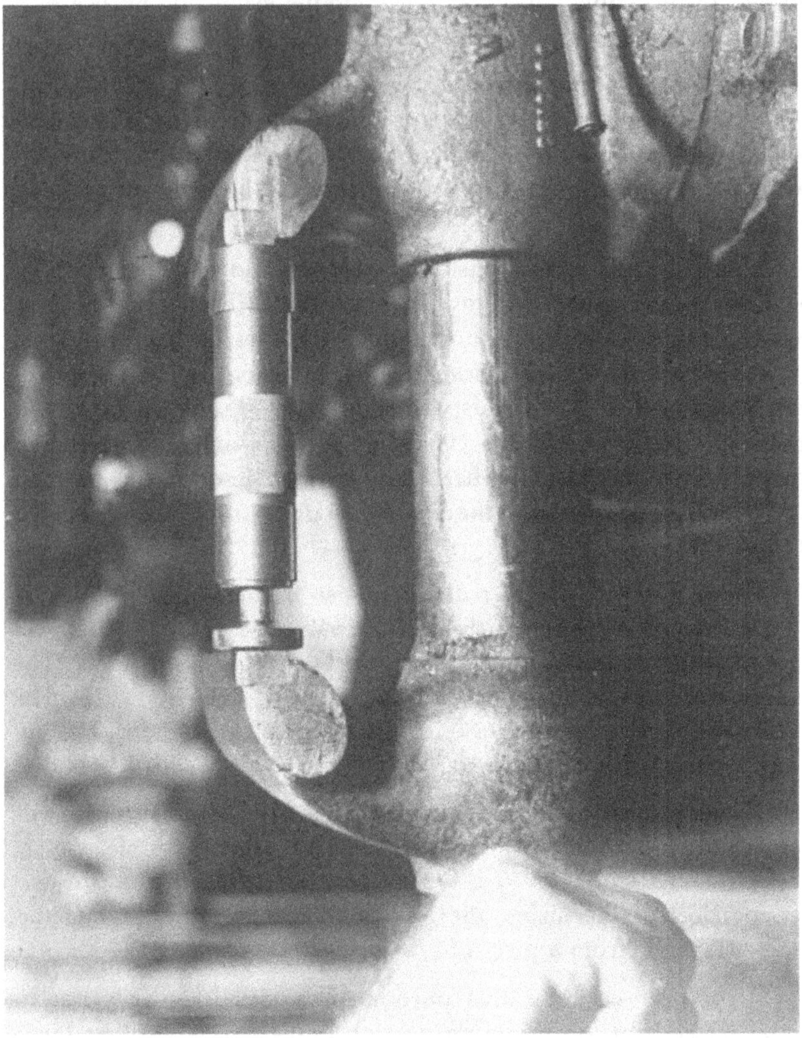

Figure 7.

LOADING DIES 231

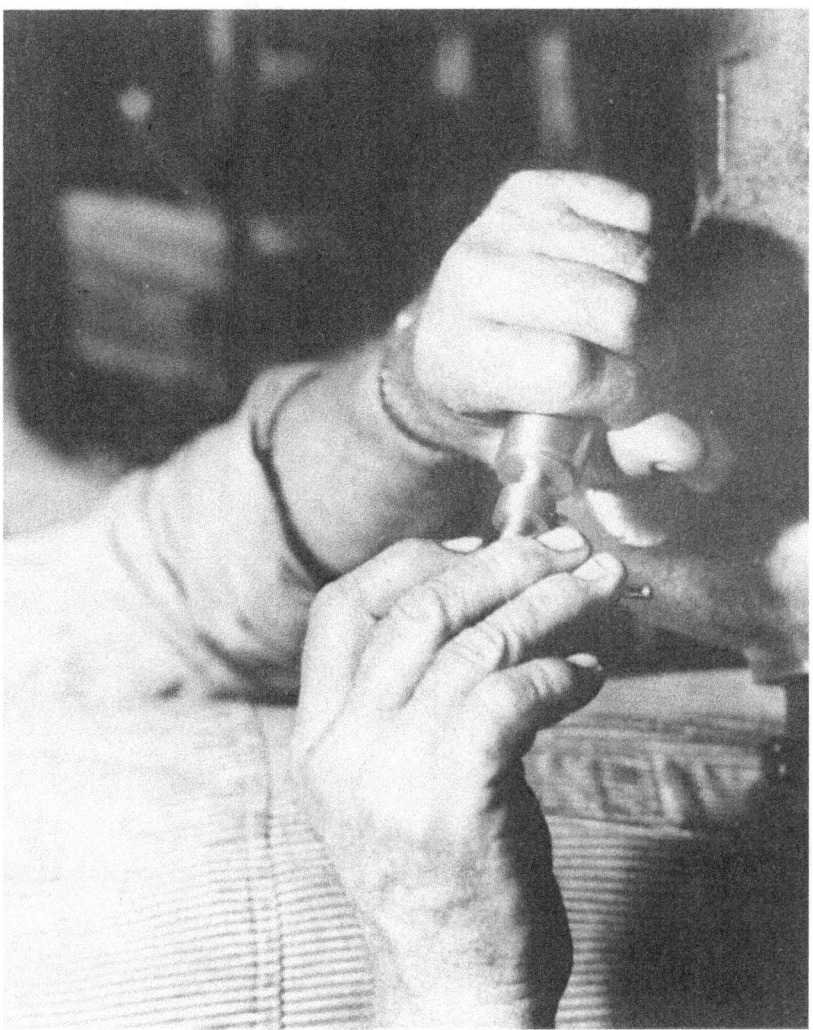

Figure 8.

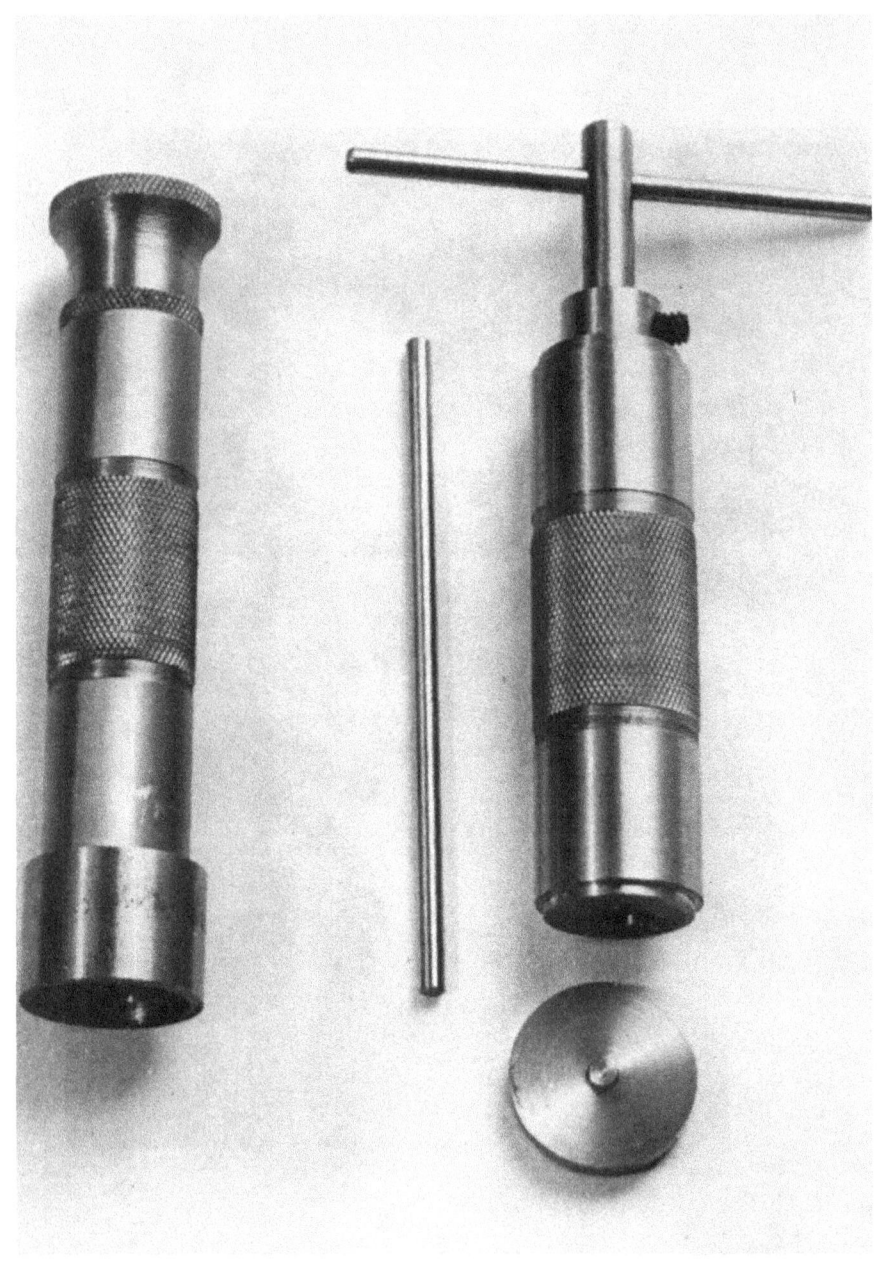

Figure 9.

loading tool. (In the illustration there is a short piece of drill rod shown. This is used to punch the sized case out of the sizing die.)

The Vickerman seating die, which is made with the standard 7/8" x 14 threads, works on the same principal as the hand type just described.

Figure 10 shows the Vickerman seater in place in a standard bench loading tool. There is a small guide which can be seen in *Figure 11* into which the neck and shoulder of the case fit as they are raised up into position by the operation of the lever of the tool. The bullet is dropped into the cut away portion of the die which is reamed to bullet diameter in exactly the same manner as described for the hand seating die. The seating punch is adjustable for seating depth, and is of standard design, but it is concealed in the illustration in the solid portion of the die above the bullet. As the handle of the tool is raised, the sliding portion of the seating die is pushed upward along with the bullet until the bullet comes in contact with the seating punch which then seats the bullet in the same manner as in the hand seater.

Here again, the obvious advantages are plain. The bullet can be dropped into the die above the charged case and becomes perfectly aligned with the axis of the case before it comes in contact with the seating punch. Another advantage of this die is that it is not necessary to have a seating die for each calibre. For example, a die made for .30 calibre will seat bullet in almost any .30 calibre case.

It will be noticed upon studying *Figure 1,* that most sizing dies are vented. The writer's experience has been that this is an unnecessary feature, and it will be noticed that this vent is absent in the hand sizing die described. The writer has manufactured and used thousands of sizing dies, and in no instance has it been necessary to have a vent which experience has shown only serves to scar the brass without serving any useful purpose. Doubtless many will take exception to this statement, but if the two types are tried side by side, one with, and one without the vent, it will be

Figure 10.

LOADING DIES

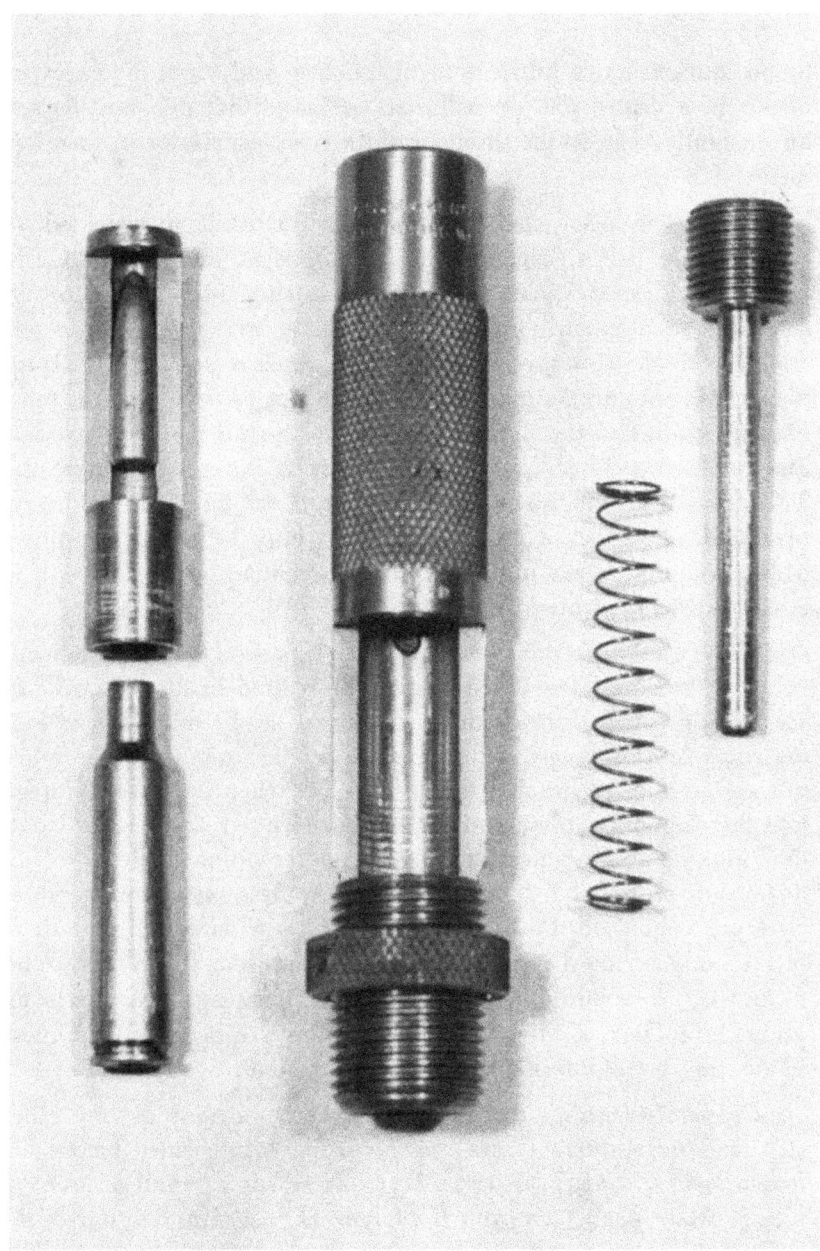

Figure 11.

found that excessive lubrication of the cases will cause the cases to buckle in a vented die. It will also be found that this vent leaves an unsightly scar on the shoulder of the case, especially in forming dies.

Many times poor workmanship of the die results in wrinkled or buckled case necks, especially in forming dies, and the trouble is laid to the lack of a vent. Poor workmanship takes many forms; such as the neck of the die being off center with the body, rough shoulder in the chamber of the die, too short a neck in the sizing die and rings in the chamber. The latter is not as serious as it may appear. Rings in the die are circular and go all the way around, and when a case is forced into the die, it is forced straight up. Therefore, these rings are of little consequence and will not be reproduced on the case unless roughness may be on the shoulder. Many complaints are made about dies because the case, after it is sized, shows numerous rings.

These rings are not caused by roughness in the die, but from rings in the chamber. When a cartridge is fired in the rifle, microscopic ridges will form on the case because the brass is forced into the rings or roughness in the chamber by the pressure. These are not apparent when the case is extracted, but when the case is forced into the sizing die, these small ridges are ironed or smoothed out, thus making them quite visible. The natural thing to do is to lay this trouble to the die probably because these microscopic ridges were not visible on the fired case before it was sized. Slight rings in the body of the die will not affect its operation in any way and those who are examining dies for microscopic rings and then complain about them, are barking up the wrong tree because roughness in the chamber of the rifle is causing the trouble.

Proper lubrication of the case is as important as any other step in handloading. Cases must be properly lubricated before full length sizing. One practice is to simply smear a small amount of lubricant on each case with the fingers. Fred Huntington, of the RCBS Company, recommends the use of a large ink pad which can be purchased in any stationery store for a reasonable price. This pad is then impregnated with case lubricant and the cases run over it. Another older method is to make a similar pad by taking a small piece of board, three to four inches wide, and eight to ten inches long, and padding it with cloth which is then impregnated with lubricant. This method is shown in *Figure 12*. The cases are simply rolled back and forth and pick up a thin coating of lubricant.

Sometimes, the necks of the cases will stick when withdrawn over the expanding plug. Fred Huntington recommends the use of a small brush which he furnishes in the proper sizes for all calibres. The use of this small brush is shown in *Figure 13*. The brush is simply covered with a light coating of lubricant and pushed into the neck of the case. Another common method is to simply dip the neck of the case into powdered graphite as shown in *Figure 14*.

By studying *Figure 1*, the design of a typical decapping pin assembly can be seen. These pins come in different shapes according to the ideas of the manufacturer, but they all serve the same purpose and usually consist of the same number of parts. The working parts of this assembly are the decapping pin and expander button marked "H". As the lubricated case is forced up into the die, the decapping pin punches out the old primer. When the case is withdrawn from the sizing die, the neck will be expanded to the proper diameter by the expander button. By lubricating the inside of the neck of the case, the sticking on this expander button will be eliminated. Care must be taken not to over-lubricate the inside of the case neck because, especially in the smaller calibres, an excessive amount of lubricant will hinder the free flow of powder into the case. This is the reason that many prefer the dry graphite method of lubrication as there is no tendency to obstruct the flow of powder into the case.

Some seating dies are equipped with a crimping device. This is usually used exclusively for loading cartridges for tubular magazine rifles, and since it is of lesser importance than other steps in reloading, it will not be discussed.

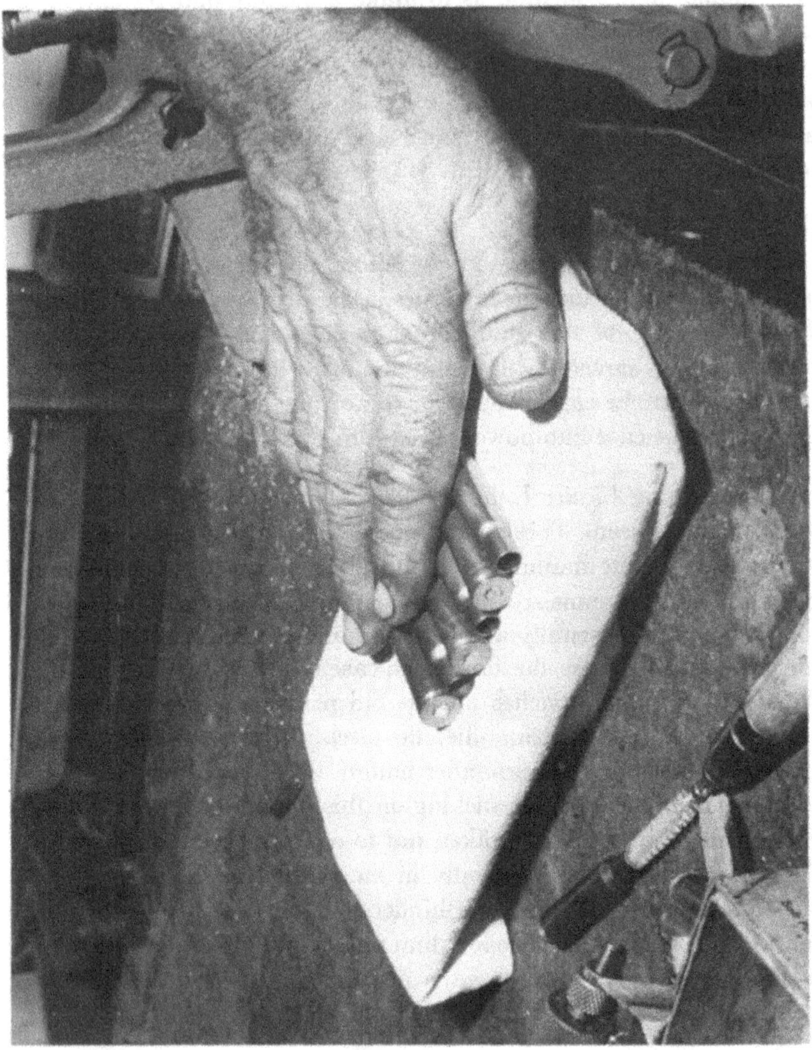

238   HANDBOOK FOR SHOOTERS AND RELOADERS

Figure 12.

LOADING DIES 239

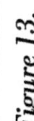

Figure 13.

Figure 14.

Of the pair of dies which consists of a sizer and seater, the full length sizer, or even just a neck sizer, is the one which causes most of the trouble. Some sizing dies are made "short". Some are made "long". The producer of the first, or short type, endeavors to produce a die which, if set down to touch the shell holder of the tool, will produce a sized case with minimum headspace. The second, or long die, when set down against the shell holder, will not touch the shoulder of the case at all and leaves the headspace unaltered, thus producing a case with the same headspace as it came from the chamber of the rifle after firing. Obviously, the short die can, and often does produce cases with headspace too short for many rifles. This results in a dangerous condition. Cases a few thousandths too short, may work for a few firings but will ultimately separate between the solid head and the body. If the case has really excessive headspace as it comes from the sizer, it definitely is dangerous to shoot and should be discarded. It is not uncommon to find dies which produce cases with almost 1/16 of an inch of headspace when set to touch the shell holder. Firing such a cartridge can and often does result in blown up guns and injury to the shooter. What this all boils down to is that all dies do not match all tools and that the tool and die combinations do not always match the rifle chamber.

The first thing is to adjust the die for the rifle for which the ammunition is being loaded. To do this, screw the sizing die into the tool until it touches the shell holder when the holder is raised to its uppermost position. Back the die off about one half turn. Run a case into the die as far as possible. Remove the case and observe on the neck where the sizing action ceased. Doubtless, the neck will show that the shoulder of the case was not touched. Turn the die in a little and repeat. Continue this procedure until the shoulder of the case is barely touched by the die. This is for cases previously fired in the rifle. If the cases have been fired in some other rifle, or a number of rifles, such as cases picked up on rifle ranges, use the same procedure but try the sized case in the rifle each time. It is best to remove the firing pin so that a better "feel" is possible when the bolt is turned down on the case. Set the die so that the bolt can be closed on the sized case with a slight "feel". If the bolt "falls down" on the case or can be moved back and forth when closed on the case, the case is too short and actually there is too much headspace. This condition can be caused by firing the cartridge in a rifle with minimum headspace, then trying to use it in a rifle with maximum or excessive headspace. Cases fired in chambers with minimum headspace should never be used in rifles with normal or excessive headspace.

If the rifle has normal headspace and the bolt fails to close on a case sized in a die set as close to the shell holder as possible, the die is too long. This is a very common occurrence, and the die suppliers are constantly confronted with the problem in the form of dies returned for replacement often accompanied with a sarcastic query as why such dies were sent out in the first place, or why the maker doesn't learn to make dies, etc. The solution, of course, is a shorter die which can be ADJUSTED for the individual gun. The die can simply be cut off slightly at the bottom to allow the case to be forced a little further into the die. This general problem is hard to solve because there are too many variables involved and often aggravated by the ignorance of the owner as to how the die should work, or what it actually is supposed to do.

Another common difficulty experienced by handloaders is the failure of the sized case to enter the chamber in which the case was fired. Dies come in minimum and maximum diameters as well as lengths. The manufacturer either makes or buys his reamers. Either way, the reamer for the sizing die is made maximum and then is used over a period of time to make a certain number of dies until the tool has worn down to minimum. In other words, it is imperative for the manufacturer to realize a reasonable life out of each tool. Thus, the first dies made with a reamer will size the cases down to SAAMI specifications given for the maximum cartridge, then as the tool wears, the last dies made with the reamer will bring the cartridge down to minimum specifications. This is just as true of rifle manufacturers who also have a set minimum and maximum tolerance.

When a rifle with a maximum chamber is wedded with a die of minimum dimensions, the honeymoon gets off to a poor start. Everyone is in trouble. The die maker probably blames the rifle maker. The rifle maker blames the die maker. The shooter blames everyone but himself. Getting back to the sized case failing to enter the chamber, sometimes the minimum die will reduce the body of the case enough to microscopically bulge the shoulder, thus preventing the bolt from closing altogether, or only with difficulty. Again, the solution is to shorten the die sufficiently to allow the die to touch the shoulder of the case enough to "straighten" it out. Here again, the short die obviously has the advantage because it can be adjusted to cope with the situation, but its disadvantage is just as obvious unless the operator understands how to make this adjustment. He cannot simply screw the die into the tool and hope for the best. He must adjust the die correctly, or take a chance on blowing his unused brains out.

Rifles, in the process of manufacture, are subjected to many gauging operations—especially for headspace. Headspace can be a matter of LIFE and DEATH, whether it involves the chamber in the rifle barrel or in the sizing die. Each manufacturer has his own set of tolerances for headspace. Each die manufacturer has his own set of tolerances. This means that there can be quite a gap between the minimum headspace tolerance of the die maker and the maximum tolerance of the rifle maker or vice versa. So-called custom rifles are sometimes the worst from the headspace tolerance standpoint. The word CUSTOM has become indiscriminately used in conjunction with guns produced in small shops often operated by inexperienced tinkerers. Shortly after the war, the word "custom" was almost a "fighting" word, especially in areas adjacent to some of the gunsmithing schools, where thousands of lunkers were sold to a gun-hungry public. Tolerances ceased to mean anything and, with such arms, understanding and proper adjustment of loading dies is doubly important. Even the widest tolerances in headspace can often be safely compensated for by proper die adjustment for the individual rifle chamber.

Headspace, when being discussed in conjunction with "wildcat" cartridges, is a different proposition than with a standard cartridge. The standard cartridges are built to certain tolerances by the factories and all factories recognize more or less the same standards. In "wildcat" rifles this is quite different because "wildcats" are made by a great number of custom gunsmiths. Sometimes there is a great difference of opinion among these gunsmiths as to what the headspace of a certain "wildcat" should be. In other words, most "wildcats" are not very well standardized and owners of "wildcat" calibres must understand headspace in order to make his own cartridges to fit his own rifle.

Whenever a shooter buys a rifle in a "wildcat" calibre he obviously intends to make his own cases and load his own ammunition. When the set of hand tools, described previously, is furnished with the rifle and adjusted for that chamber, there is no way that even an inexperienced handloader can make his cases wrong if he does not alter the dies, but with commercial dies, which are used in standard bench tools, he must have a thorough understanding of how to make cases with the proper headspace for his own individual rifle.

This means that headspace for "wildcat" rifles is of no great importance so far as uniformity is concerned. That is, it does not have to be just like some other rifle of the same calibre, because if the owner has an understanding of headspace he will be able to make his ammunition correctly. If he does not have an understanding of headspace he could not make ammunition correctly whether the headspace in the rifle is standard or not.

Anyone contemplating the purchase, or who is already an owner of a rifle for a "wildcat" cartridge should learn to make cases with the proper headspace for the rifle without regard to what the headspace actually measures in the chamber of the rifle.

The use of forming dies is probably one of the most difficult phases of handloading to understand. Too many assume that forming dies are of the correct length as they come from the factory and will need no further adjustment to make cases for his rifle. It is a common practice for many handloaders to make brass for common cartridges such as the 8x57 out of easily obtained .30/06 brass. Almost all brass must be made by the handloader himself for his "wildcat" rifle. With a "wildcat" rifle especially, care must be taken to adjust the forming die correctly for headspace, one reason being that most shooters who are playing with "wildcat" rifles are hotrodders at heart, and we can usually assume that they are going to load ammunition to the maximum. Therefore, no one should EVER assume that any forming die produced commercially will make cases which will exactly fit his rifle. It is of special importance that he set his forming dies correctly for the headspace correct for his rifle, because headspace can be a matter of life or death.

This is especially true of rimless cartridges, the headspace for which is measured by the length of the case from the base of the datum line which is some point on the shoulder as indicated on the various sheets furnished by SAAMI. Naturally, the headspace measurement varies among individual rifles as well as among individual dies.

With belted or rimmed cases, this headspace adjustment is not of as grave importance as the rimless type because even though the shoulder might be set back excessively, the headspace is determined by the thickness of the rim, or by the width of the belt, and if the dies are made so that none of these measurements are altered, there is not much trouble with headspace adjustment. In rimmed, or belted cases, if the shoulder is set back a fraction of an inch, it will not result in a dangerous condition, although it can shorten the life of the brass. When a belted or rimmed case with the shoulder set back too far is fired, it simply blows out to take the shape of the chamber in which it is fired. If it is set back too far it can result in a ruptured shoulder which does little harm except to destroy cases for further use.

Forming dies are sometimes used singly. For example, the 8 x 57 cases can be made by using one form and trim die, and trimmed to length in that die, and the same die can later be used as a trim die when required. Others require two, three or perhaps four forming operations. For example, a magnum case necked to .22 calibre could require as many as four forming dies. A .25 Magnum usually takes three forming dies in addition to the full length sizer.

When setting the forming dies for making rimless cases; for example, the 8x57 from .30/06, the die should be set with a slight space between the shellholder and the bottom of the die as shown in *Figure 15*, and the cases run through it and cut off with a fine tooth hacksaw, as shown in *Figure 16*, then filed flush with the die as shown in *Figure 17*.

The case should then be tried in the rifle and doubtless it will be too long to allow the bolt to be closed. The case can then be run through the die again after the die has been set a little closer, and this process repeated until a case is finally produced with the headspace which will allow the bolt to be closed quite easily, but with a definite "feel". When this adjustment has been accomplished, the lock ring should be turned down into position and securely locked so that the adjustment will not change whenever the die is reset.

Forming cases such as the .25 Magnum is a little more complicated process. Using the .257 Weatherby Magnum for example, the number one forming die is set in the tool so that it will touch the shellholder and all of the cases run through it and cut to length. The number two die is then put in the tool and the same process repeated, and again repeated in the number three die which should complete the making of the case with the exception of running the case through the full length sizer; which should also be done with all cartridges such as the 8x57 described previously. This will iron out the neck and expand it to accept the bullet.

The following is a description furnished by Fred Huntington for forming Magnum cases, based on *Figure 18*.

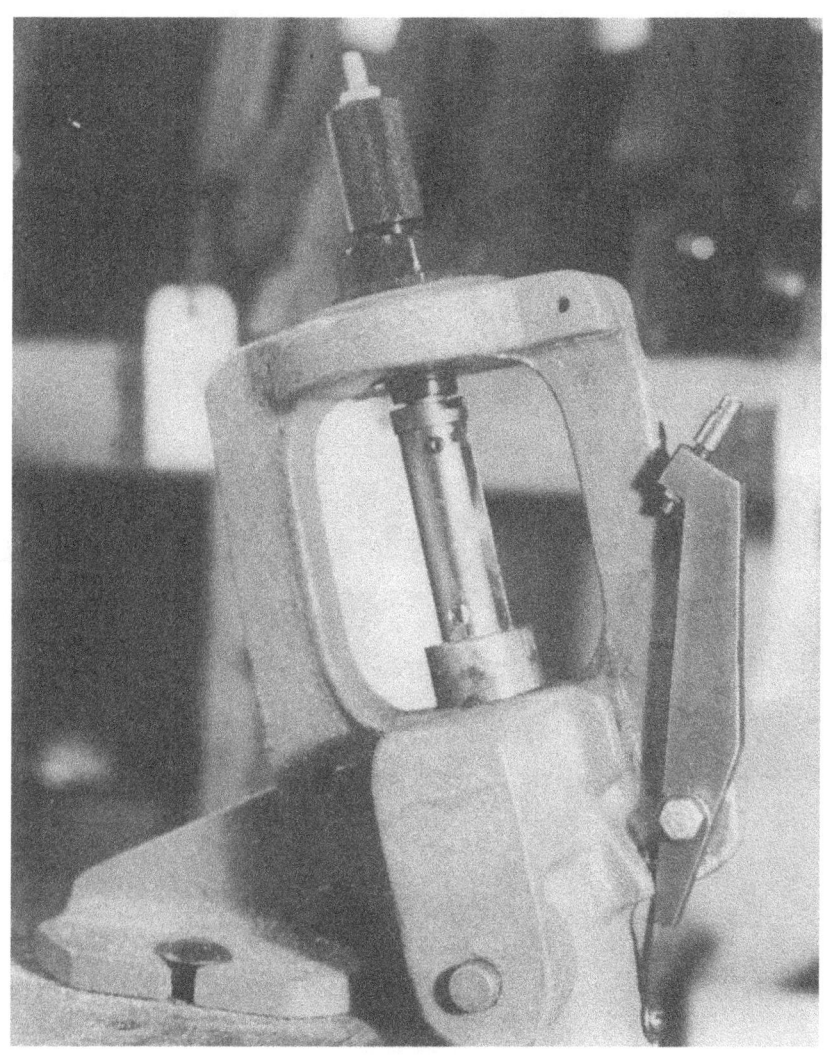

Figure 15.

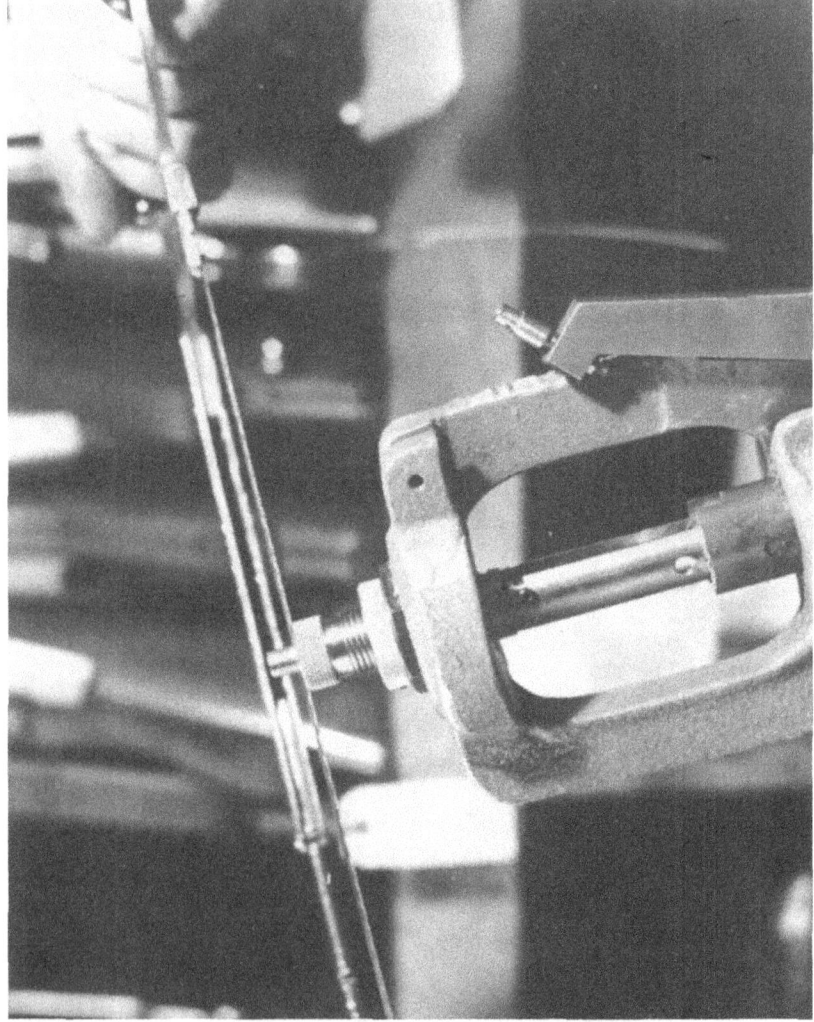

Figure 16.

LOADING DIES

Figure 17.

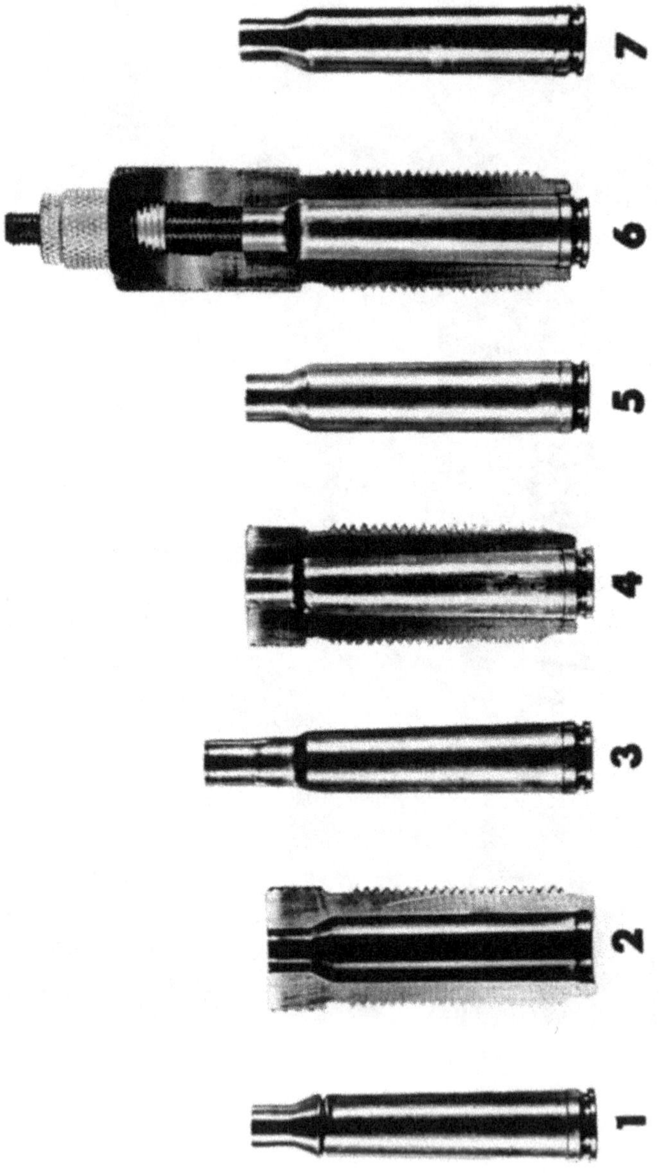

Figure 18.

1. This .300 H&H Magnum case has been formed in the wrong die. It was formed in a file-type trim die (2) which is intended for trimming the overall length of cases that have already been fire formed. The same trouble would occur if one were to form this case in a .30 Short Magnum sizer die such as die 6.

2. This is a file-type trim die intended only for trimming overall length. The shellholder should touch the bottom of the file-trim type die. Then run cases into the die and file off that portion of the case that sticks up above the die. This die is not a forming die, although from all outward appearances it may look like one.

3. This is a .300 H&H case properly formed in the forming die (4). This is the first stage in necking .300 H&H cases to .30, 7mm, .270 or .25 calibre Magnums. Note the top part of the case is somewhat smaller than the newly formed portion.

4. The forming die (4) is the right die for the first forming operation to take .300 H&H cases to .30 short Magnum. Here, again, the case forming die should touch the top of the shell holder. Then, when a case is run into the die, the portion of the case sticking up above the die is cut off with a hack saw (32 teeth to the inch) about 1/32" above the face of the die. The case mouth will be uneven, so a 1/4" diameter by 6" long rod is used to roll the case neck out to the top of the die face edge. Next the remaining 1/32" of case neck is filed off level with the face of the die with a smooth mill file. *Figure 17.* These dies are specially hardened to reduce damage caused by cutting or filing; however, it is advisable to use as little pressure as possible against the face of the die and extra caution is needed to prevent the set of the hack saw blade from hitting the inside of the hole in the top.

After the case is formed, cut and filed, it is ready to be full length sized in the sizer die (6). This sizes the neck properly, sets the shoulder headspace and rounds out the neck as it comes out over the expander ball.

If one were to form down to 7mm, .270 or .25 calibre Magnums, additional case forming dies are needed. All have the same body dimensions. However the headspace will differ and the neck diameter will be reduced in each successive operation.

The final forming operation will be in the full length sizer die of the proper calibre as outlined above.

5. This case has been properly formed in the forming die (4) and then full length sized in the sizer die (6) and then fireformed in the rifle chamber. It is now ready for reloading.

6. This is the full length sizer die with a case that has been properly formed, cut and filed in the case forming die (4). If this die is used as the sole forming die, the results will be much the same as pictured in (1).

7. This case, like (5) has been formed, cut, filed, formed in the full length sizer die and then fireformed. When cases (5) and (7) are compared with cases (4) and (6) in their respective dies, note the difference in body dimensions.

One of the most important prerequisites in case forming is to have a press of sufficient leverage and one that will not spring during the case forming operations. Proper lubrication is also extremely important. RCBS lubricant applied to a Carter's uninked stamp pad, or a homemade pad, is very convenient to use, distributes the lubricant evenly and keeps it from getting ahead of the shoulder. When the case is rolled across the pad *Figure 12*, it picks up just enough lubricant to do a good case forming job. Extremely small amounts of lubricant are needed—too much will cause dents and dimples in the case. For a lubricant in cold and damp climates we recommend Anderol case sizing lube and Lubriplate #130AA.

The preceding picture sequence has shown how to neck down the .300 H&H brass to the .30 Belted Newton. The manufacturer of the dies can make forming dies for any of the short Magnums with the same reamer used on this job. But of course the headspace would have to be adjusted to the particular version of the .30 Short Magnum.

We do not recommend forming Norma straight drawn brass below .35 calibre and better still .375 calibre in either the Magnum or .30/06 types as it requires an excessive number of forming dies as well as a neck ream die and reamer. To us, neck reaming is an unnecessary evil and if you stay away from it, do so.

We recommend .375 H&H brass rather than .300 H&H brass when forming the .338 Winchester Magnum cases.

Dies manufactured by RCBS marked with the calibre and word "TRIM" are intended for trimming fireformed cases. However, in some instances it is possible to form cases with a "TRIM" die—.30/06 to 7mm or .257 Roberts to name two. Case forming dies are marked with the calibre and the word "FORM" on the top of the die. Case forming dies are also marked, (1), (2) and (3). And are used in that sequence—(1) takes the .300 H&H case to the .30 short Magnum; (2) takes the .30 short Magnum case to the 7mm and .270 short Magnum; (3) takes the 7mm and .270 short Magnum cases down to the .25 calibre short Magnum. Always be sure to full length size the final formed case in the full length sizer die of the proper calibre before fireforming. While forming dies do set the headspace to a certain point, the final headspacing point is reached only in the correct sizer die.

Not much has been said about body support in forming dies. For example, .300 H&H Magnum when being reformed for something like the .257 Weatherby or similar cartridges. The forming die must have the same body taper as the original .300 H&H Magnum case. Without body support, cases cannot be necked down or formed without buckling. This is the reason that cases cannot be necked down in a full length sizer die for cartridges like the .257 Weatherby which must be fire formed as the last operation. If a .300 H&H Magnum case is forced into a .257 Weatherby full length sizing die very little forming or necking down will take place. The brass will simply buckle in a way quite similar to (1) in *Figure 17.* Dies with the original taper support the body so that it cannot bulge out or swell out in different spots which results in buckling.

Some "wildcat" cases can be made in the regular full length sizing die, a good example being the .25/06 because this cartridge is not fire formed. It is simply the .30/06 case necked down. Sometimes cases can be made in the full length sizing die without the use of a former, although in this instance the use of one former is usually recommended. The forming die simply brings the neck down to .270.

Once the case is formed to smaller size with the original body taper, the fire forming step comes next. Contrary to many ideas, a light load is not good for fire forming. A good, stiff load should be used. This is especially true of rimless cases because a light load is apt to increase the headspace.

For example, if an "Improved" .25/06 is being worked with, the '06 case is first necked down to .25 with the headspace set so that the bolt will close with some difficulty. In other words, it is necessary to have a "crush" fit for fire forming rimless cartridges. A good stiff load will blow the case out to conform perfectly with the chamber. If a reduced load is used sometimes cases will appear to be perfectly formed, but at the same time it has been shortened due to a sort of "bouncing around" action. This case although appearing to be perfectly formed will be dangerous to use again. It is possible to gain as much as .040 to .050 headspace when fire forming with reduced loads, so that when a case is fired the second time with a full load, all sorts of trouble can develop. This is quite a common way to blow up guns.

With rimmed or belted cases, the use of a full load is not quite so important because the headspace is measured at the belt or rim so that the position of the shoulder is of lesser importance. Sometimes, however, when considerably reduced loads are used in a Magnum case for fire forming purposes, holes will be blown through the shoulder which would not occur if a full load was used for fire forming. (Reprinted from *Guns and Ammo,* November 1960.)

THE LOADING DATA GIVEN IN THIS BOOK SHOULD BE USED WITH CAUTION. NEVER START WITH MAXIMUM LISTED LOADS AND WHERE ONLY ONE LOAD FOR A CERTAIN BULLET OR POWDER IS USED ALWAYS START A LITTLE UNDER AND WORK UP TO MAXIMUM FOR EACH INDIVIDUAL RIFLE. THE FOLLOWING LISTS OF LOADS HAVE BEEN ASSEMBLED WITH GREAT CARE, EITHER FROM A RELIABLE SOURCE, OR ACTUAL TESTING, AND ARE BELIEVED TO BE SAFE IN ALL PROPERLY CONSTRUCTED ARMS IN GOOD CONDITION. THE AUTHOR AND PUBLISHER HAVING NO CONTROL OVER METHODS, COMPONENTS OR CHOICE OF ARMS, ASSUME NO RESPONSIBILITY IN THE USE OF THESE TABLES.

LOADING DATA

BARREL TWIST

Standard twists are given for each cartridge. Special twists are also given for cartridges which often use twists other than standard. For example, the standard twist for the .250/3000 Savage is one in 14 inches, which is intended for 87 to 100 grain bullets. Often barrels are ordered for this cartridge which will be used with heavier bullets, such as 117 to 125 grains, when a 10 inch twist barrel would be furnished. Long heavy bullets require a short or "quick" twist while light short bullets require a long or "slow" twist.

.17 CALIBRE INTRODUCTION

This is one of the smallest bore sizes being currently produced by custom barrel makers. A few years ago, even smaller sizes of barrels were available, as small as .14 calibre, but the difficulty of manufacturing barrels smaller than .17 calibre is extremely difficult and impractical in these modern times. The standard bore and groove diameter for the various .17 calibre cartridges is .168 x .172. Results are improving with these small .17 calibre cartridges now that custom barrel makers are gaining experience and developing better methods. There are numerous versions of .17 calibre cartridges but experience has shown that a case capacity greater than 25 grains is impractical. Bullets are manufactured by R. B. Sisk, Iowa Park, Texas, Fred N. Barnes, Grand Junction, Colorado, and Ted Holmes of the Holmes Gun Shop, Mattoon Illinois. Some shooters like to swedge their own bullets and for this group of shooters, .17 calibre jacket cups are available from Speer Products, Lewiston, Idaho. .17 calibre barrels seem to give the best results with a 10 or 11 inch twist, and usually the best accuracy is obtained with bullets not over 25 grain weight, but for those who are interested in experimenting with longer bullets as heavy as 45 grains in an extremely quick twist barrel, such bullets are available from Fred Barnes.

.17 Hornet (Ackley)

The .17 Hornet is one of the best balanced .17 cartridges and is simply sort of an "improved" .22 Hornet necked down to .17 calibre. This .17 cartridge can be loaded by using a compressed charge of 4198 without weighing. Up to 200 yards, the .17 Hornet has proven to be extremely deadly on small game including squirrels, prairie dogs, woodchucks, foxes, etc.

25 gr. bullet	11 gr.	4198 powder	3300 fs
	12	4198	3585
	11	4227	3390
	11.5	4227	3570

Standard twist: 10"
Special twist: 11", 12", 14"

.17 Bee (Ackley)

The .17 Bee is simply sort of an "improved" .218 Bee necked down to accept the smaller .17 calibre bullet. The capacity of this small case is almost ideal for the .17 bore and can be loaded very easily by simply pouring each case full of 4198 powder and scraping it off even with the mouth of the case, and then seating the 20, 22 or 25 grain bullet to create a compressed charge which is approximately 14 grains of 4198 which gives a velocity of 3535 foot seconds. Because of the high loading density, it is a relatively accurate little cartridge well adapted for use in densely settled communities where noise and richochet are to be avoided. Like all .17 calibre cartridges it is practically recoilless.

20 gr. bullet	9 gr.	4227 powder	3225 fs
	10	4227	3640
	11	4227	3845

MAXIMUM LOAD LISTED SHOULD BE APPROACHED WITH CARE

	12	4227	4165
25	14	4198	3535
	10	4227	3335
	11	4227	3510
	10	2400	3450
	11	2400	3800

Standard twist: 10"
Special twist: 11", 12", 14"

.17 Javelina

This cartridge is a development of the A. and M. Gunshop, Prescott, Arizona, owned and operated by Bill Atkinson and Paul Marquhart. It is a shortened, blown out .222 Remington necked down to .17 for a powder capacity of a little less than 20 grains. It has been used for all kind of small game, and has been quite successful on some larger animals including small deer. Naturally a .17 calibre cartridge is not recommended for use as a big game rifle, but the .17 Javelina has proven that small bullets at high velocity can be extremely deadly. Its name was derived because of its deadliness on the small wild pig called the Javelina. Ballistics for this cartridge are practically the same as those given for the .17/222, and as a rule, loading data is interchangeable for these two cartridges. the .17 Javelina has been chronographed at 3850 fs with 18.6 grains of 3031 powder with the 25 grain bullet. Some difficulty has been experienced by some laboratories obtaining an accurate reading for the .17 calibre cartridges because of the extremely small bullet. However, lately new developments consisting of foil screens have made it possible to get more accurate readings.

25 gr. bullet	15 gr.	4198 powder	3225 fs
	16	4198	3510
	17	4198	3705
	15	3031	3075
	16	3031	3335

MAXIMUM LOAD LISTED SHOULD BE APPROACHED WITH CARE

LOADING DATA

17	3031	3570
18	3031	3704
18.5	3031	3845

Standard twist: 10"
Special twist: 11", 12", 14"

.17/.222

The .17/222 cartridge is the .222 Remington necked down to .17 calibre. There are numerous versions of this particular cartridge, mostly varying in length. Some experimenters have used shorter versions, while others have used the full length "improved" version, but experience has shown that the .222 Remington simply necked down without any other change is about the best, and most easily made since it requires no trimming or fire forming. This cartridge is about maximum capacity for the .17 bore and only a slight increase in velocity has been possible by necking down larger cases such as the .250/3000 and the .220 Swift, and these larger versions have proven to be quite inflexible thus rendering them rather impractical from the standpoint of ease of handloading and also barrel life.

20 gr. bullet	15 gr.	4198 powder	3572 fs
	16	4198	3960
	17	4198	4166
	18	4198	4348
	19	4198	4644
25 gr. bullet	15	4198	3226
	16	4198	3510
	17	4198	3704
	18	4198	3638
	13	3031	3077
	16	3031	3333
	17	3031	3572
	18	3031	3704
	18.5	3031	3846

Standard twist: 10"
Special twist: 11", 12", 14"

MAXIMUM LOAD LISTED SHOULD BE APPROACHED WITH CARE

.20/.222

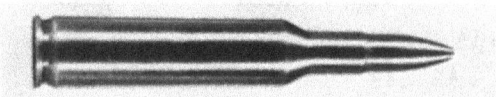

This small .20 calibre cartridge is made by necking the .222 Remington case down to .20 calibre. An even better cartridge might be made by necking down the .222 Remington Magnum, and a still more interesting one might be made by swaging a belt on the .25 or .30 Remington cases and necking to .20 calibre thus coming up with sort of a miniature .20 Belted rifle cartridge. The following loading data was developed by C. H. Stocking of Hutchison Minnesota and chronographed on an electric chronograph, which is the only authentic data available for the .20/.222 illustrated above. The bullet diamter is .204.

45 gr. bullet	18 gr.	4198 powder	3300 fs
	20	4198	3450
	22	Ball C	3450
48	18	4198	3335
	20	4198	4335
	22	Ball C	3335

.22 Hornet

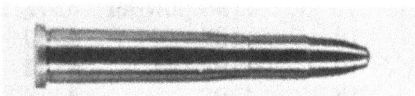

The .22 Hornet cartridge was developed during the early thirties by employees at the Springfield Arsenal. Names such as Wotkyns, Whelen and many others appear in the history of the Hornet. The .22 Hornet is a modern version of the old Winchester .22 center fire cartridge. Although over thirty years old, the .22 Hornet is still popular. Being an extremely small capacity case, it is necessary to use what might be termed as a "hot" fast burning powder.

40 gr. bullet	8.5 gr.	2400 powder	2525 fs
	10.5	2400	2775
	11	4227	2665

MAXIMUM LOAD LISTED SHOULD BE APPROACHED WITH CARE

45	8	2400	2375
	10	2400	2660
	11	4227	2590
50	11.5	4227	2625
55	9	2400	2390

The following loads are recommended for Norma and Nobel powders.

45 gr. Cast Gas-check bullet

	4 gr.	Shotgun Ballistite	1500 fs
48 gr. Gas-check	7	Shotgun Ballistite	1600
45 gr. Jacketed	10	Hercules 2400	2675
	11	4227	2560
	10	Nobel's Hornet	2600
	9	Norma M1 Carbine	2500

Standard twist: 16"

.22 K Hornet

The K Hornet is the most popular version of a multitude of improved Hornet cartridges. All of these improved versions use a minimum body taper, sharp shoulder and short neck in order to increase powder capacity as much as possible. The K Hornet was originated by Lysle Kilbourn and it was one of the very first blown out fireformed cartridges. It immediately caught on with shooters and is still popular.

40 gr. bullet	12 gr.	2400 powder	3000 fs
	13	4227	2950
	14	4198	2800
45	11.5	2400	2900
	12.5	4227	2875
	14.5	4198	2800
50	11	2400	2700
	12	4227	2675
	14	4198	2690
55	13.5	4198	2550
	11	4227	2405

Standard twist: 16"

MAXIMUM LOAD LISTED SHOULD BE APPROACHED WITH CARE

.22 ICL Gopher

The .22 ICL Gopher is an "improved" version of the .22 Hornet similar to the K Hornet, and is the smallest of a line of "improved" cartridges originated and developed by Mr. Arnold Juenke, Reno, Nev. Mr. Juenke originally operated the Santa Monica Gun Shop, using "Saturn" as his trade mark. Mr. Robert Hutton, technical editor of "Guns and Ammo" magazine and owner and operator of the Hutton Rifle Ranch of Topanga, California has done a great deal of testing of the ICL line of cartridges as well as many others. The ICL line closely resembles the older Ackley line of "improved" cartridges. They utilize the minimum body taper and sharp shoulder principle to a slightly greater degree and probably represent about the maximum for these two characteristics, sample fired cases showing about the same taper to the inch as the Ackley line, but a 45° shoulder, instead of the Ackley 28° or 40° shoulder angle. The ICL line is somewhat more complete than some other lines of "improved" or wildcat cartridges. The loading data given below was furnished by Mr. Juenke, and further information can be obtained by writing direct to him at 210 West Commercial Row, Reno, Nevada. Unlike most other lines of wildcat cartridges the ICL line has been named after various animals. Cases for the .22 ICL Gopher are made by firing factory loads in the ICL chamber. Like other "improved" versions featuring minimum body taper and sharp shoulder, cases do not stretch, and can be loaded many times. Loads recommended for the K Hornet can be used in the ICL .22 Gopher.

40 gr. bullet	10 gr.	4227 powder	2515 fs
	11	4227	2705

Standard twist: 16"

.218 Bee

MAXIMUM LOAD LISTED SHOULD BE APPROACHED WITH CARE

LOADING DATA

This cartridge was developed from the old .25/20 or .32/20 case. The forerunner was the .22 Neidner, made by simply necking the .25/20 repeater cartridge down to .22. Later the Winchester Repeating Arms Company developed what is now known as the standard .218 Winchester Bee, and was expressly produced for the Model 65 Winchester, which has been since discontinued and replaced by the new Model 43 Winchester bolt action.

The .218 Bee possesses extremely sharp body taper, and has never been too satisfactory for handloading, expecially in lever action rifles, such as the Models 92 and 65, and the later Model 43. Cases have a tendency to stick, and separated heads are common after a few loads.

When the .218 Bee is improved in some way, such as the Mashburn and similar versions, this tendency is greatly reduced and creates a case much more satisfactory for handloading, especially in lever action rifles, as well as single shot, and bolt action rifles.

40 gr. bullet	11 gr.	2400 powder	2790 fs
	12	2400	2925
	14	H4227	3100
	15	H4227	3300
	12	4227	2560
	13	4227	2910
	14	4227	3090
	14	4198	2860
	14.5	4198	2850
45	10.5	2400	2650
	11.5	2400	2840
	13	H4227	2845
	14	H4227	2950
	11.5	4227	2615
	13	4227	2850
	13.5	4227	2950
	14	4198	2700
	14.5	4198	2800
50	8	2400	1945
	8.5	2400	2005
	9	2400	2150
	9.5	2400	2245
	10	2400	2310
	12.5	4227	2660
	13.5	4227	2875
	14	4198	2650
	12.5	H4227	2700

MAXIMUM LOAD LISTED SHOULD BE APPROACHED WITH CARE

	13.5	H4227	2850
55	11	2400	2300
	12	H4227	2575
	13	H4227	2650
	13	4227	2700
	12.5	4198	2325
	13.5	4198	2520
	14	4198	2620

The following loads are recommended for Norma and Nobel powders.

	45 gr. Cast Gas-check bullet		
	5.5 gr.	Shotgun Ballistite Powder	
			1800 fs
	45 gr. Cast Gas-check bullet		
	9	Nobel's Hornet	1700
	45 gr. Jacketed bullet		
	12.5	Nobel's Hornet	2750
	12.5	Norma M1 Carbine	2750
	13.5	Norma 200	2850
50	13.5	Norma 200	2700
55	13.5	Norma 200	2500

Standard twist: 16″

.22 Carbine

This is a small .22 cartridge made by necking the M1 .30 Carbine cartridge down to .22. It is a good small cartridge comparable the the K Hornet and the same loads can be used in both cartridges for practically the same velocities.

M1 Carbines can be re-barrelled or the original barrel re-lined and the actions will work fairly satisfactorily. The Carbine can also be transformed into a manually operated repeater by leaving the gas port out of the new barrel. This makes it easier to save fired cases for reloading.

45 gr. bullet	14 gr.	4227 powder	2815 fs
	13	4198	2500

Standard twist: 16″

MAXIMUM LOAD LISTED SHOULD BE APPROACHED WITH CARE

Mashburn Bee

Like the K Hornet, the Mashburn Bee is a fire formed or "improved" version and like the K Hornet, cases are made by simply firing factory ammunition in the Mashburn chamber. The Mashburn Bee was originated many years ago by A. E. Mashburn of the Mashburn Arms Company of Oklahoma City, Oklahoma and this cartridge has, and still does enjoy a relatively high degree of popularity. This is a very nice small varmint cartridge, and very accurate. In the midwest is has been used on prairie dogs and jack rabbits, crows, hawks and chucks.

Bullet	Powder charge	Powder	Velocity
45 gr. bullet	16 gr.	4227 powder	3242 fs
	16.3	4227	3319
50	17.3	4198	3300
55	16.5	4198	3005
	16.75	4198	3063
	17.1	4198	3068
	17.3	4198	3316

Standard twist: 16"

.22 Improved Jet (Ackley) (.22 Sabre) (.22 Super Jet)

There are several versions of this cartridge but they are all enough alike so that loading data should be interchangeable. The Ackley version came into being ten years ago when a customer ordered a .17 calibre rifle chambered for the .357 Magnum necked down for the small bullet. It proved to be virtually impossible to neck the cases smaller than .22 therefore, the project was abandoned. With the advent of the .22 Jet factory cartridge these .17/.357 tools were brought out and fitted with .22 pilots to create tools for the "improved" .22 Jet. The Super Jet designed by Dan Cotterman and described in the July 1962 issue of "Gun World" has a 30° shoulder

MAXIMUM LOAD LISTED SHOULD BE APPROACHED WITH CARE

angle. The .22 Super Jet is made from the .22 Remington Jet case, while the .22 Sabre version described in the September 1962 issue of "Guns" like the Ackley version, uses the .357 Magnum case. The .22 Sabre is not quite, but almost identical to the Ackley version. Either version should be equally good.

.22 Super Jet

45 gr. bullet	17 gr.	4198 powder	3300 fs
	16.5	4227	3385
50	21	Ball C	2975
	16	4227	3195

.22 Sabre (by Christian H. Helbig, E.B.A.)

35 gr. Sisk	17	4198	3020
	13	H240	3065
	14	H240	3240
	14.5	H240	3400
	17	4227	3380
40 gr. Sierra	14	H240	3220
	14.5	H240	3390
	17	4227	3325
	17.5	4198	3145
	5	Unique	2000
41 gr. Sisk	17	4227	3295
	14	H240	3165
	15	2400	3100
45 gr. Remington HP			
	19.1 gr.	Ball C	2750
	19.5	Ball C	2835
	17.3	4198	3020
	17.5	4198	3050
	16.5	4227	3160
	14.5	H240	3190
50 gr. Hornady SP			
	16.6	4227	3040
	17.5	4198	2975
	14	H240	2975
	14.3	H240	3065

Standard twist: 16"
Special twist: 14"

*All .22 Sabre loads can be used in the Ackley Improved .22 Jet, giving the same ballistics.

MAXIMUM LOAD LISTED SHOULD BE APPROACHED WITH CARE

.218 ICL (Bobcat)

This is the ICL Improved Bee, and is similar to the Mashburn Bee, and other versions. This version produces ballistics similar to the once extremely popular R-2 Lovell, but it has the advantage of factory loads which can easily be fire formed.

40 gr. bullet	14 gr.	4227 powder	2675 fs
	15	4227	3125

Standard twist: 16″

R-2 Lovell

There are a large number of versions of the so-called .22/3000 Lovell. The original .22/3000 was made by Hervey Lovell. As soon as this original cartridge appeared, numerous gunsmiths and experimenters grabbed the idea and brought out their own versions. The most popular of these was the R-2. The word "was" is used because the popularity of the .22/3000 has dropped off a great deal in favor of the more powerful rimmed .22 cartridges such as the Wasp and Improved Zipper. Nevertheless, the R-2 is still a very good cartridge and primed empty cases are still available from Griffin and Howe. Before the advent of the Griffin and Howe factory brass, cases were made by necking the old .25/20 brass to .22. The original .22/3000 Lovell was the .25/20 case necked to .22 using the original shoulder angle and long neck. The R-2 has a shorter neck, longer body and sharper shoulder. This little cartridge is highly efficient, flexible, and accurate and one of the best varmint cartridges for thickly settled areas where reasonably high velocity with mild report is desirable. During the extensive experimentation with different versions of the .22/3000 several versions known as the "Maximum Lovell" appeared. These maximum cases have very short necks, absolute minimum body taper and sharp

MAXIMUM LOAD LISTED SHOULD BE APPROACHED WITH CARE

shoulders for the greatest capacity possible. Some held as much as 20 gr of 4198.

40 gr. bullet	14 gr.	2400 powder	3100 fs
	16	4227	3400
	17.5	4198	3340
45	8	4227	1880
	16	4227	3280
	17.5	4198	3150
50	16	4227	3100
	17	4198	3050
55	17	4198	3050
	12	2400	2660

Standard twist: 14″

.222 Remington

The .222 Remington is one of the later commercial introductions in .22 calibre. It is a small rimless cartridge midway in size between the .218 Bee and the .22/250. The popularity of this cartridge among bench rest shooters is gaining rapidly and it is proving to be a very fine varmint cartridge especially in the eastern part of the country. There are a few so called "improved" versions but none produce much over the standard version.

45 gr. bullet	20 gr.	4198 powder	3000 fs
	20.5	4198	3095
	21	4198	3230
	21.5	4198	3295
	18	4227	3250
	21.5	3031	2660
	22	3031	2775
	22.5	3031	2845
	23	3031	2905
	23.5	3031	2955
	24	3031	3090
50	19.5	4198	2870
	20	4198	2955
	20.5	4198	3060

MAXIMUM LOAD LISTED SHOULD BE APPROACHED WITH CARE

	21	4198	3130
	24	4320	2765
	24.5	4320	2840
	25	4320	2945
	25.5	4320	3005
55	19	4198	2855
	19.5	4198	2950
	20	4198	3010
	20.5	4198	3095
	21	4198	3165
	22	4320	2525
	22.5	4320	2580
	23	4320	2685
	15.5	4227	2685
	16	4227	2695
	16.5	4227	2785

The following loads are recommended for Norma and Nobel powders.

48 gr. Cast Gas-check bullet

	7 gr.	Sporting Ballistite powder	
			1800 fs
	10	Nobel's Hornet	2000
45 gr. Jacketed	22	Norma 200	3250
50	16	Nobel's Hornet	3000
	21.5	Norma 200	3200
	15.4	Norma 202	2900
55	20	Norma 200	3000

Standard twist: 14", 16"

.222 Remington Improved

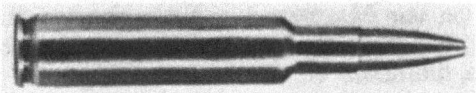

There are numerous versions of the "improved" .222 Remington cartridge all of which are about the same. The idea of the "improved" .222 Remington is namely to increase the capacity of the case to give a corresponding increase in velocity. Accuracy is probably unchanged. The following loading data is for the Kilbourn or "K" version.

MAXIMUM LOAD LISTED SHOULD BE APPROACHED WITH CARE

50 gr. bullet	16 gr.	4198 powder	3230 fs
	20	4198	3425
	19	HiVel#2	3220
	23	HiVel#2	3410
	22	4895	3150
	26	4895	3360
	20	3031	3210
	24	3031	3480
	21	4064	3180
	25	4064	3350
	23	4320	3165
	27	4320	3340
	23	H380	3025
	27	H380	3225
55	15	4198	3065
	19	4198	3290
	21	4895	2935
	25	4895	3140
	23	3031	3240
	26	HiVel#2	3030

Standard twist: 14", 16"

.222 Remington Magnum

This is the latest Remington .22 cartridge. It is very similar to the .222 Remington except in length. It is .1993 longer from the base to the top of the shoulder and is .150 longer overall. This means the neck on the Magnum is a little shorter than the neck on the original .222, but that the case holds measureably more powder. The head or rim diameter of the two cartridges is the same; they have the same shoulder angle and the same body taper. .222 chambers can easily be deepened to accept the longer and more powerful .222 Remington Magnum. It is not practical to try to change rifles which use a clip or detachable box type magazine, but the 722 Remington rifle requires minimum action work to convert it to accept the 222 Magnum. Like the original .222 Remington, this new .222 Magnum is a very fine varmint cartridge, and doubtless is just as accurate as the shorter cartridge.

MAXIMUM LOAD LISTED SHOULD BE APPROACHED WITH CARE

LOADING DATA 271

45 gr. bullet	24 gr.	4198 powder	3670 fs Maximum
50	22	4198	3305
	23	4198	3460
	26	Ball C	3150
	27	Ball C	3300
	28	Ball C	3450
	25	3031	3308
	26	3031	3458
	26	4320	3050
	27	4320	3158
	28	4320	3406
55	21	4198	3174
	22	4198	3299
	23	4198	3424
	26	Ball C	3125
	27	Ball C	3299
	28	Ball C	3373
	26	4895	3227
	27	4895	3370
	27	4320	3207
	28	4320	3325
	29	4320	3444

Standard twist: 14", 16"

.222 Remington Magnum Improved (Ackley)

This cartridge is exactly the same as the "improved" or K .222 Remington except for its greater overall length and resulting greater capacity. Since this version has been made only by request, no loading data is available but loads for the standard .222 Remington Magnum can be increased about 5%. This should make an exceptionally fine 6mm cartridge for use with light or medium weight bullets from 60 to 80 grains.

Standard twist: 14"
Special twist: 16"

MAXIMUM LOAD LISTED SHOULD BE APPROACHED WITH CARE

5.7 x 43 (.222 Eichhorn Lynx)

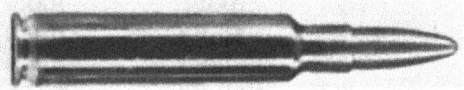

This is a cartridge developed by Dr. Edgar L. Eichhorn of Arcadia, California, otherwise known as the .222 Eichhorn Lynx. It is sort of an "improved" .222 but the length of the body is the same as the .222 Magnum with the neck shortened so that the overall length of the case is the same as the .222 Remington. This blown out version uses the common minimum body taper design with 40° shoulder. It has proven to be a very efficient little cartridge. Cases are easily made by simply shortening the standard .222 Remington Magnum to the proper length of 43mm and then fire forming in the usual manner, so common with other "improved" cartridges, in rifles which accept factory loads. This cartridge could easily become of interest to bench rest shooters because of its high flexibility and exceptional accuracy.

45 gr. bullet	25 gr.	3031 powder	3405 fs
	26	3031	3580
50 gr. bullet	23.5	Ball-C #2	2640
	24.5	Ball-C #2	2780
	25.5	Ball-C #2	2940
53.6 (diepressed)			
	24.6	H380	2500
	26.8	H380	2660
	28.6	H380	2850
56	18	4198	2720
	19	4198	2865
	20	4198	2965
	21.5	4198	3105

Standard twist: 14"
Special twist: 10", 12"

.224 ICL Benchrester

MAXIMUM LOAD LISTED SHOULD BE APPROACHED WITH CARE

LOADING DATA

The ICL Benchrester is an extremely short, straight bodied and sharp shouldered cartridge of relatively small powder capacity. It is supposed to have about the same capacity as the .219 Wasp, and is made by necking down and shortening the .250/3000 case to produce sort of a rimless version of the popular target cartridge. This small case was designed with sharp shoulder and minimum body taper for use with the slower burning powders, such as 4320 and 4350. Cases are relatively difficult to form, and this or similar cartridges are not recommended for shooters without a great deal of experience. Many similar versions have made their appearance from time to time over a period of many years, several being made from the .220 Swift and .30/06 cases.

Bullet	Charge	Powder	Velocity
45 gr. bullet	25 gr.	3031 powder	3341 fs
	28	3031	3721
	29	3031	3921
55	25	3031	3341
	28	4320	3461
	30	4320	3586
	31	4320	3721
	26.5	4895	3231
	30	4350	3236
	31	4350	3291
	31.5	4831	3211
63	29	4350	2996
	30	4350	3041

Standard twist: 14″

Donaldson Wasp

There have been many versions of the so called Wasp cartridge. The late Vernor Gipson claimed to be the originator, but as the idea gained popularity, especially among the bench rest clan, the Donaldson version has become the most popular and may well be termed "standard" so far as the Wasp cartridge is concerned. The Donaldson Wasp is considered to be one of the very best and most accurate target cartridges and of course, is as well adapted to varmint shooting as it is for target work. Its bench rest suitability is probably mostly due to its more or less ideal capacity for the .224 bore.

MAXIMUM LOAD LISTED SHOULD BE APPROACHED WITH CARE

Actually there is nothing startling in its design which might be termed conservative and sound. Cartridges of this type derive the greater part of their reputation for accuracy from the great care taken in loading the ammunition and the great care in the selection of components which go into the highest grade target rifles made for it. Actually quite similar results are possible from a variety of cartridges in this class when the same care is exercised in making both the ammunition and rifles. Cartridges like the Wasp, .22/250, Arrow (the Wilson Arrow is a target version of the .22 Swift), .222 Remington and others have their periods of popularity among target and bench shooters. Wasp cases are made by necking .219 Zipper brass back to relocate the shoulder at the proper point and the necks trimmed off to produce correct over all length. Cases can also be made from any other case with the same rim diameter and thickness (except the .303 Savage). These include .22 Savage HP, .25/35, .30/30 etc. The number of dies necessary varies from one or two to several depending on which cases are started with. Most shooters of Wasp rifles go to great lengths to produce cases of identical capacity, with reamed necks to insure neck concentricity. A multitude of loads have been developed for the Wasp cartridge, only a few of which will be given here. The Wasp is a fire formed case and good snappy charges do the best job of fireforming.

45 gr. bullet	31 gr.	4320 powder	3560 fs
	31	4064	3640
	30	3031	3780
	25	4198	3610
50 gr. bullet	27	3031	3573
	29	3031	3685
	29	4064	3420
	32	4064	3605
	28	3031	3600
	29	3031	3685
55 gr bullet	27	3031	3350
	28	3031	3500
	29	4064	3355
	30	4320	3435
63 gr. bullet	27.5	3031	3485

The following loads are recommended for Norma and Nobel powders.

MAXIMUM LOAD LISTED SHOULD BE APPROACHED WITH CARE

LOADING DATA

48 gr. Cast Gas check bullet			
	10 gr.	Nobel Hornet Powder	1180 fs
	7 gr.	Sporting Ballistite	1550
45 gr. Jacketed	31	Nobel 41	3600
50	31	Nobel 41	3510
55	29	Nobel 41	3550

Standard twist: 14"

.219 Zipper

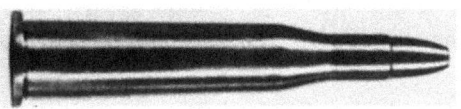

The .219 Winchester Zipper was introduced by the Winchester factory in 1937, and came out for use in the modernized version of the familiar Model 94 Winchester known as the Model 64. The .219 Zipper is simply the necked down .25/35 with slightly shorter neck. The forerunner of this cartridge was the old .22/4000 Neidner which is practically identical and was used for many years before the introduction of the Zipper for a target and varmint cartridge. The .22/4000 like the Zipper was made from .25/35 brass and this .22/4000 was made in a rimless version as well. The rimless version was the .25 Remington necked down to .22 and gave identical ballistics to the rimmed version.

45 gr. bullet	20 gr.	4198 powder	3125 fs
	22.5	4198	3400
	22	HiVel‡2	3200
	26	HiVel‡2	3500
	23	3031	3205
	26	3031	3600
	28	H380	3385
	31	H380	3565
	32	H380	3660
50	28	H380	3350
	30	H380	3475
	31	H380	3550
	25	4320	2950
	29	4320	3400
	24	3031	3200
	26	3031	3450
	23	4895	3200

MAXIMUM LOAD LISTED SHOULD BE APPROACHED WITH CARE

	28	4895	3425
	23	HiVel‡2	3170
	26	HiVel‡2	3420
55	28	H380	3200
	31	H380	3350
	25	4320	2950
	29	4320	3350
	23	4895	3035
	28	4895	3200
	26	3031	3300
	25	HiVel‡2	3260

The following loads are recommended for Norma and Nobel powders.

48 gr. Cast Gas-check bullet			
	7 gr.	Sporting Ballistite powder	1500 fs
	11	Nobel's Hornet	1900
50 gr. Jacket	28	Nobel 41	2975
55	27	Nobel 41	3000

Standard twist: 16"

.22/4000 (Senior Varminter)

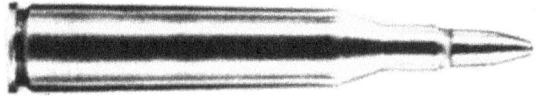

The .22/4000 and its commercial counterpart, the .219 Zipper has proven to be a satisfactory and accurate cartridge, and a good choice for use both on target shooting and varmint shooting. The .219 Zipper gained a rather poor reputation for accuracy because of the lever action rifle for which it was developed. This inaccuracy was due entirely to the rifle and should not have a reflection on the cartridge itself, and it is a very good selection for use in single shot rifles based on the Martini, Winchester, Remington and other good single shot actions.

45 gr. bullet	40 gr.	3031 powder	3750 fs
	43	3031	4000
55 gr. bullet	41	3031	3660
	45	4064	3862

MAXIMUM LOAD LISTED SHOULD BE APPROACHED WITH CARE

63 gr. bullet	36	3031	3240
	38	3031	3346

Standard twist: 16"

.219 Zipper Improved (Ackley)

Introduced in 1938, the Ackley Improved Zipper developed into a popular wildcat cartridge for use in single shot actions, Krag actions and Model 54 Winchesters made for the .30/30 cartridge. There are several other versions equally good such as the Mashburn and K Zipper. Originally it was simply a fire forming proposition. After world war two the brass furnished by the factories does not have the "stretch" necessary, therefore cases are best made by reforming and shortening .30/30 or .32 Special brass. This requires a pair of forming dies. The capacity of the case is about midway between that of the Wasp and Swift. It is a very satisfactory cartridge producing satisfactorily high velocities for the highest order of varmint rifle. Exclusive of the difficulty of forming cases since the last war, this cartridge can be recommended without reservation.

45 gr. bullet	27 gr.	4198 powder	3630 fs
	32	3031	3740
	34	3031	3950
	35	4064	3918
	36	4320	3780
	37	4320	3930
	35	4895	3781
50 gr. bullet	32	3031	3713
	33	3031	3782
	34	4064	3759
	35	4064	3817
	35	4320	3700
	34	4895	3583
55 gr. bullet	31	3031	3431
	34	4320	3450

Standard twist: 14"

MAXIMUM LOAD LISTED SHOULD BE APPROACHED WITH CARE

.219 ICL Wolverine

This is the ICL version of the Improved .219 Zipper. It is quite similar to, but a little more radical, than the older, and quite popular Ackley version. Ballistics of most of the versions of the Improved Zipper are similar to the popular .22/250. Modern brass doubtless will give trouble fire forming the ICL version, as it does with the others. Some years ago, standard factory Zipper ammunition would fire form with little difficulty. In late years, this has not been the case, probably being due to a change in the factory brass. It is best to make cases from .30/30 brass, by using a set of forming dies to neck and shorten the cases to the correct dimensions. All Improved Zippers, including the ICL, are relatively efficient cartridges, and have always given a good account of themselves in compeiton with the various popular varmint and target cartridges such as the .22/250, Wasp and Swift.

45 gr. bullet	32 gr.	4895 powder	3750 fs
50	30	4895	3575
55	32	4320	3450

Standard twist: 14"

.22/30/30 Improved (Ackley)

This cartridge uses the full length 30/30 case necked to .22 and blown out with minimum body taper and 40° shoulder. This one was developed after the post war brass began to give fire forming troubles in the Zipper. It has proven to be a very fine and practical cartridge for the same actions for which the Improved Zipper or Wasp is used. It develops appreciably higher velocities than either of these two cartridges, actually velocities almost equal the standard Swift. It is a very fine long range varmint cartridge. Like the Improved Zipper, it can be used in the Model 99 Savage actions.

MAXIMUM LOAD LISTED SHOULD BE APPROACHED WITH CARE

LOADING DATA

45 gr. bullet	38 gr.	4895 powder	3972 fs
	38	4064	4050
	38	4320	3980
50 gr. bullet	38	4895	3926
	38	4064	4030
	36	3031	4010
	34	3031	3800
	36	4320	3680
	38	4320	3890
55 gr. bullet	35	4895	3500
	36	4895	3605
	37	4320	3650
	36	4064	3810

Standard twist: 14″

.22 Varmint-R

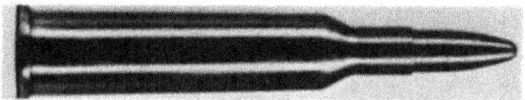

The .22 Varmint-R is a cartridge which was originally designed by the late G. B. Crandall of Woodstock, Ontario, Canada. Mr. Crandall was a famous Canadian gunsmith who decided to develop a good .22 cartridge based on the .303 brass which is so easily obtained in all the British Commonwealth countries. He necked the .303 British down and shortened it to an overall length of 2.31 with a 29° shoulder angle. The idea was to develop a rimmed cartride based on the .303 British case very close to the .22/250. Most loads recommended for the .22/250 except the heaviest can be used in the .22 Varmint-R for about the same velocity.

40 gr. bullet	38 gr.	4320 powder	3860 fs
50	34	3031	3532
	35	3031	3650
	36	4320	3730
55	30	3031	3380
	34	4320	3490
	35	4320	3530
63	34	4320	3375

Standard twist: 14″

MAXIMUM LOAD LISTED SHOULD BE APPROACHED WITH CARE

.22/.303 (Sprinter)

The .22/.303 (Sprinter) was originated by Australian gunsmiths to create a high powered .22 cartridge at less cost than imported .22 calibre cartridges. It is made by shortening the .303 case and necking down to .224 and is a very efficient cartridge. As most of the rifles chambered for this cartridge are based on the SMLE action, the loads are kept to a low pressure level.

Bullet	Charge	Powder	Velocity
48 gr. Cast Gas-check bullet	7 gr.	Sporting Ballistite Powder	1500 fs
	11.5	2400	1850
	11	4227	1700
	11	Nobel Hornet	1800
45 gr. Jacketed	33	4895	3650
	32	4740	3600
	33	3031	3600
	33	4064	3200
	CD	Nobel 41	3350
50	31	4895	3500
	30	4740	3450
	30	3031	3375
	33	4064	3150
	33.5	Nobel 41	3250

Standard twist: 14"
Special twist: 16"

.22/250

Also known as the .22 Varminter and the .220 Wotkyns Original Swift (.220 WOS). The .22/250 is one of the most flexible and accurate varmint cartridges ever designed and has won as many or

MAXIMUM LOAD LISTED SHOULD BE APPROACHED WITH CARE

LOADING DATA

more bench rest matches than any other cartridge. It is better adapted to reduced loads than the standard Winchester .220 Swift and is one of the over all satisfactory cartridges in .22 calibre for all types of varmint shooting. It has also been used with good success on large game such as deer. It was originated by Cap. Wotkyns and further developed by J. E. Gebby and J. Bushnell Smith. Gebby named the cartridge the Varminter and copywrited the name. This is the reason other gunmakers have mostly called it the .22/250 because it is simply the .250 Savage case necked to .22 with a 28° shoulder.

Bullet	Powder chg.	Powder	Velocity
40 gr. bullet	29 gr.	4759 powder	3990 fs
	40	4320	4580
45	33	4320	3440
	35	3031	3775
	37	3031	3995
	36	4895	3830
50	33	3031	3680
	35	3031	3925
	36	3031	3955
	35	4320	3625
	38	4320	3965
	15	4759	2570
	34	4895	3570
	35	4895	3675
	38	4064	3880
55	31	3031	3485
	32	3031	3580
	23	4198	3040
	25	4198	3190
	34	4320	3550
	36	4320	3640
	38	4320	3845
63	37	4350	3350
	39	4350	3580
	31	3031	3590

The following loads are recommended for Norma and Nobel powders.

Bullet	Powder chg.	Powder	Velocity
45 gr. cast gas-check bullet			
	8 gr.	Sporting Ballistite powder	1600 fs
	11	Nobel Hornet	1800
45 gr. Jacketed			
	35	Nobel 41	3650
50	36	Norma 103	3700

MAXIMUM LOAD LISTED SHOULD BE APPROACHED WITH CARE

	38	Nobel 41	3800
55	36.5	Nobel 41	3675
63	39	Norma 204	3600

Standard twist: 14"

.22/.250 Improved

Two versions of the Improved .22/250 are illustrated. One has the less radical 28° shoulder like the regular version of the .22/250 or .22 Varminter. The other has the more radical slightly venturified 40° shoulder. Both are very good cartridges and both use standard .220 Swift loading data giving practical identical ballistics. There is little choice between the two shoulder angles or any in between. Such a choice is always influenced by the shooter's own ideas and preferences. The cases are made by necking .250/3000 Savage brass down to .22 then firing it in the improved chamber to fire form. Good stiff loads are best for fireforming. Very few or no cases are lost in the fire forming step. The minimum body taper and sharp shoulder angle minimize the forward flow of brass or lengthening of the cases to the extent that case trimming is rarely necessary.

Use standard Swift loading data.

Standard twist: 14"

.22/303 (.22 Rocket or .22/4000)

This is a .22 cartridge made by necking the .303 British case down to .22 without any other change. It produces a cartridge in the Swift or Varminter class as is adapted for use in single shot rifles, and bolt or lever action rifles designed for use with long rimmed cartridges. It was originally designed in Australia for use

MAXIMUM LOAD LISTED SHOULD BE APPROACHED WITH CARE

on Australian varmints and has gained wide popularity in other countries where the .303 British cartridge is common and easily obtained. This cartridge is very similar to many American versions made by necking .30/40 brass.

48 gr. Cast Gas-check bullet

	9 gr.	Sporting Ballistite powder	1800 fs
	11	2400	1800
	11.5	4227	1750
	11	Nobel Hornet	1775

45 gr. jacketed

	35	4895	3575
	35	3031	3550
	30	4740	3200
	34	4740	3500
	37	4064	3650
	35	4320	3600
	37	Nobel 41	3600
50	35	4895	3450
	33	4740	3400
	36	4064	3740
	36	Nobel 41	3675
55	32	4895	3300
	32	4740	3350
	35	Nobel 41	3500

Standard twist: 14"
Special twist: 16"

.220 Swift

This is the original factory "hot rod." It is still one of the hottest and still travels in the fastest company no matter how wild a "wildcat" is put against it. The Swift case is maximum for a .224 bore and with top loads, the barrel life is relatively short. When handloaded to speeds 200 to 300 foot seconds under maximum, barrel life is fairly good and the loads are still powerful enough for almost any varmint shooting. It has proven to be extremely deadly on deer in spite of what some authorities want to think and

MAXIMUM LOAD LISTED SHOULD BE APPROACHED WITH CARE

would like to have their readers think. Of course, the .220 Swift will produce outstanding failures on big game just as the larger calibres do and critics of high velocity (progress) have been quick to pounce on such failures and publicize them to the utmost. The same authorities have the same type of failures with larger cartridges but always are able to produce an alibi for the big ones. If a hundred head of deer could be killed under average conditions with the .220 Swift and another hundred head killed with the .30/06 under the same average conditions, it is quite likely that the Swift would come off the winner. Many states have legislated against the Swift and similar cartridges for use on deer and larger game. It is very doubtful that very many of the legislators making these regulations ever hunted with a Swift. (Doubtless, most of them belong to the .30/30 fraternity.)

The .220 Swift was supposedly originated by Wotkyns but he used the .250/3000 cased necked to .22. Winchester finally used the 6mm Lee Navy cartridge necked to .22 and modified it by making it a semi-rimmed case with standard rim diameter. The Wotkyns version became known later as the .22/250, Varminter and Wotkyns Original Swift (WOS).

29 gr. bullet	40 gr.	3031 powder	4620 fs
	42	3031	4665
45	36	3031	3575
	38	3031	3825
	42	4064	3950
	40	4320	3925
50	38	3031	3975
	40	4064	4010
	39	4320	3865
	38	4895	3845
	34.5	HiVel#2	3530
	37	HiVel#2	3790
55	37	4064	3705
	38.5	4064	3865
	36.5	4895	3690
	41	4895	3860
	34.5	HiVel#2	3510
	43	4350	3650
63	36	4064	3480
	40	4350	3420

The following loads are recommended for Norma and Nobel powders.

MAXIMUM LOAD LISTED SHOULD BE APPROACHED WITH CARE

48 gr. Cast Gas-check bullet

	11	Sporting Ballistite powder	1880 fs
	9 gr.	Nobel Hornet	1800
45 gr. Jacketed			
	41	Nobel 41	3900
	37	4740	3800
	40.9	Norma 203	4110
50	39	Nobel 41	3860
55	35	4740	3540
	37	Nobel 41	3675
63	39	Norma 204	3425

Standard twist: 14"

.220 Swift Improved

The illustration shows the Ackley version. There are many others which are quite similar or almost identical, and with similar characteristics. There is little advantage in any "improved" Swift unless it may be some version which features a shortened case of lesser capacity. Such a case would be a Wildcat and not an "improved," since an "improved" cartridge is one whose chamber will still accept factory ammunition. The three best known versions are the Ackley, Weatherby Rocket and the Kilburn. This family of cartridges is slightly overbore capacity and consequently not as efficient or flexible as some of the smaller ones such as the .22/250, "improved" Zipper, etc. Their only advantage is mechanical. They extract better and cases last longer for the hand loader. The standard Swift cases lengthen and require frequent trimming which finally results in case separation near the solid head. Ballistics are not much superior to the standard cartridge unless it might be with relatively heavy bullets with slow burning powders.

50 gr. bullet	34 gr.	HiVel‡2 powder	3630 fs
	38	HiVel‡2	4000
	37	4895	3680
	41	4895	4050
	35	3031	3615
	39	3031	3985

MAXIMUM LOAD LISTED SHOULD BE APPROACHED WITH CARE

	41	4064	**3980**
	42	4320	4100
	45	H380	3905
55	34	HiVel#2	3550
	38	HiVel#2	3920
	37	4895	3555
	41	4895	3980
	39	3031	3900
	41	4064	3880
	42	4320	4020
	44	H380	3825
63	40	4350	3300
	43	4350	3675

Standard twist: 14″

.224 Durham Jet

This is a .22 cartridge developed by Charles Durham of the Custom Rifle Shop, 4550 East Colfax Avenue, Denver 20, Colorado, who has developed a full line of cartridges from .22 to .375 calibre. The entire Durham line is what can be described as "improved" since they utilize minimum body taper and sharp shoulder design. All of the Durham Magnum series have a well adjusted bore and case capacity ratio. None are what can be termed overbore capacity, therefore they are all relatively efficient. The .224 Durham Jet is based on the .243 Winchester case necked down to .22, but with the neck lengthened to .300. This is done by setting the front of the shoulder back. It has a 40° shoulder angle and an overall length of 2.045. Mr. Durham recommends relatively heavy .22 calibre bullets beginning with the 55 grain and extending up through 70 grains, but he gives no loading data for bullets heavier than 63 grains. The new .224 Sisk bullet weighing 70 grains should be very well adapted for this Durham cartridge. The following loads are recommended by Mr. Durham and they were made in a 22¼ inch barrel with a 12 inch twist. Loads are near maximum and should be approached with caution.

MAXIMUM LOAD LISTED SHOULD BE APPROACHED WITH CARE

55 gr. bullet	46 gr.	H380 powder	3980 fs
60	46	H380	3780
63	45	H380	3740
	46	4350	3710
	47.5	4350	3790

Standard twist: 14″

.224 ICL Marmot

The ICL Marmot is an Improved Swift, but unlike some other versions, factory loads cannot be fired in the ICL chamber. Doubtless this is a good idea, because the standard Swift is certainly maximum capacity for a .224, and when blown out, without shortening, it becomes quite badly over bore capacity. By shortening the case in order to keep the capacity to a better level, a good efficient cartridge is the result, possessing the advantages of an "improved" design, without getting over bore capacity, which always happens when the original length Swift case is blown out.

50 gr. bullet	38 gr.	4895 powder	3875 fs
55	36	4895	3755

Standard twist: 14″

.22 Hi-Power

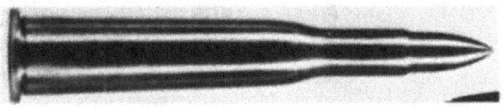

The .22 Hi-Power Savage cartridge was designed by Charles Newton before 1900 and was one of the original high velocity cartridges introduced to American shooters. About the time of World War I it created a great deal of controversy among hunters. There were a great many arguments pro and con and being something new, many old timers strenuously objected to the high velocity principle. It soon became nicknamed the "Imp," and for many

MAXIMUM LOAD LISTED SHOULD BE APPROACHED WITH CARE

years the cartridge was often referred to as the .22 Savage Imp. The original cartridge was loaded with the 70 grain bullet for a velocity of approximately 2800 fs, and this was in the first days of jacketed bullets and some trouble was experienced with the bullets disintegrating upon impact which is a phenomenon now encountered in rifles such as the .220 Swift, and like the Swift it is important to use good bullets in the .22 Hi-Power which will hold together. Some difficulty was experienced with accuracy mostly due to the fact that the only rifle available was the featherweight take-down Model 99 Savage. This cartridge has now become obsolete and has been legislated out of use in many states mostly through the ignorance of the legislators who have little conception of what the potentialities are of this and similar cartridges when they are loaded with good bullets which will react as all good bullets are intended. Even though ammunition is no longer available cases are easily made by simply necking .25/35 brass, or with the proper set of dies, cases can be fairly easily made from .30/30 or .32 Special brass. The .22 Hi-Power does not use standard .22 calibre bullets. The standard bullet diameter for the .22 Hi-Power is .227-.228 as compared to .224 for a .22 cartridge such as the .220 Swift.

45 gr. bullet	17 gr.	2400 powder	3100 fs
55	22	HiVel‡2	2560
	24	HiVel‡2	2795
	25	4895	2800
	28.5	4895	3100
	25	3031	2860
	29.5	3031	3200
70	21	4198	2700
	22	HiVel‡2	2660
	24	HiVel‡2	2900
	25.4	HiVel‡2	3070
	25	4895	2575
	26	4895	2690
	27	3031	2990
	30	4320	2930

The following loads are recommended for Norma and Nobel powders.

60 gr. Cast Gas-check bullet			
	12 gr.	Nobel's Hornet powder	
			2000 fs
70 gr. Jacket	25.5	4740	2750
	29	Nobel 41	2800

Standard twist: 12″

MAXIMUM LOAD LISTED SHOULD BE APPROACHED WITH CARE

.22 Hi-Power Improved

The Improved .22 Hi-Power was developed many years ago and was one of the first of the Ackley series of "improved" cartridges and although it never gained any great popularity it is still one of the best .22 cartridges for use with relatively heavy bullets. It is very well adapted for use in single shot rifles as well as the Savage Model 99 rifle. This cartridge is similar to the more popular .22/30/30 except it uses the .227-.228 bullets of 60 and 70 grain, and bullets should be of the heavy jacketed variety when used for hunting big game such as deer. Cases were made by simply firing factory ammunition in the improved chamber, but this can no longer be done, so cases must be made from .30/30 brass, and this is done by using the regular set of .22/30/30 forming dies.

60 gr. bullet	30 gr.	4320 powder	2900 fs
	35	4320	3480
70	32	3031	3250 est.
	34	3031	3450 est.
	36	4320	3250 est.
	38	4320	3425 est.

Standard twist: 12"
Special twist: 10"

.228 Belted Express (Ackley)

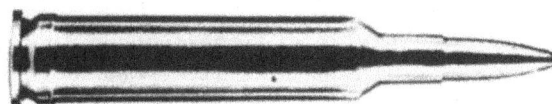

This is an Ackley cartridge made by swaging a belt on the .30/06 case and then shortening and necking the case to accept the .227 bullet. This cartridge appeals to shooters who prefer a belted case. They feel the belt affords a better headspace adjustment and produces a stronger case. This version is better and more efficient than the standard .228 and produces identical velocities, but it is a very difficult case for the average handloader to

MAXIMUM LOAD LISTED SHOULD BE APPROACHED WITH CARE

make correctly and very few shooters are interested in making cases which require so many dies and so many operations. At least three swaging operations are necessary to belt the cases. Another three are required to neck down and cut the cases to length. If a shooter is willing to go to all this trouble and bother, the Belted Express can be highly recommended. Formed cases are now available from Nonte-Taylor, 1112 Buena Vista, Decatur, Illinois. Other cartridges have been developed on the 06 belted case to make a series of belted express cartridges (Ackley and Hightower). The series included the .224 Belted Express (similar to the .22/250), .228 Belted Express described above, the 6mm or .243 Belted Express and the .25 Belted Express. The 6mm version used both the shortened .228 belted case necked up and a full length 06 case. The .25 used the full length case only. Col. E. L. Lyman, USMC retired, has used the .228 Belted Express on big game in many parts of the world and highly praises this cartridge.

70 gr. bullet	44 gr.	4350 powder	3415 fs
	45	4350	3660

Standard twist: 10"
Special twist: 9", 12"

.22 Newton

The .22 Newton was originated many years ago by Charles Newton, the originator and manufacturer of Newton rifles. This cartridge is simply the 7x57 (7mm Mauser) necked down to accept a 90 gr .228 bullet. The original .228 Ackley was the same cartridge except for the bullet which was a .227, 70 gr. The Newton company manufactured only a very few rifles in this calibre and the company went out of existence before it was fully developed. The long pointed 90 gr bullet required an 8 inch twist and it was quite effective on fairly large game. The velocity of the .22 Newton as claimed by the factory was 3103 fs. Little loading data is available but doutless good loads could be developed using the 90 gr Barnes bullet and either 4350 or 4831 powders. Barnes bullets are available in this diameter up to 150 gr in weight, but for those over 90 gr it would

MAXIMUM LOAD LISTED SHOULD BE APPROACHED WITH CARE

doubtless be necessary to use .50 calibre machine gun powder. (Available from Hodgson.)

Original load was 40 gr Dupont 15½ for 3103 fs
Dupont 15½ powder has been replaced by 4064

Standard twist: 8"

.228 Krag (Ackley)

This is a .228 cartridge with ballistics similar to the .228 Belted Express. It is a very fine cartridge for actions requiring a rimmed case. Actions such as the high side Winchester single shot, Remington Hepburn, Sharps Borshardt, Farquharson, P14 Enfield and others. Cases are relatively easy to make up by using a set of three forming and trimming dies.
Standard twist: 9," 12"

.228 Ackley Magnum

This is one of the older Wildcat cartridges. Introduced in 1938, it has enjoyed a small degree of popularity as a combination varmint and big game rifle. Its record on big game, including Alaskan and African varieties has been impressive. This is mainly due to the fact that almost all bullets made for this calibre have been made of heavy tough jacket type of a special controlled expansion design. The 70 gr bullet has been most popular and has been the one used on big game mostly. Top velocity for this weight of bullet is about 3650 fs although a few rifles have been tested which would better this velocity substantially. (There are other rifles which would not reach this velocity, also, hence the average figure of 3650 fs.) The use of this cartridge on big game all over the world has proven the effectiveness of a small calibre high velocity bullet provided a bullet of CORRECT DESIGN AND CONSTRUCTION is used.

MAXIMUM LOAD LISTED SHOULD BE APPROACHED WITH CARE

Cartridges of this class are often ineffective on big game because thin jacketed bullets disintegrate upon impact thus producing superficial or surface wounds. This invariably leads to the condemnation of high velocity bullets for use on big game by certain "authorities" who either do not have the imagination or the gumption to make further tests with correct components, or they do not want to admit high velocity bullets are any advance over medieval ideas. The only door open to improvement in ballistics is by way of higher velocities and bullet manufacturers will be forced to change their 19th century ideas in the not too distant future.

Cases for the .228 are made by necking down and shortening the common .30/06 brass for a capacity of around 55 gr. This is definitely over bore capacity for the .228 bore, therefore the cartridge is relatively inefficient and barrel life is not too good. The case was made as large as possible with the idea of sacrificing efficiency and barrel life in favor of the highest practical velocity for a 70 gr bullet. Also, the longer case functions through standard bolt actions better than extremely short ones thus making it more reliable in the field. Bullets are currently produced by Sisk and Barnes, and factory bullets made for the .22 Savage HP by the factories can be used, but with the latter, powder charges have to be reduced slightly and they are definitely good only for varmint shooting.

60 gr. bullet	46 gr.	4064 powder	3900 fs
	44	3031	4010
70 gr. bullet	44	4350	3451
	46	4350	3650
	35	3031	3300
75 gr bullet	44	4350	3325

Standard twist: 9," 12"

.226 Barnes QT

The .226 Barnes QT is a highly specialized cartridge developed by Fred N. Barnes, maker of the Barnes Custom Bullets of Grand Junction Colo. It is based on the regular .257 Ackley "improved" case which is necked down to accept the .226 bullet, commonly referred to as ".228." Like the larger Barnes 6.5 Magnum QT, it requires an extremely short twist and it has been found that a 5½

MAXIMUM LOAD LISTED SHOULD BE APPROACHED WITH CARE

inch twist is required for the extremely long 125 grain .226 bullet which is about 1¾ inch in length. This cartridge has proven to be very deadly on big game at extreme ranges because of its high sustained velocity and also because of the extremely tough Barnes bullet.

        125 gr. bullet   49 gr.   .50 Cal MG powder   2700 fs
Standard twist: 5.5"

.230 Ackley

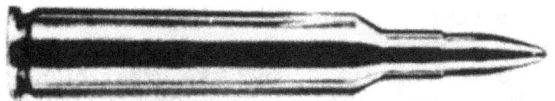

This is a recent development and has been brought out since some states have enacted laws requiring a minimum calibre of .23. The standard case is the old .228 Ackley magnum necked up very slightly to accommodate the .23 calibre bullet. Cases are made by necking and shortening the .30/06 case. Bullets are available with heavy jackets in 60, 70 and 75 grain weights. Also, they will be available in the same weights with thin jackets for varmint shooting. Although only a few of these rifles have been made, several reports on game show clean one-shot kills and judging by the results on big game with the original .228 over a period of almost twenty years it is bound to be extremely effective on all kinds of big game found in the United States. It actually shoots flatter over game ranges than such cartridges as the .250 Magnum, and like the .228, it is one of the flattest shooting cartridges yet introduced. In addition to its extremely flat shooting qualities, it is extremely pleasant to shoot, especially by recoil conscious shooters.

bullet	powder charge	powder	velocity
60 gr. bullet	41 gr.	4064 powder	3660 fs
	45	4064	3990
	47	4350	3675
	48	4350	3760
70	45	4350	3510
	47	4350	3580
	49	4350	3685
	48	4831	3450
75	45	4831	3185
	47	4831	3335
	44	4350	3395
	46	4350	3510

Standard twist: 10"

MAXIMUM LOAD LISTED SHOULD BE APPROACHED WITH CARE

.230 LLF

This is a .230 cartridge which was developed by the L.L.F. Die Shop, Eugene, Oregon. It is simply the .243 Winchester case necked down to accept the .23 calibre bullet with no other alteration. This small cartridge has given extremely good results on deer and antelope at long range, and like other high velocity cartridges, only well constructed bullets should be used for big game. The L.L.F. Die Shop specializes in the manufacture of bullet swaging dies and most of the loads which have been developed for this cartridge have been with the well designed bullets made in the L.L.F. swaging dies. Most of the work so far has been done with the 70 grain L.L.F. bullets. Bullets are also available from R. B. Sisk and Fred N. Barnes. The L.L.F. Die Shop is developing 60 and 65 grain bullets. These light bullets made in the L.L.F dies are showing promising results especially for varmint shooting, but they have not yet been tried on big game.

70 gr. bullet	47 gr.	4350 powder	3665 fs
	48	4350	3733
	49	4350	3805
	47	4831	3475
	49	4831	3575
	44	4895	3735
	45	H380	3635
	51	H450	3600

Standard twist: 10″

Special twist: 9″, 12″

MAXIMUM LOAD LISTED SHOULD BE APPROACHED WITH CARE

LOADING DATA

6 x 47 Remington

This is a cartridge which has been made in limited numbers by custom gunsmiths ever since the introduction of the .222 Remington Magnum, and even before that, the standard .222 Remington was necked up to 6mm. Recently the Remington Arms Company has become interested in this small 6mm cartridge and has been building a few target rifles on a custom basis which have been used in bench rest matches. This will very likely prove to be a very fine cartridge for bench rest, target and varmint shooting. As yet there is not a very complete list of loads available, but the Remington Company recommends the following.

    75 gr. bullet 25.5 gr. 3031 powder 2550 fs
                      26.5   3031   2650

Standard twist: 14″

.240 Madame

The .240 Madame is a small 6mm cartridge which incorporates the best features of the various "improved" series of cartridges, but has only a 30 grain powder capacity and designed for use with light and medium weight bullets. It was designed by M. J. Foerster of Laramie, Wyoming. The case is made by necking down and shortening .25 Remington, or with additional forming dies from .30 to .32 Remington brass. This is a relatively new

MAXIMUM LOAD LISTED SHOULD BE APPROACHED WITH CARE

cartridge and not too large a list of loads have been developed, but a test gun gave the following loads.

70 gr. bullet	28 gr.	3031 powder	3110 fs
	30	3031	3340

Standard twist: 10"

6mm/.30/30

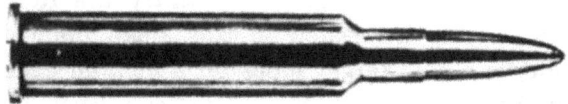

The 6mm/.30/30 is identical to the .22/.30/30 except for the neck diameter and this is an even better cartridge than the .22.30/30 and has proven to be highly satisfactory for use in lever action and single shot rifles. For example, the Model 99 .22 Highpower rifle can easily be converted to 6mm/.30/30 by reboring and rechambering the barrel and make a very slight adjustment in the action to create a rifle which for all practical purpuses is equal to the .243 Winchester. In states where the .22 Highpower has been outlawed, the 6mm/.30/30 offers a solution to the problem. Cases are made by necking .30/30 or .32 Special to 6mm which normally requires three operations, plus fire forming. The 6mm/.30/30 has a case capacity which is almost ideal for the 6mm bore.

75 gr. bullet	36 gr.	3031 powder	3430 fs
	37	3031	3450
85	34	3031	3025
	35	4895	3150
	37	4895	3300
90	35	4320	2920
	37	4320	2990
	39	4320	3110
	41	4320	3345
105	34	4320	2430
	36	4320	2885
	38	4320	3015

Standard twist: 10"

MAXIMUM LOAD LISTED SHOULD BE APPROACHED WITH CARE

6mm/250

This is simply the .250/3000 necked down or the .22/250 necked up. Many owners of shot out .22/250's have their barrels rebored and the chamber left original except necked up to accept the 6mm diameter bullet. This should be a very efficient cartridge and of special interest to target shooters interested in the 6mm bore. Very fine hunting rifles could be made up on the Model 99 Savage action made for the .250 or .300 Savage cartridges.

80 gr. bullet	36 gr.	3031 powder	3235 fs
90 gr. bullet	33	3031	3020
	36	3031	3200

Standard twist: 10"

6mm HLS

The 6mm HLS is a new 6mm cartridge developed by the Consolidated Armslube Company of Alamogordo, New Mexico. This company is composed of three partners and the HLS designation refers to the three originators. Their aim was to produce a cartridge of ideal capacity for the 6mm bore for use with light and medium weight bullets from 60 to 90 grains, which in the writer's opinion is about the best range of bullets for any 6mm cartridge. They also kept in mind longer case life and better barrel life than is possible with the various commercial 6mm cartridges. The case is about the overall length of the original .250/3000, but actually it is simply the .244 Remington shortened to .250/3000 length so that any one chambering for this cartridge can use standard .244 Remington reamers and simply run them in only to the correct depth for this shorter cartridge. And, in a pinch, standard .244 Remington dies can be shortened and utilized for the HLS cartridge. Being nearly ideal capacity for

MAXIMUM LOAD LISTED SHOULD BE APPROACHED WITH CARE

the 6mm bore it is an extremely efficient cartridge as well as being flexible and accurate. Although this is a relatively new development, it is already beginning to show up very well in bench rest matches as well as proving itself to be a highly satisfactory cartridge.

60 gr. bullet	33 gr.	4320 powder	3243 fs
	38	3031	3772
75	38	3031	3561
85	38.8	4064	3333

Further testing by Bob Hutton of "Guns and Ammo" developed the following loads:

60 gr. bullet	34 gr.	4320 powder	3145 fs
	39.2	4320	3515
	41.2	4320	3700
	45.3	4320	4070
75	39.7	4320	3360
	42	4320	3560

Standard twist: 12"
Special twist: 14"

6mm Donaldson International

The 6mm Donaldson International was designed by Harvey Donaldson of Fultonville, New York who had an idea that a more efficient cartridge could be developed for bench rest and varmint shooting. Like the Remington International, the Donaldson case is also derived from the .250/3000 brass, but could also easily be made out of .30/06 or other brass with standard head size. The 6mm Donaldson International has a conventional body taper which can be described as quite normal and has a 30° shoulder which is also quite normal. Unlike the Remington version, the Donaldson version has a more conventional neck length and the overall result is a very attractive little cartridge.

MAXIMUM LOAD LISTED SHOULD BE APPROACHED WITH CARE

LOADING DATA

60 gr. bullet	30 gr.	3031 powder	3330 fs
	32	3031	3650
	33	Ball C	3330
100	33	4320	3125
	36	4350	3225

Standard twist: 14"

6mm Remington International

The 6mm Remington International is a necked down and shortened version of the old .250/3000 case, and made by necking the .250/3000 brass to 6mm and at the same time setting the shoulder back a considerable distance in order to produce a case of lesser capcity. The cartridge is peculiar because it has such a long neck, being left the same length as the original .250/3000. It should also be noted that this cartridge is almost the direct opposite of many of the "improved" lines of wildcats in that it has a very steep body taper. The parent .250/3000 case was originally designed with excessive body taper and since the diameter at the shoulder remains the same on the Remington International, the steepness of the body taper is exaggerated by the shorter body. The design in general however produces an effective cartridge because the loading density is high, and has proven quite successful for target shooting.

65 gr. bullet	36 gr.	3031 powder	3720 fs
75	35	3031	3450
	36.6	4064	3360
82	34.5	3031	3425
	36.6	4064	3310
90	32	3031	3250
	36	4064	3240
100	34.5	4064	3065

Standard twist: 12"

MAXIMUM LOAD LISTED SHOULD BE APPROACHED WITH CARE

6mm Durham International

This is a small well designed 6mm cartridge based on the .243 Winchester brass, but shortened to an overall length of 1.875. The shoulder angle is 40° and has the typical minimum body taper feature. This cartridge has a relatively long neck and the general overall design should make it a practical target cartridge as well as a good varmint cartridge. It is quite similar to the 6mm Donaldson International. The following loads were developed in a 22 inch barrel with 10 inch twist.

75 gr. bullet	38.5 gr.	3031 powder	3440 fs
	41.5	H380	3370
100	41	4350	3130
	38	H380	2970

Standard twist: 12"

6mm Lee Navy

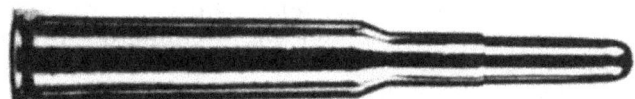

This cartridge was once the official cartridge used by the U. S. Navy. There were several rifles produced for this cartridge the most common being the Winchester Lee which was a straight pull bolt action. The service cartridge was loaded with 112 gr full patch bullet at 2560 fs. Barrels were made with a 7½ inch twist. Regular sporting ammunition with a 112 gr soft point bullet was made for many years and this little cartridge accumulated a fine record on many types of American game. It came twenty five years before modern powders and therefore had a struggle for survival. It was finally made obsolete and no longer is there any ammunition for it available. A few shooters who still have cases reload for it, and the following loads have been developed.

MAXIMUM LOAD LISTED SHOULD BE APPROACHED WITH CARE

LOADING DATA 301

75 gr. bullet	35 gr.	3031 powder	3150 fs
	37	3031	3300
112	28	3031	2500
	30	3031	2650
	32.6	HiVel#2	2710
	27	4064	2200
	32.5	4064	2540

all velocities estimated.
Standard twist: 6.5"

.240 Cobra

This was one of the most popular 6mm wildcats before the introduction of the two new factory cartridges. The 240 was originated by Homer Brown and the cases are made by necking the .220 Swift cases up to 6mm and fire forming them to final shape. This cartridge has almost ideal capacity for the 6mm bore and produces relatively high velocity with good barrel life. Being a semi-rimmed case, it requires some magazine alteration on standard bolt actions to make it feed reliably.

75 gr. bullet	43 gr.	4064 powder	3550 fs
	42	4350	3430
85	42	4895	3790
	43	4895	3406
	47	4064	3406
95	48	4350	3540

Standard twist: 12"

.243 Winchester

MAXIMUM LOAD LISTED SHOULD BE APPROACHED WITH CARE

The .243 Winchester was introduced in 1955 by the Winchester factory and was one of the first factory 6mm's. It has attained great popularity and has been used very successfully on big game. It is proving to be as effective on all species of game found in the United States, as many larger cartridges. It was introduced about the same time as the .244 Remington and the ballistics of the two cartridges are very similar. In fact, with identical bullets these two cartridges should be equally satisfactory in the field. The .243 is simply the .308 Winchester necked to 6mm. Another cartridge made by necking the .308 case is the .25 Souper and there is no reason why this same one necked to .270 should not prove to be equally good. A .270 on this case would produce ballistics a little stronger than those given for the .270/3000 Savage shown in this book.

70 gr. bullet	36 gr.	3031 powder	3375 fs
	38	3031	3520
	40	3031	3650
	39	4064	3410
	40	4064	3530
	42	4064	3700
	42	4320	3505
	44	4320	3650
	45	4320	3700
	47	4350	3480
75	35	HiVel‡2	3150
	37	HiVel‡2	3300
	37	3031	3310
	39	3031	3440
	38	4064	3260
	39	4895	3250
	41	4895	3365
	40	4320	3310
	46	4350	3415
	46.5	4350	3510
80	41	4320	3320
	45	4350	3360
85	38	3031	3310
	39	3031	3375
	38	4064	3135
	39	4064	3175
	41	4064	3345
	42	4320	3375
	44	4350	3180
	45	4350	3360

MAXIMUM LOAD LISTED SHOULD BE APPROACHED WITH CARE

87	38	4064	3120
	43	4350	3150
90	35	3031	3000
	36	4064	3005
	37	4895	2995
	38	4320	3050
	42	4350	3105
	45	4350	3240
100	35	3031	3045
	36	3031	3100
	37	4064	2950
	39	4320	3000
	40	4350	2865
	41	4350	2975
	41.5	4350	3010
	42	4350	3060
	44	4350	3165
105	40	4350	2880
	42	4350	2980
	44	4831	2850
	46	4831	2970

The following loads are recommended for Norma and Nobel powders.

75 gr. bullet	37 gr.	4740 powder	3350 fs
	40	Nobel 41	3325
	42.1	Norma 203	3500
80	42.5	Norma 103	3450
	36	4740	3300
	40	Nobel 41	3300
	45	Norma 204	3400
90	36	Nobel 41	3000
100	43.2	Norma 204	3070

Standard twist: 10″

.243 Winchester Improved (Ackley)

MAXIMUM LOAD LISTED SHOULD BE APPROACHED WITH CARE

The Ackley "improved" .243 Winchester is quite similar to the Mashburn version with little or no preference between the two. The Ackley version was created by popular demand, not with the idea of greatly improving on the original .243 Winchester which itself might be termed an "improved" cartridge. The following loads are a combination of tests made by the author in a 26 inch barrel, and results from tests made at the Hutton Rifle Ranch by Bob Hutton of "Guns and Ammo."

60 gr. bullet	50 gr.	4350 powder	3930 fs
	42	4320	3460
	45	4320	3860
	47	4320	3930
	48	4320	4170
75	39	4895	3390
	41	4895	3550
	43	4895	3630
	45	4350	3400
	47	4350	3655
	49	4350	3720
	50	4350	3765
	42	4064	3495
	44	4064	3710
	42	H375	3390
	44	H375	3495
90	39	4895	3225
	41	4895	3500
	44	4350	3310
	46	4350	3390
	47	4350	3460
	48	4350	3575
	46	4831	3310
	48	4831	3420
	49	4831	3490
	39	4064	3270
	49	H450	3310
	39	H380	3025
	40	H380	3090
100	41	4350	2910
	42	4350	3040
	43	4350	3135
	44	4350	3175
	45	4350	3235
	46	4350	3290
	47	4350	3400

MAXIMUM LOAD LISTED SHOULD BE APPROACHED WITH CARE

LOADING DATA

105	45	4831	3090
	48	4831	3135
	50	4831	3340
	37	4895	2885
	39	4895	2960
	45	4350	3265
	45	4831	3040
	48	4831	3290
	46	4064	2960
	49	H450	3180

Standard twist: 10″

.243 RCBS

The .243 RCBS is an "improved" version of the **.243 Winchester** developed by Fred Huntington of the R.C.B.S. Gun and Die Shop of Oroville, California. It is similar to the Ackley version except that it does not use as steep a shoulder angle. The following list of loads was submitted by Mr. Huntington.

75 gr. bullet	47 gr.	4350 powder	3660 fs
	48	4350	3750
	49	4350	3850
80	47	4350	3590
	48	4350	3685
	49	4350	3730
85	46	4350	3530
	47	4350	3585
	48	4350	3655
90	46	4350	3430
	47	4350	3525
	48	4350	3580
100	43	4350	3150
	44	4350	3235
	45	4350	3300
	46	4350	3380

MAXIMUM LOAD LISTED SHOULD BE APPROACHED WITH CARE

The following loads were tested by the Hutton Rifle Ranch in a 26 inch barrel,

105 gr. bullet	41 gr.	4350 powder	2790 fs
	42	4350	2870
	43	4350	2995
	44	4350	3040
	45	4350	3135
	46	4350	3235

Standard twist: 10"

.243 Improved (Epps)

This is an "improved" version of the .243 Winchester developed by Ellwood Epps of Clinton, Ontario, Canada. It is the .243 Winchester with a slightly steeper shoulder angle which allows slightly increased loading. Mr. Epps states that standard loads can be increased about two grains for a corresponding increase in velocity. Canadian shooters interested in the Epps line of cartridges should write to Ellwood Epps, Clinton, Ontario and request a copy of his new catalog which should be of great interest to the Canadian sportsman.
Standard twist: 10"

.243 Winchester Improved (Mashburn)

the Mashburn Improved .243 is a blown out version of .243 Winchester with relatively sharp 30° shoulder and minimum body taper. Made by firing factory loads in the Mashburn chamber.

70 gr. bullet	43 gr.	4895 powder	3735 fs
	43	3031	3735
	45	4064	3800

MAXIMUM LOAD LISTED SHOULD BE APPROACHED WITH CARE

LOADING DATA

	47	4320	3825
	49	4350	3600
	49	4831	3575
75	42	4895	3650
	42	3031	3650
	44	4064	3725
	46	4320	3735
	49	4350	3565
	49	4831	3550
85	42	4895	3485
	42	3031	3485
	44	4064	3465
	47	4320	3495
	49	4350	3535
	49	4831	3455
100	38	4895	3165
	38	3031	3165
	39	4064	3135
	41	4320	3145
	45	4350	3215
	47	4831	3245

All data furnished by Mashburn Arms Co. Only MAXIMUM loads given. Start well under MAXIMUM and work up. Standard twist: 10"

.243 Winchester Reynolds Special

The .243 Winchester Reynolds Special was developed by Bob Reynolds who owns and operates a custom gun shop in Tyler, Texas. It is very similar to the Ackley "improved" .243 Winchester but has a 40° shoulder and what can be described as absolute minimum body taper. The body is slightly longer than the Ackley version thus producing a slightly larger capacity case. Mr. Reynolds has been extremely happy with the results obtained with this cartridge and like other "improved" versions of the .243 Winchester, it makes for better mechanical operation including better brass life, extraction etc. Reamers for this version are available from the H. & M. Tool Company. Obviously this is a relatively efficient 6mm cartridge.

MAXIMUM LOAD LISTED SHOULD BE APPROACHED WITH CARE

75 gr. bullet	50 gr.	4831 powder	3320 fs
	44	4064	3510
	46	4064	3580
	43	4895	3415
90	50	4831	3320
	49	4350	3345
100	47	4350	3290

Standard twist: 10″

6mm Belted Express (Ackley)

This is one of the Ackley series of Belted Express cartridges made by belting and shortening the .30/60 case, then necking to hold the desired diameter bullet. This particular cartridge is identical to the .228 Belted Express described previously, except it accepts the standard 6mm bullets instead of the .228 series of bullets. Except for the difficulty of forming or making cases, it is one of the finest of all 6mm "wildcat" cartridges. It has about the ideal maximum capacity for the 6mm bore and the case is a very strong one when properly formed and belted. Formed cases are available from Nonte-Taylor, 1112 Buena Vista, Decatur, Illinois.

75 gr. bullet	40 gr.	4064 powder	3200 fs
	41	4064	3400
	42	HiVel‡2	3580
	40	3031	3390
	45	4350	3390
	44	4064	3500
90	41	4350	3045
	45	4350	3345
	47	4350	3440
100	40	4320	3130
	46	4350	3060

Standard twist: 10″

MAXIMUM LOAD LISTED SHOULD BE APPROACHED WITH CARE

6mm Krag (Ackley short version)

This cartridge is especially adapted to the better single shot actions which require a rimmed case. This medium capacity cartridge is relatively efficient and has been used very successfully on many varieties of big game. It can be highly recommended for the above type of actions for shooters who prefer the 6mm bore. Cases are made by necking and shortening .30/40 Krag brass. It is best to use three forming dies plus the full length sizing die when making cases for a total of four operations.

85 gr. bullet	40 gr.	4350 powder	2958 fs
	36	4064	3045
90 gr. bullet	40	4350	2994
100 gr. bullet	40	4350	3046

Note that the heavier bullets show higher velocity with 4350 than the lighter bullets with the same powder charge. Probably due to heavier bullets building up more pressure for more efficient burning. Doubtless much better loads can be developed for this cartridge. Velocities could be comparable with the commercial 6mm cartridges with properly developed loads.

Standard twist: 10″

.243/.303

The .243/.303 is a fairly recent development of Australian gunsmiths to provide a 6mm cartridge based on the .303 British cases which are so easily obtained in that country. This cartridge gives excellent results on kangaroos and pigs in Australia, and is used in the SMLE actions, but performs even better in the P14 Enfield action. Ballistics are very similar to the factory .243 Winchester cartridge.

MAXIMUM LOAD LISTED SHOULD BE APPROACHED WITH CARE

75 gr. bullet	33 gr.	4740 powder	3200 fs
	33	3031	3175
80	32	4740	3000
	34	Nobel 41	3150
90	34	Nobel 41	2850

Standard twist: 10"
Standard twist: 12"

6mm Krag (Ackley Improved)

This 6mm cartridge was developed for a few 6mm enthusiasts who were interested in a single shot 6mm rifle with high velocity. Cases are made by necking the regular 30/40 Krag to accept the 6mm bullet, then fire forming to produce a case with sharp shoulder and minimum body taper. It has maximum capacity for the 6mm bore.

75 gr. bullet	51 gr.	4350 powder	3809 fs
85	50	4350	3484

Standard twist: 10"

.240 Page Pooper

This is the forerunner of the .243 Winchester factory cartridge, and was originated by Warren Page, the ARMS Editor, of FIELD and STREAM. Mr. Page cooked up the name as a wise crack on the once highly touted .25 Souper, but, the name actually caught on.

The Page Pooper was first made from the 7.62 Nato, which later became the commercial .308 Winchester. The .30 calibre case was necked down with a considerably sharper shoulder, leaving the body the original length. This resulted in a modern sharp shouldered case with a sufficiently long neck.

MAXIMUM LOAD LISTED SHOULD BE APPROACHED WITH CARE

The Page Pooper was considered by the factory, but it was finally decided to use the original shoulder angle, and simply neck the .308 to 6mm. Thus the .243 Winchester came into being with its rather short neck, which makes it less appealing to handloaders. Since the .243 Winchester came out as a factory cartridge, the .240 Page Pooper was never pushed enough to permit the accumulation of any amount of loading data. Actually all loads shown for the standard .243 Winchester, can be used in the .240 Page Pooper.

Standard twist: 10″

6mm Arch

A great deal of work has been done by Dr. E. L. Arch of Wenatchee, Washington with the 6.5x55 Swedish cartridge. He has experimented in great length with an "improved" version in the various bore diameters from 6mm to .30 calibre. This cartridge employs the regular minimum body taper so common to the various "improved" cartridge designs with a very sharp 44° shoulder angle. All of the experimenting has been done with Norma brass and the results have been highly satisfactory; and the Swedish military actions in which most of the tests have been made have proven to be extremely strong. Dr. Arch has even gone so far as to rebarrel one of these actions for the .264 Winchester Magnum, and the action so far has shown no weakness. The following loads were developed in a 12 inch twist 24 inch barrel.

60 gr. bullet	49 gr.	4320 powder	4030 fs
	50	4320	4055
	51	4320	4115
	51.5	4320	4157
	52	4320	4213
	52.5	4320	4248
	53.5	4320	4291

Standard twist: 10″
Special twist: 12″

MAXIMUM LOAD LISTED SHOULD BE APPROACHED WITH CARE

.244 Remington

The .244 Remington is a development made by Remington Arms Company. It is simply the .257 Roberts case necked down to 6mm and increasing the shoulder angle to 26°. The forerunner of the .244 Remington was the .243 Rockchucker originated by Fred Huntington of the RCBS Gun and Die Shop Oroville, California. The original .244 Remington rifles were furnished with a 12 inch twist barrel which probably affected its popularity because handloaders often used bullets heavier than 90 grains and the 6mm barrel with a 12 inch twist will not handle 100 grain or heavier bullets accurately. Therefore, the Winchester .243 with the standard 10 inch twist barrel handled a wider variety of bullets which made it more popular among handloaders. Never the less, the .244 Remington is a very fine cartridge and one which should deserve greater popularity than it has enjoyed since used in a 10 inch twist barrel it is one of the most desirable 6mm cartridges especially well adapted for handloading.

Bullet	Powder charge	Powder	Velocity
70 gr. bullet	35 gr.	4895 powder	3260 fs
	42	4895	3715
	38	4064	3250
	45	4064	3780
	42	3031	3715
	47	4320	3830
75	40	H380	3320
	42	H380	3500
	40	4320	3430
	42	4320	3525
	36	3031	3300
	37	HiVel#2	3300
	39	4895	3290
	46	4350	3435
80	45	4350	3370
	48	4350	3475
	49	4831	3300
	51	4831	3450
	41	H380	3370
	40	4320	3375

MAXIMUM LOAD LISTED SHOULD BE APPROACHED WITH CARE

LOADING DATA

	37	4895	3100
	41	4895	3365
	37	4064	3150
	40	4064	3410
	33	3031	3040
	37	3031	3350
	35	HiVel#2	3240
	37	HiVel#2	3375
85	36	4895	3130
	40	4895	3425
	36	3031	3135
	41	3031	3450
	39	4064	3125
	43	4064	3450
	43	4350	3050
	48	4350	3400
90	40	4350	3000
	43	4350	3150
	45	4350	3275
	45	4831	3000
	48	4831	3200
	50	4831	3360
	34	4895	2880
	37	4895	3100
	39	4895	3230
	35	H380	2810
	38	H380	3000
	40	H380	3100
	30	HiVel#2	2800
	33	HiVel#2	2890
	35	HiVel#2	2870
	36	3031	3110
100	38	4350	2750
	41	4350	2850
	45	4350	3120
	42	4831	2850
	45	4831	3125
	34	H380	2650
	36	H380	2740
	32	4895	2865
	38	4895	3125

MAXIMUM LOAD LISTED SHOULD BE APPROACHED WITH CARE

The following loads are recommended for Norma and Nobel powders.

75 gr. bullet	39 gr.	4740 powder	3400 fs
	42.3	Norma 203	3500
	47.5	Norma 104	3400
	42	Nobel 41	3350
80	41	Nobel 41	3300
	46	Norma 104	3375
90	44.2	Norma 204	3200
	40	Nobel 41	3150

Standard twist: 12"
Special twist: 10"

.240 Page Super Pooper

This cartridge can best be described as another "improved" version of the .244 Remington. It uses more or less the conventional shoulder angle of 28° with the accepted minimum body taper design. The case holds up to 10% more powder than the standard .244 Remington. This like the other "Improved" .244 versions is best used with relatively heavy bullets with slow burning powder.

75 gr. bullet	49 gr.	4831 powder	3280 fs
	51	4831	3410
	45	4350	3210
	47	4350	3350
	40	4064	3300
	42	4064	3465
	40	4895	2550
	42	4895	2660
	37	HiVel#2	3330
90	48	4831	3170
	45	4350	3180
	38	4064	3100
	38	4895	3120
105	45	4831	2900
	42	4350	3000

Standard twist: 10"

MAXIMUM LOAD LISTED SHOULD BE APPROACHED WITH CARE

.244 Remington Improved (Ackley)

The original Improved .244 Remington used the original 26° shoulder with a minimum body taper. Later the more radical version with the 40° shoulder cartridge was introduced by request of several shooters who prefer the extremely sharp shoulder. Since the standard factory .244 Remington cartridge is about the maximum capacity for the 6mm bore, only a modest increase in velocity is possible by any so-called improvement and this increase is only possible by the use of considerably more powder. Cases are made for either version by simply firing factory loads in the improved chamber. Loads for either version.

Bullet	Powder charge	Powder	Velocity
75 gr. bullet	39 gr.	3031 powder	3374 fs
	41	3031	3492
	41	4064	3452
	43	4064	3553
	46	4064	3704
	45	HiVel#2	3775
	44	4895	3539
	46	4895	3610
	49	4350	3598
	52	4831	3550
90	35	4064	3000
	37	4064	3110
	38	4895	3125
	43	4350	3222
	45	4350	3311
	48	4831	3250
	50	4831	3337
	40	HiVel#2	3308
	42	HiVel#2	3452
105	37	4320	2779
	40	4350	2831
	42	4350	2921
	45	4831	2881
	47	4831	2984

Standard twist: 12"
Special twist 10"

MAXIMUM LOAD LISTED SHOULD BE APPROACHED WITH CARE

.244 Remington Improved (Mashburn)

Like the Improved .243, this case is made by fire forming regular factory loads. Mr. Mashburn states that this is the most powerful 6mm cartridge he has tested which can be fire formed from regular factory cartridges.

Bullet	Charge	Powder	Velocity
70 gr. bullet	45 gr.	4895 powder	3820 fs
	45	3031	3820
	47	4064	3865
	48	4320	3885
	52	4350	3785
	52	4831	3765
75	43	4895	3750
	43	3031	3750
	45	4064	3780
	47	4320	3815
	51	4350	3700
	52	4831	3700
85	44	4895	3525
	44	3031	3525
	45	4064	3515
	46	4320	3510
	50	4350	3610
	52	4831	3640
100	39	4895	3140
	39	3031	3140
	42	4064	3145
	43	4320	3150
	47	4350	3400
	49	4831	3450

Standard twist: 12"
Special twist: 10"

MAXIMUM LOAD LISTED SHOULD BE APPROACHED WITH CARE

.243 Rockchucker

This is a very fine cartridge designed by Fred T. Huntington. It is simply the standard .257 Roberts necked down with a 32° shoulder. Before the advent of the .244 Remington cartridge the .243 Rockchucker was gaining wide popularity as a varmint and big game cartridge. Since the introduction of the .244 Remington which is identical for all practical purposes (the only difference being 6° in the shoulder angle) almost all shooters interested in this class of cartridge settle on the Remington because of the availability of factory ammunition. Handloading data should be identical and interchangeable.

bullet	powder charge	powder	velocity
70 gr. bullet	40 gr.	3031 powder	3595 fs
	42	3031	3715
	43	4064	3630
	45	4064	3780
	45	4320	3630
	47	4320	3830
75	50	4350	3672
	51	4350	3615
	53	4831	3432
	44	4320	3519
	44	4895	3505
	46	4064	3752
	42	3031	3540
85	39	3031	3330
	41	3031	3460
	41	4064	3285
	43	4064	3445
	42	4320	3280
	44	4320	3440
	46	4350	3275
	48	4350	3400
100	37	3031	3095
	39	4064	3045
	40	4320	3045
	44	4350	3060

Standard twist: 10″

MAXIMUM LOAD LISTED SHOULD BE APPROACHED WITH CARE

.243 JS

The .243 JS is the smallest of the belted Jerry Shannon series of cartridges based on '06 brass and very similar to the Ackley 6mm Belted Express. It is a very interesting cartridge for handloaders who enjoy the complex process of producing belted cases out of rimless brass. Formed cases are available from Nonte-Taylor, 1112 Buena Vista, Decatur, Illinois. The following loads were developed in a 26 inch barrel.

75 gr. bullet	45.5 gr.	4895 powder	3615 fs
	47.5	4895	3700
85	50	4350	3600
	53	4831	3590
87	52	4350	3670

Standard twist: 10"

.243 RKB

.243 RKB has been developed by Mr. Jerry Shannon of Spanaway, Washington. Mr. Shannon has developed a rather complete line of cartridges among which he has developed a series based on the .30/40 Krag, another series on the .30/06 or .270 Winchester and a third series of belted cases based on '06 brass with a belt swaged on very similar to the Ackley line of Belted Express cartridges, and Mr. Shannon has come to the same conclusion concerning belted '06 cases; that they are not practical for the average handloader because of the great difficulty of swaging the belt properly and the great deal additional work of forming the cases properly. Like the Ackley Belted Express series, the Shannon belted cartridges are exceptionally strong durable cases especially well adapted for handloading once the excessive

MAXIMUM LOAD LISTED SHOULD BE APPROACHED WITH CARE

amount of work necessary to make up a batch of cases has been done.

The .243 RKB is a 6mm cartridge of very nearly ideal capacity for highest velocity in the 6mm bore. It is very similar to the short 6mm Ackley Krag and equally satisfactory for the P14 Enfield actions especially which are designed for rimmed cartridges and also good single shot actions. The following loads were tested in a 28 inch barrel.

85 gr. bullet	43 gr.	4895 powder	3500 fs
	50	4350	3550
	52	4831	3500

Standard twist: 10″

.240 Nitro, sometimes called .240 Apex

This is a British cartridge which has been on the market for many years thus proving there is nothing new about the 6mm calibre. This cartridge is about the same length as the full length .30/06, but has a little more body taper thus cutting the capacity somewhat. Although not much work has been done in this country with this cartridge, it should be an excellent one for those desiring a 6mm with maximum capacity for reasonable efficiency, one which should function very smoothly in standard bolt actions because of its long slender, rather streamlined shape. British cases have Berdan primers but cases can be made by belting and necking down 06 brass. Belting method is the same as described for the .228 Express and others of the Ackley-High-Power belted express series. British factory ammunition is available from importers handling English imports. Kynoch loads the 100 gr spitzer bullets to 2900 fs. Doutless, with our own components and with cases formed from 06 brass, velocities could be boosted to the level of the .243 Winchester or better.

Standard twist: 10″

MAXIMUM LOAD LISTED SHOULD BE APPROACHED WITH CARE

.240 Super Varminter

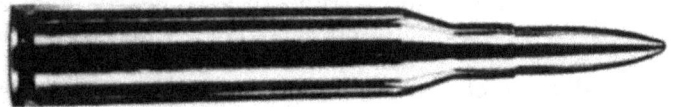

This is a large 6mm cartridge introduced by Jerry Gebby some years ago. It is made by necking the .270 Winchester down to 6mm, (or .30/06) with no other change. It is somewhat over bore capacity but has enjoyed some degree of popularity. With the right bullets such as Barnes or Nosler, it should be one of the finest long range rifles for deer and antelope. Barrel life is relatively short.

Bullet	Powder charge	Powder	Velocity
75 gr. bullet	53 gr.	4064 powder	4008 fs
	54	4064	4100
	60	4350	4000
87	56	4350	3733
100	45	4350	2997
	50	4350	3197
	52	4350	3310
	54	4831	3208
	55	4831	3269

The above loads were gathered from various sources and since compiling them we have had a test gun made and had some of the loads checked with the following results. It will be noted that our test gun did not begin to handle the top loads indicated in the above table which was exactly as expected. In fact, the top loads indicated in the following list could easily be too hot for some individual rifles, therefore special caution should be used with the loads in the preceeding list.

Bullet	Powder charge	Powder	Velocity
75 gr. bullet	46 gr.	4064 powder	3400 fs
	47	4064	3517
	48	4064	3619
	49	4064	3678 MAXIMUM
90	44	4350	2967
	46	4350	3159
	47	4350	3208
	49	4350	3278
	50	4350	3391
	51	4350	3412

Standard twist: 10″

MAXIMUM LOAD LISTED SHOULD BE APPROACHED WITH CARE

.240 Mashburn Falcon

This is a 6mm case made by necking down and shortening the .270 Winchester or .30/06 case. Like all Mashburn cartridges it features the 30° shoulder. It is slightly more powerful than the Improved .244 but it is somewhat over bore capacity which could result in less flexibility and shorter barrel life. This cartridge is quite similar to the older .240 Super Varminter.

Further information is available from the Mashburn Arms, Oklahoma City, Oklahoma.

Standard twist: 10"

.240 Gibbs

The Gibbs line of cartridges was developed by R. E. Gibbs of Viola, Idaho. Essentially the Gibbs line consists of a number of super "improved" versions, all based on the full length .30/06 brass. Cases are made by necking down and fire forming for the ones under .30 calibre and for .30 calibre or larger, the bullets are seated out far enough to firmly fit in the throat and then fired to accomplish the fire forming operation. The design of the Gibbs cartridges employ an absolute minimum body taper with sharp shoulder and extremely short neck which means that the shoulder has been moved forward measurably to create a long body thus increasing the capacity of the case to a considerable greater volume than the original .30/06. Mr Gibbs offers the following information and we quote from his circular.

"It is a well known and proven fact that with any good bolt action rifle the weakest link in the whole pressure chain is the case head itself. It is equally well known that *good case life with repeated loading, accompanied by smooth and easy extraction are the final and controlling factors in working out safe maximum*

MAXIMUM LOAD LISTED SHOULD BE APPROACHED WITH CARE

loads. Under ordinary conditions when a handloader is working out his safe maximum loads, he starts well under what is considered maximum, increases the powder charge a grain at a time, and watches for the usual pressure signs: such as, excessive flattening of primers, ejector marks on the case heads and difficult extraction. These pressure signs are not always infallible since ejector marks will show up much quicker on some makes of brass than on others. The fired primers in G.I. brass, somehow always appear much flatter than in commercial brass." . . . "Though these pressure signs are often misleading, the handloader can *always* depend on good case life with repeated loading, regardless of what brass, powder, primer and bullets he is using in a good bolt action rifle.

It is also well to remember that loads proven to be safe maximum with Super-X or Super Speed brass will be excessive when using Remington or G.I. brass, due to the fact that this brass holds approximately two grains *less* powder.

In *fire forming the* 30 *Gibbs cases*, I have always recommended seating the bullets out to where they firmly, and definitely engage in the rifling when the bolt is closed, though a lot of fellows owning the 30 Gibbs rifles on Springfield, Enfield, 30-S Remington, 98 Mauser, Husqvarna and Model 70 Winchester actions, reported that they had no difficulty in using the regular 30/06 ammunition just as it is. As a matter of interest on this subject of fire forming, I took an Enfield, that had been converted to the 30 Gibbs, and with several clips of G.I. ammunition proceeded to test this method of fire forming for myself and after successfully fire forming the 254 rounds, found that it can be done, though personally I still prefer pulling the bullets and seating them out for the fire forming operations, since this method also works with the Remington 721 30 Gibbs.

Author's note: These directions or suggestions apply equally well to *all* cartridges whether standard, wildcat or improved.

Chamber specifications are not printed in this book by the request of the originator."

The .240 Gibbs is the smallest cartridge of the Gibbs line, and as mentioned it is the full length '06 case necked to 6mm and then fire formed to a much larger capacity than the original '06.

75 gr. bullet	64 gr.	4831 powder	3840 fs
85	62.5	4831	3662
100	61	4831	3450

Standard twist: 10″

MAXIMUM LOAD LISTED SHOULD BE APPROACHED WITH CARE

6mm Magnum (Ackley)

This is another over capacity case which in no way compares to the .243 Winchester and the .244 Remington in their various versions. Cases are made by necking and shortening .300 Magnum brass to accept the 6mm bullet. This case is fire formed the first time it is fired which results in lessening the body taper for better extraction. The 6mm Magnum is not recommended because of its inefficiency, hard to make and expensive brass, and its lack of flexibility. No reliable loading data available, but data given for the .240 Super Varminter can be used as a starter and loads worked up for each individual rifle. Barrel life is relatively short.

Standard twist: 10"

.244 Durham Magnum

The .244 Durham Magnum case is made by shortening and necking down the .300 H&H Magnum case to an overall length of 2.250. This cartridge also utilizes the minimum body taper with 40° shoulder desgin with a medium length neck. Mr. Durham considers this to be about the finest 6mm cartridge available. This cartridge should be a very good long range varmint cartridge as well as a big game cartridge when used with suitable bullets. The following loads were developed in a 24 inch barrel with 10 inch twist, and Mr. Durham states that these loads are maximum and should be approached with caution.

70 gr. bullet	60 gr.	4350 powder	4140 fs
85	57	4350	3850
90	55	4350	3610
100	54	4350	3470

Standard twist: 10"

MAXIMUM LOAD LISTED SHOULD BE APPROACHED WITH CARE

.244 H & H Magnum

This is a British development. It is simply the .375 Magnum necked to 6mm using the original taper. The original factory load is supposed to develop 3500 fs with the 100 gr bullet. This is probably true since some kind of extremely slow burning powder is used. Since its introduction in this country, handloaders have been experimenting with 4350, 4831 and .50 calibre machine gun powders with all weights of 6mm bullets. This is probably the most impractical 6mm commonly available to American shooters from the standpoint of flexibility, barrel life and safety. There have been instances when rifles have blown up using this large case when loaded with a somewhat reduced load. For example, one rifle shot very well with 68 gr of .50 calibre powder, then when the powder charge was reduced 10 gr, the rifle completely disentegrated. This has happened numerous times with other over bore capacity cases when relatively light loads were being used. Several explanations have been advanced but the most sensible one seems to be that slow burning powders should be used in compressed or near compressed charges and when they are used with a large air space there is sometimes an air-powder mixture which creates a detonating effect. Also, like other large capacity cases necked to accept small diameter bullets there is a great variation among individual rifles. One rifle will accept extremely heavy loads while another which checks out the same would be dangerous with the same loads. This is true of all cartridges but becomes more noticeable as the case capacity is increased for any given bore. Barrel life is extremely short. This large cartridge is no good with light bullets and bullets lighter than 90 gr are seldom used. Barrels are usually made with an 8 inch or 10 inch twist. Recent magazine articles have described loading procedures which certainly didn't work for us in our experiments. One load mentioned in one of these articles completely wrecked a perfectly good Enfield action. This cartridge can be recommended only for very specialized use.

75 gr. bullet	73 gr.	4831 powder	3787 fs
90	68	4831	3389
	70	4831	3414

MAXIMUM LOAD LISTED SHOULD BE APPROACHED WITH CARE

	71	4831	3615
105	66	4831	3197
	68	4831	3309
	70	4831	3397

The above velocities were obtained in a 26 inch, 10 inch twist barrel. Other rifles were tried and some would accept the maximum loads shown with similar velocities but a few rifles would not accept the heaviest loads without losing the primers. Obviously great care should be exercised in working up loads. If 4350 powder is used, the loads should be reduced 5% or so under those given for 4831 then carefully work up to maximum for the individual rifle.

Mr. Martin E. Alger, Madison Heights, Michigan, has done a great deal of work with this cartridge, and has obtained a pair of barrels made from the latest Timken steel. These barrels are 28 inches long, with a 10 inch twist. He has submitted the following results from these barrels to date.

70 gr. bullet	77 gr.	4831 powder	3997 fs
85	81	.50 cal M.G.	3629
105	65	.50 cal M.G.	2794
	77	.50 cal M.G.	3416
	81	.50 cal M.G.	3572

On one shot, using the 70 gr. bullet and 77 gr. 4831 powder, Mr. Alger failed to settle the powder in the rear of the case. It produced sort of a sick sounding report and 3292 fs velocity.

After approximately 115 shots, the barrels show up to 2 inches of throat erosion, an indication that barrel life will be well under the 500 round mark.

Standard twist: 10″

6mm Atlas

The 6mm Atlas is a cartridge developed by H. R. Baker, 72 East Second Street, Corning, New York. It is made by necking down the .264 Winchester to 6mm thus producing a badly overbore capacity case which has to be loaded with extremely slow burning powders

MAXIMUM LOAD LISTED SHOULD BE APPROACHED WITH CARE

to get a degree of efficiency. Mr. Baker has experimented quite extensively with duplex loads using mixtures of powders such as 4831 and H570 but concluded that the idea is not practical and that the duplex method is extremely hard on barrels. Good accuracy has been obtained with bullets from 90 to 105 grains. This cartridge could be of interest to wildcatters who are interested in the highest possible velocity out of the 6mm bore. It is probably superior to the .244 H&H which is another cartrigde of this class.

90 gr bullet	81 gr.	H570 powder	3820 fs
100	80.5	H570	3760

MAXIMUM LOAD LISTED SHOULD BE APPROACHED WITH CARE

.25 Hornet

The .25 Hornet is simply the .22 Hornet necked up to a .25 which produces sort of a .32/20 in miniature. This is probably a very old cartridge but it was publicized to some extent by H. R. Longo who developed his version of the cartridge for use in relatively weak single shot rifles such as the Ballard. It is a good cartridge to use to bring these old rifles back to life. This cartridge can be loaded with 12 grains of 2400 powder with the 67 grain bullet for a velocity of 2000 fs and this load develops very low pressure making it easy on actions which are not too strong.

60 gr. bullet	8 gr.	2400 powder	1525 fs
	11	2400	2035
86	6	2400	955
	10	2400	1675

Standard twist: 16″

.256 Winchester

The .256 Winchester is a pistol cartridge made by necking the .357 Magnum down to .25 calibre. This was a Winchester factory project which so far has never been completed, therefore, at present it is classed as a "wildcat" cartridge. It is quite an interesting cartridge for use in single shot rifles and repeating models such as the Model 92 Winchester and Model 94 Marlin. This cartridge does not seem to be very successful for use in revolvers. The following

MAXIMUM LOAD LISTED SHOULD BE APPROACHED WITH CARE

loads were checked in a Model 92 Winchester rifle with a 20 inch barrel.

60 gr. bullet	14 gr.	4227 powder	2450 fs
	15	4227	2520
	18	4198	2725
75	14	4227	2225
	17	4198	2385

Standard twist: 16″

.25/20 Single Shot

This cartridge is supposed to be the oldest .25 calibre centerfire cartridge having been introduced in 1882. It was loaded with 67 and 77 grain bullets. Later it was made with the 86 grain bullet by UMC in 1886. It has been a long time since rifles have been made for the cartridge although at one time all of the rifle makers and manufacturers made their finest models for this and similar numbers. The .25/20 Single Shot is now obsolete, but not forgotten by old time target shooters. This same old .25/20 Single Shot was the basis for the series of .22/3000 cartridges which were so popular in the '30's. The most popular of this series was the R-2 Lovell and .22/3000. R-2 Lovell brass is still available from Griffin and Howe. These R-2 cases can be necked up to make brass for the .25/20 Single Shot. The .25/20 Single Shot cartridge is longer, smaller diameter and has a thinner rim than the currently manufactured .25/20 Repeater cartridge.

60 gr. bullet	8 gr.	2400 powder	1535 fs
	14	2400	2500
	6	Unique	1700
86	5	Unique	1200
	10.8	2400	1880
	8.5	4227	1400

Standard twist: 16″

MAXIMUM LOAD LISTED SHOULD BE APPROACHED WITH CARE

.25/20 WCF

The .25/20 WCF is an old cartridge introduced many years ago by the Winchester Repeating Arms Company for use in their Model 92 rifle. For many years it was used extensively for a woodchuck and other small game cartridge in the Model 92, and it was often used for a deer rifle, although it is considered to be too small for game as large as deer. There are numerous versions of the "improved" .25/20 WCF. Among these are the .255 Dean which is a sharp shoulder short neck version which makes possible a very noticeable increase in velocity. The .255 Dean has been chronographed at 2800 fs with the 60 grain bullet, or at about 25% higher velocity than the standard .25/20 WCF.

60 gr. bullet	11.5 gr.	2400 powder	2200 fs
	12.5	4227	2150
86	8	2400	1476
	9.5	2400	1740
	8.5	4227	1400
	10.5	4227	1725
	5.5	Unique	1795

The following loads are recommended for Norma and Nobel powders.

70 gr. Cast Gas-check bullet
    5 gr. Shotgun Ballistite Powder 1400 fs
    8   Nobel's Hornet 1600

86 gr. Cast Gas-check bullet
    4.5 Shotgun Ballistite 1300
    8   Nobel's Hornet 1575

60 gr. jacketed bullet
    10   Nobel's Hornet 2000

96 gr. jacketed bullet
    9.5 Nobel's Hornet 1700

Standard twist: 16"

MAXIMUM LOAD LISTED SHOULD BE APPROACHED WITH CARE

.25/35 WCF

The .25/35 WCF is also an old cartridge introduced many years ago by the Winchester Repeating Arms Company. It belongs to the .30/30 family of cartridges designed for the familiar Model 94 Winchester. A cartridge introduced about the same time by the Marlin factory was known as the .25/36 and was exactly the same as the .25/35 except slightly longer which allowed the use of 36 grains of black powder instead of 35 grains. The .25 Remington is the Remington version and is a rimless cartridge which was designed for use in the Model 14 Remington pump action rifle, and for the Model 8 Remington automatic. All three of these .25/35 cartridges use the same loading data.

60 gr. bullet	12 gr.	2400 powder	1870 fs
	17	2400	2500
	20	2400	2870
	21	HiVel‡2	2260
	26	HiVel‡2	2840
	31	3031	2940
87	21	4198	2500
	29	4895	2700
	30	3031	2795
	32	4320	2730
100	21	4198	2360
	25	HiVel‡2	2450
	27	3031	2450
	29	4895	2400
	29	4320	2465
117	22	HiVel‡2	2100
	25.5	4895	2300
	26.5	3031	2350

The following loads are recommended for Norma and Nobel powders.

MAXIMUM LOAD LISTED SHOULD BE APPROACHED WITH CARE

LOADING DATA

```
110 gr. Cast Gas-check bullet
      13 gr. Nobel's Hornet powder   1900 fs
100 gr. jacketed bullet
      26    4740                     2400
      28    Nobel 41                 2400
117 jacketed bullet
      25    4740                     2250
      27    Nobel 41                 2200
```

Standard twist: 8"
Special twist: 10"

.25/35 Improved (Ackley)

The Improved .25/35 is another .25 calibre cartridge best adapted to use in good single shot and lever action rifles. Originally it was fire formed in the same manner as the Improved .257 and others which are made by firing factory loads in the improved chamber, however, post war brass will not fire form without rupturing at the shoulder thus resulting in almost complete loss of brass. It is not dangerous to fire factory cartridges in the improved chamber despite the shoulder rupture, but results are disappointing and erratic. This makes it necessary to form the cases from .30/30 or .32 Special brass. This requires two forming dies. Once the cases have been fire formed, they last very well. This medium capacity case is surprisingly efficient and produces velocities practically equal to the standard .250/3000 and .257 Roberts. Even in lever actions such as the Winchester Model 94 or the later Model 64 satisfactorily high velocities can be obtained. It is especially interesting for Savage Model 99 actions. Many states have outlawed the .22 Savage HP. .22HP barrels can easily be rebored and rechambered for the .25/35 Improved with a minimum of action alteration, thus placing this light, handy rifle in a relatively high powered, long range class.

```
69 gr. bullet   39   gr.  3031 powder   3800 fs
                39.5      3031          3850
75              39        3031          3600
87              38        3031          3300
                41        4895          3400
```

MAXIMUM LOAD LISTED SHOULD BE APPROACHED WITH CARE

90	34	3031	3045
	37	3031	3235
	39	3031	3295
	40	4320	3135
100	42	H380	3085
	36	3031	3060
	36	4064	2975
	38	4230	3130
125	32	3031	2635
	34	4320	2575
	36	4320	2765
	36	4350	2575

Standard twist: 10″

.25/35 ICL Coyote

The ICL Coyote is very similar to the Ackley Improved .25/35. Both cartridges are made by fire forming standard .25/35 factory loads. As with the Zipper, brass of recent manufacture is apt to give trouble fire forming, but cases can easily be made by necking down the .30/30 brass. The ICL Coyote and similar Improved .25/35's, are efficient, and surprising cartridges.

87 gr. bullet	32 gr.	4320 powder	2860 fs
	35	4320	3125
	30	3031	3030
	32	4350	2900
	37	4350	3200
100	34	4350	2690
	35	4350	2705
	30	4320	2565
	32	4320	2600

Standard twist: 10″

MAXIMUM LOAD LISTED SHOULD BE APPROACHED WITH CARE

.250/3000 Savage

The .250/3000 Savage was designed by Charles Newton in 1914 to drive an 87 grain bullet at 3000 fs for Savage Arms Corporation. It had the highest velocity of any commercial cartridge at the time of its introduction. It gained immediate popularity in both the 1899 Savage and the Model 1920 bolt action Savage and it is still quite popular. It is a relatively small capacity case which makes for good efficiency and flexibility. It has always been a successful target cartridge also, and is probably still the equal of any standard or wildcat .25 calibre cartridge for bench rest shooting.

Bullet	Charge	Powder	Velocity
60 gr bullet	38 gr.	3031 powder	3550 fs
	35	HiVel‡2	3600
	33	4198	3530
	41	H380	3429
87	30	4198	2940
	35	HiVel‡2	3500
	35	3031	3093
	36	4064	2980
	38	4064	3210
	37	4895	3002
	37	H380	2887
100	36	4320	2850
	37	4064	2925
	34	HiVel‡2	2880
	39	4350	2750
	35	4895	2860
	34	H380	2654
117	28	HiVel‡2	2460
	32	3031	2575
	35	4320	2650
125	38	4350	2675
	42	4831	2700

MAXIMUM LOAD LISTED SHOULD BE APPROACHED WITH CARE

The following loads are recommended for Norma and Nobel powders.

```
80 gr Cast Gas-check bullet
       10 gr. Shotgun Ballistite Powder  1800 fs
       11      Nobel's Hornet            1850
       15      Norma 200                 1600
70 gr. Jacketed bullet
       36      4740                      3250
87 gr. Jacketed bullet
       35      4740                      3000
       37      Nobel 41                  3000
       35.4    Norma 203                 3030
100 gr. Jacketed bullet
       35.4    Norma 203                 2820
       32      4740                      2750
       36      Nobel 41                  2800
120 gr. Jacketed bullet
       31.3    Norma 203                 2645
```

Standard twist: 14"
Special twist: 10", 12", 16"

.250/3000 Improved (Ackley)

This is one of the best of the so called Improved cartridges. It shows a greater percentage of increase in velocity than almost any other. In spite of its superlative characteristics it is the least heard of cartridge in the entire series. There are two styles of the Improved .250 like the Improved .244 Remington. Namely one with the original shoulder angle with the body blown out to minimum taper and the other with the 40° shoulder (illustrated) common to many of the Ackley improved cartridges. The Improved .250 is especially fine for the Savage 99 lever action rifle. Velocities possible with this cartridge in the Model 99 more than equals the standard .257. Used in conjunction with good bullets, it is a very fine big game rifle. Being of almost ideal capacity for the .25 bore it is very efficient and flexible and deserving of much greater popularity than it has heretofore enjoyed.

MAXIMUM LOAD LISTED SHOULD BE APPROACHED WITH CARE

90 gr. bullet	42 gr.	4895 powder	3108 fs
	44	4895	3312
	45	4320	3391
	43	4350	3336
100	42	4350	3129
	43	4350	3276
	38	4064	3130
	40	4064	3271
125	34	4064	2606
	40	4350	2637
	41	4350	2744
	42	4350	2952

Standard twist: 10"
Special twist: 12", 14"

.257 Roberts

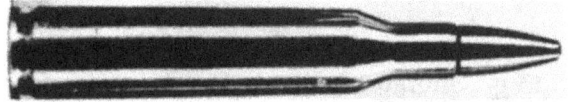

The standard .257 Roberts is shown here for comparison purposes. This is a cartridge originated by N. H. Roberts. In the early thirties he had several fine custom rifles made for the original version which was the 7x57 case necked to .25 using a long sloping shoulder. Later the factories decided to manufacture the cartridge as well as rifles for it. The factories elected to simply neck the 7mm to .25 using the original 21° shoulder which was probably an improvement over the original version. The factory version of the .257 Roberts has proven to be an exceptionally fine cartridge, both for varmint shooting and big game. Case capacity is near maximum for the .25 bore which results in fairly high velocity with good barrel life and flexibility. While studying all available manuals and hand loading books, it was found that wide discrepancies exist for identical loads. For example, one shows a velocity of 2738 fs for the 100 gr bullet and 39 gr of 4064, while another gives this same load 3138 fs or a difference of 400 fs. One shows 44 gr of 4350 driving the 125 gr bullet at 2645 fs, another shows the same load at 2800 fs. The loading data presented here is an approximate average for the available figures for each load in an effort to present velocity figures reasonably close to what may be expected from the average rifle.

MAXIMUM LOAD LISTED SHOULD BE APPROACHED WITH CARE

87 gr. bullet	39 gr.	4895 powder	3100 fs
	36	3031	2820
	41	3031	3200
	39	4064	2900
	42	4064	3150
	42	4320	3200
100	38	4320	2850
	41	4320	2950
	36	4064	2770
	41	4064	3050
	44	4350	2880
	46	4350	3050
120	35	4320	2570
	37	4320	2650
	43	4350	2725
125	44	4350	2725

The following loads are recommended for Norma and Nobel powders.

100 gr. Cast Gas-check bullet			
	11 gr.	Shotgun Ballistite Powder	1800 fs
	15	Nobel's Hornet	1650
	20	Norma 200	1900
87 gr. jacketed bullet			
	40	4740	3150
	41	Nobel 41	3100
100	37.8	Norma 203	2900
	41.2	Norma 204	2900
	40	Nobel 41	2875
117	45	Norma 204	2900
120	36.6	Norma 203	2645
	43	Norma 204	2700

Standard tiwst: 10"
Special twist: 12", 14"

.257 Roberts Improved (Ackley)

MAXIMUM LOAD LISTED SHOULD BE APPROACHED WITH CARE

LOADING DATA

The cartridge illustrated is the Ackley Improved .257. There is a multitude of similar designs although it is doubtful if any other version has gained the world wide popularity attained by this version. Cases are made by firing factory ammunition in the improved chamber. It has the familiar 40° shoulder and minimum body taper. It is a relatively efficient cartridge, flexible and comes close to the mythical "all around cartridge." It is considered to be about the maximum capacity for the .25 bore and still produce satisfactory performance and good barrel life. Like other improved cartridges, rifles chambered for it will still accept factory ammunition which appeals to many shooters who do not wish to re-load all of their ammunition. It is always an advantage in a pinch to be able to purchase a box of cartridges over the counter. The Improved .257 can be readily recommended.

Bullet	Powder charge	Powder	Velocity
60 gr. bullet	50 gr.	3031 powder	3860 fs
	62	4064	3868
	56	4320	3960
	53	H380	3751
87	42	3031	3245
	44	3031	3347
	47	4064	3285
	49	4064	3405
	46	4320	3120
	48	4320	3220
	53	4350	3336
	55	4350	3477
	48	4895	3445
	37	H380	3092
100	44	4064	3088
	43	3031	3165
	46	4064	3165
	50	4350	3257
	47	4320	3322
	42	H380	2862
117	49	4350	3120
	40	H380	2570
125	47	4350	2970
	48	4350	3050

Standard twist: 10"
Special twist: 12", 14"

MAXIMUM LOAD LISTED SHOULD BE APPROACHED WITH CARE

.257 ICL Whitetail

The ICL Whitetail is an Improved .257 Roberts, almost identical to the older Ackley version, the only difference being in the shoulder angle. All improved .257's are extremely good cartridges, and the Whitetail is no exception. Cases are made by firing factory loads in the ICL chamber. This and similar cartridges are especially well adapted to the slow burning powders like 4350.

100 gr. bullet	51 gr.	4350 powder	3215 fs
	46	4064	3225
117	48	4350	3040

Standard twist: 10"
Special twist: 12", 14"

.25 Souper

This cartridge is quite similar to the Improved .250/3000 but came at a much later date and did not gain popularity to any degree. It is made by necking the .308 Winchester case to .25 with no other change. Coming after the introduction of such fine and popular cartridges as the Improved .257 and of course the very fine standard .257, it was not much more than "just another wildcat" with little to recommend it over existing .25 calibre cartridges similar in design and capacity.

60 gr. bullet	45 gr.	4320 powder	4000 fs
	19	2400	2600
87	39	4320	3125
	43	4320	3400
	19	2400	2400
	39.5	HiVel#2	3190
	41	HiVel#2	3270

MAXIMUM LOAD LISTED SHOULD BE APPROACHED WITH CARE

	40	3031	3195
	42.5	3031	3375
	44	4064	3335
	44	4350	3205
100	39	4320	3000
	41	4320	3150
	37.5	3031	2980
	41	4895	3000
	40	4064	3055
	44	4350	3035
	47	4350	3160
	49	4831	3020
117	41	4350	2900
	43	4350	3025
120	44	4350	2755
	44	4831	2780
125	42	4350	2850

Standard twist: 10"
Special twist: 12", 14"

.257 Durham Jet

The .257 Durham Jet is a cartridge based on the .243 Winchester case necked up to .25 calibre with a 40° shoulder minimum body taper design. The neck is lengthened to .300 by setting the shoulder back, thus producing sort of an "improved" .25 Souper which has already proven itself to be an efficient cartridge. The Durham Jet being of a little more modern design should be an even more efficient one. The following loads were developed in a 21 inch barrel with 10 inch twist.

100 gr. bullet	44.5 gr.	H380 powder	3180 fs
	48.5	4350	3330
	49.5	4831	3240
115	51	H450	3100
	52	X573	3150
117	46	4350	3110
	47	4831	3055

Standard twist: 10"
Special twist: 12", 14"

MAXIMUM LOAD LISTED SHOULD BE APPROACHED WITH CARE

.257 Arch

This is another cartridge developed by Dr. E. L. Arch. It is identical to the 6mm Arch except for the neck diameter which is .257. The cartridge has been experimented with all weights of bullets up to and including the 160 grain. The longest bullets were used in a 24 inch barrel with 7 inch twist, while conventional weight bullets were used in a 26 inch barrel with 10 inch twist.

Bullet	Powder charge	Powder	Velocity
60 gr. bullet	54 gr.	4895 powder	4162 fs
	55	4320	4284
75	51	4895	3782
	49.5	4064	3763
	57	4350	3780
87	51	4064	3741
	54	4350	3520
	56	4831	3456
	48.5	4064	3582
	49.5	4895	3579
100	54	4831	3358
117	52.5	4831	3174
120	61	H870	2932
	51	4831	3031
160	50	4831	2699
	61.5	H870	2672

Standard twist: 10"
Special twist: 7", 12", 14"

.25 Short Krag (Ackley)

The .25 short Krag (Ackley) was originally developed for use in single shots for shooters who desired relatively high velocity from a cartridge designed for this type of action and it has proven

MAXIMUM LOAD LISTED SHOULD BE APPROACHED WITH CARE

to be very successful for use in the P14 Enfield giving velocities equal, if not superior to the "improved" .257 Roberts. This medium size .25 calibre case holds slightly over 50 grains of 4350 powder, or about 4 grains less than the "improved" .257 Roberts.

87 gr. bullet	49 gr.	H380 powder	3460 fs
	51	H380	3650
100	43	4064	3265
	44	4064	3287
	49	H380	3412
	50	H380	3460
	49	4350	3300
117	50	4831	3285

Standard twist: 10"
Special twist: 12", 14"

.25/.303 British

The cartridge illustrated is simply the .303 British necked down to .25 calibre and was submitted by James A. Thompson of New South Wales, Australia. This cartridge has proven to be highly satisfactory in Australia and other countries of the British Commonwealth such as Canada and New Zealand, where large numbers of rifles are available for the .303 British service cartridge. Among these are the British Enfield of the various SMLE types and the very fine P14 Enfield, as well as many single shot rifles based on the Martini, Farqharson and other single shots. Cases are easily made by simply necking the .303 British to .25 without any other change. This results in a cartridge which is quite similar to the well known .257 Roberts and is suitable for the same types of game, but the loads are usually kept to the approximate level of the .250/3000. The following loads are recommended for the P14 Enfield, Model 98 Mauser and other strong actions, and for the SMLE type of rifle it is recommended that these loads be cut about 3 grains. The case length is 2.185 and the shoulder angle is 24°.

MAXIMUM LOAD LISTED SHOULD BE APPROACHED WITH CARE

80 gr. Cast gas-check bullet

	10 gr.	Shotgun Ballistite powder	1800 fs
	15.5	2400	2100
	13	Nobel Hornet	1900
70 gr. jacketed	36	4740	3200
87	30	4740	2850
	35	4740	3000
	35.5	4064	3010
	35	4895	3000
	35	3031	3000
	36	Nobel 41	3000
100	28	4740	2600
	33	4895	2750
	34	3031	2800
	35	4064	2800
	35	Nobel 41	2800

Standard twist: 10″
Special twist: 12″, 14″

.25 Krag Improved (Ackley)

This version of the .25 Krag is based on the full length .30/40 Krag case necked down to .25 and blown out by fire forming to create a cartridge with minimum body taper and 40° shoulder. Velocity is relatively high and the case, although being of maximum capacity for the .25 bore, is reasonably efficient and fairly easy to load. (The Improved .25 Krag is too hot with maximum loads, for the standard Krag action and should never be considered for use in this action.) The P14 Enfield and the better single shot actions are best for it. With careful loading this cartridge will nearly equal the .250 Magnums. Loading data for the Improved .257 can be used for this cartridge as well as the loads given for it, since these two cartridges have exactly the same capacity.

87 gr. bullet	48 gr.	4064 powder	3360 fs
	50	4064	3500
	49	HiVel#2	3610
100	50	4350	3090
	52	4350	3270

MAXIMUM LOAD LISTED SHOULD BE APPROACHED WITH CARE

LOADING DATA

	49	4895	3414
	50	4895	3509
125	47	4350	2780
	50	4350	3000
	51	4350	3090

Standard twist: 10"
Special twist: 12", 14"

.257 Big Horn

The .257 Big Horn is a cartridge which has been developed by John C. Ochocki of Pound Ridge, New York. This cartridge was originally made in the .228 Ackley forming dies so that the headspace and case capacity is the same as the .228 Ackley, but the neck was left longer to utilize the full length '06 case. This makes quite an interesting .25 calibre cartridge and appeals to some shooters who prefer cartridges with long necks which many feel reduces throat erosion. It is what can be termed as maximum capacity for .25 calibre thus producing a relatively efficient .25 cartridge suitable for long range big game hunting such as deer, sheep or goats. The following loads have been developed by Mr. Ochocki. The velocities are estimated but should be nearly correct for the average rifle.

87 gr. bullet	45 gr.	4320 powder	3325 fs
	45	4895	3320
	51	4350	3300
	57	4831	3310
120	42	4320	2745
	42	4895	2710
	48	4350	2870
	52	4831	2910

Standard twist: 10"
Special twist: 12", 14"

MAXIMUM LOAD LISTED SHOULD BE APPROACHED WITH CARE

.25 Neidner (standard .25/06)

For those wishing to use full length .30/06 cases necked to .25, this version should prove more satisfactory in the long run than the "improved" version. Cases are made by simply necking '06 cases to .25 without any other change. Although this is probably a more efficient cartridge than the "improved version," it is still probably inferior to the Improved .257 which is considered to be just about maximum capacity for best results in the .25 bore. The standard .25/06 is one of the oldest wildcats using '06 brass. Like other overgrown cases it is best with slow burning powders and relatively heavy bullets.

Bullet	Charge	Powder	Velocity
87 gr. bullet	43 gr.	4064 powder	3229 fs
	43	4895	3204
	45	4320	3307
	54	4350	3345
100	42	4064	3038
	42	4895	2978
	44	4895	3094
	44	4320	3064
	53	4350	3188
	58	4831	3245
120	48	4350	2825
	50	4350	2935
	55	4831	3038
	57	4831	3101

Standard twist: 10″
Special twist: 12″, 14″

.25/06 Vickery

MAXIMUM LOAD LISTED SHOULD BE APPROACHED WITH CARE

This is another version of the "improved" .25/06, and was designed by W. F. Vickery, famous gunsmith in Boise, Idaho. He has been able to obtain very satisfactory results. By comparing the illustration, it will be noted that the main difference between the Vickery design, and other "improved" .25/06 cartridges like the Ackley or ICL, is the venturified shoulder. The only loading data available, is as follows.

100 gr. bullet	55 gr.	4831 powder	3014 fs
	55	4350	3447
	57	4831	3369

Standard twist: 10"
Special twist: 12", 14"

.25/06 Improved (Ackley)

The Improved .25/06 has gained a measure of popularity all over the country and has been used very successfully on all types of big game. Cases are made by necking the standard .30/06 brass to .25 calibre and then fire forming. Cases can be made in two operations. First neck to .270 in a standard .270 Winchester sizing die, or forming die then down to .25 in the full length .25/06 sizer. Great care should be taken to get correct headspace. This cartridge has proven quite dangerous when it is fire formed with a reduced load. Fire forming should be done with a full charge because light loads have a tendency to shorten the cases. In spite of the fire formed cases appearing to be fully formed they may have .050 or more headspace which can be disastrous the second time they are fired. The fire formed case is somewhat over bore capacity which results in close to maximum velocity for the .25 bore, but at the same time makes it critical and hard on barrels. It is not well adapted for reduced loads and should be used with fairly heavy or near maximum loads. Barrels are usually made with 10" twist suitable for the heavier bullets from 100 to 125 gr. In the original Ackley handbook this cartridge was left off the recommended list of wildcat cartridges in favor of the more versatile and more satisfactory Improved .257. This action was quite widely criticized by some users of this particular cartridge

MAXIMUM LOAD LISTED SHOULD BE APPROACHED WITH CARE

as well as by some gunsmiths, however it is still not recommended as being the over all satisfactory cartridge that the Improved .257 is. It is recommended for shooters desiring the highest velocity from the .25 bore regardless of other considerations.

87 gr. bullet	52 gr.	3031 powder	3600 fs
100	55	4350	3450
	47	HiVel#2	3350
117	52	4350	3200
	53	4350	3275

Loads reported by Bob Hutton.

87 gr. bullet	62 gr.	4350 powder	3856 fs
	65	4831	3920
100	58	4831	3561
	60	4831	3441
117	50	4350	3051

Like other over bore capacity cases there is a great deal of variation in the loads that individual rifles will safely accept. Also, seemingly identical rifles will show excessive differences in velocity with identical loads. Handloaders are cautioned to start with somewhat reduced charges and work up to the maximum for each individual rifle.

Standard twist: 10″
Special twist: 12″, 14″

.25/.270 ICL Ram

This cartridge is made by necking down, and blowing out or fire forming in the ICL chamber. Although quite impressive claims are made for this cartridge, it doubtless has the same faults that the Ackley Improved 25/06 has. Many feel these faults outweigh the good points. Like the Ackley version, it appeals to shooters who are interested in the highest velocity possible from a rimless .25 calibre cartridge, without too much consideration for other factors.

MAXIMUM LOAD LISTED SHOULD BE APPROACHED WITH CARE

LOADING DATA

64 gr. bullet	64 gr.	4350 powder	4200 fs
	56	4064	4200
87	62	4350	3845
	63	4831	3710
	65	4831	3920
100	55	4350	3330
	58	4350	3575
	59	4350	3710
	59.5	4350	3750
	63	4831	3710
117	61	4831	3450

Standard twist: 10"
Special twist: 12", 14"

.25/06 Mashburn

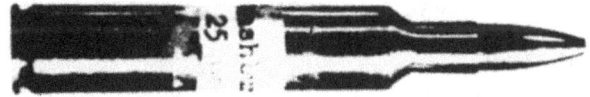

The Mashburn .25/06 can be described as an "improved" .25/06 with 30° shoulder. It is quite similar to the Ackley version, the main difference being the steeper 40° shoulder on the Ackley version. Ballistics for the two cartridges should be the same or about the same and any comments about one also applies to the other. Except for the very MAXIMUM loads, loading data should be interchangeable.

87 gr. bullet	45 gr.	4895 powder	3250 fs
	47	4895	3400
	45	3031	3250
	47	3031	3400
	48	4064	3375
	50	4064	3560
	49	4320	3395
	51	4320	3570
	55	4350	3445
	57	4350	3500
	57	4831	3475
	59	4831	3559
100	41	4895	3050
	43	4895	3200

MAXIMUM LOAD LISTED SHOULD BE APPROACHED WITH CARE

	41	3031	3050
	43	3031	3200
	44	4064	3050
	46	4064	3200
	45	4320	3095
	47	4320	3240
	51	4350	3200
	53	4350	3375
	53	4831	3225
	55	4831	3400
117	52	4350	3200
	54	4831	3250
120	52	4350	3200
	54	4831	3220

Standard twist: 10″
Special twist: 12″, 14″

.250 Durham Magnum

The .250 Durham Magnum was developed as a combination varmint and big game cartridge. This cartridge is exactly the same as the 6mm Durham Magnum except for the bullet diameter. The following loads were developed in a 24 inch barrel with 10 inch twist.

75 gr. bullet	60 gr.	4350 powder	3950 fs
87	58	4350	3800
100	57	4350	3590
117	55	4350	3330

Standard twist: 10″
Special twist: 12″, 14″

MAXIMUM LOAD LISTED SHOULD BE APPROACHED WITH CARE

.250 Bennett Magnum

The .250 Bennett Magnum is a cartridge designed by Byard Bennett, Box 2055, Roswell, New Mexico, who has designed a series of cartridges, all of the same design except the neck diameter. The series consists of .250, .275 and .300 Magnums. All of these cartridges could be described as "short" Magnums. The .250 is quite similar to the .25 Ackley Magnum except that it has slightly lesser case capacity. Mr. Bennett recommends the same loads as given for the .25/06. It is likely that these loads could be increased slightly to be equal to the loads recommended for the .250 Ackley Magnum.
Standard twist: 10″
Special twist: 12″, 14″

.25 Ackley Magnum

This cartridge is made by necking .300 Magnum cases to .25 calibre and shortening. The capacity of this case is less than most of the .257 Magnum family but still large enough to be badly over bore capacity and thus relatively inefficient. See description for .25 Weatherby Magnum.

87 gr. bullet	52 gr.	HiVel#2	3636 fs
	55	4895	3395
	54	4064	3462
	55	4320	3422
	60	4350	3436
	62	4350	3537
	67	4831	3489
100	60	4350	3368
	62	4350	3446

MAXIMUM LOAD LISTED SHOULD BE APPROACHED WITH CARE

120	54	4350	3054
	62	4831	3235
125	60	4350	3200

Standard twist: 10"
Special twist: 12", 14"

.257 Weatherby

The .257 Weatherby is a large capacity belted Mangum .25 calibre cartridge. It was originally made by necking down and shortening .300 H&H Magum cases, using the rounded or venturified shoulder. It is similar or identical ballistically to other versions of the .25 or .257 Magnums such as the Mashburn, O'Neil, Ackley, Holmes, Gipson and a multitude of others introduced during the .25 Magnum epidemic a few years ago. The .257 Weatherby however is the only one of the list which has become a factory cartridge. Like all of the .250 Magnums it is badly over bore capacity and relatively inefficient. It should be loaded with slow burning powders using full charges, preferably with medium and heavy wight bullets. The .257 Weatherby like other .25 Magnums has been used on the heaviest game throughout the world but the effectiveness of this cartridge is likely dependent on the design of the bullet. Only the best bullets should be used when hunting big or dangerous game. Some type of controlled expansion bullet is surely in order for this type of cartridge. The .25 Magnum cartridges as a class are extremely hard on barrels, which makes them somewhat impractical for use in a varmit rifle since the barrel life is extremely short.

87 gr. bullet	52 gr.	3031 powder	3412 fs
	54	3031	3487
	58	4895	3582
	47	4064	3523
	59	4320	3545
	68	4350	3762
	71	4831	3732
100	56	4895	3322
	53	4064	3219

MAXIMUM LOAD LISTED SHOULD BE APPROACHED WITH CARE

LOADING DATA

	56	4320	3338
	66	4350	3592
	68	4831	3461
117	62	4350	3208
120	61	4350	3221
	65	4831	3250

Standard twist: 10"
Special twist: 12", 14"

.257 Critser Magnum

This is a slightly shortened blown out .300 H&H Magnum developed by Carlos Critser for long range game and target shooting. The following loads were developed in a 26 inch barrel with a 9 inch twist, and accuracy up to 1000 yards was reported as excellent. The case is 2.6" with a 53° shoulder and a neck length of .250.

bullet	powder		velocity
60 gr. bullet	62 gr.	4320 powder	4010 fs
	65	4320	4200
	70	4350	3980
	70	4831	3640
	75	4350	4300
	75	4831	3800
87	60	4895	3700
	65	4350	3750
	65	4831	3510
	70	4350	3900
	70	4831	3640
	75	4831	3850
100	60	4831	3140
	65	4831	3510
	68	4350	3725
	70	4831	3705
	75	4831	3890
	75	H570	3210
120	65	4350	3400
	80	H570	3350

Standard twist: 10"
Special twist: 12", 14"

MAXIMUM LOAD LISTED SHOULD BE APPROACHED WITH CARE

.257 Condor

This is a special cartridge designed by Dr. Ramon Somovia of Hollister, California, for use with extremely long heavy .25 calibre bullets weighing at least 160 grains. .257 Condor cases are made by simply necking down the 7x61 S&H brass. This is very similar to the Barnes 6.5 QT (quick twist). .257 Condor barrels are made with a 7 inch twist for the 160 grain .25 calibre bullet as compared to 5½ inch twist in the 6.5 Barnes QT for use with the 6.5 200 grain bullet. Rifles for the .257 Condor are made by the Adobe Walls Gun Shop operated by Gene Bustine of Santa Monica, California. There is very little loading data available. The most successful load are

160 gr. bullet	56 gr.	4831 powder	2730 fs
	57	4831	2920
	54.5	4350	2920
	58	4350	3305
	60	4350	3395

Standard twist: 7"

.258 Condor

The .258 Condor is a large maximum capacity cartridge made by necking down the "improved" .300 Ackley Magnum to .25 calibre. A very similar cartridge could be made by necking down the .300 Weatherby. This cartridge was also designed by Dr. Ramon Somovia. Like the .257 Condor, barrels are made with a 7 inch twist for the 160 grain bullet. Much of the ground work on the Condor line was done by the A. & M. Gunshop of Prescott, Arizona.

160 gr. bullet	75 gr.	Machine Gun Powder	3120 fs

Standard twist: 7"

MAXIMUM LOAD LISTED SHOULD BE APPROACHED WITH CARE

6.5 x 54 Mannlicher Schoenauer

The 6.5 x 54 Mannlicher Schoenauer is a small 6.5 cartridge especially designed for the Mannlicher Schoenauer action, and it might be mentioned here that Mannlicher Schoenauer actions made for the 6.5 x 54 can be converted for larger cartridges only with the greatest difficulty, and such conversions are not recommended. This means that such actions should be rebarrelled for the original cartridge. Although the 6.5 x 54 is a small cartridge, it has given an exceptional account of itself all over the world, even on game as large as elephant. This cartridge has a slightly smaller head than so-called standard cartridges such as the 7 x 57, .30/06, etc., which is the reason for the difficulty in converting Mannlicher Schoenauer actions. The 6.5 Mannlicher Carcano was the official Italian military cartridge used extensively in World War II, and although it is perceptibly shorter than the 6.5 x 54, loading data should be interchangeable.

77 gr. bullet	40.5 gr.	Norma 203 powder	3115 fs.
120	31	HiVel #2	2450
	35	4895	2675
	36	4064	2700
130	34	4895	2400
	37	3031	2550
	38	3031	2610
	39	HiVel #2	2500
	35	4064	2290
	40	4064	2575
139	37.8	Norma 203	2580
140	36	HiVel #2	2475
	35	4895	2400
	36	3031	2450
	39	4064	2480
156	37.4	Norma 203	2460
160	37	4064	2260
	33	HiVel #2	2200

European twist: 7.5"
Standard twist: 9"
Special twist: 10"

MAXIMUM LOAD LISTED SHOULD BE APPROACHED WITH CARE

6.5 Jap Arisaka

This cartridge, one of the Japanese service cartridges, is often referred to as the .25 Jap. It is actually a .256 or 6.5mm using all standard 6.5 bullets measuring .263 - .264. Some of these rifles are extremely accurate, while a few were anything but accurate, mainly because of the over size bores. Many times when reboring these barrels to 7 mm, there is a good amount of rifling left after being reamed to .276. Naturally none of these barrels can be expected to be accurate with the standard .257 bullets which many owners of these rifles attempt to use. The Jap cartridge is of the semi-rim type. Some shooters form cases by working over the .220 Swift and sometimes .30/06 brass is converted in powerful presses. Norma brass is now available for the 6.5 Jap and when properly loaded, and used in a normal barrel, good results can be expected. The 6.5 Jap action is one of the strongest but of such a design as to make it difficult and expensive to convert into a satisfactory sporting rifle.

Bullet	Charge	Powder	Velocity
87 gr. bullet	38 gr.	4320 powder	3050 fs
	36	4064	3000
	36	3031	3120
	38	HiVel #2	3170
	39	4895	3260
100	37	4320	2600
	40	4350	2775
	37	4895	2800
120	36	4320	2720
	36	4895	2780
	35	HiVel #2	2800
	39	4350	2640
	36	Nobel 41	2780
139	33	Nobel 41	2500
	32.8	Norma 203	2430
140	34	4895	2530
	39	4350	2630
	40	4831	2500
156	29.3	Norma 203	2065

Twist - Custom: 9", 10"

MAXIMUM LOAD LISTED SHOULD BE APPROACHED WITH CARE

6.5 Spence Special

This is a cartridge which Mr. George Spence, Steele, Missouri, claims to have developed; however, many others make the same claim and it is known by a multitude of other names. It is similar if not identical to the original 6.5 x 57 Mauser which has been with us for forty years or more. Regardless of the name, this cartridge is simply the .257 Roberts necked up to accept the 6.5mm (.256) bullet, or the 7mm Mauser necked down to accept the same bullet. (The .257 Roberts and 7 x 57 Mauser are identical except neck diameter). This cartridge gained popularity in this country with the advent of a flood of 6.5 Jap Arisaka rifles brought into this country after World War II. No ammunition was available for those rifles but they could be easily rechambered for the Spence Special. This is a good efficient, flexible cartridge and one well worth considering for target shooting and hunting.

Bullet	Charge		Powder	Velocity
87 gr. bullet	42	gr.	H380 powder	2955 fs
	44		H380	3110
	46		H380	3225
	37		HiVel #2	2900
	39		HiVel #2	3060
	41		HiVel #2	3225
120	36		H380	2370
	38		H380	2480
	40		H380	2620
	33		HiVel #2	2460
	35		HiVel #2	2590
	37		HiVel #2	2700
140	32		HiVel #2	2300
	34		HiVel #2	2415
	36		HiVel #2	2520

Standard twist: 9", 10"

MAXIMUM LOAD LISTED SHOULD BE APPROACHED WITH CARE

.263 Express

This cartridge is made by necking the .308 Winchester case down to accept the standard 6.5 bullets. (Can also be made by necking .243 Winchester cases up.) The largest amount of development work has been done by Kenneth L. Waters, of New Canaan, Connecticut, and the loading data submitted below, was developed by him.

This cartridge should be relatively efficient, because of the favorable bore-case capacity. It was developed for hunting big game in the antelope, deer and black bear class. Being short, the cartridges will work in short actions, as well as standard length actions. Also, it can be used in rifles like the Savage 99 and the Winchester 88, which was designed for the .308 length. (Only Model 99's made for the .243 or .308.)

There is a wide range of bullets available, from 77 gr. to 160 gr. (even up to 200 gr.). Mr. Waters selected the .263 diameter for the following reasons:

1. .270 and 06 cases were too long for use in "short actions", especially for long, heavy bullets.
2. The .250 Savage case lacked the capacity for the flat trajectory.
3. The 6.5 Mannlicher case also lacked the capacity for flat trajectory.
4. The .243 Winchester had both accuracy and the velocity, but could not be loaded with a heavy enough bullet.

The 6.5 was selected in preference to the .270 or 7MM, because it was felt that with equal weight bullets, the greater sectional density would produce greater penetration, and flatter trajectory over long ranges.

Author's note: Conversely, the .270 or the 7mm, with equal weight of bullets, presents greater gas area and will produce greater muzzle velocities, which could make them measureably flatter over practical ranges. The term "long range" is quite indefinite. In this book it is considered to be something beyond 300 yards, which is in excess of the average hunter's ability to correctly identify game, and make effective hits.

MAXIMUM LOAD LISTED SHOULD BE APPROACHED WITH CARE

LOADING DATA

Within 300 yards, or even considerably in excess of that, a 140 gr. .270 bullet, for example, has a measureably shorter time of flight than a 140 gr. 6.5 bullet when driven at the maximum velocity from identical cases. The flatter trajectory of the smaller diameter bullets comes only at ranges far in excess of those at which the average man in the field, can make effective hits. Actually, the .308 case necked to .270 or 7MM (or the .243 necked up), should make a worthwhile addition to the family of cartridges having the .308 case as a basis.

Other experimenters have worked with this same cartridge. The RCBS Company offers for sale, loading dies designated 6.5-.308. Doubtless dies are available from other makers, under this, or other names.

The following loading data was submitted by Mr. Waters for the .263 Express. He warns against the use of maximum loads.

Bullet	Powder charge (gr.)	Powder	Velocity
87 gr. bullet	37	4320	3000 fs
	41	4320	3300
	35	3031	3000
	39.5	3031	3275
	36	4064	3000
100	36	4320	2650
	38	4320	2800
	39	4320	2785
	41	4320	3000
	42	4320	3100
120	40	4350	2700
	41	4350	2750
	42	4350	2825
	41	4831	2750
	43	4831	2900
	36	4064	2700
	39	4064	2850
140	38	4350	2600
	39	4350	2650
	40	4350	2700
	41	4350	2750
	42	4350	2800
	43	4350	2850
	40	4831	2600
	41	4831	2650
160	37	4350	2500
	39	4350	2600

Standard twist: 9", 10"

MAXIMUM LOAD LISTED SHOULD BE APPROACHED WITH CARE

.260 A.A.R.

This is a very fine 6.5mm cartridge. It is a cartridge introduced by Apex Rifle Company and is designated by them as the "all around rifle". It probably meets this requirement as well as any cartridge could although some states have legislated against the smaller bores; therefore, the slightly larger Improved 7 x 57 would be the next logical choice in states requiring larger bores. Actually the .260 AAR is the Improved .257 necked up to accept the 6.5 bullet (or the Improved 7mm necked down). This creates a very fine trio of cartridges all on the same basic case and the choice between the three would be determined by the nature of the game to be hunted. The owner of this trio would be well fixed for any North American game hunting as well as target shooting. The .270-.257 Improved could well be added to the trio to form a quartet. The Apex Company gives the following data for the .260 AAR. The .260 AAR is a very fine cartridge for the 6.5 Jap rifle. The conversion can be made by re-chambering the original barrel and minor action alterations.

100 gr. bullet	47.5 gr.	4064 powder	3305 fs.
120	51.5	4350	3160
129	49	4350	2813
	44	4895	2940
	46	4895	3080
140	48	4350	2767
	49	4350	2883

Standard twist: 9", 10"

6.5 x 55

The 6.5 x 55 is the Norwegian and Swedish service cartridge. The service load is a 156 gr. bullet at around 2450 fs. Since the Norwegian and Swedish rifles have been sold in great numbers in the United States, the 6.5 is assuming greater importance than heretofore.

MAXIMUM LOAD LISTED SHOULD BE APPROACHED WITH CARE

The Norwegian service rifle is a Krag, very similar to the U. S. Krag service rifle, except, it is designed for use with rimless cartridges and differs in minor details. It is a relatively strong action, and is better than many of the foreign service rifles for use as a sporting arm.

The Swedish rifle is built on the Model 1896 Mauser, which is about the same as the Models 93 and 95 Mausers, the main difference being the guide rib on the bolt. These actions are well made, but seem to vary considerably in heat treatment. Doubtless they can be recommended for the same cartridges that are recommended for the Model 93 and 95 Mausers. Some difficulty is experienced when attempting to re-chamber the original barrels for wildcat cartridges based on standard American cartridges like the .30/06, because the 6.5 x 55 chamber is somewhat larger near the base, causing a sloppy condition, when standard cases are chambered.

Many use ammunition made from American brass, such as the .30/06, .257, 7MM, etc., but it could hardly be called a safe practice. Only 6.5 x 55 brass should be used in the original chambers. This brass is now being made by Norma and is available in this country. Empty cases as well as loaded ammunition is available in most large sporting goods stores. Norma cases are made for standard American primers.

Author's note: During the past few months there has been an increasing interest in the 6.5 calibre, otherwise called the .256. All sorts of designs, in a multitude of capacities are being advertised by enthusiastic promoters. There are several fine wildcat cartridges now being used, as well as the various foreign imports like the 6.5 Jap, 6.5 x 55, 6.5 x 52 (Italian) and 6.5 x 54 Mannlicher, an old but extremely effective little cartridge.

Among the better Wildcats in the 6.5 size we have the Spence Special which could also be described as the 6.5 x 57 made by simply necking up standard .257 Roberts cases, or necking down the 7 x 57mm brass. The .260 AAR is one of the best 6.5 wildcats and this case is simply the improved .257 Roberts case necked up to 6.5 or the improved 7mm necked down to 6.5. There is also a multitude of 6.5 wildcats based on .270 Winchester or .30/06 brass in full length versions, short versions and blown out versions.

Of the whole batch, the old conservative, soundly designed .256 Newton is about the maximum capacity for the best results in the .256 bore. It is almost perfectly designed, to feed through

MAXIMUM LOAD LISTED SHOULD BE APPROACHED WITH CARE

almost all suitable actions with a minimum of alteration, and develops almost ideal velocities for available bullets.

Too much cannot be said for the cartridges of Charles Newton for use with modern powders. His fine .30 and .35 Newtons are not described in this book because no brass is being made and there is no existing cartridge from which the .30 or .35 Newton cases can be formed. The next best, or closest thing we can get to the original Newtons, are wildcat cartridges, like the .35 Belted Newton, the short .30 Magnums, like the Ackley, Mashburn and Apex and the short .35 Magnums, in their various versions. It can only be hoped that some enterprising manufacturer will see his way clear to again produce the .256, .30 and .35 Newton cases for handloaders.

87 gr. bullet	44	gr.	4320 powder	2980 fs.
	47		4320	3100
	49		4320	3220
	43		4064	2955
	46		4064	3100
	48		4064	3200
	43		4895	2955
	46		4895	3060
	48		4895	3170
	45		H380	2950
	48		H380	3130
	50		H380	3200
	40		HiVel #2	3025
	43		HiVel #2	3220
	45		HiVel #2	3360
120	38		4320	2510
	41		4320	2690
	43		4320	2750
	38		H380	2415
	41		H380	2550
	43		H380	2670
	38		4064	2550
	41		4064	2700
	43		4064	2770
	38		4895	2490
	41		4895	2660
	43		4895	2740
	35		HiVel #2	2525
	38		HiVel #2	2685
	40		HiVel #2	2800
	45		4350	2520
	48		4350	2690
	50		4350	2780

MAXIMUM LOAD LISTED SHOULD BE APPROACHED WITH CARE

140 gr. bullet	35 gr.	H380 powder	2190 fs.
	40	H380	2400
	41	4350	2280
	43	4350	2390
	46	4350	2530
	32	HiVel #2	2250
	35	HiVel #2	2400
	37	HiVel #2	2500
	46	4831	2375
	49	4831	2540
	51	4831	2635
160	37	4350	2030
	42	4350	2325
	43	4831	2190
	48	4831	2440

The following loads are recommended for Norma powders.

77 gr. bullet	37.8 gr.	Norma 200 powder	3120 fs.
93	45.2	Norma 203	3150
139	46.6	Norma 204	2790
156	44.2	Norma 204	2495

Custom barrel twist: 9", 10"

6.5 x 55 Improved Arch

This is the original Arch cartridge which was the forerunner of all of the other Arch "improved" cartridges based on the 6.5 x 55 Swedish military cartridge. A large amount of work has been done with this cartridge using a 26 inch barrel with 9 inch twist and a 24 inch barrel with 7 inch twist, the latter being employed for testing the extremely long bullets from 160 to 200 grains. Another barrel with 5-1/4 inch twist was also used for testing the 200 grain Barnes bullet.

87 gr. bullet	57 gr.	4831 powder	3458 fs.
100	52.5	4831	3107
	58	H450	3359
120	51.5	4831	3059
	56	H450	3140
139	50	4831	2890

MAXIMUM LOAD LISTED SHOULD BE APPROACHED WITH CARE

140 gr. bullet	47.5 gr.	4350 powder	2898 fs.
	54	H450	2908
160	48	4831	2604
	61.5	H870	2745
	52	H450	2740
	50	4831	2719
	52.5	4831	2796
200	61.5	H870	2624

Standard twist: 9", 10"
Special twist: 5.5", 7"

.256 Newton

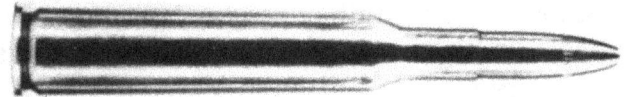

This is one of the finest cartridges in its class. It was originated prior to World War I by the late Charles Newton who later invented and manufactured the very fine Newton rifles. Both the cartridge and the rifle were many years ahead of their time. For some years the .256 Newton cartridge was manufactured by the various ammunition manufacturers but prior to World War II, it was declared obsolete and the manufacture was discontinued. It now is necessarily classed as a Wildcat cartridge. Originally the .256 Newton was loaded with a 129 gr. bullet at 3100 fs. Many still consider it superior to either the .257 Roberts or the .270 Winchester. Cases can easily be made from .30/06 or .270 Winchester brass by the use of a pair of forming dies.

87 gr. bullet	49 gr.	3031 powder	3366 fs.
	52	4895	3295
	52	4064	3415
100	46	4064	3090
120	47	4895	2767
	54.5	4350	2955
	48	4064	2892
140	45	4895	2604
	45	4064	2663
	53	4350	2853
	58	4350	2952
150	50.5	4350	2870
160	46	4064	2550

Standard twist: 10"

MAXIMUM LOAD LISTED SHOULD BE APPROACHED WITH CARE

.26 Epps

The .26 Epps is the Elwood Epps version of the 6.5/06. Mr. Epps being located in Clinton, Ontario, Canada caters especially to the Canadian trade. This .26 Epps is quite similar to the .256 Newton except it utilizes the full length 06 case. Like other versions of the 6.5/06, it is a highly effective cartridge on all kinds of big game and especially well adapted for extreme ranges.

129-130 gr. bullet	52 gr.	4350 powder	2935 fs.
	55	4350	3250
	50	4064	3225
140	55	4831	3126

Standard twist: 10"

6.5/06

The standard 6.5/06, sometimes called the .256/06 is simply the standard .30/06 case necked to 6.5. Being a slightly larger bore it is somewhat superior to the .25 Neidner otherwise known as the standard .26/06. Since the popularity of the 6.5 bore in general has increased markedly during the last few years, the 6.5/06 has become a relatively popular Wildcat cartridge and is sufficiently powerful for almost any game found in North America if the correct bullet is used. It is a very flat shooting long range cartridge very well adapted for open country as well as brush hunting with the heavier bullets which are available up to 160 grain.

87 gr. bullet	48 gr.	4064 powder	3425 fs.
	50	4064	3610
	48	HiVel #2	3700
	54	4350	3425
	56	4350	3610

MAXIMUM LOAD LISTED SHOULD BE APPROACHED WITH CARE

100 gr. bullet	47 gr.	4064 powder	3340 fs.
	47	HiVel #2	3500
	53	4350	3340
	55	4350	3495
120	52	4350	3180
	54	4350	3310
140	53	4350	3175
150	49	4350	2860
	51	4350	2970

Standard twist: 10"
Special twist: 12", 14"

.256/06 Improved

The 6.5 x 06 Improved, sometimes called the .256/06 Improved is obviously not as efficient as the standard 6.5/06 which tends to indicate that the maximum efficient case capacity has been reached and that the 6.5/06 Improved is somewhat over bore capacity thus resulting in not quite as efficient cartridge as the standard version. The following loads bear this out because these were made in the same barrel, by first chambering the barrel for the standard 6.5/06, then later it was rechambered for the "improved" version so that a good comparison was obtained for the two cartridges in the same barrel.

120 gr. bullet	53 gr.	4350 powder	3100 fs.
	55	4350	3275
140	51	4350	2920
	53	4350	3095
	53	4831	2950
	55	4831	3065
150	49	4350	2780
	51	4350	2915
	51	4831	2760
	53	4831	2915
165	46	4350	2550
	48	4350	2600
	48	4831	2550
	50	4831	2650

Standard twist: 10"
Special twist: 12", 14"

MAXIMUM LOAD LISTED SHOULD BE APPROACHED WITH CARE

.263 Sabre

The .263 Sabre developed by Jerry Shannon of Spanaway, Washington is based on the full length '06 brass with relatively the same body taper as the original cartridge but designed with a sharp 35° shoulder for a more positive headspace adjustment. This cartridge could well be described as sort of a mild "improvement" on the 6.5 x 06 and for all practical purposes loading data should be interchangeable. The sharp shoulder angle should in a measure at least reduce the stretching of the brass as compared to the same cartridge possessing the more sloping shoulder. The following loads were developed in a 26 inch barrel.

100 gr. bullet	62.5 gr.	4350 powder	3710 fs.
	64	4831	3690
	54	4895	3650
120	58.5	4350	3400 estimated
125	58	4350	3350 estimated
129	58	4350	3300 estimated
140	56.5	4350	3200
	59.2	4831	3150
160	54	4350	2950

Standard twist: 10"

6.5 ICL Boar

This ICL cartridge is the same as the preceding .25/.270 Ram, except the neck is larger to accept the slightly larger 6.5 bullet. Doubtless this cartridge has the same characteristics of the .25 calibre version with the same faults, but to a lesser degree. Case capacity is too large for the best efficiency, but certain results with heavy bullets, and the slow burning powders are possible. It is the opinion of many shooters that the '06 case simply necked down, is somewhat over maximum capacity for the .25 or 6.5 calibre bores.

MAXIMUM LOAD LISTED SHOULD BE APPROACHED WITH CARE

150 gr. bullet	54 gr.	4350 powder	2885 fs.
156	54	4350	2973
	55	4350	3030

Standard twist: 9", 10"

.264 Williams

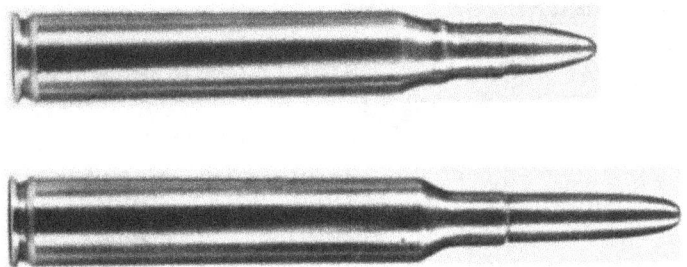

This is the latest development of W. H. (Bill) Williams of Odessa, Texas and was introduced in 1951. It is a full length '06 case necked down and blown out so as to move the shoulder forward. It is a conservative design with a 28° shoulder and can be described as a minimum body taper cartridge. The illustration shows one cartridge fully fire formed and the other necked down to form the proper headspace and loaded ready for fire forming. This same system is the best one to use when fire forming any cartridge where the body has to be blown forward to create a longer body and shorter neck. For example, this is the best method to use when forming .280 Remington brass out of '06 cases.

77 gr. Norma	56 gr.	4895 powder	3750 fs. estimated
100	55	4895	3300 fs. estimated
129	56	4350	3125 fs. estimated
140	52	4350	3000 fs. estimated
	54	4350	3100 fs. estimated
160	54	4350	2800 fs. estimated
	56	4831	2800 fs. estimated

Standard twist: 9", 10"

MAXIMUM LOAD LISTED SHOULD BE APPROACHED WITH CARE

LOADING DATA

.264 Short Magnum (Connell)

This is a shortened version of the .264 Winchester designed to get 3100 foot seconds with the 140 grain bullet. This cartridge was designed by Calvin C. Connell, 2520 East Street, Warren, Michigan for use in a double barrel rifle. The following loads have been developed preparatory to sending the information, reamers, etc., to Austria. Further information can be obtained by writing direct to Mr. Connell.

Bullet	Charge	Powder	Velocity
100 gr. bullet	51 gr.	4064 powder	3340 fs.
	52	4064	3460
	53	4064	3500
	54	4064	3780
120	49	4064	3080
	51	4064	3245
	46	4320	2910
	47	4320	2980
	48	4320	3010
	49	4320	3080
	50	4320	3110
130	47	4064	2935
	48	4064	2995
	49	4064	3010
	51	4064	3115 Maximum
140	54	4350	3095
150	45	4350	2545
	47	4350	2625
	48	4350	2650
	49	4350	2730

Standard twist: 9", 10"

.264 Durham Magnum

The .264 Durham Magnum utilizes the same case as the 6mm and .25 Durham Magnums except for the larger bullet diameter.

MAXIMUM LOAD LISTED SHOULD BE APPROACHED WITH CARE

The overall length is 2.270 and being of lesser capacity than the .264 Winchester Magnum and similar cartridges, it should be more efficient than these .264 Magnums. As mentioned above, this case is the same as the two smaller Durham Magnums except that the neck is slightly longer to accept the longer bullet. The .264 Durham Magnum was used with considerable success by Melville Haskill of Tucson, Arizona in Africa. The rifle was used for medium size African game including zebra, impala, dik dik, Thompson's gazelle and similar animals.

100 gr. bullet	60 gr.	4350 powder	3640 fs.
120	58	4350	3390
129	57	4350	3240
140	56	4350	3130
160	55	4350	2950

Standard twist: 9", 10"

6.5 Brooks

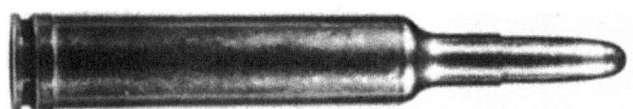

The 6.5 Brooks Magnum developed by G. L. (Roy) Brooks of Las Vegas, Nevada, could be just as well called a 6.5 or .256 Weatherby Magnum since it is simply the .257 Weatherby case necked up to accept the slightly larger 6.5 bullet. Cases can be made by either necking up .257 Weatherby, or necking down the .270 Weatherby brass. This cartridge should be quite similar to the .264 Winchester Magnum in general characteristics. The following two loads were the average of ten shots on the Weatherby chronograph.

140 gr. bullet	63 gr.	4350 powder	3125 fs.
156	64	4831	2890

Standard twist: 9", 10"

MAXIMUM LOAD LISTED SHOULD BE APPROACHED WITH CARE

6.5 Barnes QT

This is one of the first experimental cartridges of this type which has come to the writer's attention and it was developed by Fred N. Barnes of Grand Junction, Colorado. The name "QT" means quick twist. The first barrel was made with a 6-1/4 inch twist for use with 200 grain 6.5 bullets. This barrel was made in 1946. The load first used was 60 grains of .50 calibre machine gun powder which gave a velocity of 2650 fs, and was almost 200 fs over the expected velocity when the cartridge was designed. The case is simply the .250 Ackley Magnum necked up to accept the slightly larger 6.5 bullet. After testing the first barrel in 1946, it was found that a still sharper twist was needed and a 5-1/2 inch twist finally became standard. Experiments are now going on to a limited extent using the .264 Winchester Magnum case which should give practically the same results. Obviously this type of cartridge which requires such a rapid twist barrel is a highly specialized one. It will handle nothing except the very longest bullets. Standard weight bullets will not hold together if fired at relatively high velocity in a 5-1/2 inch twist barrel.

200 gr. bullet 60 gr. .50 Cal. MG powder 2650 fs.
                64   .50 Cal. MG powder 2700

Standard twist: 5.5"

6.5 x 68

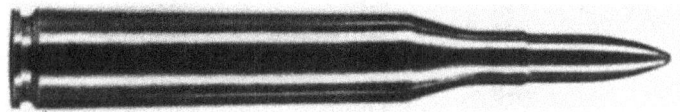

The 6.5 x 68 is a European cartridge for which Mannlicher Schoenauer rifles are currently being manufactured in Europe and marketed by the Stoeger Arms Corporation of South Hackensack, New Jersey, This cartridge is quite similar to the more recently introduced .264 Winchester Magnum. It has the same capacity, but is a conventional rimless case rather than a belted case. Factory loads are available with 93 and 123 grain bullets, but other

MAXIMUM LOAD LISTED SHOULD BE APPROACHED WITH CARE

weight bullets were tested in a rifle furnished by the courtesy of Stoeger Arms. This rifle was a standard Mannlicher Schoenauer with a 25 inch barrel. The twist in this barrel is relatively slow, nearly one in twelve inches, therefore it was not successful with heavy pointed bullets such as the 160 grain which had a tendency to keyhole. This means that Mannlicher Schoenauer rifles chambered for the 6.5 x 68 should be used with light and medium weight bullets. The 93 grain factory load is listed at 3933 foot seconds and the 123 grain factory load at 3440 foot seconds. This compares quite favorable with the .264 Winchester Magnum factory loads which are listed at 3700 foot seconds for the 100 grain bullet, and 3200 foot seconds for the 140 grain bullet. The following loads were developed with 93 grain RWS bullets, 140 grain Speer and 150 grain Barnes.

Bullet	Powder (gr)	Type	Velocity (fs)
93 gr. bullet	52	3031 powder	3220 fs.
	55	3031	3400
	57	3031	3550
	58	4895	3500
	68	4350	3510
	72	4350	3850
	72	4831	3745
	73	4831	3780
120	62	4350	3095
	64	4350	3235
	66	4350	3400 Maximum
	62	4831	3105
	64	4831	3185
	66	4831	3280
130	65	4350	3280
	67	4350	3425 Maximum
	67	4831	3310
	68	4831	3335
140	59	4350	2950
	61	4350	3080
	63	4350	3150
	62	4831	3080
	64	4831	3100
	66	4831	3185
150	56	4350	2800
	58	4350	3000
	58	4831	2770
	61	4831	2925

Standard twist: 12"
Special twist: 9", 10"

MAXIMUM LOAD LISTED SHOULD BE APPROACHED WITH CARE

.264 Winchester

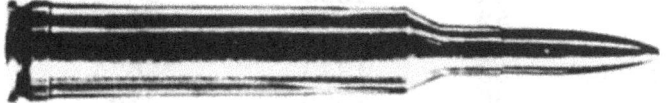

The .264 Winchester Magnum cartridge is simply the .338 Winchester Magnum necked down to accept the regular 6.5mm bullet. 6.5 bullets are available in a variety of weights, ranging from 87 to 200 grains, the latter being available from Fred Barnes of Grand Junction, Colorado. The original 6.5 QT (quick twist) as made by Barnes was based on the .250 Ackley Magnum case necked up to .264 and loaded with .50 calibre machine gun powder.

The .264 Winchester Magnum, although not identical to the 6.5 Ackley and other similar "wildcat" 6.5 Magnums, is so similar that loading data given for these short 6.5 Magnum can be used in the .264 Winchester, but the Winchester case being of slightly greater capacity would show a slightly reduced velocity as for example, compared with the 6.5 Ackley or Apex, which are slightly shorter. Like all over bore capacity cases, the .264 Winchester is relatively inefficient as compared to a cartridge such as the .260 AAR, and has comparatively short barrel life. The .338 Winchester is a relatively efficient and well adjusted case. Since this is true, it could not also be true when the case is necked down to accept a bullet only slightly larger than the standard .25 calibre.

The factory aims for a muzzle velocity of 3250 foot seconds with the 140 grain bullet, which in our tests, as well as some other experimentors, have so far been impossible to obtain with conventional components.

87 gr. bullet	70	gr.	4831 powder	3535 fs.
	74		4831	3780
	64		4350	3570
	68		4350	3760
	57		4895	3540
	60		4895	3650
100	61		4350	3185
	65		4350	3390
	55		H380	3245
	59		H380	3450
	67		4831	3130
	71		4831	3325

MAXIMUM LOAD LISTED SHOULD BE APPROACHED WITH CARE

120 gr. bullet	54 gr.	4895 powder	3115 fs.
	58	4895	3315
	52	3031	3265
	56	3031	3460
	53	4350	3025
	60	4350	3280
	62	4350	3350
	64	4831	3260
	66	4831	3380
	69	4831	3450
	50	4895	3045
	52	4895	3130
	54	4895	3225
	49	4064	3045
	52	4064	3200
	49	HiVel #2	3200
	52	H380	2970
	57	H380	3165
140	56	4350	2890
	60	4350	3100
	62	4831	3000
	65	4831	3140
	48	4895	2735
	52	4895	2925
	50	H380	2660
	54	H380	2855
	44	HiVel #2	2840
	46	HiVel #2	2950
160	54	4350	2615
	58	4350	2810
	46	4895	2515
	50	4895	2725
	58	4831	2660
	62	4831	2865
	48	H380	2570
	52	H380	2720
	41	HiVel #2	1485
	45	HiVel #2	2680

The following loads were developed for the .264 Winchester Magnum by Dr. E. L. Arch of Wenatchee, Washington, in a 24 inch barrel with 7 inch twist.

165 gr. bullet	70 gr.	H870 powder	3035 fs.
	76	5010	3145

The following loads for the 200 grain bullet were developed in a 26 inch barrel with 5 inch twist.

MAXIMUM LOAD LISTED SHOULD BE APPROACHED WITH CARE

200 gr. bullet 65 gr. H870 powder 2705 fs.
               70   5010   2770
               78   H202   2810

Standard twist: 9"
Special twist: 5", 7"

6.5 Apex Magnum

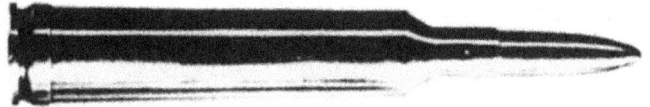

These cartridges are the development of the Apex Rifle Company, Sun Valley, California. These cartridges, with the exception of the .300 Super are made by shortening and necking down the .300 H & H brass. The .300 Super is identical to the standard .300 H & H except the shoulder angle which is somewhat sharper. The 6.5, .300 and .35 Apex cartridges are quite similar to the Ackley line in powder capacity but are slightly longer overall and feature considerable more body taper.

Like the 6.5 Ackley and several other quite similar 6.5 Magnum cartridges, the Apex is doubtless quite badly over bore capacity and not as efficient as the same cartridge necked up to 30 or larger. Such cartridges appeal to shooters who are more interested in maximum velocity to the exclusion of the other considerations.

(Loads worked out by H. C. Carey — Tested by Robert Hutton)

120 gr. bullet 60 gr. 4350 powder 3225 fs.
               61   4350   3330
               60   4831   3125
140   56   4350   2940
               58   4350   3030
               59   4350   3125
               60   4350   3225
               58   4831   2860
               60   4831   3030
               61   4831   3125
160   59   H570   2565
               62   H570   2780
               64   H570   2860
               58   4831   2860
               59   4831   2940
               60   4831   2985
               54   4350   2860

Standard twist: 9", 10"

MAXIMUM LOAD LISTED SHOULD BE APPROACHED WITH CARE

6.5 Super Magnum (Mashburn)

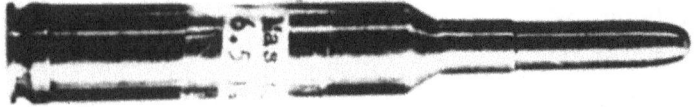

The Mashburn 6.5 Magnum is made by necking down and shortening .300 H&H cases to 2.630". It is very similar to the 6.5 Apex Magnum. See description of 6.5 Apex.

Bullet	Powder charge	Powder	Velocity
87 gr. bullet	77 gr.	4350	4050 fs.
	77	4831	3960
100	71	4350	3720
	75	4831	3780
120	67	4350	3500
	68	4350	3550
	71	4831	3565
	72	4831	3640
129	64	4350	3310
	66	4350	3400
	68	4831	3360
	70	4831	3440
140	64	4350	3290
	68	4831	3345

Standard twist: 9", 10"

6.5 Critser Express

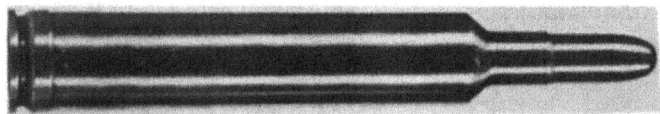

The 6.5 Critser Express is a full length .300 H&H Magnum case necked down to 6.5 and blown out for maximum capacity with a 42° shoulder and a neck length of .325. The loads given below were developed in a 26 inch barrel with 9 inch twist, and the test gun gave excellent accuracy up to 1000 yards.

Bullet	Powder charge	Powder	Velocity
87 gr. bullet	65 gr.	4350	3910 fs.
100	65	4831	3710
	67	4350	3840
120	67	4350	3720
	70	4831	3810
140	65	H570	2910

Standard twist: 9", 10"

MAXIMUM LOAD LISTED SHOULD BE APPROACHED WITH CARE

6.5/.300 Weatherby-Wright Magnum

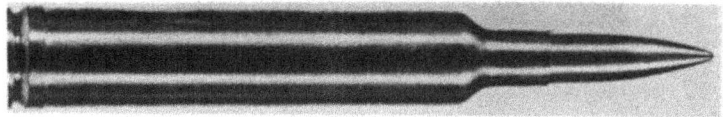

This is an extremely large cartridge and for ordinary powders it is badly over-bore capacity and very likely quite inefficient. It was developed for one purpose only, namely, 1000 yard target shooting where barrel life is not a prime consideration. Extensive tests show that by using proper powders of the slow burning type that this is an absolute maximum case capacity for the 6.5 bore. In tests where pressures have been maintained at almost 55,000 psi the following loads were developed.

139 gr. Norma Match bullet	87 gr.	202 (Hodgdon)	3429 fs.
	84	H870	3400

The above loads were developed and tested for pressure and velocity by B. E. Hodgdon, Merriam, Kansas. The second load shown above was used by Lt. Col. Paul Wright of Silver City, New Mexico for 1000 yard match shooting. Colonel Wright was looking for a cartridge with reasonable recoil and the highest possible velocity at safe working pressure. Further tests by Mr. Hogdon prove that a large capacity case such as the .378 Weatherby Magnum necked down to 6.5 would give no more velocity even though more powder could be used. For example, the 6.5/.378 Weatherby Magnum required 106 grains of IMR 6915 for a velocity of 3440 fs at a pressure of 55,000 psi.

Standard twist: 9", 10"

MAXIMUM LOAD LISTED SHOULD BE APPROACHED WITH CARE

.270 Savage

This cartridge is made by necking the .300 Savage down to .270. Like a few others, this development has been jealously claimed by a number of gunsmiths; therefore, it goes by numerous names. It became quite well known during the last war, having been advertised quite extensively by the late F. R. Krause, famous custom loader of Albuquerque, New Mexico. In about 1945, Roy Triplett of Cimarron, New Mexico also a custom hand loader, advertised it and rebarrelled a few Model 99 Savages for it. About this time Charles A. Evans also developed a version which he called the .270 Evans and still later Bliss Titus started working with it, thus it is also known as the .270 Titus. Doubtless, like most other Wildcats, it was created years before any of these individuals ever though of it. Usually there are a number of enterprising gunsmiths who have new Wildcats cooked up well before new commercial cartridges are even on the market. All that is needed is an announcement by a factory that a certain new cartridge will be put on the market on a certain date. As soon as the announcement appears a Wildcat epidemic starts.. It is necessary to be a real early bird to really come up with something new. In spite of the claims and counterclaims by the "originators," the .270 Savage makes a fine efficient .270 cartridge well adapted for both target and game shooting. A similar cartridge could be created by necking the .308 Winchester to .270 or 7mm.

Bullet	Charge	Powder	Velocity
100 gr. bullet	39 gr.	HiVel #2	2925 fs.
	39	3031	2950
	42	4064	3107
130	37	HiVel #2	2727
	39	4064	2763
	40	4895	2703
	37	3031	2701
150	36	4064	2385
	39	4895	2555
	43	4350	2574

Standard twist: 10"
Special twist: 12"

MAXIMUM LOAD LISTED SHOULD BE APPROACHED WITH CARE

.270/.303

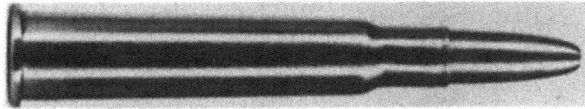

This is a good efficient .270 cartridge made by necking the .303 British case to .270. An equally good or better cartridge could be made by necking the .303 British to 7mm. The .270/.303 is a very popular cartridge in Australia for use on kangaroo, pig, etc., but should be a fine cartridge for deer and other big game. A similar and equally good cartridge can be made by necking the .30/40 to .270 or 7mm, and is especially well adapted for use in single shot and P14 Enfield rifles. These cartridges are also of special interest to New Zealanders and Canadians.

Bullet	Charge	Powder	Velocity
100 gr. bullet	37.5 gr.	Modified Cordite powder	2850 fs
	38	4740	2730
	39	4740	2900
	38	HiVel #2	2800
	40	Nobel 41	2850
130	36	4740	2600
	38	4895	2625
	39	4064	2700
	39	Nobel 41	2675
150	34	4740	2325
	36	Nobel 41	2375
	42	Norma 104	2550

Standard twist: 10"

.270/.308

This is a very fine efficient .270 cartridge made by simply necking the common .308 Winchester case to .270. It resembles the .270 Savage, but being slightly larger, it produces somewhat higher velocities, and these velocities compare very favorably with the standard .270 Winchester, and a multitude of the larger .270 cartridges, including the Magnums. The .308 necked to 7mm is quite similar to the .270 version, but it handles the heavier bullets at very satisfactory velocities.

MAXIMUM LOAD LISTED SHOULD BE APPROACHED WITH CARE

130 gr. bullet	38	gr.	3031 powder	2814 fs.
	39		3031	2935
	42		4320	2950
	48		4350	3136
140	44		4350	2809
	46		4350	2880
150	44		4350	2728
	45		4350	2782

Standard twist: 10"
Special twist: 12"

.270/.257 Improved (Ackley)

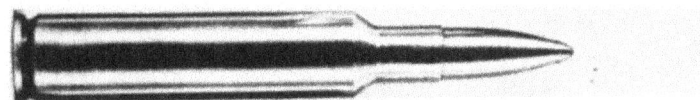

The cartridge illustrated is the Ackley Improved .257 necked up or the Improved 7 x 57 necked down to accept the .270 bullet. The same can be done with any of the other versions of these two cartridges, with similar results. Like the .270 Savage, this case is of lesser capacity than the standard .270 Winchester thus producing a more efficient cartridge. The standard .270 is somewhat over bore capacity and not as efficient as slightly smaller cases. Actually, the .270/.257 Improved produces velocities fully as good as the standard .270 with slightly less powder. It is a cartridge which can be highly recommended for all types of American game.

100 gr. bullet	43	gr.	HiVel #2	3187 fs.
	41		3031	3103
	46		4895	3144
	46		4064	3263
	48		4320	3292
	55		4350	3263
130	38		3031	2735
	41		4320	2779
	43		4895	2882
	51		4350	3032
	55		4831	3027
150	39		4064	2541
	46		4350	2679
	48		4350	2760
	51		4831	2728
	53		4350	2849

MAXIMUM LOAD LISTED SHOULD BE APPROACHED WITH CARE

170 gr. bullet	36 gr.	HiVel #2 powder	2449 fs.
	38	HiVel #2	2531
	40	4064	2486
	42	4064	2554
	47	4350	2575
	49	4350	2690
	51	4831	2583
	53	4831	2681

Standard twist: 10"
Special twist: 12"

.277 ICL Flying Saucer

This is one of the most efficient, and flexible of all the .270 cartridges. It is identical to the Ackley .270/.257, and loading data is interchangeable. Cases are made by necking up .257 Robers brass and then firing in the ICL chamber. Ballistically this cartridge duplicates the .270 Winchester, and seems to have ideal capacity for the .270 bore.

110 gr. bullet	48 gr.	4831 powder	2631 fs.
	40	4895	2791
	42	4895	2951
	44	4895	3135
	46	4895	3186
	48	4895	3236

Standard twist: 10"
Special twist: 12"

.277 Brooks Short Magnum

This is a short cartridge with a case length of approximately 2.0 developed by G. L. (Roy) Brooks of Las Vegas, Nevada. This 2.0 length produces an overall length suitable for use in Model 88 Winchester and other short actions. Cases are usually

MAXIMUM LOAD LISTED SHOULD BE APPROACHED WITH CARE

made by shortening .257 Weatherby cases, but of course cases can also be made from .300 H&H Magnum or other Magnum brass. Dies are available from R.C.B.S. Gun and Die Shop. This short cartridge maintains the typical Weatherby shoulder design. Mr. Brooks gives no ballistic data for this short .270 Magnum except to mention that it is very similar to the standard .270 Weatherby when loaded with 55 grains of 4831 powder and the 130 gr. bullet; therefore, we can assume that this short Magnum develops velocity somewhat in excess of 3000 fs. with the 130 gr. bullet. Standard twist: 10"

.270 Winchester

The ever popular .270 Winchester cartridge is presented here for the purposes of comparison. The loading data given for this standard factory cartridge can be compared to the Wildcat .270's with lesser case capacity and the .270 Magnums with greater case capacity. Actually the standard .270 is probably slightly over bore capacity for best efficiency since the slightly smaller cases produce almost equal velocity with less powder. It can also be noted that the largest magnums produce only a meager increase in velocity over the standard .270 Winchester even with a greatly increased powder charge.

100 gr. bullet	47 gr.	3031 powder	3370 fs.
	49	3031	3455
	49	HiVel #2	3396
	51	4895	3418
	51	4064	3410
	53	4064	3534
120	51	4064	3250
130	46	3031	3014
	48	3031	3123
	47	4895	2927
	48	4064	3028
	50	4064	3121
	53	4350	3038
	57	4350	3171
150	46	4895	2785
	45	4064	2766
	54	4350	2903
	56	4350	3010

MAXIMUM LOAD LISTED SHOULD BE APPROACHED WITH CARE

LOADING DATA

160 gr. bullet	53	gr.	4350 powder	2800 fs.
170	43		4064	2439
	45		4064	2532
	44		4895	2510
	46		4895	2591
	50		4350	2556
	52		4350	2656
	55		4831	2570
180	54		4831	2650
	49		4350	2600

The following loads are recommended for Norma and Nobel powders.

125 gr. Cast Gas-check bullet			
	13 gr.	Nobel's Hornet powder	1450 fs.
	18	Norma 200	1550
100 gr. Jacketed bullet			
	48	4740	3200
	53	Nobel 41	3450
110	51.9	Norma 203	3250
	57.9	Norma 104	3250
	47	4740	3150
130	56	Norma 104	3140
	50	Nobel 41	3100
150	51	Norma 104	2800
	46	Nobel 41	2800

Standard twist: 10"
Special twist: 12"

.270 ICL Jaguar

This is the ICL version of the Improved .270 Winchester. Cases are made by firing factory loads in the ICL chamber. It is another of the ICL line which is quite similar to the Ackley Improved .270, and doubtless the same comments apply equally well to both cartridges. It has been the opinion of the author that the standard unaltered .270 Winchester cartridge is slightly over bore capacity and not much can be gained by increasing the capacity by blowing the case out. It is possible a slight advantage would be gained, when using heavy bullets with slow burning powder.

MAXIMUM LOAD LISTED SHOULD BE APPROACHED WITH CARE

110 gr. bullet	50 gr.	4064 powder	3080 fs.
	58	4064	3575
	62	4350	3515
130	59	4350	3200
	52	4320	3080
	54	4320	3200
	60	4831	3080
	65	4831	3390
150	56	4350	2950
	58	4350	3030
	62	4831	3150
	68	50 MG	2860

Standard twist: 10"

.270 Winchester Improved (Ackley)

This is a fire formed .270 made by firing factory cartridges in the improved chamber. Since the original .270 is over bore capacity, little improvement can be expected although some shooters say it is a fair cartridge for bullets heavier than 150 gr. Due to its relative inefficiency, it is not recommended. The standard .270 in unaltered form should be better, therefore no loading data is given.

Standard twist: 10"
Special twist: 12"

.270 Ackley Magnum

There are numerous versions of .270 Magnums designed and introduced by various gunsmiths and experimentors similar to this cartridge and some are so near like it that ballistics are about the same. Cases are made by necking and shortening .300 H&H Magnum brass. This is done in three operations. It is then fire formed to final shape. Full loads should be used for fire forming.

MAXIMUM LOAD LISTED SHOULD BE APPROACHED WITH CARE

Because it is about the smallest .270 Magnum Wildcat it is better than most, but is still what can be described inefficient and can be recommended to only a few shooters who are not concerned with barrel life or flexibility. This class of shooters are interested in top velocity at any cost and work on the theory that the more coal, the more steam, without regard to the law of diminishing returns. This class of cartridge is sometimes advocated for use on big game such as goat and sheep with bullets such as the 160 gr. Barnes or the new 170 gr. Speer bullet.

100 gr. bullet	58	gr.	HiVel #2 powder	3567 fs.
	60		HiVel #2	3659
	60		4895	3487
	59		4064	3513
	61		4320	3470
120	58		4064	3107
	64		4350	3343
130	54		4064	3045
	56		4064	3155
	65		4350	3225
	67		4350	3310
	69		4831	3245
150	52		4895	2821
	51		4064	2821
	60		4350	2969
	65		4831	3058
160	58		4350	2950
170	45		3031	2506
	49		4895	2578
	57		4350	2718
	65		4831	2833
	51		4064	2680

Standard twist: 10"
Special twist: 12"

.270 Durham Magnum

The .270 Durham Magnum is a slight departure from the normal Durham design in that it has slightly more body taper, but the same sharp shoulder. This cartridge falls into the same class as the .270 Magnums, among which we find the .270 Ackley,

MAXIMUM LOAD LISTED SHOULD BE APPROACHED WITH CARE

Weatherby and short Mashburn Magnums. This cartridge is a good one to use for rechambering standard .270 Winchester barrels since it has about sufficient overall length to clean up the Winchester .270 chamber without setting the barrel back. The overall length of the .270 Durham Magnum is 2.535. The following loads were developed in a 22 inch barrel with 10 inch twist and are considered maximum and should be approached with caution.

    100 gr. bullet 71 gr. 4350 powder 3740 fs.
    130 68 4350 3410
    150 65 4350 3125
    170 64 4350 2950

Standard twist: 10"
Special twist: 12"

.270 Mashburn Magnum (short)

This .27 short Magnum is similar to the .270 Ackley and uses the same loading data. It was originated by A. E. Mashburn, Oklahoma City. There is little choice between the Ackley and short Mashburn .270 Magnums.

Standard twist: 10"
Special twist: 12"

.270 Weatherby Magnum

The .270 Weatherby Magnum started out as a "wildcat" cartridge and later it was developed into a factory cartridge. It is quite similar in ballistics to other .270 Magnums like the Ackley .270, Mashburn and other versions. It was originally made by necking down and shortening .300 Magnum cases. It has the characteristic Weatherby curved shoulder design found on all Weatherby cartridges. The following loads are all recommended

MAXIMUM LOAD LISTED SHOULD BE APPROACHED WITH CARE

LOADING DATA

for cases made from Remington or Winchester .300 Magnum brass. Norma brass being thicker will not accept the maximum loads recommended for the domestic brass. Like all .270 Magnum cartridges it is somewhat over bore capacity, and relatively inefficient. It is recommended mostly with slow burning powder and full charges. All Weatherby Magnum rifles are free bored and the maximum charges listed for Weatherby rifles must be reduced slightly when used in rifles without free boring.

Bullet	Charge	Powder	Velocity
100 gr. bullet	61 gr.	3031	3573 fs.
	66	4895	3620
	66	4064	3716
	73	4350	3650
	77	4831	3635
130	54	3031	3135
	58	4064	3199
	68	4350	3366
	74	4831	3453
150	57	4895	2920
	56	4064	2938
	66	4350	3178
	70	4831	3144
170	53	4895	2659
	52	4064	2618
	61	4350	2765
	66	4831	2768

Standard twist: 10"
Special twist: 12"

.270 Super Magnum (Mashburn)

The Masburn .270 Super Magnum appears to be the same case as the Mashburn 6.5 Magnum except for neck diameter. It should be slightly more efficient than the 6.5 but still somewhat over bore capacity. Statistics are quite similar to other .270 Magnums such as the Ackley and the Weatherby.

Bullet	Charge	Powder	Velocity
100 gr. bullet	74 gr.	4350	3660 fs.
	76	4350	3775
130	69	4350	3375
	71	4350	3495

MAXIMUM LOAD LISTED SHOULD BE APPROACHED WITH CARE

	75	gr.	4831 powder	3467 fs.
	77		4831	3590
150 gr. bullet	68		4350	3195
	70		4350	3280
	71		4831	3210
	73		4831	3325

Standard twist: 10"
Special twist: 12"

.270 Mashburn Magnum (long)

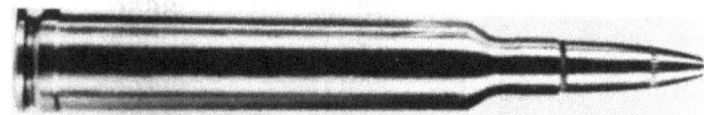

This .270 Magnum is based on the full length .300 H&H Magnum case. It is badly over bore capacity and not as efficient as the short Mashburn. It appeals to the class of shooters who look for top velocity regardless. No loading data given but data for the .270 Weatherby Magnum should be all right.

Standard twist: 10"
Special twist: 12"

MAXIMUM LOAD LISTED SHOULD BE APPROACHED WITH CARE

7 x 57mm Mauser

The 7mm Mauser is the official cartridge for numerous armies and has proven to be one of the best military and hunting cartridges ever developed. It has been used successfully on all types of big game throughout the world including elephant. It is considered by many to be the best "all around cartridge". This case has almost ideal capacity for the .276 bore for best over all results. No better choice could be made for North American hunting if a commercial cartridge is desired. The 7 x 57 case has been the basis of innumerable Wildcats such as the .257 Roberts which later became a commercial cartridge, .22/4000 .22 Newton, 6.5 Spence Special and many others. Commercial ammunition is available at present loaded only with the 175 gr bullet, but there is a wide variety of custom bullets available in weights ranging from 120 to 195 gr.

Bullet	Charge	Powder	Velocity
120 gr. bullet	46 gr.	4064 powder	2990 fs
	48	4064	3130
	42	3031	2910
	44	3031	3080
	45	4895	3015
130	44	4064	2870
	40.5	3031	2750
	42	3031	2865
	45	4895	2890
	43	4320	2910
139	42	4320	2680
	46	4320	3015
	38	HiVel #2	2635
	42	HiVel #2	2840
	37.5	3031	2610
	40	4064	2625
	46	4064	3000
140	43	4320	2690
	42	4064	2655
	38.5	HiVel #2	2650
	40	HiVel #2	2690
	38	3031	2605

MAXIMUM LOAD LISTED SHOULD BE APPROACHED WITH CARE

Bullet	Charge	Powder	Velocity
145 gr. bullet	41.5 gr.	4320 powder	2605 fs
	41.5	4064	2625
154	47	4350	2575
	40.5	4064	2520
160	39	4064	2420
	40.5	4064	2520
	45	4064	2560
	45.5	4350	2525
	47	4350	2665
	49	4350	2750
	42	4895	2625
175	33	3031	2210
	40	3031	2530
	39	4320	2335
	40	4320	2400
	42	4320	2580
	38	4064	2320
	41	4064	2530
	45	4350	2415
	46	4350	2525
	48	4350	2635
	36	HiVel #2	2310
180	43	4350	2325
	36	4064	2200
195	44	4350	2400

The following loads are recommended for Norma and Nobel powders:

Bullet	Charge	Powder	Velocity
130 gr. Cast Gas-check bullet			
	14 gr.	Nobel's Hornet powder	1700 fs
	17	Norma 200	1700
110 Jacketed bullet			
	45.8	Norma 203	3070
	43	4740	3000
120	42	4740	2950
	46	Nobel 41	3000
139-140	43	Nobel 41	2750
	39	4740	2740
150	44.1	Norma 203	2755
	41	Nobel 41	2625
175	42.3	Norma 203	2490
	45.1	Norma 104	2490

European twist: 8.66"
Standard American twist: 10"

MAXIMUM LOAD LISTED SHOULD BE APPROACHED WITH CARE

7mm ICL Tortilla

This is the ICL version of the "improved" 7 x 57 and it is practically identical to the Ackley version except it has a slightly sharper shoulder angle of 45°. Like all other "improved" 7 x 57 versions it is an extremely good cartridge and one that could be recommended for almost any kind of North American game. The various 7 x 57 "improved" cartridges have an almost ideal powder capacity for this size bore which results in a very flexible and efficient cartridge with almost any available weights of bullets.

120 gr. bullet	48 gr.	4831 powder	2860 fs
140	55	4831	3150
160	53	4831	3080
173	53	4831	2740
175	47	4831	2565

Standard twist: 10"

7 x 57 Improved (Ackley)

The improved 7mm is one of the better so called improved cartridges. Cases are made by simply firing factory loads in the improved chamber. Of course, cases can also be made by necking and shortening .30/06 brass. It has almost ideal powder capacity for the 7mm bore and produces very satisfactory ballistics. It is powerful enough for all North American big game when good bullets are used. There are many similar versions by other gunsmiths and experimenters which have similar characteristics. The Ackley Improved 7mm is identical to the Ackley Improved .257 and Improved .270/.257 except in neck diameter.

MAXIMUM LOAD LISTED SHOULD BE APPROACHED WITH CARE

130 gr. bullet	46 gr.	4895 powder	2923 fs
	48	4320	3056
	48	4895	3038
	54	4350	3129
	46	4320	2935
	56	4350	3211
140	45	HiVel #2	3064
	46	HiVel #2	3120
	45	3031	3124
	58	4350	2774 powder compressed
	49	4064	3008
145	43	HiVel #2	2878
	44	4064	2802
	48 gr.	4895 powder	2941
	46	4320	2819
	53	4350	3005
	58	4831	2973
160	42	HiVel #2	2669
	43	4064	2633
	44	4895	2678
	45	4320	2680
	51	4350	2791
	56	4831	2783
	55	4350	2965
175	50	4350	2694
	52	4350	2784

Standard twist: 10"

7mm/.308

The 7mm/.308 is a very fine "wildcat" made by necking the .308 Winchester case to 7mm, and of course it is very similar to the same case necked to .270. Being nearly ideal capacity for the 7mm bore it makes a very efficient cartridge and almost equal to some of the 7mm Magnums. It compares very favorably to the .270 Winchester and .280 Remington cartridges but can be used in short actions including some of the late model lever actions.

MAXIMUM LOAD LISTED SHOULD BE APPROACHED WITH CARE

LOADING DATA

139-140 gr. bullet	41 gr.	4831 Powder	2400 fs
	51	4831	2630
	45	H380	2630
	46	H380	2685
	41	3031	3030
	43	4350	2500
	51	4350	2915
	41	HiVel #2	2885
	42	HiVel #2	2940
	43	HiVel #2	3000
	44	HiVel #2	3030
	42	4064	2885
	43	4064	2900
	44	4064	2910
	45	4064	2940 Max.
160 gr. bullet	43	H380 powder	2510
	44	H380	2685
	39	3031	2595
	39	4350	2290
	49	4350	2785
	51	4350	2855 Max.
175	48	4831	2565
	42	H380	2410
	43	H380	2430
	34	4350	2000
	44	4350	2565

Standard twist: 10"

7mm Improved Arch

The 7mm Improved Arch is the same cartridge as the 6.5 Arch except it is necked up to accept the larger 7mm bullet. This is another very efficient cartridge especially well adapted for use in short and medium length actions.

139 gr. bullet	49 gr.	4895 powder	3005 fs
	55	4350	3129
	58	4831	3033
	58.5	H450	2931
145	55	4350	3090
	56	4350	3106
	57	4350	3156

Standard twist: 10"

MAXIMUM LOAD LISTED SHOULD BE APPROACHED WITH CARE

.285 O.K.H.

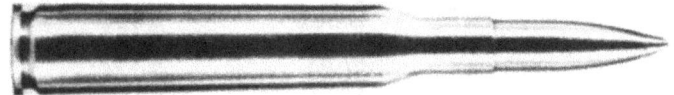

This is a cartridge introduced some years ago by O'Neill, Keith and Hopkins. Actually it is simply a 30/06 necked to 7mm and could be and is called the standard 7mm/06. This is not a bad cartridge, being identical to the standard .270 Winchester in case design, shoulder angle, capacity, etc. The two differences are the neck length which is a little longer in the .270 and of course the bullet diameter which is .284 as compared to .277-.278 for the .270 Winchester. With this case capacity, the advantage is bound to be with the larger diameter no matter how small the difference is. There is a wide variety of 7mm bullets available to handloaders in 120 to 195 gr. The original .285 OKH was designed around the 180 gr bullet, and the loading was the so-called duplex. The case had an extended flash tube which ignited the powder further forward than is possible with conventional methods. Certain advantages were claimed by the originators, but the idea has died out to the extent that mostly conventional loading methods are used. This cartridge can be recommended for use on all types of North American big game as well as many types of big game found throughout the world.

Bullet	Powder charge	Powder	Velocity
130 gr. bullet	48 gr.	4895 powder	2931 fs
	48	4064	3047
	54	4350	3071
	56	4350	3146
145	47	4895	2827
	46	4064	2938
	54	4350	3023
	58	4831	3020
160	43	4064	2616
	45	4320	2637
	52	4350	2828
	54	4350	2902
	56	4831	2782
175	47	4064	2520
	49	4895	2710
	53	4350	2665
	55	4350	2720

Standard twist: 10"

MAXIMUM LOAD LISTED SHOULD BE APPROACHED WITH CARE

7mm/06 (Mashburn)

The Mashburn 7mm/06 is the .30/06 case necked down to 7mm without any other change. This makes it identical to the .285 OKH and the .280 Remington. It is a relatively good cartridge and loading data is the same as for the .285 OKH or .280 Remington.

Standard twist: 10"

7mm/06 Improved (Ackley)

This is a blown out (fire formed) version of the 30/06 case necked to 7mm. A slight increase is possible with this case over the standard, especially with the heavier bullets. Loading data given for the standard cartridge can be used plus an increase of 5% or more.

Bullet	Powder charge		Powder	Velocity
140 gr. bullet	54	gr.	4064 powder	3123 fs
	50		3031	3132
	55		4350	3040
160	57		4350	3010
	60		4831	3000
175	56		4350	2930
180	58		4831	2818
195	56		4831	2700

Standard twist: 10"

MAXIMUM LOAD LISTED SHOULD BE APPROACHED WITH CARE

.280 Remington

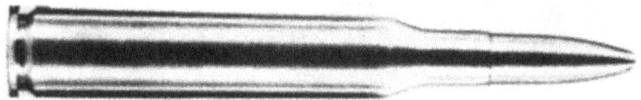

The .280 Remington is a new 7mm cartridge developed and introduced by Remington Arms for use in the Remington Model 740 auto loading rifle. Although introduced late in 1957 as a new development there is not much new about the idea. It is nothing more or less than the .285 OKH or its duplicate the standard 7mm/06. Actually the .280 Remington has slightly greater powder capacity because the body of the case is some .052 longer which means that it cannot be chambered in a 30/06 rifle. Also, supposedly a .270 Winchester cartridge cannot be fired in the .280 chamber, however this claim is not true as indicated by actual tests where .270 cartridges were fired in the .280 chamber. This is a dangerous practice because of the excessive headspace with the shorter bodied .270. Although cases for the .270 can be made by re-forming .270 or 30/06 brass it results in an amount of work all out of proportion to the rewards. This is because the .270 or 06 brass must be necked up to .35 or .40 calibre, then necked back down to 7mm with the proper headspace. Doubtless, the .280 Remington will be a better choice for many shooters interested in a 7mm/06 because of the availability of factory ammunition.

130 gr. bullet	46 gr.	4320 powder	2850 fs
	47	4320	2910
	49	4320	3000
	45	H380	2700
	46	H380	2785
	50	H380	2940
	41	HiVel #2	2840
	46	HiVel #2	3015
	45	4895	2875
	50	4895	3080
	45	4064	2900
	46	4064	2950
	48	4064	3040
	53	4350	3000

MAXIMUM LOAD LISTED SHOULD BE APPROACHED WITH CARE

LOADING DATA

Bullet	Charge	Powder	Velocity
130 gr. bullet	54 gr.	4350 powder	3050 fs
	56	4350	3170
	57	4831	2950
	58	4831	3000
	60	4831	3100
140	42	H380	2475
	43	H380	2525
	45	H380	2610
	47	H380	2690
	43	4895	2660
	45	4895	2740
	48	4895	2900
	50	4350	2850
	51	4350	2900
	53	4350	2985
	54	4831	2770
	55	4831	2820
	58	4831	2960
160	40	H380	2450
	41	H380	2500
	43	H380	2550
	45	H380	2610
	42	4895	2500
	43	4895	2550
	46	4895	2675
	49	4350	2670
	50	4350	2720
	53	4350	2960
	53	4831	2655
	54	4831	2700
	57	4831	2800

Standard twist: 10"

.280 Remington Improved

This is simply a blown out version of the .280 Remington, similar to the Ackley 7MM/06 or similar versions. The only difference being the slightly longer case resulting in a very slight increase in capacity over the 7MM/06 Improved.

MAXIMUM LOAD LISTED SHOULD BE APPROACHED WITH CARE

For shooters wishing to get the top velocity out of a 7MM cartridge, this could be a good choice since it is still possible to use the factory ammunition in the improved chamber. Cases are made by the simple expedient of shooting the factory loads in the improved chamber.

All loads shown for the Ackley Improved cartridge, can be used in this one. The following data is the latest received from the R.C.B.S. Company, obtained in their new modern laboratory. An interesting comparison can be made by studying these figures with those for the various 7MM Magnums, like the Weatherby or Ackley. It will be quickly noticed that there is very little difference between the top velocities for the .280 Improved, and the Magnums, plainly demonstrating that there is little advantage in using a belted Magnum case, for anything under .30 calibre.

Bullet	Powder charge	Powder	Velocity
140 gr. bullet	63 gr.	4350 powder	3320 fs
145	61	4831	3120
154	60	4831	2920
	60	4350	3070
175	58	4350	2850

Standard twist: 10"

Wade Super Seven

The Wade Super Seven was developed by Fred Wade of Wade's Gun Room of Phoenix, Arizona for use in bolt action rifles. Cases are made by turning off the rim of the .348 Winchester, transforming it into a rimless cartridge. It is necked down to 7mm and blown out to the conventional "improved" design. This cartridge is very similar to the 7mm Gradle except that it has the more desirable characteristics of the sharp shoulder and minimum body taper. The following loads were developed in a 21-1/2 inch barrel.

Bullet	Powder charge	Powder	Velocity
110 gr. bullet	60 gr.	4895 powder	3570 fs
	70	4831	3420
	73	4831	3540

MAXIMUM LOAD LISTED SHOULD BE APPROACHED WITH CARE

	74	4831	3680
	75	4831	3735
	72	4350	3710
139-140	67	4350	3390
	68	4831	3335
	69	4831	3400
	70	4831	3430
160	74	H570	3000
	64	4831	3070
	64	4350	3185
175	64	4831	3005
	73	H570	2900
	73	Machine Gun	2960

Standard twist: 10"

7mm Express

The 7mm Express was originated by the famous gunsmith, Roy Gradle of Santa Barbara, California, who is now retired. Rifles for this cartridge are now being made by Ralph M. Payne, of 1005 North Ventura Avenue, Ventura, California. Cases are made by making extensive changes on the .348 Winchester case, the method for which is essentially as follows:

Neck the case to .30 calibre. Fill the case with lubricating oil and place in a chamber made with a chambering reamer which is attached to an air cylinder. The cylinder is equipped with a two-way valve. The upper part of the die is fitted with a 1/2-inch piston which the air drives into the case filled with oil. The pressure being applied slowly allows sufficient time for the brass to flow into the chamber and form perfectly. The cases are removed, cleaned and then run through the standard full length sizing die. After the cases are formed, they are placed in a special collet and the rims turned off, and a new extracting cannelure cut in one operation. The result is a completely different case in 7mm calibre, with a radius shoulder (no sharp corners).

The general appearance of the case is on the fat, stubby side. Higher velocities are claimed with the relatively short fat case, as compared with the longer, and slimmer cases of equal capacity. The 7mm Express has proven highly successful on big game all over the world. The following

MAXIMUM LOAD LISTED SHOULD BE APPROACHED WITH CARE

loading data was developed in a 26 inch barrel with 12 inch twist.

bullet	powder			
139 gr. bullet	57 gr.	4064 powder	.... fs.	max.
	64	4350	3525	
140	57	4064	....	max.
	64	4350	3525	
154	63	4350	3325	
156	63	4350	3325	
	64	4350	....	max.
160	63	4350	3300	
	64	4350	....	max.
175	62	4350	3125	
	63	4350	....	max.

Standard twist: 10"

7mm Venturan

The 7mm Venturan is a short 7mm Magnum designed by Ralph M. Payne of Ventura, California. This cartridge has the same general design as the 7mm Express originated by Roy Gradle, however it is a little longer and is made by necking down and shortening .300 Magnum brass in a special tool to produce a radius shoulder. Cases can also be made from .264 Winchester, .338 Winchester or .375 H&H brass. The case is 2.235 inches long with .020 taper. The following loads were obtained in a 25 inch barrel with 10 inch twist.

139 gr. bullet	65 gr.	4350 powder	3345 fs.
140	65	4350	3345
154	64	4350	3185
	69	4831	3250
160	64	4350	3235
	69	4831	3290
175	63	4350	3135
	66	4831	3090

Standard twist: 10"

MAXIMUM LOAD LISTED SHOULD BE APPROACHED WITH CARE

.276 Carlson Magnum

This is a short 7MM Magnum cartridge, made by necking down and shortening the .300 H&H brass. It was originated by Richard Carlson, Corvallis, Montana. This cartridge has proven to be effective on all types of big game in North America, and is especially recommended for long range work. It is practically identical to the 7MM Ackley Magnum, both cases having essentially the same overall length, same body length and same shoulder angle. The main difference is that the Carlson Magnum has approximately .020 greater body taper than the Ackley case. The following list of loads for the .276 Carlson Magnum were chronographed by the H. P. White Laboratory and Phil Sharpe.

From upwards of twenty years of experience it appears that this general design and size of case which includes such cartridges as the Carlson, Ackley, Sharpe and Hart, Mashburn etc. are about the best for a 7MM Magnum, based on .300 H&H Magnum brass. If loading data tables for these various similar versions are compared, it can be seen that they all produce essentially identical results, and the small variations could easily be due to the differences in barrel length, local conditions, etc.

Bullet	Powder charge	Powder	Velocity
139 gr. bullet	56 gr.	4064 powder	3111 fs
160	60	4350	3052
173	58.5	4350	2896
180	57	4350	2830
195	54	4350	2657

Standard twist: 10"

.276 B-J Express (Barnes-Johnson)

This is a cartridge designed by Barnes and Johnson

MAXIMUM LOAD LISTED SHOULD BE APPROACHED WITH CARE

and is being currently furnished by Fred N. Barnes, Grand Junction, Colorado, the famous bullet maker. The B-J line can be described as "short" magnums and were designed for use with heavy bullets primarily. Barnes recommends only one load but data for the 7mm Weatherby will work for other bullet weights.

180 gr. bullet   81 gr. Machine Gun Powder   3100 fs

Standard twist: 10"

.275 H&H Magnum

The .275 Magnum was at one time a factory cartridge in the United States and still is in England. The manufacture of ammunition in this size was discontinued some time before the last war in this country, therefore it is now classed as a wildcat. Cases can be made by necking and shortening .300 Magnum brass. Although the oldest of the 7mm Magnum family it is still as good as any. It is somewhat over bore capacity but not as bad as some of the later 7mm Wildcats. Loads for the .275 and .276 DuBiel, another old time 7mm Magnum wildcat are identical and loads given for either of these cartridges can also be used in the 7mm Ackley Magnum and 7 x 61 S&H with practically the same velocities. A study of the chamber data will show the similarity between these cases.

Bullet	Powder charge	Powder	Velocity
136-140 gr. bullet	48 gr.	4064 powder	2810 fs
139-140	52	4064	3087
160	51	4064	2860
	59	4350	3050
175	50	HiVel #2	2720
	46	4064	2800
	58	4350	2850
180	48	4064	2580
	57	4350	2805
195	52	4350	2671

Standard twist: 10"

MAXIMUM LOAD LISTED SHOULD BE APPROACHED WITH CARE

7 x 61 Sharps and Hart

This is another short 7mm Magnum made by necking down and shortening .300 H&H Magnum brass. Recently factory cases and loaded ammunition has been made available. This ammunition is manufactured by Norma and is loaded with a 160 gr. bullet to about 3100 fs. Long experience has proven that it is difficult to drive a 160 gr. bullet in 7mm faster than 3100 fs despite the claims of advocates or originators of various versions of the 7mm Magnum. This also applies to the .270 Magnum family of cartridges. The 7 x 61 S&H is very similar to the original .275 H&H Magnum which is still manufactured in England. Because of the availability of formed cases and loaded ammunition the 7 x 61 could be said to be more practical than most of the other 7mm Magnums. Other than this, there is nothing to recommend it over similar versions some of which are probably better designed.

Bullet	Powder charge	Powder	Velocity
120 gr. bullet	67 gr.	4350 powder	3408 fs
130	54	4064	3160
	55	4895	3163
	62	4350	3233
	67	4831	3225
145	53	4064	3000
	54	4320	3045
	63	4350	3187
	66	4831	3128
160	52	4064	2857
	53	4895	2880
	53	4320	2860
	60	4350	2936
	64	4350	3185
	66	4831	3128
	60	Norma 204	3100
175	60	4350	2955

Standard twist: 10"

MAXIMUM LOAD LISTED SHOULD BE APPROACHED WITH CARE

Reynolds 7mm Magnum

The Reynolds 7MM Magnum, developed by Bob Reynolds of Tyler, Texas, is simply the .264 Winchester Magnum necked up to 7mm to produce what is now commercially available known as the 7mm Remington Magnum, however, the Reynolds version came out considerably ahead of the Remington commercial cartridge. The following loads were developed by Mr. Reynolds. Standard 7mm Remington Magnum loads can be used since the two cases are the same thus making the loading data interchangeable.

Bullet	Powder Charge	Powder	Velocity
120 gr. bullet	73 gr.	4350 powder	3635 fs
150	74	4831	3345
160	73	4831	3345
175	70	4831	3085

Standard twist: 10"

7mm Mashburn Magnum (short)

The 7mm Mashburn short Magnum is very similar to the Ackley, S&H, .285 Luft and other short 7mm Magnums. Its general characteristics are similar. Cases are made from .300 H&H Magnum brass and loading data for the Ackley, S&H, and .275 H&H can be used for the Mashburn.

Bullet	Powder Charge	Powder	Velocity
130 gr. bullet	58 gr.	4064 powder	3170 fs
	59	4895	3160
	64	4350	3258
	71	4831	3354
145	53	4064	2907
	54	4895	2942
	62	4350	3085
	68	4831	3180

MAXIMUM LOAD LISTED SHOULD BE APPROACHED WITH CARE

LOADING DATA

160 gr. bullet	52 gr.	4895 powder	2734 fs
	52	4320	2747
	61	4350	2938
	67	4831	3020

Standard twist: 10"

.284 Williams

The .284 Williams designed by W. H. (Bill) Williams of Odessa, Texas, was introduced in 1945 and produces ballistics closely to those of the short 7mm Magnums in the various versions, such as the 7mm Ackley Magnum, the 7x61 S&H and the 7mm Weatherby, and loading data for the Williams and Ackley should be interchangeable. Cases are made by necking down and shortening .300 H&H Magnum brass. Mr. Williams has worked out the following loads:

112 gr. bullet Ideal Gas check #287-129 hollowpoint
    22 gr. H375 powder 2000 fs est.
140 gr. bullet Ideal Gas check #287-422 hollowpoint
    30 H380 2000 fs est
129 gr. jacketed bullet

	64	4350	3050
	70	H570	3100 est.
130	66	4831	3125 est.
154	66	4831	2950 est.
160	62	4350	2850 est.
175	70	H570	2750 est.
	58	4350	2800 est.
	65	4831	2775 est.

Standard twist: 10"

7mm Ackley Magnum

MAXIMUM LOAD LISTED SHOULD BE APPROACHED WITH CARE

This is one of the shortest 7mm Magnums made by necking the .300 H&H Magnum brass to 7mm and shortening it to hold a little less than 70 gr. Although one of the shortest 7mm Magnums, it is still badly over bore capacity, a characteristic it shares with all 7mm Magnums. The Ackley 7mm Magnum is the same case as the .270 Ackley Magnum except the neck is large enough to accept the slightly larger 7mm bullet. For this reason, the 7mm Magnum is slightly more efficient than the .270. Of course, for practical use, there is not much difference between the .270 Magnums and the 7mm Magnums. The 7mm Magnums are called by various names such as .276 Magnum and .285 Magnum. This 7mm Magnum can be recommended the same as the .270 Magnum. From the standpoint of the average shooter, the 7 x 57 Improved should prove to be a much more interesting cartridge because it drives the various weights of bullets nearly as fast as the Magnums with considerably less powder, it is more flexible and barrel life is much better, and after all, the 7mm Improved with the right bullet is sufficiently powerful for almost any type of big game.

139 gr. bullet	60 gr.	4350 powder	3200 fs
	65	4350	3450
	55	4064	3100
	58	4064	3300
160	64	4350	3124
175	60	4350	2950

All loads for the 7 x 61 S&H can be used for equal velocities. Standard twist: 10"

7mm Weatherby Magnum

This is another quite popular 7mm Magnum. It can also be made by necking down and shortening .300 H&H Magnum brass and like the 7 x 61 S&H, it has the advantage of the availability of factory cases and loaded ammunition. Being a larger capacity case than the Ackley or S&H it is a little less efficient but because of this larger capacity it will handle somewhat more powder for a slightly higher velocity with the attendant decrease in barrel life, etc.

MAXIMUM LOAD LISTED SHOULD BE APPROACHED WITH CARE

130 gr. bullet	60 gr.	4895 powder	3218 fs
	61	4320	3247
	59	4064	3226
	69	4350	3460
139	65	4350	3184
	68	4350	3330
145	58	4064	3137
	67	4350	3255
154	66	4350	3123
160	55	4064	2902
	65	4350	3110
	70	4831	3098
175	63	4350	2903

Standard twist: 10"

.284 Jet (7mm) Durham Magnum

This cartridge is based on the .264 Winchester Magnum necked up to 7mm and for all practical purposes, it should be identical to the new Remington 7mm Magnum recently introduced by the Remington factory. The Durham utilizes a 35° shoulder angle which is sharper than the Remington and it has an overall case length of 2.490. The following loads are maximum and should be approached with caution.

140 gr. bullet	77 gr.	4831 powder	3560 fs
160	74	4831	3305
	75	4831	3365
173	74	4831	3250
175	63	4871	3170

Standard twist: 10"

7mm ICL Wapiti

MAXIMUM LOAD LISTED SHOULD BE APPROACHED WITH CARE

This is the ICL version of the 7MM Magnum. Cases are made by necking down .300 Magnum brass, trimming to proper length, and fire forming. This is a more radical cartridge, than some of the older versions, such as the Ackley, or Weatherby, but likely has the same characteristics, and comments made concerning the others should apply to the ICL version. The ICL Wapiti should appeal to hunters intrested in the maximum velocity with the long heavy 7MM bullets.

130 gr. bullet	65 gr.	4064 powder	3450 fs
	74	4350	3515
147	72	4350	3300
156	68	4350	3080
	70	4350	3225
	74	4831	3300
160	70	4831	3125
	72	4831	3225
	74	4831	3280

Standard twist: 10"

.275 Bennett Magnum

The .275 Bennett Magnum is the second of a series developed by Byard Bennett of Roswell, New Mexico and like the .25 Bennett Magnum it is quite similar to the Ackley 7mm Magnum. Mr. Bennett recommends 7mm/06 loading data for this cartridge which means that any loads given for the .285 OKH, or .280 Remington could also be used and very likely the loads could be increased to about the same level as recommended for the 7mm Ackley Magnum.

Standard twist: 10"

7mm Super Magnum (Mashburn)

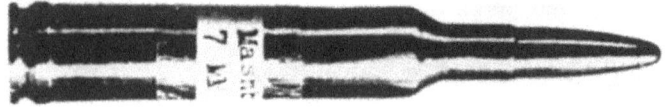

MAXIMUM LOAD LISTED SHOULD BE APPROACHED WITH CARE

LOADING DATA

This, again, is the same case as the .270 and 6.5 Mashburn Magnums except for neck diameter and because of the larger bore it is slightly more efficient than the other two.

139 gr. bullet	70 gr.	4350 powder	3375 fs
	72	4350	3500
	73	4831	3395
	75	4831	3550
160	68	4350	3165
	70	4350	3240
	72	4831	3195
	74	4831	3270
175	66	4350	2950
	68	4350	3085
	71	4831	3035
	73	4831	3175

Standard twist: 10"

7mm Mashburn Magnum (long)

This 7mm Magnum is made by necking the .300 H&H Magnum case to 7mm and leaving it full length. It is longer and has greater capacity than the 7mm Weatherby and for that reason probably less efficient with little or no higher velocity. Doubtless it is inferior to the Mashburn short 7mm.

No loading data available. Use Weatherby data.

Standard twist: 10"

.280 Ross (.280 Nitro)

MAXIMUM LOAD LISTED SHOULD BE APPROACHED WITH CARE

The .280 Ross was developed in Canada some fifty years ago. At the time of its introduction, it received a great deal of attention because of its high velocity and long range characteristics. Just prior to World War II it again received some attention in the form of the .280 Halger. Great claims were made by Harold Gerlich who subsequently was unable to prove any of the claims he made for it. There is still some interest in this cartridge and it is still being manufactured in England under the name of .280 Nitro. According to modern ideas it is a poorly designed case. It has the greatest or sharpest body taper of any existing cartridge which results in excessive bolt thrust. In Canada, the Ross rifle was made for it for many years. The Ross rifle gained a bad reputation supposedly because it was a straight pull bolt action which could be so assembled as to allow the bolt to be closed without locking and still could be fired. Actually this fault was greatly exaggerated and it has been hard to pin down actual or authentic instances when blow ups could be blamed on this failure to lock. Actually any rifle action can be blown up because of carelessness on the part of the shooter or handloader.

140 gr. bullet	60 gr.	4064 powder	3200 fs
	57	3031	3050
	56	HiVel #2	3240
160	62	4350	2965
	59	4350	2835

Standard twist: 8.66"

.288 Barnes Supreme

This is a full length blown out Magnum. Cases can be made from .300 or .375 H&H Magnum brass. Special Barnes bullets with thick jackets are available from Fred N. Barnes, Grand Junction, Colorado. This cartridge was designed for use with heavy bullets and very slow burning powder. Being a highly specialized cartridge, it is used only for long range big game shooting.

200 gr. bullet	90 gr.	M.G. powder	3050 fs

7mm Remington Magnum data on page 566.

MAXIMUM LOAD LISTED SHOULD BE APPROACHED WITH CARE

7.35 Terni

LOADING DATA

The 7.35 Terni is sometimes referred to as the 7.35 Italian Mannlicher Carcano. This is a relatively small center fire cartridge used by the Italian Army during World War II. The bullet is slightly smaller than .30 caliber in diameter but larger than the 7mm. Being a cartridge of fairly small capacity, it is a relatively efficient one and although the Mannlicher Carcano action has been called relatively weak, tests have not shown this to be true. Although the 7.35 could only be described as an odd ball, there are a large number of the rifles floating around. Dies are obtainable for reloading and bullets are available from several sources including Speer and Hornady. Hornady produces a very fine 128 grain bullet for which loading information is given below. Speer produces a special 150 grain bullet and Speer recommends that cases be made by necking up 6.5 x 54 Mannlicher Schoenauer brass which is available from all dealers carrying Norma products and Norma cases all accept standard American primers. The following loading data has been worked out by Hornady for the 128 grain bullet and by Speer for the 150 grain bullet.

128 gr. bullet	32	gr.	4198 powder	2490 fs
	33		4198	2555
	34		4198	2600
	37		3031	2505
	38		3031	2555
	39		3031	2630
	39		4895	2525
	40		4895	2585
	41		4895	2635
	38		4064	2425
	39		4064	2470
	40		4064	2535
	41		4064	2635
	36		HiVel #2	2475
	37		HiVel #2	2530
	38		HiVel #2	2580
150	38		H380	2355
	40		H380	2455
	42		H380	2525
	40		4320	2545
	42		4320	2620
	40		4895	2520
	42		4895	2595
	39		4064	2415
	41		4064	2555
	38		3031	2495
	40		3031	2580
	37		HiVel #2	2550
	39		HiVel #2	2580

MAXIMUM LOAD LISTED SHOULD BE APPROACHED WITH CARE

.30 M1 Carbine

The .30 Carbine cartridge is one of the official U. S. cartridges for the armed forces. It is in the same category as the .32/20 or the now obsolete .32 Winchester self-loader. Many U.S. carbines have been and are still being sold to American shooters. It cannot be classed as a varmint or big game cartridge but actually it is used quite extensively for both. This cartridge has been used to a degree by handgunners. Numerous gunsmiths have converted Colt Single Action revolvers to take the M1 Carbine cartridge. The military cartridge is loaded with the 110 grain bullet to 1975 foot seconds.

93 gr. bullet	14 gr.	2400 powder	2000 fs
100	15	4227	1975
	17	4227	2200
	15	2400	2100
110	13	2400	1900
	14	4227	1950 est.

Standard twist: 20"
Special twist: 10", 14", 16"

.30/30 Winchester

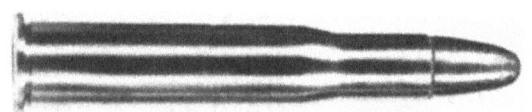

The .30/30 is probably the best known of all cartridges. Actually there are hundreds of thousands of rifles in use chambered for this cartridge. The .30 Remington is the rimless version and ballistics for the two cartridges are practically identical. All of the existing arms companies in the United States have made and are still making rifles for this cartridge. In addition many foreign manufacturers have made rifles for it. The .30/30 has a reputation for

MAXIMUM LOAD LISTED SHOULD BE APPROACHED WITH CARE

being relatively inaccurate. This is not true because when it is put in a good rifle such as the old Model 54 Winchester, it does as well as any other .30 calibre cartridge. The reputation comes from the rifles themselves. Most ".30/30's" are of the lever action type or some extremely low quality bolt contraption. These rifles are accurate enough for practical hunting but seldom possess target accuracy. The .30/30 case can be blown out to form an improved version with a sharp shoulder, shorter neck and minimum body taper and handloaded to almost equal the .300 Savage. Two other cartridges in this same class and with practically identical ballistics are the .32 Special and the .32 Remington. These two cases are the same as the .30/30 and .30 Remington except for the neck diameter which is .012 larger to accommodate a .32 calibre bullet. Shot out .30/30's can be rebored to .32 Special.

110 gr. bullet	21 gr.	2400 powder	2400 fs
	32	4198	2700
	26	4895	2600
150	24	2400	2210
	31	HiVel #2	2315
	35	3031	2450
	30	4895	2250
	33	4064	2200
170	30	HiVel #2	2180
	33	3031	2190
	30	4895	2200
	28	4198	2275

The following loads are recommended for Norma and Nobel powders:

170 gr. Cast Gas-check bullet
        16 gr.   Nobel's Hornet powder   1700 fs
        26   Norma 200   2000
150 gr. Jacketed bullet
        31 gr.   4740   2400
170 gr. Jacketed bullet
        30 gr.   4740   2150
        32.4   Norma 201   2220

Standard twist: 12"
Special twist: 10"

MAXIMUM LOAD LISTED SHOULD BE APPROACHED WITH CARE

.30/30 Improved (Ackley)

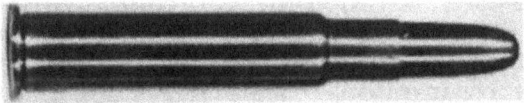

The Improved .30/30 in its various versions, all of which are quite similar to the one illustrated, is quite decidedly a surprising cartridge. With its minimum body taper design it can be loaded relatively "hot" and still work fine in lever action rifles. It is an easy cartridge to handload and can be highly recommended.

Bullet	Powder charge	Powder	Velocity
77.2 gr. bullet	38 gr.	4227 powder	3710 fs
110	30	4227	3280
	36	4198	3175
125	39	3031	2940
	35	4198	2940
150	34	4198	2700
	36	3031	2535
	37	HiVel #2	2700
	38	3031	2700
	40	4320	2500
	43	H375	2535

Standard twist: 10"

.30 Lever Power

This is a cartridge developed by Fred Wade of Wade's Gun Room, Phoenix, Arizona. Cases are made by turning down the rim of .303 British or the .30/40 Krag, then shortening the overall length of the case to standard .30/30 length. This could be called in "improved" version since it utilizes the sharp shoulder and minimum body type of "improved" cartridges. It was designed especially for use in Model 94 Winchester, Models 93 and 336 Marlin and the Model 99 Savage rifle made for the .30/30 series

MAXIMUM LOAD LISTED SHOULD BE APPROACHED WITH CARE

of cartridges. This cartridge is especially well adapted for brush shooting. The following loads were tested in a Model 94 Winchester with a 20" barrel. Mr. Wade will chamber rifles in any calibre for this cartridge. That is, he can furnish chambers in .25, .30, .32, .38, also in 6mm, .270 etc. This means that if one has a .25/35 and desires more "poop", it can be rechambered for this more powerful cartridge in .25 calibre and very nearly equal a bolt action.

150 gr. bullet	41 gr.	4064 powder	2670 fs
	42	4064	2700
	43	4064	2770

Standard twist: 10"

.308 x 1.5 Inch

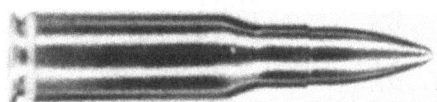

The .308 x 1.5 Inch cartridge was designed by Frank C. Barnes of Santa Fe, New Mexico in March 1961. It is based on the .308 Winchester case shortened to 1.50 inch. Other dimensions are the same except the body taper. Many Wildcat cartridges are based on Military cases, but this is probably the only Wildcat Military cartridge ever designed. It is an assault rifle cartridge similar to the German 7.92mm Kurtz and the Russian 7.62mm (M-43).

With all the blown out, expanded, lengthened and magnumized cartridges being developed, the .308 x 1.5 inch is definitely counter to the trend of the times. However, these small cartridges are extremely efficient and deliver performance out of proportion to their size. The .308 x 1.5 Inch will actually deliver initial velocities greater than the .30/30 WCF. Recoil and muzzle blast are quite moderate and these small cartridges are unusually well adapted to short actions and ultra light rifles. In field tests several deer and antelope were killed cleanly by this little cartridge using the 150 grain Nosler bullet at 2532 fs. With bullets of 100 to 125 grains it is a fine varmint cartridge out to 250 or even 300 yards. It has proven to be unusually accurate and and several heavy bench rest and target rifles have been

MAXIMUM LOAD LISTED SHOULD BE APPROACHED WITH CARE

made up in this calibre. It may be that its most important role will be as an International Match cartridge. Several individuals working on assault rifle designs are using the .308 x 1.5 Inch.

Bullet	Powder charge	Powder	Velocity
80 gr. bullet	25 gr.	Ball C powder	2140 fs
	33	Ball C	2750
	28	4198	2875
	29	4198	2938
93	33	Ball C	2651
	28.5	4198	2835
100	33	Ball C	2612
	28.5	4198	2808
125	32	Ball C	2428
	24	H380	1680
	30	H380	2015
	28	3031	2300
	29	3031	2352
	22	4198	2155
	27	4198	2557
	28	4198	2641
150	29	Ball C	2160
	23	H380	1589
	28	3031	2371
	27	4064	2032
	21	4198	2027
	26	4198	2456
	27	4198	2532
170	27.5	3031	2112
	24.5	4198	2233
180	26	3031	2035
	24.1	4198	2180

Standard twist: 10"
Special twist: 12"

.30/40 Krag

This is one of our best and most famous .30 calibre cartridges. It is known by several names as .30 Army, .30/40 Krag, and .30 USA. It was designed for use in

MAXIMUM LOAD LISTED SHOULD BE APPROACHED WITH CARE

the various models of Krag rifles used by the U.S. Army from 1893 until the adoption of the Model 1903 Springfield. Several sporting rifles have been made for this cartridge, the most famous of which is the Model 95 Winchester box magazine lever action rifle. Thousands of Krag rifles have been sold by the DCM with a good percentage still in use. The .30/40 is a very good cartridge for handloading and one of the most effective .30 calibre cartridges for use on big game.

Bullet	Powder charge		Powder	Velocity
100 gr. bullet	35	gr.	4198 powder	2695 fs
	37		4198	2860
	40		3031	2615
	45		3031	2945
150	38		HiVel #2	2320
	40		HiVel #2	2440
	40		3031	2520
	42		3031	2645
	40		4064	2300
	45		4064	2590
180	36		HiVel #2	2240
	38		HiVel #2	2360
	40		4064	2340
	40		4320	2335
200	37		4320	2035
	42		4350	2010
	47		4831	2160
220	39		4320	2190
	43		4350	2250

Standard twist: 10"

.30/40 Improved (Ackley)

The Improved .30/40 is one of the best of the "Improved" cartridges but it has never gained popularity because of the lack of suitable actions. It is a very fine cartridge for the better single shot actions like the Hi-wall Winchester, Sharps Borchardt or the P14 Enfield. There is also a number of the old Winchester Model 54's in .30/30 calibre which can easily be converted for the Improved

MAXIMUM LOAD LISTED SHOULD BE APPROACHED WITH CARE

.30/40. Due to the wide rim and relatively strong case, it handles high pressures well and loads equalling the standard .300 Magnum have been used for a long time by owners of rifles chambered for the cartridge. Cases are made by fire forming factory loads in the improved chamber.

150 gr. bullet	53 gr.	HiVel #2	3287 fs
180	54	4350	2740
	56	4350	2920
	50	4064	2902
220	58	4350	2603

Standard twist: 10"

.300 Savage

The .300 Savage is a relatively short rimless cartridge with the regular .30/06 head diameter especially designed for the Model 99 Savage lever action rifle. This cartridge has been very successful on all types of North American game and other types of big game throughout the world. It became extremely popular among lever action rifle fans for use on all kind of big game. For practical purposes it comparess favorably to the .30/40 or even the .30/06 under average hunting conditions. It is still a very good cartridge even though it has been somewhat supplanted by the recently introduced .308 Winchester. The .300 Savage is a very good cartridge to consider for shot out .250/3000 Savage rifles. These rifles can easily be rebored and converted to take the .300 Savage which is approximately the same length and will work through the action with minimum alteration. This short .30 calibre cartridge is best adapted for bullets no heavier than 150 grains, although heavier 180 grain bullets are often used.

100 gr. bullet	46 gr.	4895 powder	2880 fs
	45	4064	3025
	42	3031	2975
110	33	4198	2690
	38	4198	3000
	43	H380	2675

MAXIMUM LOAD LISTED SHOULD BE APPROACHED WITH CARE

	gr.		
	48	H380 powder	2925 fs
	50	H380	3000
	42	3031	2890
	44	3031	2975
	42	4895	2730
	46	4895	2935
	47	4895	2870
125-130	41	H380	2590
	47	H380	2790
	41	3031	2860
	40	4895	2450
	46	4895	2780
	40	HiVel #2	2700
150	39	H380	2300
	42	H380	2450
	44	H380	2650
	38	4320	2320
	43	4320	2570
	45	4320	2530
	37	4895	2330
	42	4895	2500
	34	HiVel #2	2450
	36	HiVel #2	2550
	38	HiVel #2	2650
	39	HiVel #2	2700
165	39	4064	2450
	41	4064	2560
	43	H380	2390
	42	4320	2525
	37	HiVel #2	2650
180	45	4350	2420
	41	H380	2275
	34	HiVel #2	2320
	37	HiVel #2	2470

Standard twist: 10"

7.5 Swiss

This is a very nicely designed cartridge and has become more important to American shooters during the last two or three years during which the country has been flooded

MAXIMUM LOAD LISTED SHOULD BE APPROACHED WITH CARE

with these rifles. There seems to be no commercial brass made in this country which can be used for making these cases. The diameter at the base is larger than the .30/06 and smaller than our Magnum brass. The owners of these rifles just about have to use Swiss ammunition which is loaded with Berdan primers, thus making it difficult to reload. It is also difficult to convert the Swiss rifle to handle any American cartridge and after a conversion has been accomplished for something like the .308 Winchester, the owner still has a very clumsy rifle impractical for hunting purposes. The best advice to the shooting public is to let these military rifles alone except for collections. The sale of the Swiss, Italian and similar military rifles has been pushed by certain dealers, mostly because there is a lot of money in imported surplus weapons which can be bought for practically nothing and sold to American shooters at a profit many times higher than could possibly be made on sporting rifles of American manufacture. This does not apply to all imported surplus rifles. Many thousands of Mexican Mausers, German Mausers, some types of Mannlichers, many models of European single shot rifles, and many others can form the foundation of very fine rifles because they have well designed, strong actions which can readily be converted to sporting use. If a prospective customer is not familiar with imported items such as the Swiss and Italian, he should consult a competent gunsmith before investing in one.

The following loads were developed by Arthur E. Anderson, a gunsmith who specializes in converting these rifles. Further information can be obtained by writing direct to Arthur E. Anderson, 1128 Los Olivos Avenue, San Luis Opispo, Los Osos Station, California.

150 gr. bullet	46 gr.	4064 powder	2750 fs est.
	47.5	4320	2700 est.
	45	4895	2500 est.
180	51.5	4831	2550 est.
	49	4350	2450 est.

The above loads were developed with .3085 bullets and Winchester 120 primers. Mr. Anderson reduced all of the above loads one grain with Berdan primers. Unprimed brass for standard American or boxer primer is available from Golden State Arms Corporation, 386 West Green Street, Pasadena, California.

MAXIMUM LOAD LISTED SHOULD BE APPROACHED WITH CARE

7.62 Russian

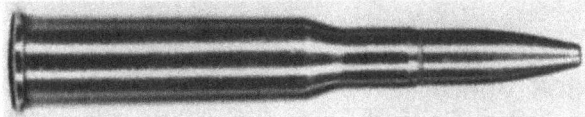

The 7.62 Russian is the official Russian military cartridge and it came to the attention of the American shooter just after World War I when large numbers of Russian rifles were dumped on the American market by the DCM. Many American shooters purchased these rifles for $2.00 each and converted them to sporters. About that time the American ammunition manufacturers started producing sporting ammunition but later discontinued the manufacture, and for a long time the cartridge has been more or less dormant. During the last two or three years numbers of Russian automatic rifles and other models of Russian rifles have again been sold in the United States thus once again reviving the 7.62 Russian cartridge. This is a rimmed cartridge of fairly good design and develops ballistics quite similar to the standard .30/06. The 7.62 Russian can be loaded with the standard .308 diameter or .30 caliber bullet.

Bullet	Charge	Powder	Velocity
110 gr. bullet	56 gr.	4831 powder	3140 fs
	53	4895	3185
	50	3031	3125
	54	H380	3150
150	56	4831	2675
	47	HiVel #2	2765
	50	4895	2735
	49	4064	2740
	54	4350	2700
	51	H380	2695
180	55	4831	2645
	50	4320	2685
	52	4350	2640
	50	H380	2650

MAXIMUM LOAD LISTED SHOULD BE APPROACHED WITH CARE

.308 Winchester (7.65 Nato)

The .308 Winchester was introduced by the Winchester Repeating Arms Company a few years ago and it has gained wide popularity. It is the best factory cartridge available for the 7.7 Jap rifle. The 7.7 Jap barrel can be set back and rechambered for the relatively powerful .308 for a low labor charge to produce a low cost rifle which is safe and fairly accurate. Many gunsmiths are requested to change the Model 99 Savage in .300 Savage to handle the slightly longer .308 but this cannot be done. Savage 99 actions made for the .300 Savage cannot be altered, therefore this conversion should not be considered. There is a Model 99 now being produced for the .308 but this action is different than the others.

Bullet	Charge	Powder	Velocity
93 gr. bullet	49 gr.	3031 powder	3340 fs
110	49.5	Ball C	2790
	41	4198	2895
	42.2	4198	2985
	43	4198	3095
	45	4198	3325
	48	HiVel #2	3100
	50	HiVel #2	3200
	46	3031	3100
	48	3031	3185
	26.5	2400	2590
	49	4895	3020
	50.5	4064	3065
	52	4064	3155
125	49.5	Ball C	2855
	40	4198	3025
	45	3031	2510
	50	4320	3000
140	48	Ball C	2740
	41.3	4198	2955
150	46.5	Ball C	2655
	47	4198	2600
	33	HiVel #2	2185
	41.5	HiVel #2	2710

MAXIMUM LOAD LISTED SHOULD BE APPROACHED WITH CARE

LOADING DATA 421

	gr.	powder	fs
	43	HiVel #2 powder	2660 fs
	45	HiVel #2	2800
	44	3031	2800
	44.5	3031	2815
	46.5	4895	2860
	46	4064	2850
	48	4320	2750
152	46.5	Ball C	2670
	39.6	4198	2680
	46.5	4895	2680
	46.5	4320	2785
166	42.6	Ball C	2430
	46.8	4320	2695
172	42	Ball C	2365
	46.8	4320	2670
180	35	4198	2360
	38	HiVel #2	2475
	40	HiVel #2	2560
	48	4350	2425
	50	4350	2510
	51.5	4350	2625
	41	4895	2270
	43	4895	2415
	41	4064	2360
	43	4064	2505
	43	4320	2450
	45	4320	2550
200	41	4320	2245
	43	4320	2360
	45	4350	2230
	47	4350	2305
	48	4350	2470
	41	4320	2245
	43	4320	2360
220	45	4320	2375
160 gas check	20.5	4198	1580
195 gas check	30.4	4895	1880

The following loads are recommended for Norma and Nobel powders:

150 gr. Cast Gas-check bullet
        16 gr.   Nobel's Hornet powder 1800 fs
110 gr. Jacketed
        46   4740   3000
        40.5   Norma 200   2900
        44.4   4740   2900

MAXIMUM LOAD LISTED SHOULD BE APPROACHED WITH CARE

150 gr. Jacketed
- 43 — 4740 powder — 2750 fs
- 46 — Nobel 41 — 2850
- 45.5 — Norma 201 — 2860

180 gr. Jacketed
- 42.5 — Nobel 41 — 2500
- 44.3 — Norma 203 — 2610

Standard twist: 10"

7.65 MM Mauser

The 7.65 MM Mauser is a military cartridge used by several different European nations. It is sometimes referred to as the 7.65 Belgian and the model 1889 Belgian Mauser was designed for this cartridge. Rifles have been manufactured in the United States for this cartridge, mainly the old Model 54 Winchester and the Remington 30S, and both companies manufactured ammunition for many years. It became almost a forgotten number until recently when large numbers of these rifles were imported into this country chambered for the 7.65 MM, notably the Model 1891 and the Model 1909 Argentine Mausers. The Model 1891 is similar to the 1889 Belgian model. Both have the vertical magazine in front of the trigger guard while the 1909 Model Argentine Mauser has the hinged floor plate identical to the commercial Mauser hinged floor plate made before World War II. The Model 1891 is best left in its original calibre while the Model 1909 can be converted to .30/06 by simply rechambering the barrel or it can be re-barrelled for almost any modern cartridge. The Model 1889 and 91 Mausers are relatively strong actions but not desirable as a basis for a custom rifle. Loaded ammunition is now manufactured by Norma and cases are very easily made by re-forming .30/06 brass. This cartridge comes midway between the .308 Winchester and the .30/06.

100 gr. bullet
- 46 gr. — 4895 powder — 2980 fs
- 50 — 4895 — 3130
- 45 — 4064 — 3035

MAXIMUM LOAD LISTED SHOULD BE APPROACHED WITH CARE

	47	gr.	4064 powder	3140 fs
	45		3031	3150
150	48		4350	2500
	50		4350	2630
	43		H380	2450
	45		H380	2550
	43		4895	2530
	45		4895	2650
	45		4320	2710
	39		HiVel #2	2750
	40		3031	2700
	44		4064	2675
180	44		4350	2200
	46		4350	2350
	42		4320	2440
	39		4895	2280
	41		4895	2340
	42		4320	2440
	39		4064	2400
	42		4064	2525
	37		3031	2390
	36		HiVel #2	2400

Standard twist: 10"

.30 Improved Arch

The .30 Improved Arch employs the same design as the other "improved" Arch cartridges with the exception of the body length which has been increased noticeably. Since the overall length is the same as standard 6.5 x 55, the .30 Arch has a shorter neck, but consisting of all of the same characteristics of the other Cartridges in the Arch line, and this is a relatively efficient .30 calibre cartridge, developing velocities comparable to the standard .30/06. Like the 7mm Arch Improved, it provides a solution for rejuvenating Swiss rifles which have been shot out, by simply reboring the old barrel to larger size and rechambering which is a great deal more economical than a new barrel job.

MAXIMUM LOAD LISTED SHOULD BE APPROACHED WITH CARE

130 gr. bullet	52.5 gr.	4320 powder	3163 fs
	60	4350	3100
150	58	4350	3010
	50.5	4320	2946
165	49	4320	2833
	53	4350	2720
	54	4350	2791
180	53.5	4350	2663
200	49.5	4831	2363

Standard twist: 10"

.300 ICL Tornado

This is the same case as the .277 ICL Flying Saucer, except, necked up to .30 calibre. Doubtless this could be developed into one of the very finest of the .30 calibre cartridges. It is quite similar to the .308 Winchester and being of the so-called improved design, it would doubtless be more satisfactory for handloading. It could easily duplicate the .30/06 ballistics.

125 gr. bullet	52 gr.	4350 powder	2791 fs
	54	4350	2871
	50	4320	2941
	41	4895	2792
	56	4831	2716
150	48	4350	2576
	52	4350	2790
	54	4350	3041
	45	4320	2791
	48	4320	2951
180	50	4350	2646
	51	4350	2716
	52	4350	2791
220	44	4350	2186
	46	4350	2336

Standard twist: 10"

MAXIMUM LOAD LISTED SHOULD BE APPROACHED WITH CARE

.30/06

This old standby is shown for purposes of comparison. The loading data which follows can be compared with the various smaller and larger .30 calibre wildcats. It is also interesting to compare this data to the loading data for the .270 Winchester. It will be seen that the .30/06 is a lot more gun over the average hunting ranges than the .270 is with equal weight bullets. Of course the .270 150 gr. factory load may be flatter at ranges out beyond 1000 or 1500 yards than the .30/06 150 gr. factory load but very few shooters are able to hit a flock of circus tents at these ranges without first sighting in. Within game ranges the 150 gr. .30/06 bullet is quite noticeably flatter and has more oomph when it arrives. This does not mean that the .270 is not a good killer because it has sufficient power for all practical hunting. The .30/06 is not only a good practical big game gun, it is also the mother and father of a countless number of good, bad and worthless wildcat kittens.

110 gr. bullet	57	gr.	4895 powder	3330 fs
	48		HiVel #2	3165
	54		HiVel #2	3300
	53		3031	3330
	54		3031	3375
	57		4320	3235
125	48		HiVel #2	3140
	55		4320	3130
	55		4064	3100
	59		4350	3200
130	51		3031	3090
	52		3031	3155
150	44		3031	2550
	45		3031	2610
	50		3031	2975
	51		3031	2990
	47		4064	2540
	50		4064	2720
	52		4064	2880

MAXIMUM LOAD LISTED SHOULD BE APPROACHED WITH CARE

	53 gr.	4064 powder	2940 fs
	54	4064	3000
	48	4320	2630
	52	4320	2820
	53	4320	2905
	53	4895	2905
	55	4895	3010
	54	4350	2680
	56	4350	2715
	57	4350	2760
	59	4350	2945
	61	4350	3045
	37	HiVel #2	2295
	43	HiVel #2	2590
	44	HiVel #2	2610
	46	HiVel #2	2875
	47	HiVel #2	2915
200	52	4350	2515
	56	4350	2715
220	50	4350	2385
	52	4350	2425
	58	4350	2600
	49	4320	2415
	41	HiVel #2	2355
250	54	4831	2450

The following loads are recommended for Norma and Nobel powders:

150 gr. Cast Gas-check bullet
- 20 gr. Nobel's Hornet powder 1800 fs
- 20   Norma 200   1400
- 27   Norma 200   2000

110 gr. Jacketed bullet
- 50   4740   3000

130 gr. Jacketed bullet
- 50   4740   3000
- 57.5 Norma 203   3280

150 gr. Jacketed bullet
- 46   4740   2800
- 53   Nobel 41   2900
- 54.7 Norma 203   2970

180 gr. Jacketed bullet
- 44.5 4740   2550
- 50   Nobel 41   2700
- 50   Norma 203   2700

220 gr. Jacketed bullet
- 47.3 Norma 203   2410

Standard twist: 10"
Special twist: 12"

MAXIMUM LOAD LISTED SHOULD BE APPROACHED WITH CARE

.30/06 ICL Caribou

The ICL Caribou is an Improved .30/06, and is a very good efficient cartridge. All improved '06 cartridges are especially good with the 180 gr. or heavier bullets, in combination with slow burning powder. They easily equal .300 H & H factory loads. (Please note that the words "factory loads" are always used when comparisons are made between Improved .30/06 and .300 Magnum cartridges, because very likely the .300 Magnum can be steamed up to velocities which conceivably would be unattainable with the Improved .30/06). When properly loaded with suitable bullets, the ICL Caribou and similar versions, is adequate for any North American game.

150 gr. bullet	57 gr.	4895 powder	3150 fs
	60	4064	3360
	61.5	4350	3235
172	58	4350	2866
	62	4350	3076
180	60	4350	2950
	61	4350	2996
	61.5	4350	3030
	64	4831	2940
220	58	4350	2800

Standard twist: 10"

.30/06 Improved (Ackley)

This and similar improved version of the well known .30/06 have developed into quite controversial cartridges. Actually they have a great deal of merit and for handloaders they can be highly recommended. Various articles

MAXIMUM LOAD LISTED SHOULD BE APPROACHED WITH CARE

have appeared in sporting magazines written by individuals who do not believe in the "improved" idea. Invariably loads appear in these articles which do no credit to the cartridge while the loads which really show something have been carefully left out. A cartridge which has gained such world wide popularity does not do it without merit. Since its introduction just after World War II (some versions came before that, but did not catch on) it has become one of the most popular of all wildcat or improved cartridges. Cases are made by firing factory loads in the improved chamber, and of course factory ammunition can regularly be used in the improved chamber without serious loss in velocity. This cartridge is particularly good with bullets of 180 gr. or heavier and with these bullets it equals the standard factory .300 H&H Magnum factory loads.

Bullet	Powder charge	Powder	Velocity
150 gr. bullet	50 gr.	HiVel #2 powder	2915 fs
	52	HiVel #2	3100
	55	HiVel #2	3215 too hot for some guns
	52	4895	2960
	54	4895	3035
	50	4064	2960
	55	4064	3150
180	55	4350	2720
	60	4350	2920
	61	4350	3053
220	50	4350	2420
	53	4350	2500
	55	4350	2645

Standard twist: 10"
Special twist: 12"

.30 Howell

This is a short cartridge designed by John A. Howell of Havana, Kansas. It is based on the .348 Winchester case necked down and shortened and Mr. Howell has found that Winchester brass is thicker, thus creating a smaller capacity case than Remington brass. The case was designed

MAXIMUM LOAD LISTED SHOULD BE APPROACHED WITH CARE

for 100% loading density, and he uses Remington brass which has greater powder capacity with light bullets and the Winchester brass for heavier bullets. This allows him to use a case full of powder for each weight of bullet. His rifle is built on a P14 Enfield action and like the .30/.378 Arch, it should give uniform ignition and pressure which should result in fine accuracy. Mr. Howell has found that when using Ball powder that finely ground spheres will find their way down into the flash hole and into the primer thus creating ignition trouble. To prevent this Mr. Howell inserts a small cellophane disc in the primer pocket ahead of the primer. He uses CCI Magnum primers, and when the cellophane disc is used very uniform pressure is obtained. After experimenting with this cartridge Mr. Howell feels it would be a good idea for the factories to introduce cartridges with a capacity which would assure 100% loading density, and then produce cases with thin side walls and with thick side walls for use with light and heavy bullets. He feels that a large diameter powder column with Magnum primers help burn a large percentage of powder in the case without raising pressure too fast. He also feels that such a cartridge should be quite efficient in relatively short barrels.

Bullet	Powder charge	Powder	Velocity
100 gr. bullet	56 gr.	4895 powder	3350 fs
	60	4320	3500
	50	3031	3300
	54	3031	3560
110	56	4320	3350
	59.5	4320	3500
125	55	4064	3300
130	54	4320	3250
	57	4320	3400
150	65	4831	3200
	56	4350	2800
	58	4350	2950
	60	Ball C	3200
165	63	4350	3150
180	54	4350	2650
	63	4350	3100

Standard twist: 10"

MAXIMUM LOAD LISTED SHOULD BE APPROACHED WITH CARE

.300 Bennett Magnum

The Bennett Magnum is the third of the series developed by Byard Bennett. This should be an extremely good efficient cartridge probably somewhat superior to the two smaller Magnums since this cartridge would have an almost ideal maximum case capacity for the .30 calibre bore. Mr. Bennett recommends .30/06 loading data but it is quite obvious that loading data listed for the #1 short .30 Ackley Magnum could also be used with safety.

Chambering reamers for the Bennett Magnum series are available from Keith Francis of Talent, Oregon. Mr. Francis also manufactures a very complete line of fine chambering reamers and is always willing to make special reamers if specifications are furnished with the order.

Standard twist: 10"

.30 short Magnum No. 1 (Ackley)

This is one of the shortest if not the shortest .30 Magnum Wildcat cartridges. It is the same as the .270 or 7mm Ackley Magnums except for neck diameter. Because it is relatively short and has a powder capacity of less than 70 gr (maximum for .30 calibre for best efficiency) it is a cartridge which can be highly recommended for use on big game. It produces practically the same ballistics as the standard .300 H & H with less powder and it is short enough to work through standard actions without alteration except for opening the bolt face for the larger head. .30/06 barrels cannot be rechambered for this No. 1 Short .30 Magnum without setting the barrel back one thread. This

MAXIMUM LOAD LISTED SHOULD BE APPROACHED WITH CARE

prevents the accidental firing of .30/06 cartridges. One forming and trimming die is necessary to form cases from .300 Magnum brass. Cases are fire formed and a good stiff load is best for the fireforming step. This is a very satisfactory cartridge.

110 gr. bullet	67 gr.	4064 powder	3650 fs
125	62	3031	3560
150	64	4064	3245
	68	4350	3220
180	58	4064	2940
	63	4350	2950
	67	4350	3050
220	62	4350	2704

Standard twist: 10"

.30 short Magnum No. 2 (Ackley)

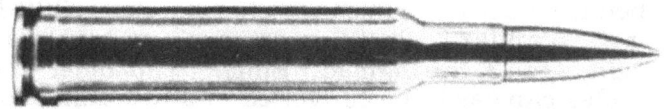

This cartridge is of the same design as the No. 1 Short .30 Magnum except its length has been increased enough to make it possible to rechamber standard .30/06 barrels without setting them back. It is not as an efficient case as the No. 1, but not so badly over bore capacity that flexibility is lost and barrels wear out too quickly. There are many similar versions originated by other gunsmiths. The .30 Luft and the .300 Apex Magnums are very similar and loading data can be interchanged. Since there are several of these cartridges so similar, no one of them could be recommended over another.

150 gr. bullet	58 gr.	4895 powder	3100 fs
	67	4350	3190
180	54	4064	2810
	67	4350	3060
220	64	4350	2650

Standard twist: 10"

MAXIMUM LOAD LISTED SHOULD BE APPROACHED WITH CARE

.30 Belted Newton

The .30 Belted Newton is also known as the .30-.338 which means that this cartridge is simply made by necking down the .338 Winchester Magnum case to .30 calibre to produce a cartridge very similar but not quite identical to the older #2 Short .30 Ackley Magnum, and the later .308 Norma Magnum. All three cartridges are very similar and all produce practically the same results in the field. The .30 Belted Newton became quite popular just after the introduction of the .338 Winchester Magnum, but shortly after that the .308 Norma Magnum became available which has the advantage of factory loaded ammunition and factory cases. This is a very good long range .30 calibre cartridge being somewhat superior to the standard .300 H&H Magnum. Standard .30/06 rifles such as high number Springfield, O3A3 Springfield, Enfield and other similar .30/06 rifles can easily be converted and rechambered. Standard twist: 10"

.300 Durham Magnum

The .300 Durham Magnum is made by shortening the .300 H&H Magnum cases to an overall length of 2.510. This cartridge is what could be described as a short .30 Magnum and should have just about the maximum capacity for the .30 calibre bore. It is a very fine cartridge to use where standard .30/06 rifles have to be rechambered. It has sufficient power for all North American game. The following loads were developed in a 24 inch barrel with 10 inch twist, and are near maximum, therefore should be approached with caution.

MAXIMUM LOAD LISTED SHOULD BE APPROACHED WITH CARE

125 gr. bullet	72 gr.	4320 powder	3660 fs
150	74	4350	3310
180	71	4350	3090
200	69	4350	2935

Standard twist: 10"

.300 Apex Magnum

The .300 Apex Magnum is the same case as the 6.5 Apex, but necked up to accept .30 calibre bullets. This should be a fine cartridge of about maximum capacity for the .30 bore. It is noticeably longer than the No. 2 short .30 Ackley Magnum, but otherwise of almost identical design.

125 gr. bullet	69 gr.	4895 powder	3686 fs
150	65	4895	3480
172	70	4350	3203
180	69	4350	3213
220	68	4350	2885
	69	4831	2780

Loads shown for the No. 2 short Ackley .30 Magnum can also be used.

Standard twist: 10"

.300 Wade Magnum

The .300 Wade Magnum was developed by Fred Wade of Wade's Gun Room of Phoenix, Arizona, and could be described as a "short" .30 Magnum. It is practically the same as the #2 short .30 Ackley Magnum, both of these cartridges being just long enough to clean up old .30/06

MAXIMUM LOAD LISTED SHOULD BE APPROACHED WITH CARE

chambers. Cartridges of this type have been supplanted by the .308 Norma which is only slightly longer and being commercially available it is more appealing to most shooters. However, these two shorter cartridges are a little bit more efficient than the .308 Norma and for shooters who load their own ammunition, these short Magnums are very desirable cartridges.

125 gr. bullet	66 gr.	4064 powder	3600 fs est.
150	60	4064	3200 est.
180	57	4064	2875 est.

Standard twist: 10"

.300 ICL Grizzly Cub

The ICL Grizzly Cub is a short .30 Magnum designed for use in standard length actions without alterations except the bolt face and extractor. Cases are formed from .338 Winchester, or .308 Norma brass, and this cartridge was developed by the Juenke-Saturn Gun Shop of Sparks, Nevada. Like other short .30 Magnum cartridges, the ICL Grizzly Cub can be highly recommended.

150 gr. bullet	74 gr.	4350 powder	3280 fs
	76	4350	3590
180	69	4350	3105
	71	4350	3200
220	70	4831	2705

Standard twist: 10"

.30/.348 Improved (Ackley)

MAXIMUM LOAD LISTED SHOULD BE APPROACHED WITH CARE

The .30/.348 is a cartridge designed upon request of Bob Hutton of "Guns and Ammo" magazine. It is the smallest of a series of cartridges based on the "improved" .348 case. It is a relatively efficient long range .30 calibre cartridge but has to be loaded with discretion for the lever action Model 71 Winchester rifle because of the limited diameter of the barrel in the chamber section. The following loads have proven to be safe in rifles barrelled with high tensile strength steel barrels.

170 gr. bullet	60	gr.	4350 powder	2710 fs
	61		4350	2760
	48		HiVel #2	2665
	49		HiVel #2	2710

Standard twist: 10"

.300 Mashburn Short Magnum

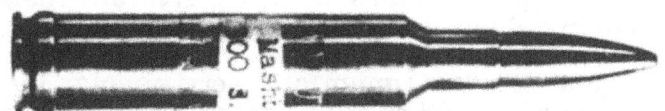

This is a true short Magnum made by necking down and shortening regular .300 H&H cases. Like all Mashburn cartridges, it has the 30° shoulder. Although slightly longer than the No. 2 Ackley Short Magnum, it is very similar to that case. The overall length of the Short .300 Mashburn (2.530) is less than the 7MM Mashburn Magnum, making it a much better balanced cartridge than the 6.5, .270, and 7MM Mashburn Magnums. The capacity of the short .300 Mashburn is about the same as the standard .300 H&H, but it is a much better designed cartridge for use with modern American powders.

130 gr. bullet	62	gr.	HiVel #2 powder	3484 fs
	60		3031	3390
	64		4064	3410
	65		4320	3415
	73		4350	3400
150	68		4350	3300
	70		4831	3350
180	66		4350	2885
	68		4831	2980

MAXIMUM LOAD LISTED SHOULD BE APPROACHED WITH CARE

220 gr. bullet	66 gr.	4350 powder	2780 fs
	69	4831	2860
250	63	4831	2470

Standard twist: 10"

.308 Norma Magnum

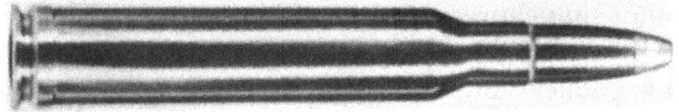

The .308 Norma Magnum is a short .30 calibre Magnum quite similar to the older #2 short .30 Ackley Magnum with the exception that the body is slightly longer thus producing slightly greater capacity. Although this slightly greater capacity makes it slightly less efficient than the other shorter .30 calibre Magnums, it has the great advantage of the availability of factory ammunition and factory components. It is a somewhat more efficient cartridge than the standard .300 H&H Magnum and very popular for converting standard .30/06 rifles to a more powerful Magnum cartridge. Like other Norma developments, ammunition and components are marketed in this country by Norma Precision, South Lansing, New York. The .308 Norma Magnum is a cartridge which could be highly recommended for all species of North American game as well as other big game throughout the world.

110 gr. bullet	66 gr.	4320 powder	3540 fs
	64	4064	3615
	66	4064	3720
	60	3031	3450
	59	HiVel #2	3550
130	74	4350	3330
	76	4350	3420
	80	4831	3290
	82	4831	3400
	64	4064	3420
	60	3031	3330
	57	HiVel #2	3310
	59	HiVel #2	3400
150	71	4350	3240
	73	4350	3290
	77	4831	3200

MAXIMUM LOAD LISTED SHOULD BE APPROACHED WITH CARE

	79 gr.	4831 powder	3265 fs
	63	4895	3140
	65	4895	3225
	62	4064	3210
	56	HiVel #2	3160
180	67	4350	2940
	69	4350	3020
	73	4831	2940
	75	4831	3025
	55	4895	2700
	57	4895	2765
	53	3031	2790
	52	HiVel #2	2830
	72.5	Norma 204	3100
200	66	4350	2815
	68	4350	2900
	71	4831	2815
	73	4831	2895
	54	4895	2670
	56	4895	2735

The following is loading data for the .308 Norma Magnum as recommended by the Norma factory:

110 gr. bullet	67.5 gr.	4064 powder	3406 fs
	68.5	4064	3484
	69.5	4064	3622
	70.5	4064	3694
130	66	4064	3380
	67	4064	3464
	68	4064	3516
150	65	4064	3156
	66	4064	3219
	67	4064	3271
180	69	4350	3006
	70	4350	3055
	71	4350	3087
	71.5	4350	3116
220	65.5	4350	2687
	66.5	4350	2720
	67.5	4350	2746

Standard twist: 12"
Special twist: 10"

MAXIMUM LOAD LISTED SHOULD BE APPROACHED WITH CARE

.300 H&H Magnum

This is another standard cartridge inserted here for purposes of comparison. It was originated by the old English firm of Holland and Holland. It was designed for Cordite powder and is not a particularly well designed case for American powders. It is somewhat over bore capacity and considerably more powder is used than the .30/06 to achieve a given velocity but because it does hold more powder it drives .30 calibre bullets somewhat faster than the 06 if enough powder is used. The relative efficiency of the two cases can be studied by comparing data tables for each. The design of the standard .300 Magnum case employs a rather steep body taper and long sloping shoulder which results in case separation just forward of the belt after the cases have been loaded a few times. This trouble is eliminated in the Improved .300 or the .300 Weatherby because of the absence of these two objectional features.

Bullet	Powder charge	Powder	Velocity
125 gr. bullet	65 gr.	3031 powder	3480 fs
150	60	HiVel #2	3195
	61	HiVel #2	3210
	62	HiVel #2	3265
172	72	4350	3160
180	55	HiVel #2	2825
	57	HiVel #2	2950
	57.5	4064	2925
	60	4064	2950
	60	4895	2915
	66	4350	2850
	67	4350	3000
	67	4831	2970
	69	4831	3055
	69.3	Norma 204	2920
200	54	HiVel #2	2620
	56	4064	2600
	57	4064	2680
	57	4320	2635
	64	4350	2705
	65	4350	2770
	66	4350	2805

MAXIMUM LOAD LISTED SHOULD BE APPROACHED WITH CARE

LOADING DATA

220 gr. bullet	55.5 gr.	4064 powder	2550 fs
	60	4350	2415
	65	4350	2710
	63.2	Norma 204	2625
250	64	4350	2500
	57	4064	2410

Standard twist: 10"

.300 Apex Super Magnum

The .300 Super Magnum is identical to the standard .300 H&H except for the sharper shoulder. This cartridge, developed by Apex, is supposed to be somewhat more efficient than the .300 H&H; however, any increase might be hard to demonstrate. Doubtless the greatest improvement is better case life due to less stretching, (forward flow) of brass because of the sharper shoulder.

150 gr. bullet	65 gr.	4064 powder	3340 fs
	70	4064	3575
180	74	4350	3280
	77	4831	3213
220	74	4831	2860

All standard .300 H&H loads can be used.

Standard twist: 10"

.300 Mashburn Super Magnum

The Mashburn Super .300 Magnum being slightly larger in capacity than the .300 Weatherby makes it possible to fire the .300 Weatherby factory loads in the Mashburn

MAXIMUM LOAD LISTED SHOULD BE APPROACHED WITH CARE

chamber, however Mashburn does not recommend deep throating or free boring as is practiced by the Weatherby factory. He feels that accuracy suffers in free bored barrels.

Bullet	Powder (gr.)	Powder type	Velocity
130 gr. bullet	82 gr.	4350 powder	3670 fs
	84	4350	3780
	88	4831	3750
	90	4831	3860
150	80	4350	3420
	82	4350	3575
	85	4831	3510
	87	4831	3630
180	74	4350	3100
	76	4350	3210
	78	4831	3125
	80	4831	3260
220	71	4350	2890
	73	4350	2975
	76	4831	2970
	78	4831	3010

Standard twist: 10"

.300 Improved Magnum (Ackley)

The Ackley .300 Improved is the same as the .300 Weatherby except for minor details. The Weatherby has what is known as a venturi shoulder (curved corners) while the Ackley has sharp corners and 40° angle. The capacity is badly exaggerated for the .30 bore and faults are more numerous than good points. There is one thing about both the Ackley and Weatherby and that is the general design of the two cartridges produces much better case life than the standard .300 H&H. Case life is better than for the standard .300 H&H which is of interest to handloaders.

Loading data is same as for the .300 Weatherby.

Standard twist: 10"

MAXIMUM LOAD LISTED SHOULD BE APPROACHED WITH CARE

.300 Weatherby Magnum

The .300 Weatherby Magnum is a full length blown out .300 Magnum with about maximum capacity possible by blowing out the .300 as large as possible. There are several similar versions such as the Ackley Improved .300 Magnum, Apex .300 Super Magnum, .300 Mashburn, .300 PMVF, .300 CCC and many others. All are badly over bore capacity and relatively inefficient compared to the standard .300 Magnum which is already over capacity for the .30 bore. Barrel life is relatively short, they have minimum flexibility and can be recommended only for specialized use.

bullet	gr.	powder	fs
150 gr. bullet	70 gr.	4320 powder	3208 fs
	67	3031	3238
	71	4895	3273
	80	4350	3314
	86	4831	3420
180	68	4895	2935
	68	4320	3015
	76	4350	3004
	78	4831	2930
200	65	4320	2878
	74	4350	2961
	76	4831	2872
220	73	4350	2950

Standard twist: 10"

.300 ICL Grizzly

The ICL Grizzly is the ICL Improved .300 Magnum. Cases are made by firing factory loads in the ICL chamber,

MAXIMUM LOAD LISTED SHOULD BE APPROACHED WITH CARE

like the Ackley Weatherby, Mashburn and others. Like other over bore capacity cases, the ICL Grizzly could not be very efficient. See the comments on the Ackley Improved .300 Magnum and the .300 Weatherby.

150 gr. bullet	80	gr.	4350 powder	3590 fs
180	75		4350	3300
	78		4350	3330
	80		4350	3395
	81		4350	3460
220	76		4350	3200

Standard twist: 10"

.30/.378 Arch

The .30/.378 Arch is a short chubby cartridge made by necking down and shortening the .378 Weatherby to an overall length of approximately 2.25 inch holding upwards of 87 gains of powder. It was developed by Dr. E. L. Arch of Wenatchie, Washington, who has also done so much experimental work with the 6.5 x 55 cartridge. This .30 calibre case was designed with the thought in mind of producing a case shape which would permit uniform ignition and burning and pressure. Dr. Arch has always questioned whether case shape is an important factor in accuracy provided uniform ignition and uniform pressure are assured, which in turn should create accuracy. This cartridge was created with the idea that perhaps it would have long range target possibilities from 800 to 1000 yards and preliminary tests have shown it to live up to the expectations. The following loads were tested by the Speer Products Company Ballistic Laboratory.

180 gr. bullet	81	gr.	4831 powder	3065 fs
	83		4831	3120
	86		4831	3250
	88		4831	3355
	89		4831	3415
250	85		H570	2980
	70		4831	3185

Standard twist: 10"

MAXIMUM LOAD LISTED SHOULD BE APPROACHED WITH CARE

.303 Savage

The .303 Savage is strictly a Savage development and a cartridge which originally made the Savage rifle famous. Although it is similar in characteristics to the .30/30 it was a little more powerful. At the time of its introduction it was designed especially for the Model 99 Savage lever action rifle. Sometimes owners of .303 rifles attempt to use .30/30 cartridges, and sometimes they get away with it, but the practice is dangerous and should never be indulged in. The .303 Savage was originally loaded with the 190 grain soft point bullet.

150 gr. bullet	26	gr.	HiVel #2 powder	1960 fs
	32		HiVel #2	2360
	35		4895	2275
	32		3031	2300
	34		4064	2325
180	30		HiVel #2	2265
	34		4895	2240
	31		3031	2250
	33		4064	2275
190	30		HiVel #2	2000
	36		4320	2145

Standard twist: 10"

7.7 x 54MM

The 7.7 x 54mm was designed by J. Pollard, of Sidney, Australia, for use in states of Australia, where the standard .303 British cartridge is illegal. The case is trimmed to 54 mm and then resized to the former .303 neck size. There is no loading data available but factory cartridges are

MAXIMUM LOAD LISTED SHOULD BE APPROACHED WITH CARE

furnished in Australia for the 7.7 x 54mm using the 140 gr. round nose bullet with 38 grains of 4740 powder for a velocity of 2500 fs.

Standard twist: 10"

.303 British

This cartridge has been the service cartridge of the British Empire for a great many years. The original service load used a 215 gr. bullet and was known as the Mark II. Later it was changed to use a 174 gr. bullet and designated as the Mark VII. Sporting ammunition has always been made by leading ammunition manufacturers in the United States, and sporting rifles have been produced for it by both Remington and Winchester. Lately, many thousands of Canadian Ross and British Lee Enfields have been imported and sold in this country, in addition to the P14 Enfields which are the same as the M17 Enfield except the mechanism is arranged to handle the rimmed .303 British cartridge, instead of the .30/06.

The .303 British cartridge is quite similar to the .30/40 Krag. It is about 1/16" longer in the body and .092" shorter over all meaning it has a somewhat shorter neck than the .30/40 Krag. It is some .010 or .011 smaller in diameter at the shoulder and nearly the same diameter just forward of the rim. This makes the capacity of the two cases almost the same, and from the ballistics standpoint, there couldn't be much difference. This means also, that the improved version of the .303 British would have to be about like the improved .30/40.

Like the .30/40, the .303 British has been eminently successful all over the world on all kinds of big game. Both of the cartridges drive relatively heavy .30 calibre bullets at optimum velocity for consistent results with regular jacketed bullets now available. They drive these bullets fast enough to produce flat enough trajectories in a large percentage of conditions, making them pretty satisfactory for all around big game rifles.

MAXIMUM LOAD LISTED SHOULD BE APPROACHED WITH CARE

LOADING DATA

Under average conditions, this class of cartridges gives very good accounts of themselves in comparison with the more modern and popular cartridge of the '06 class. The .303 British bullet measures .311, but many standard .300 bullets are fired through the .311 barrels with satisfactory results.

Bullet	Powder charge	Powder	Velocity
150 gr. bullet	46 gr.	4350 powder	2320 fs
	49	4350	2500
	40	4895	2410
	44	4895	2650
	38	HiVel #2	2420
	38	3031	2430
	40	3031	2535
174	37	3031	2150
	38	4064	2250
	40	4320	2280
180	35	HiVel #2	2218
	37	HiVel #2	2300
	36	3031	2200
	41	4320	2320
	45	4350	2258
	48	4831	2215
215	31	HiVel #2	1890
	38	3031	2100
	41	4320	2090
	46	4350	2330

The following loads are recommended for Norma and Nobel powders:

Bullet	Charge	Powder	Velocity
150 gr. Cast Gas-check bullet	12 gr.	Shotgun Ballistite Powder	1500 fs
	18	Nobel's Hornet	1700
110 gr. Jacketed bullet	43	4740	2550
130	42	4740	2700
	39.4	Norma 200	2790
150	44.6	Norma 201	2720
	38	Modified Cordite	2700
	41	4740	2500
158	37	4740	2350
174	37.5	Modified Cordite	2450
	41.5	Nobel 41	2450
	37	4740	2250
180	37	4740	2200
215	39.4	Norma 203	2180

Standard twist: 10"

MAXIMUM LOAD LISTED SHOULD BE APPROACHED WITH CARE

.303 ICL Improved

The .303 ICL Improved is an "improved" version of the .303 British very similar but not quite identical to the Epps version. This cartridge should be of interest to Canadian and other British Commonwealth shooters who have easy access to .303 British rifles of the various types such as SMLE but particularly the P14 Enfield. It is a good cartridge for good single shot actions. Ballistics are very similar to the "improved" .30/40 and the different versions of the "improved" .303 British can be considered to be about equal to similar versions of the .30/40. The following loads are recommended for the P14 Enfield, and not for actions of the SMLE type. Loads for the SMLE should be worked up carefully starting with the equivalent of the factory load.

215 gr. bullet, factory load to fire form case - 2100 fs

bullet	charge		powder	velocity
150 gr.	50	gr.	4320	2870 fs
	52		4320	2950
	50		4064	3040
	48		3031	3040
	50		3031	3190
	51		3031	3235
180	43		4320	2450
	45		4320	2580
	48		4320	2680
	50		4320	2870
	52		4320	3030
	50		4350	2680
	50		4831	2390
150	47		3031	3000 Approx. - Target Load
	45		4320	2580 Target Load

Standard twist: 10"

MAXIMUM LOAD LISTED SHOULD BE APPROACHED WITH CARE

.303 British Improved (Epps)

The .303 British cartridge has been a very popular one throughout the world for many years but in the way of ballistics it leaves quite a bit to be desired. Therefore there have been numerous "improved" versions of the .303 British. The cartridge illustrated is the Epps version developed by Ellwood Epps of Clinton, Ontario, Canada, especially for the benefit of Canadian shooters. The Epps version of the "improved" .303 British is practically identical to the Ackley version of the "improved" .30/40 with the exception that the neck is shorter therefore creating a cartridge case with a shorter overall length than the .30/40, but from a practical standpoint ballistics for the .303 British Improved are about the same as the .30/40 Improved.

Mr. Epps also uses this same case for larger bullets among which are the 8mm, .338 and .35 thus creating a line of "improved" cartridges based on the .303 British brass which cover a wide range of hunting conditions including long range open country work as well as brush shooting. Any rifle chambered for the .303 British can be rechambered for the Epps version but the SMLE type rifle will not accept as heavy charges as the P14 Enfield rifle. Loads given for the improved .30/40 can be used in the Epps Improved .303 British for identical velocities, and loads for the ICL .303 Buttress can also be used.

Standard twist: 10"

7.7 Jap

This cartridge is the other Japanese service cartridge used during World War II. It is often referred to as the

MAXIMUM LOAD LISTED SHOULD BE APPROACHED WITH CARE

31 Jap but actually it is neither a .30 or .31 calibre, but a .303, using bullets measuring .312-.314. Like the 6.5 Jap the action is strong, but not well adapted to sporting use. Neither is it well designed, and the workmanship is not as good as in the 6.5 action.

Thousands of these rifles have been re-chambered to accept the regular .30/06 cartridge, but this is a dangerous conversion without setting the barrel back at least 3/8", because the Jap chamber is oversize at the butt for our standard cartridge thus increasing the danger of ruptured cases near the head.

Both models of the Jap action handle gas about the best of any bolt action, but this is no reason to invite disaster by performing incorrect conversions. Actually, when these rifles are properly converted to handle the standard .30/06, .300 Savage, or the .308 Winchester cartridges they show surprising accuracy with standard .30 calibre bullets.

Many custom loaders produce so-called custom loads for the rifles by working over .30/06 brass. This is also a doubtful practice, both because of the oversize Jap chamber, and the quite wide variation in headspace among rifles. Also, in too many instances, the producers of this "custom" ammunition have little knowledge, or regard for headspace. Reloaders should always use bullets measuring .311, rather than the standard .308 bullet.

Bullet	Charge	Powder	Velocity
100 gr. bullet	54 gr.	H380 powder	3190 fs
	56	H380	3260
	46	3031	3070
	48	3031	3200
150	50	4350	2450
	54	4350	2750
	44	4895	2640
	46	4895	2700
	36	HiVel #2	2500
	39	HiVel #2	2580
	41	HiVel #2	2700
	37	3031	2485
	40	3031	2630
	42	3031	2730
	42	H380	2460
	45	H380	2600
180	48	4350	2380
	50	4350	2450

MAXIMUM LOAD LISTED SHOULD BE APPROACHED WITH CARE

LOADING DATA

38	gr.	4320 powder	2250 fs
41		4320	2430
43		4320	2500
33		HiVel #2	2185
36		HiVel #2	2315
38		HiVel #2	2430
37		H380	2160
41		H380	2330
40		4895	2360
42		4895	2420

The following are loads for Norma powders:

130 gr. bullet	50	gr.	Norma 203 powder	2950 fs
180	45.2		Norma 203	2495
215	43.5		Norma 203	2265

.308 B-J Express (Barnes-Johnson)

This is the .30 calibre member of the B-J family. It is the same case as the .276 B-J Express except the neck diameter which is for .30 calibre. This is quite similar to the new .308 Norma Magnum.

180 gr. bullet	76	gr.	4831 powder	3160 fs
200	74		4831	3000
250	70		4831	2610

Standard twist: 10"

.308 Barnes Supreme

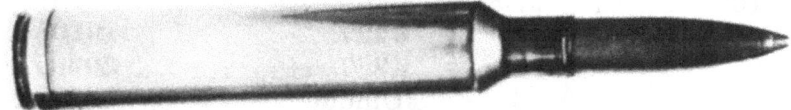

This, like the .288 Barnes Supreme is Fred Barnes' idea of what a .30 calibre cartridge should be for extremely heavy bullets and slow burning powder. No loading data is available, but with the 225 grain bullet we have an estimated speed of 3000 foot seconds.

MAXIMUM LOAD LISTED SHOULD BE APPROACHED WITH CARE

.32/20 WCF

This is a cartridge adapted to both rifles and handguns (for revolver loads, see pistol cartridge section) and some 30 or 40 years ago was quite popular as a varmint cartridge. It is not powerful enough to be classed as a deer cartridge, although many thousands of deer have been killed with it. It is now commercially available only with the 115 grain bullet, but in the past it has been commercially loaded with 80, 90 and 100 grain bullets. Many different models of rifles have been made for the .32/20, the most famous of which were the 1873 and 1892 Winchester, Model 94 Marlin and Model 25 Remington.

80 gr. bullet	10 gr.	2400 powder	1370 fs
	13	2400	1845
	13	4227	1710
	17	4227	2220
	6.6	Unique	1800
90	11.7	2400	1780
	6	Unique	1680
100	11.5	2400	1670
	12	4227	1610
	15	4227	2000
	6	Unique	1650
115	10.8	2400	1555
	7	Unique	1575
	13.5	4227	1750

Standard twist: 20", 22"

MAXIMUM LOAD LISTED SHOULD BE APPROACHED WITH CARE

.32/40

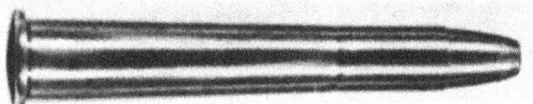

The .32/40 is one of the old reliable target cartridges, and famous rifles such as the Ballard, Remington, Winchester and others in the highest grade target rifles were chambered for the .32/40 and .38/55 cartridges. For many years the Winchester Model 94 and the Marlin Model 93 repeating rifles were very popular as deer rifles, and although the .32/40 is now considered obsolete it is still being used for deer by owners of these old rifles. Sometimes the ammunition is difficult to find and for those who own Model 94 Winchester or similar model rifles, the one thing that can be done is to rechamber these rifles for the more easily obtained .32 Special cartridge. The original .32/40 cartridge was loaded with the 165 grain bullet and 40 grains of black powder.

Bullet	Charge	Powder	Velocity
110 gr. bullet	20 gr.	4198 powder	1800 fs
	24	4198	2230
	28	3031	2155
	33	3031	2245
165	13	2400	1500
	15	2400	1600
	17	4198	1460
	22	4198	1890
	20	HiVel #2	1390
	24	HiVel #2	1850
	26	4895	1810
	30	4895	1935
	24	3031	1835
	28	3031	1950

Standard twist: 16"

MAXIMUM LOAD LISTED SHOULD BE APPROACHED WITH CARE

.32 Special

The .32 Special cartridge is identical to the .30/30 WCF except that it has a larger neck for the .32 calibre bullet and was originally brought out in the Model 94 Winchester rifle. The .30/30 and .32 Special are almost identical ballistically which makes the killing power for the two cartridges about the same. The .32 Special cartridge makes a very handy rebore job for .30/30 since all that is necessary is to ream out the barrel to .32 calibre and simply neck up the chamber for the larger bullet. The .32 Remington Rimless is simply the Remington version of the .32 Special and accepts the same loads to produce the same ballistics.

100 gr. bullet	29	gr.	4198 powder	2350 fs
	36		4198	2775
	29		HiVel #2	2100
	35.5		HiVel #2	2530
	32		3031	2050
	37		3031	2350
	32		4895	2000
	36		4895	2300
170	25		4198	2040
	27		4198	2180
	28		HiVel #2	1950
	33		HiVel #2	2200
	32		4895	1900
	37		4895	2160
	29		3031	1935
	32		3031	2150
	34		3031	2250

Standard twist: 16"

MAXIMUM LOAD LISTED SHOULD BE APPROACHED WITH CARE

8mm Mauser (8 x 57mm)

The 8x57mm has been the official German military cartridge for many years. This cartridge has gained a reputation for being inaccurate along with many other faults, but actually, it is a very fine big game cartridge and in the same class as the .30/06. Just after World War I a large number of very poor rebuilt or "customized" military Mauser rifles were imported by certain dealers who saturated the American market with "junk" but since it was sold under the name of Mauser and because these junkers were sloppily chambered for the 8mm cartridge, the reputation of both rifle and cartridge suffered. Actually, a good German military Mauser in good condition and properly chambered for the 8 x 57 cartridge makes a very good big game rifle once it has been fitted with good hunting sights and it is a rifle worth spending considerable cash on to create a fine custom sporting rifle.

Bullet	Powder (gr.)	Powder	Velocity (fs)
125 gr. bullet	46	4198	3074
	52	4895	2892
	50	3031	2897
	54	4320	2907
150-154	48	3031	2760
	50	3031	2875
	47	4320	2585
	56	4320	3040
	50	4895	2650
	50	HiVel #2	2800
	48	4064	2600
170	52	4320	2690
	48	HiVel #2	2650
	48	4895	2525
	47	3031	2660
180	52	4064	2795
200	50	4064	2500
236	46.5	4320	2385
250	50	4350	2200

Do not use in old Model 88 Mauser

MAXIMUM LOAD LISTED SHOULD BE APPROACHED WITH CARE

The following loads for Norma powders which are available from Norma Precision, South Lansing, New York:

123 gr. bullet	43.2 gr.	Norma 200 powder	2885 fs
159	50.9	Norma 203	2725
196	45.5	Norma 203	2395
	48.3	Norma 203	2525
198	49.4	Norma 203	2625
227	45.3	Norma 203	2330

European twist: 9", 10"
American-Standard twist: 12", 14"

8mm/06

The 8mm/06 is made by simply necking up the standard .30/06 case to accept the 8mm (.323) bullet. It makes a very fine big game cartridge which is both efficient and flexible. Also there is a wide variety of bullets available. In this country there is a large number of 8mm Mauser military rifles which are being used for game hunting. Many owners of these rifles feel that the standard 8x57mm for which these rifles are chambered, lacks something in power. Standard 8mm barrels can easily be rechambered for the 8mm/06 and the magazines lengthened slightly to handle the longest bullets, thus creating a rifle that is certainly the equal of the .30/06 and most likely one which is more effective for the larger types of big game. This cartridge can be considered one of the best of the large bore wildcats and certainly adequate for the largest North American big game.

125 gr. bullet	58 gr.	HiVel #2	3240 fs
	60	HiVel #2	3378
	57	3031	3278
	60	4064	3298
150	56	HiVel #2	3072
	57	4064	3020
	59	4895	3026
	61	4895	3114

MAXIMUM LOAD LISTED SHOULD BE APPROACHED WITH CARE

170 gr. bullet	56	gr.	4064 powder	2876 fs
	61		4320	2950
	58		4064	2984
200	62		4350	2740
250	63		4831	2430

Standard twist: 12"

8mm/06 Improved

This cartridge is simply the Ackley Improved 06 necked up to 8mm and is even better than the very fine standard 8mm/06. It is especially good for the heavier bullets from 170 gr. up. Since the 8mm/06 is a handloading proposition anyway, it would seem that the Improved version would be the better choice. It should be as effective on all species of big game as the standard .300 Magnum.

Use loading data for standard 8mm/06, increase 5%.

There are many other fine 8mm Wildcat cartridges such as the various short .30 Magnums previously described and even the big blown out .300 Magnum, blown out versions necked up to 8mm. Because of the larger diameter bullet these large blown out cases would be much better necked up to 8mm than left .30 calibre.

Standard twist: 12"

8mm Express

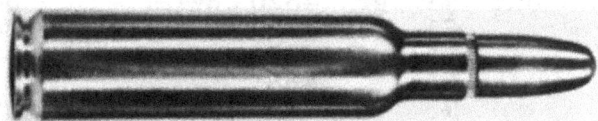

The 8mm Express is another Payne cartridge. This is the same as the 7mm Express except the shoulder is moved forward a little bit to give more volume. This cartridge

MAXIMUM LOAD LISTED SHOULD BE APPROACHED WITH CARE

has proven very effective on elk and similar game. Like the 7mm Express, cases are made from .348 brass with the rim turned off to make a rimless cartridge.

150 gr. bullet	80 gr. 4350 powder	3390 fs	compressed load
170	79 4350	3400	compressed load
175	77 4350	3190	
	79 4350	3400	Max.
200	75 4350	3095	
	76 4350	3210	Max.
	78 4831	3040	
225	74 4350	2970	
	77 4831	2865	
250	68 4350	2675	
	70 4350	2710	
	71 4350	2840	Max.
	74 4831	2765	Max.

Standard twist: 12"

8 x 62 Durham Magnum

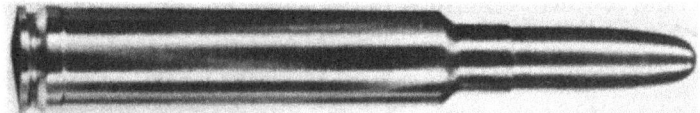

The 8 x 62 Durham Magnum is quite similar to the .30 Durham Magnum with only a slightly larger case capacity and it handles all standard 8mm bullets. Original 8mm Mauser barrels can be easily rechambered for this short Magnum which is near maximum capacity for the 8mm bore. It approximates the standard .375 H&H Magnum in killing power. The following loads were developed in a 24-inch barrel with 10 inch twist and are considered maximum, therefore should be approached with caution.

150 gr. bullet	71 gr. 4320 powder	3480 fs
175	71 4320	3467
	75 4350	3300
	75 4831	3165
196	75 4350	3294
	75 4831	3150
225	72 4350	3055
	75 4831	3066

Standard twist: 12"
Special twist: 10"

MAXIMUM LOAD LISTED SHOULD BE APPROACHED WITH CARE

8 x 68

The 8 x 68 is another cartridge furnished in the currently manufactured Mannlicher Schoenauer rifle, the agent for which in the United States is Stoeger Arms Corporation, South Hackensack, New Jersey. The 8 x 68 is the same cartridge as the 6.5 x 68 except for the bullet which is the regular .323 (8mm). The factory cartridge is loaded only with the 186 grain bullet and velocity is 3280 fs. This cartridge could be considered in the class with the .338 Winchester Magnum and .358 Norma Magnum. Like the 6.5 x 68 it is a large rimless cartridge using Berdan primers and like the 6.5 x 68, components including new empty cases, Berdan primers, etc., are available from Stoeger Arms.

Bullet	Powder charge	Powder	Velocity
150 gr. bullet	71 gr.	4350 powder	2675 fs
	72	4350	2985
	73	4350	3050
	77	4350	3205
	78	4350	3260
	75	4831	2995
180	67	4350	2750
	68	4350	2780
	69	4350	2820
	75	4831	2770
	76	4831	2800
	77	4831	2830
186-187	68	4350	2755
	69	4350	2775
	70	4350	2820
	71	4350	2885
	73	4831	2650
	74	4831	2730
	75	4831	2900
200	68	4350	2620
	69	4350	2680
	73	4831	2630
	74	4831	2650
	75	4831	2690
250	63	4350	2420
	64	4350	2435
	65	4350	2450
	71	4831	2415
	72	4831	2535

Standard twist: 12"

MAXIMUM LOAD LISTED SHOULD BE APPROACHED WITH CARE

.323 Critser Magnum

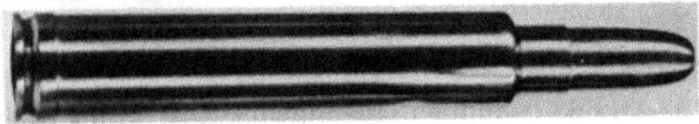

The .323 Critser Magnum is another full length blown out .300 H&H Magnum case necked up to accept 8mm (.323) bullets. This cartridge utilizes a 50° shoulder angle in conjunction with a very short neck measuring only .225 in length. Like the other Critser cartridges, this cartridge utilizes the minimum body taper design for a total body taper of about .020.

Bullet	Powder charge	Powder	Velocity
150 gr. bullet	80 gr.	4831 powder	3110 fs
	85	4831	3390
	90	4831	3600
171	75	4350	3200
	77	4350	3270
	80	4350	3350
	83	4831	3170
	85	4831	3250
	87	4831	3290
180	80	4350	3270
	94	H570	3110

Standard twist: 12"

.333 OKH

The .333 OKH is a cartridge introduced many years ago by O'Neil, Keith and Hopkins. It is made by necking up .30/06 cases with no other change. Unlike the .338 Winchester or the old .33 Winchester the bullets for which measure .338, the .333 OKH bullet actually measures .333. Like the 8mm/06 or .35 Whelen it makes a very efficient big game cartridge; however, the 8mm or .35 calibres offer a much wider range of bullet weights. It would seem since

MAXIMUM LOAD LISTED SHOULD BE APPROACHED WITH CARE

the introduction of the new .338 Winchester that it would be best to increase the bore diameter of the .333 OKH when new rifles are being made up, to accept the .338 bullet. Actually there would be no noticeable difference in ballistics but there would be a great advantage from the standpoint of bullet availability.

250 gr. bullet	57	gr.	4064 powder	2635 fs	
	62		4350	2400	est.
275	44		4064	2141 fs	
	45		4895	2202	
	45		4320	2154	
	53		4350	2250	
	60		4350	2500	est.
	57		4831	2314	
300	55		4064	2300	est.
	59		4350	2225	est.

Standard twist: 10"

.333 Short Magnum (Ackley)

The cartridge illustrated is the No. 2 Ackley short .30 Magnum necked up to .333. There are several other similar versions such as the Luft Magnum. The following data can be used for either the Luft or Ackley interchangeably for practically the same ballistics.

275 gr. bullet	51	gr.	4895 powder	2241 fs
	52		4064	2307
	54		4320	2345
	61		4350	2360
	66		4831	2478

Standard twist: 10"

MAXIMUM LOAD LISTED SHOULD BE APPROACHED WITH CARE

.333 x 61 Carlson Magnum

This is another cartridge designed by Richard Carlson of Corvallis, Montana. It is made by either necking up 7 x 61 S&H cases or by necking down and shortening the .300 H&H Magnum brass. Chamber specifications are the same as for the 7 x 61 S&H except for the larger neck diameter. Obviously this is an especially good cartridge and should be one of the very best in its class. It has a much better case and bore capacity ratio than the same case in 7mm calibre, and can be recommended for all kinds of big game hunting, especially the larger North American species.

275 gr. bullet	62 gr.	4350 powder	2500 fs
	63	4350	2535
	64	4350	2610
	64	4831	2490
	65	4831	2520
	66	4831	2580
	67	4831	2630
	68	4831	2685

Standard twist: 10"

.333 Barnes Supreme

The .333 Barnes Supreme is another Barnes full length blown out Magnum case for use with heavy bullets, and it is the same case as the other Supreme cases with sharp shoulder and minimum body taper.

300 gr. bullet   96   gr.   Machine Gun powder 2750 fs
Standard twist: 10"

MAXIMUM LOAD LISTED SHOULD BE APPROACHED WITH CARE

.333 B-J Express (Barnes-Johnson)

The .333 B-J Express is the .276 B-J Express necked up to accept the .333 Barnes bullet which was probably the first .333 bullet manufactured in the United States for use in the .33 and .334 OKH cartridges.

200 gr. bullet	82 gr.	4350 powder	3175 fs
250	78	4831	2800
300	75	4831	2600

.334 OKH

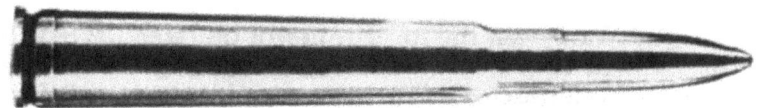

This one is made for shooters who wish to have a .333 Magnum with maximum powder capacity. Doubtless such a case is over bore capacity but should be a great deal better than the same case in .300 calibre. The original cartridge of this type to be introduced in this country was probably the .334 OKH. This cartridge is similar to the Improved .333 Magnum except the case is not blown out which means it has lesser capacity therefore better adjusted to the .333 bore.

No loading data available.

Standard twist: 10"

MAXIMUM LOAD LISTED SHOULD BE APPROACHED WITH CARE

.333 Magnum Improved (Ackley)

The illustration shows the Improved .300 Ackley Magnum case necked up to .333. Doubtless this would make an impressive cartridge for the owner to impress his friends with and it couldn't help but be a good killer. It could be concocted by necking up any of the big cases but it would be better based on one of the short Magnum cases which should create a relative satisfactory and efficient cartridge.

No loading data available.

Standard twist: 10"

.33 WCF

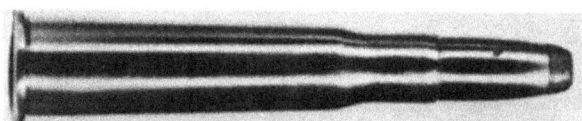

The .33 WCF was the forerunner of the later .348 Winchester. It was the last or most recent cartridge introduced by the Winchester factory for use in the old Model 86 Winchester rifle. It became obsolete in 1936, and ammunition is no longer available. Those who have Model 86 Winchester and Marlin rifles chambered for this cartridge can have the rifles rebored to .45/70, or .33 WCF brass can be made by necking down .45/70 brass. The .33 WCF was a powerful cartridge which has given a good account of itself on all types of North American game.

200 gr. bullet	42 gr.	3031 powder	2260 fs
	35	HiVel #2	2000
	43	HiVel #2	2430
	19	2400	1630
	26	2400	2100
	44	4320	2200
	46	4064	2260

Standard twist: 12"

MAXIMUM LOAD LISTED SHOULD BE APPROACHED WITH CARE

.338 Winchester

The .338 Winchester Magnum is a new cartridge developed by the Winchester Repeating Arms Company. Basically, it is what the wildcatters term a "short Magnum". It is almost the same case as the Ackley No. 2 Short .30 Magnum necked up to .338.

This Ackley No. 2 Short .30 Magnum necked up to .333 has been furnished for many years, and doubtless, numerous similar "wildcat" cartridges have been made up in the same way. Wildcatters have been using the .333 diameter bullet because of its availability, but Winchester elected to use the old .33 Winchester bullet size.

It is somewhat of a mystery why this odd size bullet was selected when so many fine .35 calibre bullets have been available for so many years. Certainly there could be little ballistic advantage. This can be seen by comparing the ballistics of the new .338 Winchester Magnum with those of any similar .35 Magnum cartridges.

The .338 Winchester Magnum is proving to be a very fine big game cartridge, large enough for all types of big game throughout the world, but of course, too large for most hunting in the United States.

Since the .338 Winchester Magnum is a "short Magnum", cases can easily be formed from .300 or .375 H&H Magnum brass, and being .30/06 length, makes it well adapted for use in standard length actions. It is a fine cartridge necked to .30 or expanded to .35, .375 or .40 etc. Having the minimum body taper design which the wildcatters have been advocating for so many years, combined with a relatively sharp shoulder (28°) similar to most "wildcats", it won't be easy to "improve" it. The capacity of the case is too large to neck down to anything smaller than .30 calibre for good efficiency, although the Winchester factory is using the same case necked down to take the 6.5mm bullets, and which is now known as the .264 Winchester.

MAXIMUM LOAD LISTED SHOULD BE APPROACHED WITH CARE

180 gr. bullet	60 gr.	4895 powder	3050 fs
	65	4895	3270
	66	4320	3048
220	63	4320	2760
	65	4350	2713
	67	4350	2815
250	60	4350	2438
	65	4350	2600
	67	4350	2680
	68	4350	2715
275	70	4831	2578
	75	4831	2838
	70	4350	2600
	73	4350	2720
	58	4320	2400
	60	4320	2475
300	60	4350	2167
	65	4350	2350
	66	4350	2375

Standard twist: 10"

.348 Winchester

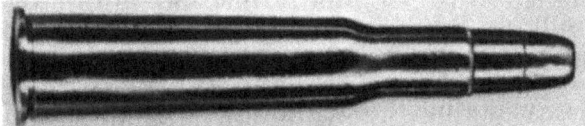

The .348 Winchester cartridge was designed for the Model 71 Winchester which was an improved version of the older Model 86 rifle and was introduced in 1936. It was intended to be an improvement over the cartridge .33 WCF which was introduced in 1902. The .348 was one of the most powerful cartridges ever developed for a lever action rifle up to the time of its introduction. The manufacture of the Model 71 Winchester rifle has been discontinued by the factory but factory ammunition is still available.

150 gr. bullet	36 gr.	4198 powder	2400 fs
	54	3031	2760
	58	4320	2800
	58	4064	2835
180	57	4895	2675
	53	3031	2700
	58	H380	2645
	59	4320	2665
	65	4350	2680

MAXIMUM LOAD LISTED SHOULD BE APPROACHED WITH CARE

200 gr. bullet	67 gr.	4831 powder	2480 fs
	48	HiVel #2	2535
	55	4895	2495
	49	3031	2480
	56	4320	2510
	56	H380	2495
220	65	4831	2290
	46	HiVel #2	2330
	52	4895	2300
	60	4350	2320
	54	H380	2300
250	62	4831	2080
	50	4895	2125
	50	4064	2150
	52	H380	2120

Standard twist: 12"

.348 Improved (Ackley)

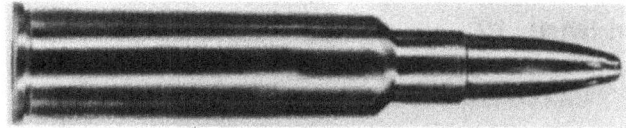

The .348 Improved was developed upon request of many shooters owning Model 71 Winchester rifles. The original .348 cartridge was very poorly designed in a way mainly because it had such a steep body taper that the bolt thrust developed was much greater than it should be, and this bolt thrust undesirable as it is, is doubly so in lever actions. The "improved" .348 combines minimum body taper and sharp shoulder design and is capable of giving a noticeable increase over the factory round. The following loads have been developed by Bob Hutton of Guns and Ammo magazine.

200 gr. factory load fired in the standard chamber-2469 fs
200 gr. factory load fired in the "improved" chamber - 2350 fs

150 gr. bullet	67 gr.	4064 powder	3175 fs
180	70	4350	2885
	58	4064	2665
	59	4064	2705
	60	4064	2740

MAXIMUM LOAD LISTED SHOULD BE APPROACHED WITH CARE

200 gr. bullet	62	gr.	4350 powder	2220 fs
	63		4350	2245
	64		4350	2300
	65		4350	2355
	66		4350	2381
	67		4350	2470
	68		4350	2500
	69		4350	2530
	70		4350	2665
	71		4350	2710
220	60		4350	2275
	62		4350	2355
	63		4350	2410
250	58		4350	2245
	60		4350	2355
	62		4350	2380
	64		4350	2470
	66		4350	2530
	60		4320	2470
	61		4320	2500

Standard twist: 12"

MAXIMUM LOAD LISTED SHOULD BE APPROACHED WITH CARE

.357 Magnum

The .357 Magnum is a pistol cartridge, but it is quite popular for use in rifles, especially the Model 92 Winchester, and it has proven to be extremely deadly on game such as deer at short range. Rifles can be made extremely short and light, and it is ideal for brush shooting. This calibre rifle is popular among trappers and law enforcement officers. Rifles converted for the .357 Magnum will also handle the .38 Special loads. The Model 92 Winchester only in .25/20 or .32/20 calibres can be converted. All good single shot rifles can be rebored or rebarrelled for the .357 Magnum. The following is a list of a few loads tested in a rifle with a 24 inch barrel.

160 gr. bullet	15.5 gr.	2400 powder	1720 fs
	17	2400	2005
	20	2400	2135
	20	4227	1990
	21	4227	2030

Standard twist: 18" to 40", according to fancy

.35 Remington

The .35 Remington is the largest member of the Remington auto loading series which originally consisted of the .25/35, .32 and .35 Remington. The .35 Remington had a head diameter midway between the .30 Remington and the .30/06 and was sort of a little 9mm. The .35 Remington made itself famous as a brush cartridge and was designed for use in the Remington Model 14 pump and Model 8 automatic rifles. The Stevens factory also produced a lever action repeating rifle chambered for the Remington series

MAXIMUM LOAD LISTED SHOULD BE APPROACHED WITH CARE

of cartridges and Marlin Firearms is currently manufacturing their Model 336 lever action for the .35 Remington cartridge.

Bullet	Powder (gr.)	Powder type	Velocity
150 gr. bullet	38 gr.	HiVel #2	2340 fs
	40	3031	2200
	36	4198	2400
180	47	H380	2175
	44	4895	2235
	37	3031	2170
	43	3031	2200
	41	4320	2120
	28	4198	2050
	34	HiVel #2	2075
200	36	3031	2065
	37	3031	2150
	40	3031	2200
	33	HiVel #2	1965
	39	HiVel #2	2215
	28	4198	1980
220	39	4320	1930
	31	HiVel #2	1825
	35.5	4064	1780
	34	3031	1940

Standard twist: 16"

.358 Winchester

The .358 Winchester is simply the .308 Winchester necked up to .35 calibre. This makes a series of three cartridges by Winchester which use the same basic case: the .243, .308 and .358. The .358, like the .35 Remington is a satisfactory cartridge for use on big game in brushy country where range is limited to 150 yards or under. It is a more satisfactory cartridge than the older .348 Winchester which it resembles ballistically. Within its range, the .358 Winchester is satisfactory for all North American big game.

Bullet	Powder (gr.)	Powder type	Velocity
180 gr. bullet	51 gr.	4320 powder	2250 fs
	53	4320	2330

MAXIMUM LOAD LISTED SHOULD BE APPROACHED WITH CARE

LOADING DATA

	51	gr.	4895 powder	2500 fs
	48		3031	2570
	48		HiVel #2	2525
200	47		HiVel #2	2440
	48		4895	2490
	51		4320	2500
	50		4064	2550
	43.1		Norma 200	2530
220	48		4064	2425
	50		4895	2410
	46		HiVel #2	2410
	46		3031	2435
250	44		HiVel #2	2350
	46		4895	2300
	47		4064	2400
	45		3031	2340
	46		4320	2260
	52		4350	2390
	47.4		Norma 203	2250

Standard twist: 14"

.35 Lever Power

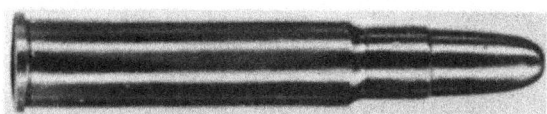

This is a cartridge developed by Fred Wade of Wade's Gun Room, Phoenix, Arizona. Cases are made by turning down the rim of .303 British or the .30/40 Krag cases then shortening the overall length of the case to about standard .30/30 length. This could be called an "improved" version since it utilizes the sharp shoulder and minimum body taper of "improved" cartridges. It was designed especially for use in Model 94 Winchester, Model 93 and 336 Marlin and the Model 99 Savage rifles made for the .30/30 series of cartridges. This cartridge is somewhat more powerful than the .35 Remington and is especially well adapted for brush shooting. The Model 336 Marlin in .35 Remington can be rechambered for this more powerful "wildcat" cartridge. The following loads were tested in a Model 94 Winchester with a 20 inch barrel.

MAXIMUM LOAD LISTED SHOULD BE APPROACHED WITH CARE

200 gr. bullet	40 gr.	3031 powder	2370 fs
	41	3031	2440
	42	3031	1440
	43	3031	2490
	44	3031	2515
	45	3031	2545
	46	3031	2600

Standard twist: 16"

9 x 57

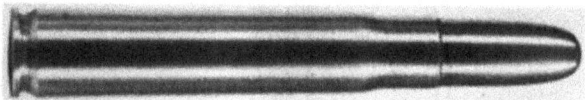

The 9 x 57 is also known as the 9mm and the 9mm Mannlicher. This is a very old cartridge quite similar to the present day "wildcat" .35 Whelen except that it is somewhat shorter than the .35 Whelen and somewhat longer than the .35 Remington. Cases are very easily made in one operation from .30/06 by using a suitable forming die which is available from any of the loading die manufacturers. This cartridge has been manufactured in the United States in the days past, and it is still very popular in other countries throughout the world. Actually this is a very hard cartridge to beat for brush shooting, being quite similar or a little better than the currently manufactured .358 Winchester.

200 gr. bullet	43 gr.	HiVel #2 powder	2200 fs
	44	3031	2185
	45	4064	2165
	45	4895	2240
220	42	HiVel #2	2150
	44	4895	2085
	44	4064	2100
250	42	3031	2075
	51	3031	2500
	43	4064	2060
	50	4064	2400
	52	4895	2400
275-280	42	4064	2000
	46	4064	2160

Standard twist: 14"

MAXIMUM LOAD LISTED SHOULD BE APPROACHED WITH CARE

.35 Whelen

Like the 8mm/06, the .35 Whelen is simply a necked up 30/06 case without any other change. It is one of the very finest of big game rifles and especially appeals to hunters who hunt big game in brushy country. This is a wildcat originally developed by Colonel Townsend Whelen and James V. Howe many years ago. It has been gaining in popularity since the war and along with the 8mm/06 it is a natural for rebore jobs on shot out .30/06 rifles. There is a very fine selection of .35 calibre bullets ranging from 180 gr to 300 gr. The Barnes .300 gr bullet is made in both solid point and soft point styles. These bullets have tough, thick pure copper jackets and makes the .35 Whelen powerful enough for any game in the world in the hands of a good shot. There is nothing to the rumor that there is not enough shoulder area to maintain headspace. Like the 8mm/06, the .35 Whelen can be recommended for big game without reservation.

150 gr. bullet	59 gr.	3031 powder	2865 fs
	60	3031	2940
	64	3031	3100
	54	4198	2875
	56	4198	3025
180	59	3031	3020
	65	4320	2935
	60	4064	2840
200	57	3031	2820
	53	4064	2475
	60	3031	2850
220	62	4350	2520
	53	3031	2639
	59	4320	2655
	59	4064	2755
250	52	4064	2485
	54.5	4320	2475
	51	3031	2450
	51	HiVel #2	2495
275	49	3031	2320
	53	4064	2370

MAXIMUM LOAD LISTED SHOULD BE APPROACHED WITH CARE

| 300 | 53 gr. 42 | 4320 powder 3031 | 2310 fs 2060 |

Standard twist: 14"
Special twist: 16"

.35 Whelen Improved

This is simply the Ackley Improved .30/06 necked up to .35 calibre. It is better from the standpoint of velocity because an increase of about 5% in loads and velocities can be realized. Use loading data for the standard .35 Whelen plus 5%. Especially good for the heavy bullets from 250 gr up.

Standard twist: 14"
Special twist: 16"

.35 Brown-Whelen

This is another .35 calibre cartridge based on the .30/06 case. It gives more velocity than the Improved Whelen but the cases are hard to make. It is necessary to neck up the 06 brass to .40 calibre (straight), then back down to .35 with a short neck. This makes a case almost exactly like the Improved Whelen except it has a longer body and shorter neck making it hold a little more powder. It is doubtful if it is as practical as either the Improved Whelen or the short .35 Magnum but it appeals to shooters who feel they have to use the 06 case and still get almost Magnum velocities. The idea of pushing the body forward on various cases to get greater capacity is rather common and some almost impossible claims have been made for such cartridges from 6mm up to .35. Most of these claims cannot

MAXIMUM LOAD LISTED SHOULD BE APPROACHED WITH CARE

be demonstrated in the average rifle and such claims should be investigated very carefully by any prospective buyer. Claims for the Brown Whelen have not been exaggerated but this is certainly not true of some of the smaller calibres on about the same case.

220 gr. bullet	70 gr.	4320 powder	2900 fs
250	71	4350	2700
300	68	4350	2525

Standard twist: 14"
Special twist: 16"

.35-.348 Improved (Ackley)

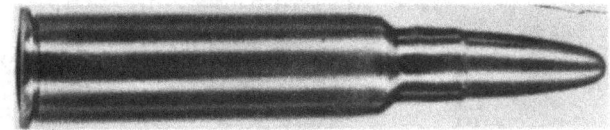

The .35-.348 Improved is simply the "improved" .348 with the neck expanded to accept standard .35 calibre bullets, producing a cartridge quite similar to the "improved" .348 with the advantage of using standard .35 calibre bullets. This cartridge should prove to be the best of the family of cartridges based on the "improved" .348 case. The following loads were developed by Bob Hutton of "Guns and Ammo".

180 gr. bullet	67 gr.	4064 powder	3007 fs
200	67	4320	2817
220	66	H380	2597
250	63	H380	2564
275	57	4320	2300
300	59	4350	2222

Standard twist: 14"
Special twist: 16"

MAXIMUM LOAD LISTED SHOULD BE APPROACHED WITH CARE

.35 Newton

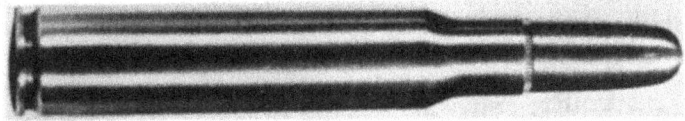

The .35 Newton cartridge came out around 1916 and was designed by Charles Newton and was his most powerful cartridge. The original factory cartridge was loaded with the 250 gr bullet for a muzzle velocity of 3000 fs and a muzzle energy of about 5000 pounds, which made it powerful enough for any game found anywhere in the world. The .35 Newton was a rimless cartridge of almost ideal capacity for the .35 calibre bore. There are several currently popular cartridges which are quite similar, among these we have the .35 Ackley Magnum and the .358 Norma Magnum.

180 gr. bullet	79	gr.	4831 powder	2522 fs
	79		4320	3175
	77		4064	3158
200	68		3031	2625
220	75		4064	3014
	81		4350	2792
250	68		3031	2760
	72		4064	2790
	81		4350	2800
275	70		3031	2615

Standard twist: 14"
Special twist: 16"

.350 Williams

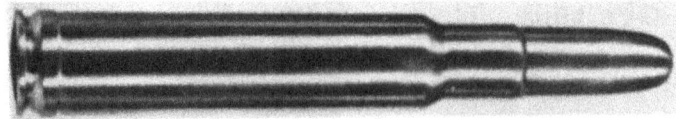

The .350 Williams was introduced in 1947 by W. H. (Bill) Williams of Odessa, Texas, and although not being identical to the older Ackley .35 Magnum it is so nearly so that the two can only be told apart by actually measuring

MAXIMUM LOAD LISTED SHOULD BE APPROACHED WITH CARE

them. Like other similar .35 Short Magnums including the .358 Norma it is an extremely good large bore cartridge and being almost identical to the .35 Ackley Magnum loading data should be interchangeable.

160 gr. bullet - Ideal #358-429 hollow point

	25 gr.	2400 powder	2500 fs est	
200 gr. jacketed bullet				
	60 gr.	HiVel #2	2650	
250	63	4350	2550	
	65	4320	2800	
275	65	4350	2600	est
300	63	4350	2500	est

Standard twist: 14"

.35 Ackley Magnum

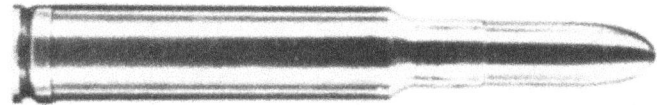

This is a short magnum made by re-forming and shortening .300 H&H or .375 Magnum brass. One forming and shortening operation is used plus fire forming. It holds over 75 gr of powder and about the maximum for best results in the .35 bore. The cartridge is still short enough to work through standard actions with a minimum of alteration. There are several very similar versions originated by other gunsmiths which are equally good. The .35 short Magnum, when loaded with suitable bullets is sufficiently powerful for any big game in the world. Since these cases have a relatively large powder capacity, they are best adapted for use with fairly heavy bullets.

200 gr. bullet	60 gr.	3031 powder	2824 fs	
	65	3031	3185	
	74	4895	3113	
250	62	4350	2700	
	65	4350	2850	
	68	4320	2920	
	70	4895	2900	
275	70	4895	2810	
300	68	4895	2670	
	74	4350	2701	

Standard twist: 14"

MAXIMUM LOAD LISTED SHOULD BE APPROACHED WITH CARE

.358 B-J Express (Barnes-Johnson)

Again, the .358 B-J Express is the same case as used for the other B-J Express line, but with neck expanded to accept the standard .35 calibre bullets. It is similar to the older .35 Ackley Magnum and to the new .358 Norma and likely would accept loads recommended for these two. A very fine big game cartridge.

Bullet	Powder charge	Powder	Velocity
220 gr. bullet	75 gr.	4064	3120 fs
250	78	4350	2900
300	76	4350	2600

Standard twist: 14"

.358 Norma Magnum

The .358 Norma Magnum is so nearly identical to the .35 Ackley Magnum that either of these two cartridges interchange and loading data for both of these cartridges is also identical. The following are a few loads recently developed for the .358 Norma Magnum by Speer Products, Lewiston, Idaho.

Bullet	Powder charge	Powder	Velocity
180 gr. bullet	76 gr.	H380	3150 fs
	78	H380	3185
	76	4320	3215
	78	4320	3290
	74	4064	3265
	76	4064	3335
	68	3031	3200
	67	HiVel #2	3325
220	79	4350	2900
	82	4831	2730
	68	4320	2885

MAXIMUM LOAD LISTED SHOULD BE APPROACHED WITH CARE

LOADING DATA

	68 gr.	H380 powder	2750 fs
	68	4895	2870
	60	HiVel #2	2905
250 gr. bullet	77	4350	2830
	82	4831	2750
	66	H380	2590
	66	4895	2720
	65	4064	2560
	58	HiVel #2	2730
	70.2	Norma 203	2790

Additional loads can be found in the Speer Manual #5.

Standard twist: 14"

.35 Belted Newton

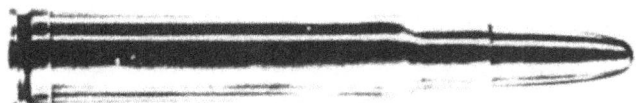

This is called a "belted" Newton because it is about as close to the original .35 Newton as it is possible to make from H&H Magnum brass. The cartridge illustrated was designed by Eldon Stephen and John Walker of Great Falls, Montana. Although not quite identical to the .35 Ackley Magnum, which was also designed with the original Newton in mind, it is so nearly so that all loads can be considered interchangeable. Like the Ackley version, it has proven to be extremely effective on all types of big game, and with good or correct bullets it is sufficiently powerful for any big game in the world. This and similar versions like the Ackley and Apex .35 Magnums, cannot be praised too highly as big game cartridges. The following loads have been worked out by owners of .35 Belted Newton rifles.

220 gr. bullet	71 gr.	4320 powder	2840 fs	est
	77	4350	2850	est
250	69	4320	2960	est
	75	4350	3000	est

Standard twist: 14"

MAXIMUM LOAD LISTED SHOULD BE APPROACHED WITH CARE

.350 Mashburn Short Magnum

This is another true short Magnum cartridge made by necking down and shortening .300 or .375 H&H brass. This cartridge is almost identical to the .35 Ackley Magnum and any comments and loading data apply to both cartridges equally.

Standard twist: 14"

.35 Apex Magnum

This is the same case as the .300 Apex except necked up to accept the .35 calibre bullets. The overall length of the .35 Apex and the .35 Ackley magnum is almost exactly the same; however, the length of the body of the Ackley case is very slightly longer which makes the capacity of the Apex case slightly less. Since this difference is hardly measurable, loading data for the two cartridges is interchangeable. For the loading data see .35 Ackley Magnum.

Standard twist: 14"

.350 Mashburn Super Magnum

This is a full length .375 H&H Magnum case necked to .35 and blown out with a 30° shoulder. It is very similar to the Ackley Improved .35 Magnum.

MAXIMUM LOAD LISTED SHOULD BE APPROACHED WITH CARE

250 gr. bullet	72	gr.	4064 powder	2784 fs
	74		4064	2831
	74		4320	2755
	76		4320	2815
	87		4350	3038
	89		4350	3076
	93		4831	3031
	95		4831	3085

Standard twist: 14"

.35 Ackley Magnum Improved

This cartridge is furnished for shooters who feel they want maximum capacity possible with the .300 Magnum blown out case in .35 calibre. It is the .300 Improved Ackley magnum necked up to .35. The same can be done with the Weatherby and others. The best use for this cartridge is for shot out .300 Magnums which can be rebored to .35 and chambered for this big .35 without going to the expense of replacing the barrel. It is doubtful if this big one is as good or as efficient as the short .35 Magnum, but it should be a great deal more satisfactory than a .30 calibre using the big case. This big one requires a long action such as the Enfield, Model 70 Magnum, FN Magnum or the genuine Magnum Mauser.

220 gr. bullet	75	gr.	4895 powder	3000 fs
	74		4064	2965
	85		4350	3010
	88		4831	2880
250	71		4064	2760
	86		4350	3000
	88		4831	2945
300	80		4350	2620

Standard twist: 14"

MAXIMUM LOAD LISTED SHOULD BE APPROACHED WITH CARE

.358 Barnes Supreme

Again, the .358 Barnes Supreme is the same case as the other Barnes Supreme cartridges but necked to .35. This cartridge is almost identical to the Ackley Improved .35 Magnum and will accept the same loads, but Barnes recommends only the heaviest bullets.

350 gr. bullet   90 gr.   4350 powder   3050 fs
Standard twist: 14"

.358 Lee Magnum

This cartridge was originated by Robert M. Lee, of Woodmere, Long Island for use mostly on African and other big game. Cases are made by necking down .425 Wesley Richards cases, and then fireforming. An unique feature of this case is the standard head or rim diameter which makes the rim smaller in diameter than the body of the case. Because of this standard rim diameter and medium over all length, it works through standard actions with a minimum of alteration. The reduced head diameter may also be a disadvantage since there is less metal around the primer. The case uses Berdan primers.

Bullet	Powder charge	Powder	Velocity
250 gr. bullet	79 gr.	4350 powder	2865 fs
	80	4350	2900
	84.5	4350	3010
275	80	4350	2630
	83	4350	2840
	87	4831	2775
300	85	4831	2700

Standard twist: 14"

MAXIMUM LOAD LISTED SHOULD BE APPROACHED WITH CARE

.38/55

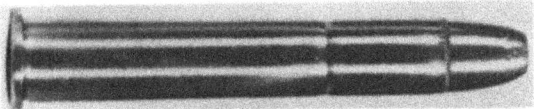

The .38/55 is another target cartridge which was a companion to the familiar .32/40. Actually there were three of these straight black powder cartridges, .28/30, .32/40 and the .38/55. All became famous for their accuracy. The .38/55 like the .32/40 was originally designed as a Ballard cartridge and many thousands of the fine Ballard rifles were chambered for this cartridge which was originally loaded with the .255 grain bullet and 55 grains of black powder. Marlin and Winchester produced their repeating rifles for the .38/55. For many years the .38/55 was extremely popular for deer hunting, and was considered superior to the .30/30 and they are still killing deer in spite of some of the state laws which prohibit its use.

The .38/56 uses the same bullet as the .38/55, but the .38/56 has the same rim diameter as the .45/70 and was designed for use in the Model 1886 Winchester. Being a bottle necked cartridge it had slightly greater capacity than the .38/55 and was originally loaded with 56 grains of Black powder behind the .255 grain bullet. Owners of .38/56 rifles, both in Winchester and Marlin make can have them rebored to .45/70, and a 38/56 case can be made by necking .45/70 brass down. .38/55 loading data can be used for the .38/56.

255 gr. bullet	30	gr.	3031 powder	1555 fs
	35		3031	1820
	18		2400	1475
	26		HiVel #2	1455
	29		HiVel #2	1645
265	20		4198	1600
	23		4198	1750
	26		HiVel #2	1455
	29		HiVel #2	1645
	30		3031	1555
	35		3031	1820

Standard twist: 18", 20"

MAXIMUM LOAD LISTED SHOULD BE APPROACHED WITH CARE

.375 Barnes Supreme

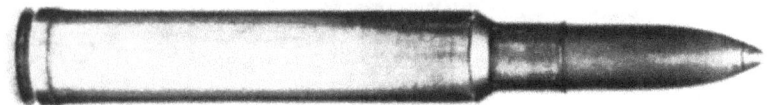

The .375 Barnes Supreme is a full length Magnum case with minimum body taper and sharp shoulder. It can be described as an "improved" .375 and cases can be made by fire forming .375 H&H Magnum factory loads. Barnes designed this cartridge for use with his 350 grain soft point or full jacket bullet.

350 gr. bullet	88 gr.	4831 powder	2650 fs

Standard twist: 12"

.375 Express

The .375 Express is a cartridge similar to the 8mm Express by Ralph M. Payne of Ventura, California, except it is necked up to accept the .375 bullet. Like the other Payne Express cartridges, the .375 Express cases are made from .348 Winchester brass with the rim turned off to create a rimless cartridge. The following loads were developed in a 25 inch barrel with 10 inch twist.

270 gr. bullet	82 gr.	4350 powder	2800 fs compressed load
	73	4064	2825
300	80	4350	2675
	80	4831	2420
	72	4064	2675

Standard twist: 12"

MAXIMUM LOAD LISTED SHOULD BE APPROACHED WITH CARE

.375 Durham Magnum

The .375 Durham Magnum is the .338 Winchester Magnum case necked up to .375 with a 35° shoulder angle to produce a very fine short .375 Magnum cartridge with an overall length suitable for use in standard actions. Ballistics are practically the same as for the standard .375 Magnum. The following loads were developed in a 20 inch barrel with 14 inch twist.

235 gr. bullet	82	gr.	H380 powder	2825 fs
270	80		H380	2725
300	78		H380	2580

Standard twist: 12"

.375 Whelen

The .375 Whelen is simply the standard '06 case necked up to .375 and could very well be called the .375/06. It can be made in both standard and improved versions. The following loads were worked out by Elwood Wimmer of Magna, Utah, who feels that this is a very fine cartridge.

235 gr. bullet	55	gr.	4895 powder	2495 fs	est.
	56		4895	2520	est.
	57		4895	2560	est.
	58		4895	2600	est.
350	52		4895	2340	est.
	57		4350	2280	est.
	58		4350	2320	est.
	59		4350	2320	est.
	56		4064	2500	est.
	57		4064	2545	est.
	52		3031	2550	est.
	53		3031	2600	est.

MAXIMUM LOAD LISTED SHOULD BE APPROACHED WITH CARE

260 Gas check Lyman #375-449
                30 gr. 4064 powder   1400 fs est.

Standard twist: 12"

.375 Whelen Improved

This cartridge is an improved .35 Whelen, necked up to accept the .375 calibre bullet. Very little loading data is available, but it has been chronographed with 51 gr of 4895 and the 350 gr. bullet to produce an approximate velocity of 2100 fs and with 55 gr. of 4895, approximately 2300 fs. Doubtless very good loads could be worked up with the various bullet weights available in .375 calibre.

Standard twist: 12"

.375 H&H Magnum

The .375 Magnum was introduced by Holland and Holland something like forty-five years ago. It has been used successfully all over the world for large game since that time. Rifles for it are currently manufactured by both Remington and Winchester in this country.

190 gr. bullet	60	gr.	4198 powder	2940 fs
	71		4064	2830
235	69		4064	2690
	75		4064	2810
	77		4064	2880
	66		HiVel #2	2700
250	62		HiVel #2	2580
	64		4895	2600
	65		4895	2615
	50		4198	2405

MAXIMUM LOAD LISTED SHOULD BE APPROACHED WITH CARE

LOADING DATA

270 gr. bullet	69 gr.	4064 powder	2650 fs
	70.5	Norma 203	2740
285	70	4320	2500
	70	4895	2520
300	70	4350	2300
	73	4350	2410
	78	4350	2550
	57	HiVel #2	2230
	62	4064	2360
	67.1	Norma 203	2550

Standard twist: 12"

.375 ICL Kodiak

This ICL Improved .375 is similar in design to the ICL Grizzly, but since it handles a much larger diameter bullet, it should be a relatively efficient large capacity cartridge, for use on the largest game. Its characteristics should be quite similar to those of the .375 Weatherby, or the Ackley Improved .375, and many other similar versions.

270 gr. bullet	84 gr.	4350 powder	2885 fs
300	81	4350	2720

Standard twist: 12"

.375 Mashburn Magnum (long)

This is simply a blown out Improved .375 Magnum with a 30° shoulder. Cases are made by fire forming factory loads. This should be a relatively efficient large capacity cartridge, like the Ackley Improved .375 and the .375 Weatherby Magnum which it closely resembles. The Mashburn .375 and similar .375 Magnums can be highly

MAXIMUM LOAD LISTED SHOULD BE APPROACHED WITH CARE

recommended for all kinds of big game found throughout the world.

235 gr. bullet	88 gr.	4064 powder	3135 fs
	90	4064	3179
270	81	4064	2825
	83	4064	2880
300	88	4350	2740
	89	4350	2773

Standard twist: 12"

.375 Weatherby

Before it became a factory cartridge, the .375 Weatherby was what could be described as an "improved" .375 almost identical to the Ackley "improved" version in performance, the main difference being a venturified shoulder of the Weatherby as compared to a sharp cornered shoulder of the Ackley. Loading data should be interchangeable for both of these cartridges. The .375 Weatherby is one of the very best of the Weatherby line and is a good efficient cartridge for all kind of big game and could be highly recommended for anyone desiring this much power. It is somewhat superior to the standard .375 H&H and any standard .375 H&H rifle can easily be rechambered for the .375 Weatherby. The following are some of the loads recommended by Roy Weatherby.

235 gr. bullet	82 gr.	4064 powder	2950 fs
	84	4064	3015
	86	4064	3060
270	80	4064	2795
	81	4064	2825
300	78	4064	2630
	80	4064	2680
	72	4350	2265
	75	4350	2310
	77	4350	2385
	80	4350	2490
	82	4350	2530

MAXIMUM LOAD LISTED SHOULD BE APPROACHED WITH CARE

84 gr.	4350 powder	2630 fs
85	4350	2655
86	4350	2675
87	4350	2730
88	4350	2740

Standard twist: 12"

.375 Magnum Improved (Ackley)

The Improved .375 Magnum is essentially the same as the Improved .300 Magnum except it handles the larger .375 bullet. Because of the larger bore, it is a much more satisfactory cartridge than the .30 calibre and handles heavy charges of powder quite efficiently. It can be recommended for use on the largest game. In North America, there are not many species of game large and tough enough to demand so much power but it is a good killer on big Alaskan bear, moose, etc., and all large varieties of African and Indian game when good bullets are used. There have been reports of failures on elephant but it has been ascertained that in most instances improper bullets were used. About the only bullet available in this country is the Barnes which is made up to 350 gr with an extremely thick, tough jacket. Barnes .375 bullets are available in soft point and solid point especially for African hunting. Loaded with the Barnes 350 gr solid nose bullet the Improved .375 is powerful enough for the largest elephant. Also Barnes bullets are made as light as 250 gr with fairly tough jackets which do not blow up badly at the relatively high velocities of which the Improved .375 is capable. Cases are made by firing factory loads in the improved chamber. There are several other versions of this cartridge like the .375 Weatherby which are equally as good as the Ackley version.

235 gr. bullet	82 gr.	4064 powder	2950 fs
	86	4064	3060
270	80	4064	2800
	81	4064	2830

MAXIMUM LOAD LISTED SHOULD BE APPROACHED WITH CARE

300 gr. bullet	78 gr.	4064 powder	2630 fs
	85	4350	2650
	88	4350	2740
350	88	4831	2650

Standard twist: 12"

.378 Weatherby Magnum

This cartridge was designed and introduced by Roy E. Weatherby for use on the largest and most dangerous game. It is actually a .375 calibre but drives the 300 grain bullet at 3000 foot seconds as compared to the Improved .375 H&H Magnum at 2800 foot seconds. The .378 produces 6000 foot pounds energy at the muzzle as compared to a little under 5000 for the Improved .375 H&H Magnum. A good example of what the extra velocity does. Here we have an increase of 200 foot seconds which increases the energy over 1000 foot pounds. To get the most out of a cartridge such as the .378 Weatherby, only the strongest bullets should even be considered. This limits the choice of bullets to a very few such as the Barnes in both solid and soft points and the steel jacketed Hornady.

270 gr. bullet	106 gr.	4350 powder	3115 fs
	107	4350	3190
	108	4350	3210
300	100	4350	2880
	101	4350	2930
	102	4350	2950
	103	4350	3020

.38 WCF

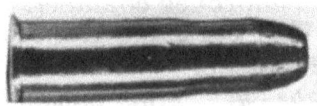

The .38 WCF, originally called the .38/40 was one of the earliest center fire cartridges and along with the .44/40

MAXIMUM LOAD LISTED SHOULD BE APPROACHED WITH CARE

it became famous especially in the old days of the west. It was originally made and brought out in the 1873 Winchester rifle, but later many other companies produced a rifle for it. Among these the most famous were the Marlin, Savage, Colt and Remington. The .38/40 like the .44/40 was also used in a large variety of revolvers which were used as companion arms to the rifle, and the old black powder cartridges could be interchanged in the rifle and revolver. Although the .38/40 is called .38 calibre it is actually .40 calibre which means that it should never be used in a true .38 calibre.

130 gr. bullet	24	gr.	2400 powder	1950 fs
	26		2400	2130
	28		4227	1950
	30		4227	2130
180	18		2400	1680
	22		2400	1870
	20		4227	1650
	26		4227	1850

Standard twist: 20" to 36"

.40-.348 Improved (Ackley)

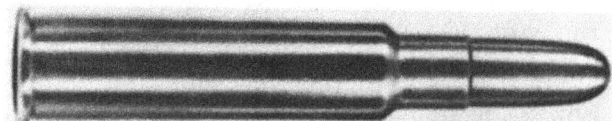

The .40-.348 Improved is similar to the Improved .348 except it is necked up to accept the .411 bullet, and like the .45/.348 it was designed by request of big game hunters who wanted a relatively larger diameter with something over two tons muzzle energy.

300 gr. bullet	72	gr.	4350 powder	2200 fs
	59		4064	1960
	69		4064	2440
	50		3031	1820
	54		3031	1925
	56		3031	2020
	58		3031	2130
	60		3031	2200
	61		3031	2180
	62		3031	2220

MAXIMUM LOAD LISTED SHOULD BE APPROACHED WITH CARE

400	63 gr.	3031 powder	2300 fs
	64	3031	2325
	65	3031	3380
	66	3031	2440
	72	4320	2355
	62	3031	2105
	60	4064	2000
	61	4064	2041
	62	4064	2105
	63	4064	2130
	67	4350	2020
	68	4350	2060

Standard twist: 16"

.400 Williams

The .400 Williams was the first Wildcat cartridge developed by W. H. (Bill) Williams of Odessa, Texas. It was originated in 1944 during wartime when materials were practically non-existent. No bullets being available during the war, .45 calibre bullets were simply swaged down to .411. After the war Fred Barnes of Grand Junction, Colorado, started to produce the .411 bullet. Cases for the .400 Williams can be made from any of the various Magnum cases but the easiest one to use is the .458 Winchester which can be necked down to .400 in one pass. It makes a very efficient practical big bore cartridge powerful enough for any North American game and probably any game in the world if loaded with the proper bullet.

208 gr. bullet - Ideal gas check #.429-.434 hollow point.
            28 gr. H240 powder 2350 fs
            30   2400   2350
234 gr. bullet - Ideal #429-421 cast
            28   H240   2200
            32   2400   2200
250 gr. Barnes 60   HiVel #2   2550 est.
                      65   4198   2400
300 gr. Barnes 66   4350   2500
400 gr. Barnes 65   4350   2150

Standard twist: 16"

MAXIMUM LOAD LISTED SHOULD BE APPROACHED WITH CARE

.404 B-J Express (Barnes-Johnson)

This .404 B-J Express cartridge is the same as the .358 B-J Express except necked for the tough .411 Barnes bullets. It is suitable for the largest game.

250 gr. bullet	77 gr.	4198 powder	3017 fs
300	85	4320	2810
400	74	4064	2425

Standard twist: 16"

.404 Barnes Supreme

The .404 Barnes Supreme is simply the .375 Barnes Supreme cartridge necked up to accept the Barnes .411 bullet.

400 gr. bullet   85 gr.   4064 powder   2550 fs

.416 Rigby

The .416 Rigby is a large English cartridge quite popular in Africa for game such as elephant, rhino and buffalo. The factory cartridge is loaded with the 410 grain bullet at about 2300 foot seconds which means that it is quite a lot less powerful than some American cartridges, which are considerably smaller. For example, the above ballistics

MAXIMUM LOAD LISTED SHOULD BE APPROACHED WITH CARE

can be compared to the .458 Winchester which is considerably smaller cartridge. The .416 Rigby cases can be made by turning the belt off on the .378 Weatherby case to produce a standard rimless case which is identical to the Rigby.

400 gr. bullet   105 gr.   4831 powder   2450 fs
                  110   4831   2600

Standard twist: 16"

.416 Barnes Supreme

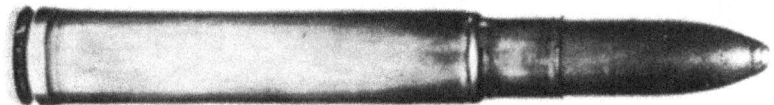

The .416 Barnes Supreme is the same cartridge as the .404 Barnes Supreme except necked up to accept the slightly larger .416 Barnes bullet.

500 gr. bullet   85 gr.   4831 powder   2400 fs

.44 WCF (.44/40)

The .44 WCF (.44/40) was the first cartridge developed for the Model 1873 Winchester rifle which figured very importantly in the development of the west, and within a very short time after its introduction the Colt factory announced their Single Action Army model for this cartridge and there are a large number of Colt revolvers still in circulation marked "Frontier Six Shooter" chambered for the .44/40. The .44/40 like the .38/40 was used extensively for deer and it still is used quite extensively for hunting deer in brushy country. When handloading for the .44/40, like the .38/40 it must be kept in mind that there are many rifles which have limited strength and loads which are safe in a Model 92 Winchester or Marlin Model 94 are not safe in

MAXIMUM LOAD LISTED SHOULD BE APPROACHED WITH CARE

the older models like the 1873 Winchester or equivalent models, for which black powder loads should be used. For the later models maximum loads listed in the various loading tables are safe.

140 gr. bullet	30 gr.	2400 powder	2425 fs
	33	2400	2720
	14.4	Unique	2035
200	25	2400	1870
	27.5	2400	2100
	27	4227	1850
	29	4227	1990
	11.3	Unique	1520

Standard twist: 20" to 36"

.44 Magnum

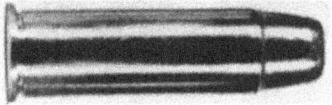

The .44 Magnum is a new and extremely powerful pistol cartridge and since its introduction quite a few rifles have been made up to handle it. The Model 92 Winchester is the most popular one for the purpose although all good single shot rifles can be rebarrelled or relined for it. The Model 92 Winchester in 38/40 and 44/40 calibres can be rebarrelled and converted to handle this cartridge. The following is a list of loads which have been tested in a rifle with a 20" barrel.

240 gr. bullet			1718 fs Factory Load
240	22 gr.	2400 powder	1638 fs
	25	2400	1827
	27	2400	1913

Standard twist: 18" to 40", according to fancy

MAXIMUM LOAD LISTED SHOULD BE APPROACHED WITH CARE

.44 Van Houten Super

The .44 Van Houten Super is a cartridge designed by Mr. E. B. Van Houten in cooperation with 'Lucky' Wade of Phoenix, Arizona. The case is a relatively efficient one and is made by necking up the .30/40 brass to .44 calibre then trimming it to 2 inches overall case length. The rim is turned off so as to work through the Model 94 Winchester for which this cartridge was especially designed.

250 gr. bullet	37 gr.	4227 powder	2255 fs
	47	4198	2355
250 gr. cast	49	3031	1970

Standard twist: 18", 20"

.424 Lee Magnum

This is essentially the same cartridge as the .358 Lee Magnum except the neck of the .425 Wesley Richards is left unchanged and the body fireformed to create what might be described as an "improved" .425 Wesley Richards. The shoulder angle is sharper (30°) and the body taper is less than on the original. This allows heavier loading as well as making the extraction easier. This cartridge has a favorable bore-case capacity ratio. Mr. Lee has used this cartridge in Africa with great success.

410 gr. bullet	84 gr.	4895 powder	2466 fs
	85	4895	2490
	86	4320	2413
	87	4320	2435

MAXIMUM LOAD LISTED SHOULD BE APPROACHED WITH CARE

.45/70

The .45/70 was the official government cartridge for many years and in addition to the service rifles many thousands of sporting rifles were manufactured by the various manufacturers of commercial rifles and ammunition. Rifles like the Model 86 Winchester and Model 95 Marlin, and many models of single shot rifles such as the Sharps, Peabody Martini, Winchester and many others were made for this cartridge. In addition all of these models were made in a variety of smaller calibres, especially .38 and .40 calibre. Since the .45/70 cartridge is the only one still being manufactured, these old .38 and .40 calibre rifles are being rebored to .45 and chambered for the old ever popular .45/70. The 45/70 is a short range cartridge judged by modern standards but for many years it has proven itself in the field on all kinds of big game all over the world.

300 gr. bullet	30 gr.	2400 powder	1875 fs
	44	HiVel #2	1920
	48	3031	1675
	58	3031	2015
400	58	3031	1900 (Barnes)
405	27	2400	1500
	36	4198	1417
	53	3031	1827

Standard twist: 20", 22"

.450 B-J Express (Barnes-Johnson)

The .450 B-J Express is the same case as the other B-J cartridges, but necked for .45 calibre bullets. This cartridge could best be described as an "improved" .458

MAXIMUM LOAD LISTED SHOULD BE APPROACHED WITH CARE

Winchester. It uses all .45 calibre bullet but especially the Barnes line which are made with both .032 and .049 thick copper jackets. These bullets are available in both soft point and solid nose types and are the toughest bullets made in the United States. The full jacket .450 Barnes bullet has proven itself many times on the largest elephants. Barnes also furnishes this design for 8mm and .375.

500 gr. bullet   78 gr.   4320 powder   2200 fs

Standard twist: 14"
Special twist: 18", 20"

.450 Alaskan

The .450 Alaskan was designed by Harold Johnson of Cooper Landing, Alaska, especially for hunters who demand a lever action rifle for the largest Alaskan game. The Alaskan cases are made by necking up and blowing out the .348 Winchester case. It can be loaded with 300, 400, or 500 gr. bullets. Velocities approach those of the .458 Winchester Magnum factory loads. It is recommended only for the Model 71 Winchester lever action rifle or the better single shot actions like the Hi-side Winchester or Sharps Borchardt. The .450 Alaskan is very similar to the .450/.348 cartridge. Both are made in the same way, but the Alaskan has about .020" greater body taper which means it is noticeably smaller in diameter at the shoulder. It has a slightly longer body which patially compensates for the reduced capacity caused by the steeper taper. Because of this greater body taper, it feeds through the Model 71 action much more easily and with considerably less action alteration than is necessary for the Ackley version. Because of this feature, it can be considered more satisfactory of the two cartridges. Because of the slightly lesser case capacity, loads shown for the .450/.348 should be reduced about 5%. This results in slightly reduced velocity, but it is more than offset by the better feeding qualities.

Standard twist: 14"
Special twist: 18", 20"

MAXIMUM LOAD LISTED SHOULD BE APPROACHED WITH CARE

.450 Barnes Supreme

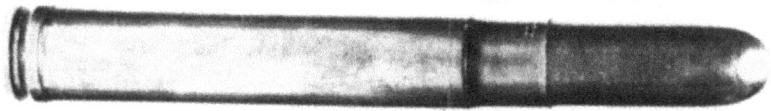

The .450 Barnes Supreme is the same as the .416 and other Supreme cartridges but necked to accept standard .45 calibre bullets, but particularly the heavy, tough jacketed Barnes line of bullets. It is very similar to the .450 Ackley Magnum and will accept the same loads. Barnes recommends the 500 grain bullet.

500 gr. bullet   95   gr.   4320 powder   2440 fs

.450 Fuller

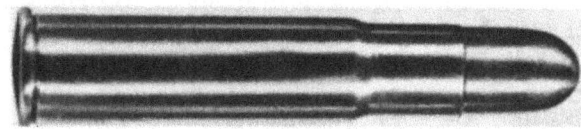

The .450 Fuller is a cartridge developed by Harold Fuller who was once a gunsmith for Harold Johnson the originator of the .450 Alaskan. Since Mr. Johnson is no longer in the gun business Mr. Fuller has carried on the Fuller Gun and Machine Shop on his own in Cooper Landing, Alaska. The .450 Fuller is quite similar to the .450 Alaskan and the .450/.348, the main difference being the 20° shoulder instead of a sharp one. It also has a slightly longer neck than the others. Mr. Fuller recommends this cartridge for use in the Model 86 Winchester. His pet load for the Model 86 Winchester is 61 grains of 4198 powder with the 350 grain bullet for an approximate estimated velocity of 2000 fs. There is one other load which he uses quite a bit—66 grains of 3031 powder with the 400 gr bullet for an estimated velocity of 2045 fs. These two loads have been recommended for use with Remington cases only.

Standard twist: 14"
Special twist: 18", 20"

MAXIMUM LOAD LISTED SHOULD BE APPROACHED WITH CARE

.450-.348 Improved (Ackley)

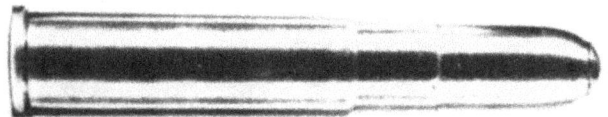

This is the oldest of the large bore cartridges based on the "improved" .348 design. It has been made for many years by request and recently revived by extensive tests by "Guns and Ammo" magazine. This is one of the most powerful cartridges available for lever action rifles and is especially adapted to the Model 71 Winchester lever action repeater. However, quite a few guns have been made on good single shot actions such as the Winchester Hiside. Standard .45 calibre bullets are used of the same quality as recommended for the .458 Winchester Magnum and this cartridge develops ballistics quite close to those of the .458. It is recommended only for the largest game and for shooters who can stand the heavy recoil. It is a cartridge of quite violent recoil especially in lever action rifles requiring special attachments for the magazine assembly. The following loads were developed by Bob Hutton of "Guns and Ammo."

Bullet	Powder (gr.)	Powder type	Velocity
350 gr. bullet	64 gr.	3031 powder	2060 fs
	66	3031	2220
	67	3031	2245
	68	3031	2275
	70	3031	2480
400	62	4064	1870 Fire Form Load
	67	4064	2020
	68	4064	2085
	69	4064	2130
	70	4064	2150
	65	3031	2130
	67	3031	2150
	68	3031	2200
	69	3031	2245
	70	3031	2275
500	62	4064	1840
	64	4064	1905
	67	4064	2000
	68	4064	2040
	69	4064	2060

Standard twist: 14"
Special twist: 18", 20"

MAXIMUM LOAD LISTED SHOULD BE APPROACHED WITH CARE

.458 American

The .458 American (.458 x 2 inch) was recently designed by Frank C. Barnes of Santa Fe, New Mexico. This is a big bore cartridge tailored strictly to North America big game and hunting conditions. It is intended for use in medium or standard length actions and is based on the .458 Winchester Magnum with a reduced case length of 2 inches. It also has a slightly smaller base and case diameter and less body taper. It is one of the shortest belted cases currently in use. Loading dies are available from R.C.B.S. and cases are made from .458 Magnum or Norma unformed Magnum brass. Maximum performance is delivered with bullets of 300, 350 or 400 grains of weight. For possibly 40 or 50 years there has been a persistent, but not overwhelming demand for an American big bore cartridge. Something adequate for the largest, most dangerous game found here under adverse conditions. The demand has been filled to some extent by the obsolete .45/70 and to some extent by various Wildcat cartridges based on necking up the .348 Winchester to .40 or .50 calibre. Almost all of these are good cartridges ballistically, but suffer from a common fault. They must be used in lever action or single shot rifles. The .458 Winchester and other Magnum big bores for bolt action rifles are all badly over powered for North American use. They can be loaded down, but are then inefficient and the ammunition, components and the rifles are expensive in the first place. The .458 American is designed to eliminate these shortcomings. It is an efficient design at full power or with reduced loading, and recoil is not completely obnoxious. It can be used in modern bolt actions and is entirely adequate for any North American big game, including the big Alaskan bears in heavy brush.

300 gr. bullet	55 gr.	HiVel #2 powder	2300 fs
	52	3031	2530
350	50	3031	2310
405	51	HiVel #2	2050

Standard twist: 14"
Special twist: 18", 20"

MAXIMUM LOAD LISTED SHOULD BE APPROACHED WITH CARE

.458 Winchester

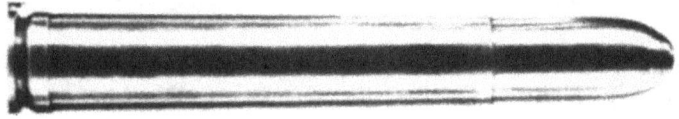

The .458 Winchester is one of the latest additions to the Winchester line of commercial cartridges. It was designed only for the largest game, especially African game and since its introduction, it has proven to be one of the best and certainly sufficiently powerful for anything. Being smaller in size than many of the overgrown (and over rated) English cartridges, it does not impress prospective African hunters as much as the large ones but actually it is more powerful than most of them. The factory loads the 500 gr soft point bullet 2125 fs velocity and the 510 gr solid point to 2125 fs. It is a very easy cartridge to handload and bullets from 300 to 600 gr are available. Also a wide variety of moulds are available with which to cast lead bullets. The .458 case is about the same length as the .30/06 but utilizes the standard belted Magnum head. Custom rifles can be made for the .458 on any good standard bolt action such as the 98 Mauser, Springfield, etc. Several improved versions have appeared which are made by firing factory loads in the improved chamber. These versions make it possible to increase the velocity slightly but it is doubtful if more power is necessary until safaris are possible on Mars or some other planet.

300 gr. bullet	80	gr.	4198 powder	2743 fs
400	75		3031	2347
	68		4198	2405
	71		4198	2449
	74		4198	2508
	77		4198	2556
500	70		3031	2172
	73		3031	2246
	75		3031	2338
	65		4198	2153
	68		4198	2363

Standard twist: 14"

MAXIMUM LOAD LISTED SHOULD BE APPROACHED WITH CARE

.450 Watts Magnum

This cartridge was developed by Mr. Watts and H. B. Anderson of Yakima, Washington. As mentioned in the description of the .450 Ackley Magnum, it was the forerunner of that cartridge. It was originally made by necking the .375 H & H Magnum case up to .45 to create a straight case similar in general appearance to the older and smaller .38/55. Needless to say, it is a good, efficient cartridge for all types of heavy game such as elephant and rhino and although slightly less powerful than the .450 Ackley Magnum and similar .450's, it certainly should be sufficient.

300 gr. bullet	85 gr.	4198 powder	2950 fs	
	90	4198	3030	
400	85	3031	2500	est
	85	4198	2670	
500	90	3031	2470	
	90	4320	2350	
	98	4320	2500	
600	80	3031	2180	
	85	4320	2190	
	90	4320	2260	

Standard twist: 14"
Special twist: 18", 20"

.450 Mashburn Magnum

This is a full length Magnum case made by necking up .375 brass or by using cylindrical Norma Magnum cases. Since it is essentially the same as the .450 Ackley Magnum all comments and loading data given for the .450 Ackley Magnum will apply equally well to the .450 Mashburn Magnum.

Standard twist: 14"
Special twist: 18", 20"

MAXIMUM LOAD LISTED SHOULD BE APPROACHED WITH CARE

.450 Magnum (Ackley)

This is one of the most powerful cartridges made in this country. Cases are made by necking .375 Magnum brass up to .450 and then fire-forming or by necking down Norma cylindral brass. The forerunner of this cartridge was the .450 Watts. The Watts cartridge is different in that it has no shoulder and appears like an overgrown .38/55. The Watts is a very good cartridge but the large .450 bore can use the extra powder capacity and since shooters wanting a rifle as large as this are looking for all the energy possible, this bottle necked version appeals to more than the straight case. There are two or three other versions of the .450 Magnum. That is, there are other names applied to .450 Magnums which appear to be identical to the Ackley version. This big cartridge with its tremendous recoil is actually too powerful for any North American hunting. In spite of this, it has gained a measure of popularity. On elephants it has proven especially effective. It has sufficient penetration with the Barnes 500 gr solid nose bullet to completely penetrate through large elephants at the shoulders producing clean one shot kills. There are few so called English "elephant guns" which approach it in power. Barnes bullets are available in 300, 400, 500 and 600 gr. The two heavier ones in both soft point and solid. Only the best actions can be used for this cartridge. Winchester Model 70 Magnum actions, Enfield, Magnum Mauser and the new Brevex Magnum are best. The Enfield is most commonly used because it is easy to get at reasonable prices.

Bullet	Powder charge	Powder	Velocity
300 gr. bullet	90 gr.	4198 powder	3033 fs
400	85	4198	2670
	100	3031	2802
500	90	4320	2350
	90	3031	2470
	95	4320	2440
600	90	4350	2100
	85	4320	2190
	87	4320	2200

Standard twist: 14"
Special twist: 18", 20"

MAXIMUM LOAD LISTED SHOULD BE APPROACHED WITH CARE

.460 Weatherby Magnum

The .460 Weatherby Magnum is described in the Weatherby book as being the world's most powerful big game rifle, and very likely, this cartridge fulfills this claim. The .460 Weatherby is the .378 Weatherby case necked up to accept the .45 calibre bullets which are available from 300 gr. to 600 gr. in weight.

There is very little loading data available for this cartridge. The following loads have been worked out and furnished by J. R. Buhmiller of Kalispel, Montana. He states that the tests are quite incomplete, however, and that the velocities are only approximate.

480 gr. bullet	115 gr.	4350 powder	2700 fs
500	115	4350	2650
	100	4320	2550

.475 Magnum (Ackley)

This is one of the largest wildcat cartridges. Cases are made by necking .375 brass up to accept the 475 bullet or by using unnecked Norma Magnum cases. These cylindrical Norma cases are exactly right without any change. The .475 Magnum is only for the very largest game. It is not as versatile as the .450 Magnum which uses all .45 bullets for velocities over 3000 fs. Only the Barnes 600 gr. bullet is available, but this one is made in both solid point and soft point types.

600 gr. bullet   90 gr.   4320 powder   2250 fs

Standard twist: 18"

MAXIMUM LOAD LISTED SHOULD BE APPROACHED WITH CARE

.475 Barnes Supreme

This is the .450 Barnes Supreme necked up to take the 600 grain bullet. It is almost identical to the older .475 Ackley Magnum for which the Barnes .475 bullet was originally designed. These .475 Magnums are among the most powerful rifles in the world and not particularly pleasant to shoot (not recommended for varmint shooting).

600 gr. bullet   90   gr.   4320 powder   2250 fs
Standard twist: 20"

.475 A & M Magnum

This is probably the largest cartridge made in this country with the exception of the .50 calibre machine gun cartridge which could hardly be called a sporting cartridge although there have been a few rifles made for it. The .475 Magnum was originated by the A&M Rifle Company. Cases are made by necking up the .378 Weatherby to accept a .475 bullet. Doubtless it is more than powerful enough for any worldly game and would appeal only to a hunter who feels he will be confronted by some wild animal with supernatural strength and that he is man enough to handle such a gun. Certainly this cartridge will separate the men from the boys in a hurry. Barnes bullets are available in 400, 500 and 600 gr sizes and with both solid and soft points. Gunmakers who claim they are making America's most powerful rifles had better take a look at the almost 10,000 lbs muzzle energy of the 500 gr .475 bullet. This same case is being necked by some gunmakers to accept the .450 diameter bullets which are also available in the same weights and types as the .475 Velocities for the .450 would doubtless be about 5% lower.

MAXIMUM LOAD LISTED SHOULD BE APPROACHED WITH CARE

```
400 gr. bullet    120 gr.   3031 powder    3227 fs
500               110       3031           2980
600               105       3031           2502
```
Standard twist: 18"

.505 Gibbs

The .505 Gibbs is shown here mostly for comparison. It is a tremendously large cartridge, the size of which is all out of proportion to its ballistics. It is, of course, for African or Indian game only. Its recoil, like that of the .450 and .475 Magnums is too much for most shooters. The overgrown size of the .505 in comparison to its ballistics is a characteristic shared by most of the other big English elephant cartridges notably the .416 Rigby which is a very large impressive looking cartridge which doesn't approach the ballistics of the smaller .450 Magnum.

```
525 gr. bullet    98  gr.   4064 powder    1970 fs
                  100       HiVel #2       2250
                  105       HiVel #2       2390
```

Only a few .505 Gibbs rifles have been built in this country. A few of these were made on the Enfield action, and others on Magnum Mausers. There has been practically no interest for this cartridge in this country for some years.

11mm Mauser

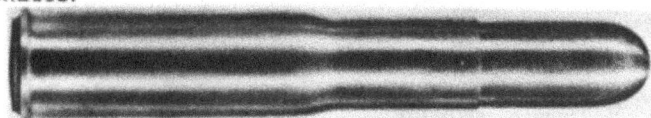

The 11mm Mauser is an old German service cartridge originally loaded with 77.16 grains of black powder with the 386 grain bullet developing a velocity of 1425 foot seconds. There are a large number of rifles floating around the United States which have been imported into this country and sold by dealers in surplus arms. There is no loading data available for this cartridge, therefore loading data for the .45/70 is recommended which will produce practically the same ballistics as listed for the .45/70 cartridge.

MAXIMUM LOAD LISTED SHOULD BE APPROACHED WITH CARE

English Cartridges for African Hunting

The following illustrated cartridges are manufactured in England for use on African big game safaris.

.400 Jeffrey

400 gr. bullet, 2125 foot seconds muzzle velocity
4020 foot pounds muzzle energy

.404 Nitro

400 gr. bullet, 2125 foot seconds muzzle velocity
4020 foot pounds muzzle energy

.470 Nitro

500 gr. bullet, 2125 foot seconds muzzle velocity
5030 foot pounds muzzle energy

.450 #2 Nitro

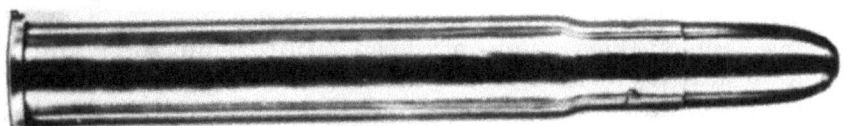

480 gr. bullet, 2150 foot seconds muzzle velocity
4930 foot pounds muzzle energy

MAXIMUM LOAD LISTED SHOULD BE APPROACHED WITH CARE

LOADING DATA

.475 #2 Nitro

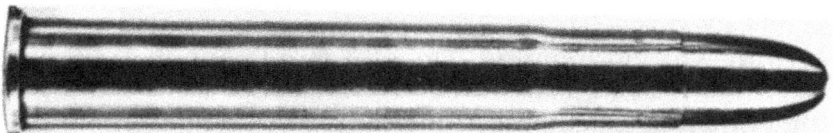

480 gr. bullet, 2200 foot seconds muzzle velocity
5170 foot pounds muzzle energy

.500 Kynoch

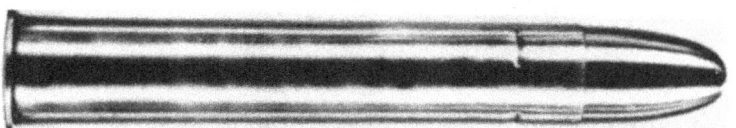

535 gr. bullet, 2400 foot seconds muzzle velocity
6800 foot pounds muzzle energy

.577 Kynoch

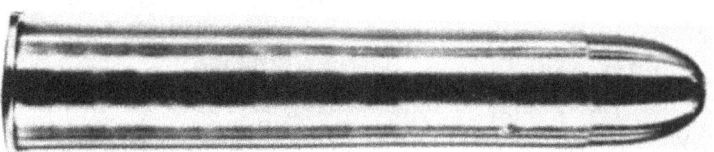

750 gr. bullet, 2050 foot seconds muzzle velocity
7020 foot pounds muzzle energy

.600 Nitro

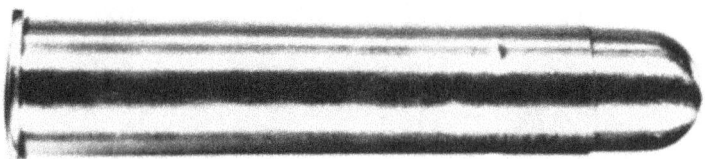

900 gr. bullet, 1950 foot seconds muzzle velocity
7610 foot pounds muzzle energy

MAXIMUM LOAD LISTED SHOULD BE APPROACHED WITH CARE

PISTOL AND REVOLVER LOADING TABLES

The following loading data for the more popular pistol cartridges is not complete. Only the more popular calibres and loads are given. For more complete information see the Lyman Reloading Handbook, or the Speer Loading Manual #5.

.22 Remington Jet

The .22 Remington Jet is a special pistol cartridge developed by Remington for use in Smith and Wesson revolvers. It is simply the .357 Magnum necked down to .22 with a long very sloping shoulder. The factory cartridge is loaded with the 40 grain jacketed bullet for a suggested velocity of 2460 fs in a 8-1/2 inch barrel revolver. Cartridges of this type are rather unpleasant to fire in revolvers because of the excessive blast, and the factory loads rated at 2460 fs actually produced about 1800-1900 fs in a revolver, but will develop very close to the claimed velocity in a short rifle barrel. It is a rather poorly designed cartridge for use in a rifle. Therefore some sort of an "improved" version is very much in order. Tests made by the Lyman Gunsight Corporation and the Speer Products produced approximately the following results. For additional loading data see the #5 Speer Manual for reloading ammunition.

Bullet	Powder charge	Powder	Velocity
40 gr. bullet	10 gr.	2400 powder	1675 fs
	10.5	2400	1750
	11	4227	1625
	13	4227	1850
	6	Unique	1490
	7	Unique	1700
45	9.5	2400	1480
	10	2400	1625
	10.5	2400	1710
	6	Unique	1445
	7	Unique	1665

MAXIMUM LOAD LISTED SHOULD BE APPROACHED WITH CARE

.22 Long Snapper

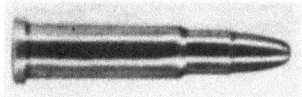

The .22 Long Snapper is a wildcat revolver cartridge based on the Hornet case and was originated by Robert Snapp of Royal Oak, Michigan. Its overall length allows it to be used in the S & W K-22, Combat Masterpiece, Colt Official Police in .22 calibre and the Ruger single six. Aluminum frame guns are not suitable for conversion to this cartridge. Good single shot rifles can be barrelled for this calibre as a companion gun to revolver. Existing .22 Long Rifle calibre rifles will not handle this cartridge. Suitable revolvers in either the .22 Long Rifle or .22 W.M.R. are used for this conversion. For further information on converting your revolvers for this cartridge, those interested can write direct to Snapp's Gunshop, 214 North Washington, Royal Oak, Michigan. Loading dies and shellholders, etc. are available from the R.C.B.S. Gun Shop of Oroville, California. Remington cases were used for all the following loads. If Winchester-Western brass is used, loads must be reduced because this brass is thicker. Barrel length - 4 inches.

40 gr. bullet	5 gr.	Unique powder	1555 fs
	8	2400	1495
	1	Bullseye	600

The following loads were developed in a 6 inch barrel and are MAXIMUM.

35 gr. bullet	9.7 gr.	2400 powder	1965 fs
	5.7	Unique	2015
37	9.5	2400	1840
	5.5	Unique	1905
40	9	2400	1745
	5.5	Unique	1905

Mr. Snapp has another "Snapper" handgun cartridge, namely the .22 Short Snapper which can be used on very short revolvers like the S&W Kit Gun, but due to its limited use there is no loading data available.

MAXIMUM LOAD LISTED SHOULD BE APPROACHED WITH CARE

.22 Williams

The .22 Williams is a pistol cartridge based on the .22 Hornet case and was developed by W. H. (Bill) Williams of Odessa, Texas. This cartridge was originated and introduced in 1944 and chamber tools are made by H & M Tool Company. It is quite similar to the blown out Kay-Chuck but apparently was originated some years before the Kay-Chuck. Mr. Williams designed a special bullet for use with this cartridge in revolvers. It is a cast bullet with a gas check and molds are now available from the Lyman Gunsight Co. as number 225-96. This cartridge has proven to be very deadly on small game and many of Mr. William's customers have had rifles made for it so that they have two guns using the same cartridge. He converts most of the better .22 revolvers such as the Colt Official Police Officer Model, Smith and Wesson K-22 and many good single action Colt revolvers. Further details can be obtained by writing direct to Mr. Williams at 1320 West 6th Street, Odessa, Texas. The following loads were developed in a 7-1/2 inch barrel.

49.5 gr. bullet	6 gr.	2400 powder	1400 fs est.
	8.8	2400	1700 est.-most accurate
	2.5	Bullseye	1050 est.-target accuracy
	4.5	Bullseye	1100 est.

.224 Critser Comet Magnum

This short cartridge was designed by Carlos Critser of Critser's Gun Haven, Phoenix, Arizona. It was designed for use in revolvers, especially for the K model .22 Smith

MAXIMUM LOAD LISTED SHOULD BE APPROACHED WITH CARE

and Wesson. The case is 1.030 long with 53° shoulder. The cartridge can also be used in rifles such as the Model 92 Winchester and single shots. The following loads were chronographed in a 6 inch Smith and Wesson K .22 revolver with .224 bullet, but .223 bullets are recommended.

40 gr. bullet	7 gr.	2400 powder	1870 fs
45	6.5	2400	1740
	7	2400	1820
50	6.5	2400	1680
	7	2400	1710

.224 Harvey Kay-Chuck

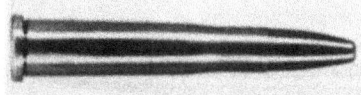

The .224 Harvey Kay-Chuck is a .22 center fire cartridge designed for use in revolvers, especially the Smith and Wesson K-22 Masterpiece. There are two versions of the Kay-Chuck, namely the standard and "improved", but the developers the Lakeville Arms, Inc. of Lakeville, Connecticut recommend the standard since it is better adapted for use in revolvers. Both are derived from the .22 Hornet rifle cartridge shortened sufficiently to work satisfactorily without excessive blast in the Smith and Wesson K-22 Masterpiece. It would seem that this is a more practical cartridge for use in a revolver than the recently developed Remington Jet because it does produce the same velocity with a much better chance of satisfactory mechanical operation of the revolver. This little cartridge would also be good in a short barrelled rifle where the shooter enjoys having a rifle and handgun using the same cartridges. The Lakeville Arms Company specializes in converting K-22 Smith and Wesson revolvers to handle the center fire .224 Harvey Kay-Chuck and complete information can be obtained by writing them direct. Lakeville Arms recommends the following loads for the standard .224 Harvey Kay-Chuck:

35 gr. bullet	2 gr.	Bullseye powder	980 fs	
	4	Bullseye	1620	
	5	Unique	1650	
	5.4	Unique	1760	
	9.7	2400	1900	Max.

MAXIMUM LOAD LISTED SHOULD BE APPROACHED WITH CARE

37 gr. bullet	2.5 gr.	Bullseye powder	903 fs	
	4	Bullseye	1600	Max.
	5.4	Unique	1750	Max.
	9.5	2400	1820	Max.
40	2	Bullseye	948	
	5	Unique	1715	Max.
	9.3	2400	1800	Max.
45	2.5	Bullseye	950	
	8.7	2400	1800	Max.
50	2.5	Bullseye	903	
	8	2400	1500	Max.

.224 Blown Out Kay-Chuck

The .224 Blown Out Kay Chuck case could very well be described as an "improved" .224 Kay-Chuck. It is the same length as the standard case. The case length for the two Kay-Chucks is 1.357, and the recommended load for fire forming the blown out Kay-Chuck is 2.5 or 3 grains of Bullseye powder, or 5 grains Unique, or 9.5 grains 2400.

35 gr. bullet	2 gr.	Bullseye powder	930 fs	
	4	Bullseye	1610	Max.
	5	Unique	1600	
	6	Unique	1650	Max.
	8	2400	1775	
	10.3	2400	1950	Max.
37	2	Bullseye	850	
	4	Bullseye	1560	Max.
	5	Unique	1560	
	6	Unique	1700	Max.
	8	2400	1550	
	8.5	2400	1650	
	10.2	2400	1840	
40	2	Bullseye	943	
	4	Bullseye	1500	Max.
	5	Unique	1600	
	6	Unique	1625	Max.
	8	2400	1600	
	9.5	2400	1750	Max.

MAXIMUM LOAD LISTED SHOULD BE APPROACHED WITH CARE

.30 Luger (7.65mm)

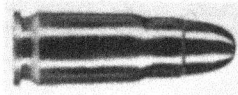

The .30 Luger is a bottle neck cartridge and compared to most pistol and revolver cartridges, it is relatively high velocity. Being a bottle neck cartridge it is necessary to full length resize for each reloading.

93 gr. bullet	3.5 gr.	Bullseye powder	1150 fs
	4	Bullseye	1170
	5	Unique	1245

.32/20 Revolver

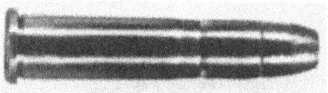

The .32/20 pistol is also known as the .32 WCF because it is widely known as both a rifle and a pistol cartridge. It was originated as a rifle cartridge for use in Model 1873 Winchester rifles but shortly after its introduction, Colt started making revolvers for it and later S&W and many other makes were made for this cartridge.

80 gr. bullet	4.2 gr.	Bullseye powder	1180 fs
	5.0	Unique	1220
90	3.6	Bullseye	1060
	5.8	Unique	1160
115	3.1	Bullseye	850
	4.5	Unique	925

MAXIMUM LOAD LISTED SHOULD BE APPROACHED WITH CARE

.32 S&W Long (.32 Colt New Police)

This is an old revolver cartridge introduced around 1895. Many, many thousands of revolvers have been manufactured for this cartridge and for the last few years it has been used quite a bit by target shooters. It is a very accurate cartridge, easy to load and easy to shoot because of its light recoil.

Bullet	Powder charge	Powder	Velocity
89 gr. bullet	2 gr.	Bullseye powder	750 fs
	3	Unique	975
	4	Unique	1000
95-98	2	Bullseye	770
	2.7	Bullseye	910
	4	Unique	940
	4.3	Unique	1010
105	2.1	Bullseye	745
	4	Unique	980

.32 ACP (7.65mm)

This little cartridge is known throughout the world except in the United States as the 7.65mm Browning. In the United States it is always known as the .32 ACP (Colt Automatic Pistol). There have been literally scads of different makes of automatic pistols manufactured around the world for this small cartridge. This is a semi-rimmed type of case.

Bullet	Powder charge	Powder	Velocity
71-74 gr. bullets	2 gr.	Bullseye powder	860 fs
	2.2	Bullseye	950
	2	Unique	600
	3.2	Unique	975
77	2.2	Bullseye	970
	3.3	Unique	950
85	1.8	Bullseye	830

MAXIMUM LOAD LISTED SHOULD BE APPROACHED WITH CARE

.357 Magnum

The .357 Magnum pistol cartridge was for a long time the most powerful commercial revolver cartridge in existence. It is identical to the .38 Special except slightly longer which prevents the .357 Magnum from being chambered in .38 Special guns. This cartridge is popular with law enforcement officers as well as target shooters. It is especially a good target cartridge when loaded with .39 Special loads.

87 gr. zinc alloy bullet 8.5 gr. Unique powder 1790 fs.

Bullet	Charge	Powder	Velocity
146 gr. bullet	4 gr.	Bullseye powder	1085 fs
	4	No. 6	1085
	15	2400	1475
148	4	5066	1000
	3	Bullseye	890
153	7	Unique	1295
	13	4759	1315
	14	2400	1560
155	6.5	Unique	1290
159	13.5	Ball C	1460
	7	Unique	1305
	15	4227	1400
160	7.5	Unique	1330
161	3.8	No. 6	1025
	5.3	5066	1090
	5	Red Dot	1045
162	12	4759	1275

.38 ACP (.38 Super)

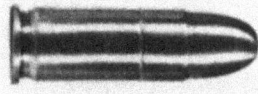

This is one of the oldest automatic pistol cartridges, having been in production since before 1900. It was first a military cartridge designed for the Colt "Military" model automatic pistol. Later the Colt Company produced the

MAXIMUM LOAD LISTED SHOULD BE APPROACHED WITH CARE

.38 Super automatic pistol for this cartridge. This late model was simply the .45 Colt automatic adapted for the .38 cartridge. Like the .38 Special, it uses bullets .357 in diameter and could be described as sort of an automatic .357 Magnum since it develops about the same ballistics as the .357 in the same length of barrel. The .38 ACP is a semi-rimless case.

130 gr. bullet	4.6 gr.	Bullseye powder	1200 fs
	5	Bullseye	1275
	4.7	Unique	880
	7.7	Unique	1310

.38 WCF (.38/40) Revolver

The .38 WCF (.38/40) cartridge is actually a .40 calibre originally designed for the Model 1873 Winchester. In the old days, many old timers would prefer to have handguns the same calibre as their rifles and the .38/40 became quite popular for rifles and revolver use.

180 gr. bullet	4 gr.	Bullseye powder	735 fs
	5.9	Bullseye	1050
	5	No. 6	730
	7.8	No. 6	1105
	8	Unique	925
	10	Unique	1285
200	8	Unique	900
	10	Unique	1175
	4.5	Bullseye	725
	5.3	Bullseye	950

MAXIMUM LOAD LISTED SHOULD BE APPROACHED WITH CARE

.38 Special Revolver

The .38 Special has long been one of the favorite handgun target cartridges, and at one time was used by the United States Army. It is an extremely easy cartridge to handload and a very accurate one.

Bullet	Powder charge	Powder	Velocity
85 gr. bullet	7 gr.	Unique powder	1430 fs
115	2	Bullseye	680
	4	Bullseye	1015
	3	No. 6	700
	4.7	No. 6	1040
141	4	No. 5	970
144	4	5066	980
146	3	Bullseye	860
	3.6	No. 6	970
148	3.2	5066	770
	2.7	Bullseye	760
140-150	2.5	Bullseye	740
	3.5	Bullseye	850
	9	2400	940
	13.5	2400	1350
	3.5	Unique	720
	6.4	Unique	1145
155	5.2	Unique	1005
158	2.5	Bullseye	720
	3.5	Bullseye	850
	5.5	Unique	910
	6.4	Unique	1145
	9.5	2400	915
	12.5	2400	1240
161	3.3	Unique	945
	5.2	Unique	970
165	2	Bullseye	640
	3.5	Bullseye	900
	5	Unique	700
	6	Unique	910
	9.5	2400	875
	10.5	2400	1025

MAXIMUM LOAD LISTED SHOULD BE APPROACHED WITH CARE

The following are a few loads recommended for the so-called .38/44 pistol cartridge which is the same as the .38 Special but especially adapted for use in special S&W heavy frame revolvers called their .38/44 Model.

bullet	powder		velocity
85 gr. bullet	15 gr.	2400 powder	1520 fs
146	6.4	Unique	1155
	11.5	S'Shooter	1210
	13.5	2400	1225
151	12	2400	1230
155	12.5	2400	1265
161	11	S'Shooter	1135
	13.5	2400	1220
162	5	5066	1040

.44 S&W Special

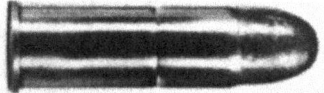

The .44 Special has been a favorite handgun cartridge for many years. It has always been considered just about the best big bore revolver cartridge for handloading.

bullet	powder		velocity
145 gr. bullet	5.5 gr.	Bullseye powder	955 fs
	7.5	Bullseye	1230
	9	Unique	1035
	11.5	Unique	1300
180	5	Bullseye	855
	6.8	Bullseye	1050
	8	Unique	900
	12.4	Unique	1400
200	4.5	Bullseye	800
	6.5	Bullseye	1000
	7	Unique	850
	9.8	Unique	1130
255	5.4	Bullseye	850
	6	Unique	735
	8.5	Unique	980

MAXIMUM LOAD LISTED SHOULD BE APPROACHED WITH CARE

.44 WCF (.44/40) Revolver

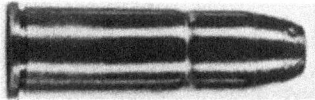

The .44/40 was a cartridge designed for the 1873 Winchester rfle but shortly after its introduction, the Colt factory produced their Single Action revolver. Many of these revolvers were known as the Frontier Six-Shooter. This rifle and pistol combination played a prominent part in the development of the west.

Bullet	Powder charge	Powder	Velocity
175 gr. bullet	6 gr.	Bullseye powder	900 fs
	8	Bullseye	1100
	9	Unique	950
	11.9	Unique	1200
240	5	Bullseye	720
	6.3	Bullseye	835
	7	Unique	760
	9.3	Unique	935
250	7	Unique	780
	9.1	Unique	940

.45 Colt

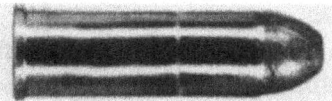

The .45 Colt has been and still is a very popular revolver cartridge. It was originally designed for the Colt Single Action in the early 1870's. Like the .44/40 this Colt gun and cartridge played a large part in the development of the West, and is often referred to as the "Peace Maker."

Bullet	Powder charge	Powder	Velocity
170 gr. bullet	6 gr.	Bullseye powder	900 fs
	7.8	Bullseye	1100
	9	Unique	1125
	11.8	Unique	1200
235	5	Bullseye	780
	6.8	Bullseye	950
	8	Unique	860
	10.7	Unique	1050

(.44 Magnum data on page 522)

MAXIMUM LOAD LISTED SHOULD BE APPROACHED WITH CARE

250 gr. bullet	5 gr.	Bullseye powder	785 fs
	6.2	Bullseye	895
	8	Unique	800
	10.3	Unique	990
260	5	Bullseye	770
	6.2	Bullseye	880
	8	Unique	790
	10.3	Unique	980

.45 ACP

This has been the standard military pistol cartridge of the United States armed forces for many years. It has been used in automatic pistols, revolvers sub-machine guns by all branches. It was brought out around 1905 and the automatic pistol developed for it finally became known as the 1911 Colt Automatic Pistol. This cartridge is rimless and has the same head diameter as the .30/06 rifle cartridge. Bullets cannot be crimped because the .45 ACP cartridge gets its headspace at the end of the case.

185 gr. bullet	4 gr.	Bullseye powder	810 fs
	5.5	Unique	850
	7	Unique	970
200	4.7	Bullseye	900
230	4.9	Bullseye	825
	6.5	Unique	760
	7.7	Unique	880
240	4.5	Bullseye	845
	5	Unique	700
	7	Unique	900
255	4.5	Bullseye	840
	6	Unique	840

MAXIMUM LOAD LISTED SHOULD BE APPROACHED WITH CARE

.454 Magnum

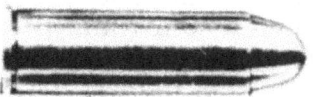

This is one of the most powerful revolver cartridges ever developed. It is also extremely powerful when used in rifles such as the Model 92 Winchester. Basically it is the .45 Colt but only solid head cases of the highest quality are used. The loads shown for this cartridge should *never* be used in a standard .45 Colt revolver.

This cartridge was developed by Jack Fullmer and Dick Casull of Salt Lake City, and they manufacture special five shot oversize cylinders, and fit them to single action Colt Frontier Model revolvers, and make certain alterations in the action, so as to accept these cylinders. The cylinders are made of special high tensile strength alloy steel, properly heat-treated to withstand the high pressure developed by the special duplex load.

Obviously, great care must be exercised when working with these duplex or triplex loads. When loading the following loads with the various powders, the powder charges are introduced into the case in the order given, and held in place by compression. The primer pockets are altered to accept the Remington 9-1/2 primers.

Bullet	Charge		Powder	Velocity
230 gr. bullet	2	gr.	Unique powder	
	25		2400	
	3		Bullseye	2000 fs
250	2		Unique	
	25		2400	
	2		Unique	1890
300	25		2400	
	2		Unique	1710

The following loads have been successfully used in a 20" barrel, Model 1892 Winchester rifle.

Bullet	Charge		Powder	Velocity
230 gr. bullet	2	gr.	Unique powder	
	25		2400	
	3		Bullseye	2315 fs
250	2		Unique	
	25		2400	
	2		Unique	2185

MAXIMUM LOAD LISTED SHOULD BE APPROACHED WITH CARE

.455 Webley Mark II

This has been, for a long time, the official British service revolver cartridge. It is quite similar to the .45 ACP from the standpoint of ballistics. However, it differs from the .45 ACP in that it is a rimmed cartridge. It has a thinner than the common rim, which hurts case life.

Bullet	Powder charge	Powder	Velocity
190 gr. bullet	3 gr.	Bullseye powder	675 fs
	4	Bullseye	770
	6.5	Unique	800
235	4	Bullseye	750
	6.2	Unique	780
250	4	Bullseye	735
	6	Unique	725

9mm Luger

The 9mm Luger is world famous as a military pistol and sub-machine gun cartridge. It is the same cartridge as the 7.65 Luger except it is straight, while the 7.65 is necked to .30.

Bullet	Powder charge	Powder	Velocity
124 gr. bullet	4.8 gr.	Bullseye powder	1120 fs
	6	Unique	1300

.44 Magnum

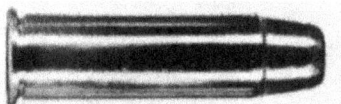

The .44 Magnum is at present the most powerful commercially loaded pistol cartridge and adapted only to revolvers made especially for it. It is quite similar to the old .44 Special but enough longer so that it cannot be chambered in revolvers made for .44 Special.

Bullet	Powder charge	Powder	Velocity
225 gr. bullet	20 gr.	2400 powder	1350 fs
	22	2400	1400
	10	Unique	1200
	11	Unique	1295
240	19	2400	1300
	21	2400	1425
	10	Unique	1190
	11	Unique	1275

MAXIMUM LOAD LISTED SHOULD BE APPROACHED WITH CARE

POWDER
by B. E. Hodgdon

Modern small arms ammunition is all loaded with smokeless powder.

In appearance, there are three general types: flake, cylindrical, and spherical. The reloader must depend upon identification by the label on the container, not by physical appearance of the powder itself.

The three companies who manufacture powder in the United States are Hercules, DuPont and Olin-Mathieson. Hercules and Olin powders are double base, containing both nitro-cellulose and nitro-glycerine. DuPont is single base, having only nitro-cellulose as its energy source. Most propellants have deterrents to assist in burning rate control. A second ingredient is present to reduce muzzle flash. A third important factor is graphite external coating. This aids in measuring during loading operation, and reduces possibility of static electricity and friction.

Black powder is a mixture of sulphur, charcoal and potassium nitrate. It was the only propellant known before about 100 years ago. As a propellant, its present use is confined to muzzle-loading, blank cartridges and twist barrels. Caution must be used during loading, since it is very easily ignited and burns extremely fast.

Burning rate, or relative quickness of various powders is established in laboratory "bomb" test.

This chart of DuPont I.M.R. rifle powders is based on 4350 as a standard of 100. This has nothing to do with pressure in rifle cartridges, but is a comparison of powders only.

Powder Number	Relative Quickness
5010	70
4831	89.9
4350	100
4320	110
4895	115
4064	120
3031	135
4198	160
4227	180

Hercules rifle powders are now confined to two. #2400 for very small cases, and HiVel #2, adaptable to medium capacity cases. Unique can be used as a very light charge propellant in most rifle cartridges. It is ordinarily considered a pistol and shotgun powder.

MAXIMUM LOAD LISTED SHOULD BE APPROACHED WITH CARE

Olin-Mathieson Ball powder is currently marketed only for pistol and shotgun.

However, Olin powder for rifle has been supplied to U.S. Ordnance in large quantities. Surplus, salvage, experimental lots, and end-of-run lots have been purchased by B. E. Hodgdon, Inc. and resold to the handloading trade. By screening and blending, the burning rate of any given number of powder has been kept within normal tolerances.

Currently available in Hodgdon's spherical powder is BL-C, H380, H450 and H870. For a rough comparison to DuPont I.M.R. it could be said that BL-C is slower than 3031, H380 slower than 4064, H450 is similar to 4831, and H870 faster than 5010. It is an important note, not to expect the same performance from two powders because they are similar or close in burning rate. The size and shape of the cartridge, bullet weight, and other factors cause powders to produce somewhat different results. So, don't guess what charge to use, refer to tested loading data tables.

Ball powder will give substantially longer barrel life. If the exact combination of the right Ball powder for the case and bullet weight can be found, a small increase in velocity can be obtained over other propellants.

GENERAL INFORMATION — SURPLUS POWDERS

Read this *BEFORE* using data. - B. F. Hodgdon

Loads marked with asterick (*) are considered strong maximum. Reduce first test load by 5% from highest shown. If air temperature is more than 20° above test temperature, reduce first test loads a second 5%. Work back up in half grain increments. If primers are loose or seat too easily on subsequent reloading of case, reduce charge about 4%. Reloaders should recognize the fact that velocities in their own guns may be somewhat different from those published. Also, that information from various laboratories will be different and still not be wrong. Using the same data with different lots of components fired in a different barrel may show over 300 feet per second different velocity. Firing in hot weather and/or with a hot barrel and chamber causes pressures to go up.

Our testing for velocity is done on the latest type of Berkeley chronograph. The first screen is 6 feet from the muzzle; the second is 10 feet from the first. The chronograph is accurate to one twenty-millionth of a second, which makes each recording a maxi-

MAXIMUM LOAD LISTED SHOULD BE APPROACHED WITH CARE

mum at 10 feet from absolute. Velocities published are instrumental. Since screens are so close, the muzzle velocities will be less than one-half of 1% faster than instrumental.

AGAIN, ALWAYS REDUCE FIRST TEST LOAD BY AT LEAST 5%!

Powders are listed according to burning rate, from fastest to slowest.

LOADING DATA FOR #5 PISTOL

Calibre	Bullet Weight	Powder charge	Velocity
.25 ACP	50 gr. Jacket	1.4 gr.	776 fs
.30 Luger	93 gr. Jacket	4.4	1170
.32 L. Colt	80 gr. Lead	2.7	835
.32 S&W	100 gr. Lead	2.6	707
.32 ACP	70 gr. Jacket	2.6	965
.32/20	80 gr. Lead	6.5	1300
.357 Magnum	145 gr. Lead	5.5	1190
	158 gr. Lead	5.0	1070
	160 gr. Lead	5.5	1160
.38 S&W	147 gr. Lead	3.8	796
.38 Special	147 gr.	4.4	840
	158 gr.	5.0	950
.38 ACP	125 gr.	5.0	1100
9 mm	127 gr.	6.0	1135
.44 Special	215 gr.	7.5	940
.44/40	200 gr.	11.5	1150
.45 Colt	200 gr.	10.5	1050
	255 gr.	8	870
.45 Auto	220 gr.	5.6	880

LOADING DATA FOR HS10

Calibre	Bullet Weight	Powder charge	Velocity
.30/06	169 gr.	10 gr.	1285 fs
		13	1502
		15	1630
.38 Special	145 gr.	4	791
		6	1086
	155	4	778
		4.5	895
		5.3	962
	167	6.5	1043
	110	6	1079
		7	1223
	120	6	1045
		7	1199
	135	6	1019

MAXIMUM LOAD LISTED SHOULD BE APPROACHED WITH CARE

LOADING DATA FOR HS10 *continued*

Calibre	Bullet Weight	Powder charge	Velocity
.38 Special (cont.)	146 gr.	5 gr.	873 fs
		5.5	956
		6	1005
	150	5.5	959
		6	1000
	155	5.5	958
	160	5	837
		5.5	933
	165	5	882
	180	4	707
.357 Magnum	167	8.5	1231
	155	8.5	1265
	146	8.5	1246
		9	1303
		9.5	1341
	160	8	1142
		8.5	1220
		9	1277
.44 Special	215	12.5	1353
	220	8	994
		8.5	1023
		9	1069
	225	7.5	913
		8	990
		8.5	1057
	230	7	865
		7.5	907
		8	950
	240	6.5	831
		7	859
		7.5	934
	250	6	715
		6.5	770
		7	805
.44 Magnum	215	10.5	1188
		16.5	1510
	225	10.5	1124
		11	1143
		11.5	1228
	235	14	1359
	240	9.5	1046
		10	1086
		10.5	1133
	250	9	938
		9.5	1029
		10	1057
		13.5	1302

MAXIMUM LOAD LISTED SHOULD BE APPROACHED WITH CARE

LOADING DATA FOR HS10 *continued*

Calibre	Bullet Weight	Powder charge	Velocity
.45 ACP	185 gr.	4.5 gr.	680 fs
		6	877
		7	993
	200	5	773
		5.5	860
		6.5	901
	215	4.5	720
		5	753
		6.5	997
	230	4	620
		5	783
	240	4	640
		4.5	712
		6	864
	255	4	642
		4.5	710

LOADING DATA FOR H4227

Calibre	Bullet Weight	Powder charge	Velocity
.218 Bee	40 gr.	12 gr.	2760 fs
	43	11	2375
	48	11	2435
.22 Hornet	40	9.5	2410
	43	10	2460
	48	9.5	2380
.22 Savage	60	13	1950
.220 Swift	48	13	1900
	55	14	2150
.222 Remington	50	14	2525
		16	2825
		18*	3131
	55	16	2710
.25/20	85	8.6	1500
.257 Roberts	85	17	1935
.270 Winchester	105	15	1600
7mm	130	14	1700
7.65 BM	311316 cast	18	1956
		12	1383
		10	1116
	311466	19	1867
	311467	19	1787
	311291	15	1881
.30/40	165	19	1740
.30/06	120	18	2000
	150	20	1700

MAXIMUM LOAD LISTED SHOULD BE APPROACHED WITH CARE

LOADING DATA FOR H4227 continued

Calibre	Bullet Weight	Powder charge	Velocity
.357 Magnum	148 gr.	16 gr.	1287 fs
	160	14	1085
		15	1274
		16	1359
	170	14	1115
		15	1193
.44 Special	250	19	1120
		20*	1209
.44 Magnum	250	21	1229
		23*	1361
.45 Colt	254	20	997
.45/70	500	26	1243
		28*	1276

LOADING DATA FOR SPHERICAL H335

Calibre	Bullet Weight	Powder charge	Velocity
.222 Remington	50 gr.	26 gr.	3232 fs
.308 Winchester	130	52	3146
	150	46	2750
		49.5	2960
	180	45.5	2564
		46	2685

LOADING DATA FOR 4895

Calibre	Bullet Weight	Powder charge	Velocity
.222 Remington	225415 cast	14 gr.	1488 fs
		15	1626
	45 gr.	25	3171
	50	24.5	3295
		25.5	3438
	55	23	2808
.222 Remington Magnum	55	29	3530
.219 Wasp	50	28	3312
	55	28	3501
.22/250	225415 cast	19	1870
	50	36	3560
	55	35	3560
.220 Swift	225415 cast	21	2299
	50	39	4028
	55	38	3819
.243 Winchester	70	39	3377
	75	38	3219
	85	35	2949
	100	34	2710

MAXIMUM LOAD LISTED SHOULD BE APPROACHED WITH CARE

LOADING DATA FOR 4895 *continued*

Calibre	Bullet Weight	Powder charge	Velocity
.243 Rockchuck	105 gr.	41.5 gr.	2969 fs
.244 Remington	70	41	3603
	75	40	3484
	85	39	3303
	100	36	2889
.244 Remington Improved	60	44	3805
.250 Savage	60	40	3667
	75	38	3380
	87	37	3208
	100	35	2988
.257 Roberts	87	42	3302
	100	38	3029
	117	34	2593
.25/06	87	47	3258
6.5 x 55	129	41	2810
	140	37	2520
	156	36	2370
6.5 Jap	129	35	2347
	156	32	2129
.270 Winchester	90	52	3337
	100	50	3345
	130	49	3158
	150	45*	2760
7 x 57 MM	130	45	2939
	139	42	2727
	140	45	2919
	160	41	2598
	175	39.5	2466
.30/30	311466 cast	30	1956
	110	30	1812
	110	38	2610
	150	35	2349
	170	30	1888
.308 Winchester	110	49	3028
	130	47	2897
	150	45	2691
	180	40	2390
.30/06	311466 cast	30	1638
	311467	32	1715
	311284	36	1834
	110 gr.	52	3017
	125	55	3197
	150	50.9	2756
	180	47	2588
	200	48	2654

MAXIMUM LOAD LISTED SHOULD BE APPROACHED WITH CARE

LOADING DATA FOR 4895 continued

Calibre	Bullet Weight	Powder charge	Velocity
.303 British	130 gr.	43 gr.	2650 fs
	150	42	2479
	180	40	2295
7.65 BM	311413 cast	26	1385
	175 gr.	26	1527
		35	2008
		37	2072
.32 Special	323470 cast	30	1889
8 mm	323470	30	1555
	125 gr.	51	2796
	150	50	2747
	165 gas check cast	30	1555
	170	46	2501
.300 Weatherby	150	72	3185
	180	68	2651
	200	63	2651
.35 Remington	200	39	2069
.375 Weatherby	235	81	2919
	289	78	2718
	300	76	2566
.458 Winchester	500	70	2048
		74	2156
.45/70	400	50	1622

LOADING DATA FOR SPHERICAL H375

Calibre	Bullet Weight	Powder charge	Velocity
.222 Remington	50 gr.	27 gr.	3033 fs
	55	27	3004
.222 Magnum	50	31	3408
	55	30	3363
		32	3534
		33	3677
.22/250	50	40	3872
	55	37	3555
	60	36.5	3494
.219 Wasp	51.5	32	3512
		33.3	3802
	55	33	3609
.220 Swift	50	41	3798
	55	39	3519
	60	37	3323
.243 Winchester	75	40	3107
	90	37.5	2858
	105	35.5	2650

MAXIMUM LOAD LISTED SHOULD BE APPROACHED WITH CARE

LOADING DATA FOR SPHERICAL H375 *continued*

Calibre	Bullet Weight	Powder charge	Velocity
.244 Remington	70 gr.	46 gr.	3714 fs
	75	44	3501
	85	40	3064
	90	39	2935
	105	36	2666
.257 Roberts	87	44.5	3148
	100	42	2925
	117	40	2659
.270 Winchester	100	57	3564
	130	51	3078
	150	49	2848
	170	47	2574
7 x 57 mm	139	41	2566
	160	38	2377
	175	37	2239
.30/06	150	55	2888
	180	50	2559
.303 British	130	47	2686
	150	45	2582
.35 Whelen	180	63	2766

LOADING DATA FOR SPHERICAL H380

Calibre	Bullet Weight	Powder charge	Velocity
.222 Remington	55 gr.	31 gr.	3255 fs
.222 Magnum	55	32	3492
	63	32	3418
.220 Swift	36	46	4392
	50	44	4074
	55	40.5	3806
		42	3910
.22/250	49	42	3831
	55	38	3577
.243 Winchester	70	45	3517
	75	42	3286
		43	3322
		44	3397
	85	38	2968
		39	2960
	90	38	2968
	105	34	2630
.244 Remington	70	47	3518
	75	45	3163
	85	41	3163
	90	40	3094
	100	37	2827

MAXIMUM LOAD LISTED SHOULD BE APPROACHED WITH CARE

LOADING DATA FOR SPHERICAL H380 *continued*

Calibre	Bullet Weight	Powder charge	Velocity
.257 Roberts	75 gr.	48 gr.	3572 fs
	87	49	3443
	100	44.5	3065
	117	41	2735
.270 Winchester	100	55	3398
	130	52	3069
7 x 57 mm	130	47	2831
7 mm	139	42.5	2597
	160	39.5	2382
	175	39	2251
.308 Winchester	150	51.5	2746
	180	46.5	2464
.30/06	150	55	2872
	180	48	2514
.300 Weatherby	150	72	3009
	180	66	2636
	200	63	2571
.375 Weatherby	235	78	2492
	300	76	2396
.35 Whelen	250	61	2564

LOADING DATA FOR 4831

Calibre	Bullet Weight	Powder charge	Velocity
.22/250	50 gr.	42.5 gr.	3557 fs
	55	42.5	3552
	60	42	3471
	63	41.5	3329
.220 Swift	50	46	3718
	55	46	3754
	60	46	3734
	63	46	3754
.243 Winchester	60	50.5	3547
	70	50	3473
	75	50	3292
	80	50	3380
	85	49	3275
	90	47	3139
	100	46	3009
	105	45	2914
.243/06 Improved	100	56	3259
.244 Remington	60	53	3584
	75	52	3659
	80	51	3638
	90	49	3426
	105	46.5	3201

MAXIMUM LOAD LISTED SHOULD BE APPROACHED WITH CARE

POWDER

LOADING DATA FOR 4831 *continued*

Calibre	Bullet Weight	Powder charge	Velocity
.250 Savage	100 gr.	42 gr.	2825 fs
		43	2922
		44	2972
	120	44	2878
.257 Roberts	60	55	3787
	75	55	3595
	87	55	3422
	100	52	3220
	117	50	3183
.25/06	75	62	2648
	87	59	3559
	100	58	3457
	117	56	3169
.257 Weatherby	75	77	3994
	87	74	3813
	100	71	3525
	120	67	3248
.257/6.5	87	52	2900
	120	51	2835
	140	50	2732
	160	46	2461
6.5 x 55	140	52	3010
	156	50.5	2846
6.5 x 06	100	66	3593
	120	60	3199
	140	59	3111
	156	58	3003
.264 Winchester	77	78	4026
	87	72	3892
	100	71	3844
	120	65	3445
	139	67	3151
	140	61	3164
	160	57	2886
.270 Winchester	90	60	3292
		65	3593
	130	60	3219
	150	59	3105
	170	58	2838
.270 Gibbs	100	66	3428
	130	64	3270
7 x 57 mm	130	55	2856
	154	52	2641
7 mm/06 Improved	160	60	2748

MAXIMUM LOAD LISTED SHOULD BE APPROACHED WITH CARE

LOADING DATA FOR 4831 *continued*

Calibre	Bullet Weight	Powder charge	Velocity
7.65 BM	311466 cast	42 gr.	1890 fs
	311467 cast	41	1906
	311291 cast	42	1809
	175 gr.	53	2456
.30/06	110	63.5	2614
	130	63.5	2654
	150	63.5	2709
	165	61.5	2706
		63.5	2869
	169 gr. cast	50	2198
	180 gr. cast	50	2201
	180	62.5	2752
	200	59.5	2671
	220	59	2500
.308 Winchester	150	53	2572
	165	53	2513
	180	53	2523
	200	51	2453
.300 H&H Magnum	110	83	3611
	125	83	3406
	130	81.5	3389
	150	78	3313
	165	77	3099
	180	75.5	3013
	200	72.5	2954
	220	71	2746
	250	69	2585
.300 Improved Magnum Weatherby Type	110	94	3877
	130	92	3713
	150	88	3559
	165	86	3423
	180	84	3304
	200	81	3128
		82	3145
	220	78	2906
.30/.338	150	80	3187
	180	80	3079
	200	80	2996
.30/30	170	39	1980
8 x 57 mm	150	57.5	2466
	170	57.5	2428
	196	57.5	2441
	225	57.5	2366

MAXIMUM LOAD LISTED SHOULD BE APPROACHED WITH CARE

LOADING DATA FOR 4831 continued

Calibre	Bullet Weight	Powder charge	Velocity
.348 Winchester	200 gr.	65 gr.	2316 fs
		67	2460
		68	2510
	220	65	2472
.35 Whelen	180	66	2375
	220	66	2360
	275	66	2364
	275	66	2316
.375 H&H Magnum	235	89	2770
	285	88	2712
	300	87	2649
.458 Winchester	500	83	1934
.45/70	500 cast	60	1383

LOADING DATA RECOMMENDED BY JACK O'CONNOR FOR 4831

Calibre	Bullet Weight	Powder charge	Velocity
.257 Roberts	100 gr.	49 gr.	3140 fs
	117	46	2925
	120	45	2875
.270 Winchester	100	60	3200
	130	60	3237
		63	3350
	140	60	3090
	150	58	3003
	180	52	2460
		54	2580
.30/06	150	60	2760
	180	58	2550
		60	2725
	220	56	2405
		57	2435
	250	52	2180
		54	2225

LOADING DATA FOR H570

Calibre	Bullet Weight	Powder charge	Velocity
.22/250	60 gr.	44 gr.	2820 fs
.220 Swift	225415 cast	30	1941
	63	46	3293
.243 Winchester	90	50	2875
	105	48	2698
.244 Remington	90	50	2910
	105	48	2783

MAXIMUM LOAD LISTED SHOULD BE APPROACHED WITH CARE

LOADING DATA FOR H570 *continued*

Calibre	Bullet Weight	Powder charge	Velocity
.25/06	117 gr.	68 gr.	3133 fs
	120	61	3024
.264 Winchester	77	81	3479
	87	79	3588
	100	79	3531
	120	77	3461
	139	80*	3347
	140	74	3257
	160	71	3067
.270 Winchester	130	64.5	2974
	150	64	2930
	170	61	2631
7 mm/06	175	62	2253
.30/06	170 Lead	56	2092
	200 Lead	52	1927
	220	61	2245
	250	57	2028
.300 H&H Magnum	150	85	2866
	200	85	2841
	220	85	2740
.300 Weatherby	180	92	2859
	220	84	2519
		86	2545
		88	2640
		90	2725
.300 Improved	180	95	3200
	200	94	3083
	220	90	2819
		94	3035
8 mm	160 cast	52	1829
.375 Weatherby	350	90	2151

LOADING DATA FOR H870

Calibre	Bullet Weight	Powder charge	Velocity
.22/.250	63 gr.	45 gr.	2766 fs
.220 Swift	63	48	3116
.243 Winchester	105	52	2778
.244 Remington	105	55	3067
.25/06	117	69	3107
6.5 x 55	156	57	2599
6.5/06	156	64	2802
.264 Winchester	77	85	3627
	120	80	3488
	139	78	3274
	140	76	3241
	160	70	2985

MAXIMUM LOAD LISTED SHOULD BE APPROACHED WITH CARE

POWDER

LOADING DATA FOR H870 *continued*

Calibre	Bullet Weight	Powder charge	Velocity
.270 Winchester	130 gr.	65 gr.	2785 fs
	150	65	2818
	170	65	2649
.30/06	200	65	3559
	220	65	2230
.300 H&H Magnum	180	90	2883
	200	90	2965
	220	90	2962
.300 Improved Magnum	180	95	2949
	200	97	3140
	220	97	3099
	250	92	2791
8 mm Hodgdon Magnum	150	69	3302

LOADING DATA FOR 5010-50 MG

Calibre	Bullet Weight	Powder charge	Velocity
6 mm	105 gr.	80 gr.	3719 fs
6 mm Improved	90	86.5	3542
	105	86	3552
.270 Winchester	150	66	2772
	170	66	2670
7 mm/06	175	62	2195
.30/06	150	60	2251
	175 Lead	56	1992
	180	60	2171
	200 Lead	56	1910
	220	60	2137
.300 Weatherby	220	94	2603

MAXIMUM LOAD LISTED SHOULD BE APPROACHED WITH CARE

QUESTIONS AND ANSWERS

One of the best ways to present information is in the form of questions and answers, and the following section is devoted to a series of Questions received from all parts of the world. Some of the answers necessarily are the personal opinion of the author, but so far as possible only factual information is used in answering questions.

QUESTION: I have a rifle which is chambered for a blown out .30/06 cartridge with a much longer body than is found on the standard '06 case, and I have been told that I can fire form cases by using factory ammunition, if I pull the bullet out far enough so that it will set up against the lands or touch the lands firmly. Is this a safe practice? WCH

ANSWER: Some recommend this way of fire forming cases, and some get away with it for a long, long time, but it could hardly be considered a safe practice. For example, I once observed this method of fire forming where the bullet was being set into the lands and the cases were blown forward about 1/8 inch in the fire forming process. This shooter got away with it for several hundred rounds, but finally one did not form correctly. The head blew off, the action was completely demolished, the barrel was blown off into the bushes ten feet away and the shooter wound up in the hospital for several weeks, and for some time there was some doubt about saving his sight. Therefore, it would be cheap insurance to first neck the cases up to larger diameter, and in this instance it would probably be .35, then neck it back down the distance equal to the headspace of the new chamber, or to a point which will allow the bolt to be closed on the new cartridge with a definite "feel". This eliminates the necessity of withdrawing the bullet far enough to engage the lands and establish a safe shoulder to headspace against. Then, the resulting cartridge can be loaded with a full load and fire formed with perfect safety.

QUESTION: Can the Krico varmint rifle in .222 calibre be rechambered for the .222 Magnum, or is the action and magazine too short? WCP, Jr.

ANSWER: I doubt if it would be practical to try to rechamber the Krico .22 to the .222 Remington Magnum because of the difficulty which would be encountered with the magazine.

QUESTION: In your article "Wildcats" in the 1962 Gun Digest you noted that the .270 WCF was maximum capacity for its bore and that little improvement could be made. What about the .270 Weatherby and the .270 Gibbs? The .270 Weatherby is advertised as moving a 150 grain bullet at 3250 foot seconds with 72 grains of 4831, while the Gibbs version is reputed to do about the same with 6 grains less of the same powder. Both are claimed at least as accurate as the standard case. Are these claims correct? WPB

ANSWER: There are a lot of ways to look at the things which you mention in your letter and when I say that the .270 Winchester is already over bore capacity, it does not necessarily mean that you cannot get a slight increase by adding a lot more powder. If you want a surprise take a .270 Magnum to someone who has a reliable chronograph and chronograph one of the loads and find out how it compares.

The thing that you must keep in mind is that a common method used by the various originators, enthusiasts and cranks who advertise their products, is to work up loads in some individual rifle which for some reason will accept heavier loads than the average gun will and even in that gun, the loads are right up to the absolute maximum and quote the figures obtained in that way. Such loads are very likely to blow the average rifle to Kingdom come. Then there is the other way which a few use, and that is to advertise velocities which they are reasonably sure the average handloader can safely obtain in the average rifle. I can assure you that there is a lot of difference between these two types of figures. For example, if you should compare the figures that I give for my own .270 Magnum to some similar cartridges there will be several hundred feet difference, while in reality the two cartridges would give exactly the same velocity under the same conditions.

There is no question but that the Gibbs cartridge will give the same performance with less powder than some of the .270 Magnums but I am very doubtful that much improvement can be made over the standard .270 except by going to a smaller case such as the Improved .257 Roberts necked up, or the .308 Winchester necked down. Such cartridges will produce velocities just as high as the .270 Winchester, but will do it with considerably less powder.

Having been in the reboring business for twenty-five years, I have a much better chance to observe barrel life than most people and most .270 Magnums or similar cartridges shoot out a barrel in a comparatively short time. For example, a .270 Magnum which could perhaps be expected to give 100 foot seconds more than the .270 Winchester, might give less than 50% barrel life. So when we look at these things from the overall standpoint, which would include the shooter's pocketbook, barrel life, efficiency of the cartridge, flexibility and things like that, everything is in favor of the smaller case which has a better adjustment between bore and case capacity.

I am very much against publicizing loads which are of such a specialized nature that the average owner of rifles of the same calibre would never be able to reproduce in any safe manner, or load which have been built up by using some surplus powder, the availability of which could cease any minute.

Accuracy claims of overbore capacity cases probably are more or less true, except that nothing is ever mentioned about the flexibility which means that usually the larger the case the harder it is to find a load which will shoot and I have seen Magnums which have been worn out before a good load could be found. In other words, they are very much more critical.

Modern advertising is more and more taking the form of creating certain impressions in the mind of the reader without actually stating very many facts, and it is the things that are not said that most shooters should know about. A good example of this is automotive advertising. For the last three years I have had two different makes of compact cars, both makers advertising up to thirty miles to the gallon. They never mention the "down to" which is actually what we want to know and the "down to" is closer to 18 miles, than the "up to" of 30 miles.

QUESTION: I have been reading recently about a brand new idea in cartridges called the .25 CONDOR. Do you have any information on this cartridge?

2. Why would Timken steel show better barrel life as mentioned in this article?

3. What do they mean by copywriting? N.S.

ANSWER: Yes, I have some information, but I would not call the idea new by any means. I suspect only the name is new. Fred Barnes brought out a similar cartridge some fifteen years ago. He called it the 6.5 QT (quick twist). It was based on the .250 Ackley Magnum, while the Condor is the 7x61 S&H case necked to .25 calibre, but since the two parent cases are very similar, results would be bound to be similar.

The Barnes cartridge used a 200 grain 6.5 bullet at over 2700 foot seconds with 64 grains of machine gun powder. Later Barnes worked out a .228 cartridge using bullets up to 150 grains. (Imagine a 150 grain .22 bullet!!!!), finally settling on a 125 grain .22 bullet. .He gets 2750 foot seconds with this bullet and 50 grains of machine gun powder. The case is the Improved .257 Roberts necked down to .22. This .22 will smash both shoulders of the largest elk. Barnes has done it. This shows the idea is not new. Doubtless it was tried many years before Barnes did it.

Such cartridges are highly specialized. They require extremely sharp twist from 5 to 6 inches, which means they will not handle normal bullets at all. They are cartridges which are built around one special load.

2. I am afraid the whole story was not told concerning the steel and barrel life. Investigation shows the first barrels which wore out rapidly were used with a steel bullet made from Shelby tubing with no gilding metal or copper plating. When the Timken barrel was installed, they switched to plated Norma bullets. Very likely the barrel steel had nothing to do with it, the whole thing being due to the difference in the bullet jackets. The first barrels, or at least some of the first ones were made of Ryerson 4140 which is identical in analysis to the Timken material with only the slightest variations, notably in the sulfur content. Sulfur is detrimental rather than beneficial. The added sulfur in the Timken material probably had no measurable effect on the overall results.

3. My observations on copywriting a name for a cartridge go back more than twenty years. It simply consists of coining a name, any name, not previously used in connection with a cartridge and then copywriting it so no one can stamp the name on their own product without permission. An old example of this is the name "Varminter", which was copywrited to identify a cartridge made by necking the .250/3000 down to .22 calibre. The result was to antagonize the trade. In reprisal, the trade started making rifles for the same cartridge like crazy, and stamped the barrels .22/250, and as a result, a great many more rifles were produced under the .22/250 designation, than under the copywrited name. Seldom is anything gained by antagonizing the competition.

Getting back to the virtues and faults of extremely long bullets, it is my personal opinion that the faults far outweigh the virtues. Since the idea is by no means new, there has been ample time to flood the market long before this but the trade has never fallen over each other to get on the band wagon. Barnes can still furnish his QT line in anything from .22 to .457. He will make a 1000 grain bullet for anyone, and a rifle to go with it, if anyone thinks he is man enough to herd such a beast.

Actually many more things enter the picture than just the sustained velocity element. First you have to have some velocity to sustain, and in this day and age, 2800 to 3000 foot seconds is nothing to make the experienced shooter write home about. Experienced hunters also know that the human element is one of the unsurmountable obstacles in the game fields. This is one factor that we can all very well believe will remain unchanged for a lot longer time than we will be around. Guess work in holding over, leading, etc., is greatly reduced by high velocity. Time of flight is of much greater importance than sustained velocity, since a high velocity bullet, even though it is only medium or light weight, has both the time of flight and actual drop factors entirely in its favor within any range at which the average shot could even hope to make a decent hit. It might be added that no matter how long the bullet, or what its velocity may be, the first requirement is to make a good hit. The following table showing theoretical drop, time of flight, etc., was submitted by Paul C. VonRosenberg. Also see Time of Flight table on page 545 for comparison between light and heavy bullets. Note especially the actual drop figures.

QUESTION: I do not normally try to correct an expert in his field, but really feel that what I am going to pass on may be of interest to you and also may well save someone a ruined gun and worse yet, actual injury.

You state in the question and answer department that you do not believe that reduced loads of 4831 powder in the .30/06 is anything to worry about. It is.

I have read quite a bit on this subject and as a result did not try to use reduced loads of 4831 even though the price made it seem tempting. However, like everyone else who thought about it I could not really see how the reduced load could kick up more pressure than a full load. In fact, I advised against it.

I believe I found that this powder will push pressures when a club member came in and asked me why his loads were taking primers right out of his cases. His normal load of about 59 grains, as I remember, caused no trouble. However either 30 or 35 grains, again I can't swear to the load he quoted, from the same can of powder expanded primer pockets. You don't do that with low pressure!

COMBINED BALLISTIC TABLE AND RANGE CHART

TABLE I

CARTRIDGE	Bullet Wt.	Muzzle Velocity	Muzzle Energy	Section Density	Ballist. Coeff.	300 YARD RANGE Vel.	Energy	Time of Flight	Drop	400 YARD RANGE Vel.	Energy	Time of Flight	Drop	500 YARD RANGE Vel.	Energy	Time of Flight	Drop
22/06 Imp.	63	4000	2240	.179	.291	2910	1190	.251	12.1	2590	940	.351	23.7	2290	735	.458	40.4
270 Imp.	100	3750	3120	.187	.306	2750	1680	.266	13.6	2450	1330	.371	26.4	2180	1055	.487	45.5
6MM/06 Imp.	85	3650	2520	.205	.334	2730	1410	.271	14.1	2470	1150	.380	27.8	2210	925	.489	46.0
25/06 Imp.	87	3650	2580	.187	.306	2650	1360	.275	14.6	2380	1100	.385	28.5	2090	845	.506	48.8
300 Mag. Imp.	150	3500	4070	.227	.369	2680	2390	.281	15.2	2430	1970	.389	29.0	2220	1640	.504	48.9
244 Imp.	85	3500	2320	.205	.334	2600	1275	.285	15.6	2350	1045	.393	29.6	2100	830	.517	51.4
334 OKH	200	3300	4840	.258	.420	2590	2980	.296	16.8	2390	2640	.403	31.2	2200	2155	.525	53.0
25/06 Imp.	100	3400	2560	.217	.352	2570	1470	.290	16.1	2310	1185	.404	31.4	2090	970	.524	52.8
270 Imp.	130	3300	3140	.243	.394	2530	1850	.298	17.0	2330	1570	.415	33.0	2120	1300	.535	55.0
300 Mag. Imp.	180	3190	4070	.272	.442	2520	2540	.308	18.2	2350	2210	.421	34.0	2160	1865	.540	56.0
270 Imp.	150	3050	3100	.279	.454	2440	1985	.320	19.7	2250	1690	.442	37.6	2070	1430	.566	61.6
7mm/06 Imp.	160	3000	3200	.282	.461	2410	2070	.323	20.0	2230	1770	.447	38.4	2040	1480	.572	62.7

NOTES: All bullets assumed to be 6 calibre radius spitzers, soft point or small hollow point similar to Barnes, Nosler, Sierra, Sisk, Speer and WTCW to which are assigned a coefficient of form of .615, which is conservative. Muzzle velocities are nominal with 24″ barrel lengths.

TABLE II

CARTRIDGE	Bullet Wt.	Muzzle Velocity	Muzzle Energy	Section Density	Ballist. Coeff.	300 YARD RANGE Vel.	Energy	Time of Flight	Drop	400 YARD RANGE Vel.	Energy	Time of Flight	Drop	500 YARD RANGE Vel.	Energy	Time of Flight	Drop
25/06 Imp.	87	3650	2580	.187	.306	2650	1360	.275	14.6	2380	1100	.385	28.5	2090	845	.506	48.8
25/06 Imp.	100	3400	2560	.217	.352	2570	1470	.290	16.1	2310	1185	.404	31.4	2090	970	.524	52.8

CARTRIDGE	Bullet Wt.	Muzzle Velocity	Muzzle Energy	Section Density	Ballist. Coeff.	600 YARD RANGE Vel.	Energy	Time of Flight	Drop	700 YARD RANGE Vel.	Energy	Time of Flight	Drop	800 YARD RANGE Vel.	Energy	Time of Flight	Drop
25/06 Imp.	87	3650	2580	.187	.306	1840	650	.629	76.0	1610	500	.763	112	1410	380	.930	166
25/06 Imp.	100	3400	2560	.217	.352	1870	780	.655	83.6	1660	610	.807	125	1490	490	.957	176

CARTRIDGE	Bullet Wt.	Muzzle Velocity	Muzzle Energy	Section Density	Ballist. Coeff.	900 YARD RANGE Vel.	Energy	Time of Flight	Drop	1000 YARD RANGE Vel.	Energy	Time of Flight	Drop
25/06 Imp.	87	3650	2580	.187	.306	1240	300	1.114	238	1120	240	1.311	330
25/06 Imp.	100	3400	2560	.217	.352	1370	390	1.164	260	1190	315	1.311	330

CARTRIDGE	Bullet weight grains	Muzzle velocity ft. seconds	Muzzle energy ft. pounds	Sectional density	Ballistic Coefficient	Vel.	Energy	Time of Flight	Drop
							300 Yard Range		
.257 Condor	160	2900	2990	.347	.563	2400	2080	.338	22.0"
.257 Condor	120	3375	3040	.260	.422	2660	1890	.299	17.2
.257 Weatherby	100	3650	2960	.217	.352	2790	1730	.272	14.2
.334 B-J Express	250	2970	4900	.322	.525	2440	3310	.333	21.3
							400 Yard Range		
.257 Condor	160	2900	2990	.347	.563	2280	1850	.463	41.1"
.257 Condor	120	3375	3040	.260	.422	2440	1590	.414	32.9
.257 Weatherby	100	3650	2960	.217	.352	2520	1410	.390	29.2
.334 B-J Express	250	2970	4900	.322	.525	2280	2890	.458	40.3
							500 Yard Range		
.257 Condor	160	2900	2990	.347	.563	2110	1580	.600	69.1"
.257 Condor	120	3375	3040	.260	.422	2260	1360	.536	55.2
.257 Weatherby	100	3650	2960	.217	.352	2280	1160	.508	49.5
.334 B-J Express	250	2970	4900	.322	.525	2100	2450	.593	67.5
							600 Yard Range		
.257 Condor	160	2900	2990	.347	.563	1990	1410	.738	104.5"
.257 Condor	120	3375	3040	.260	.422	2050	1120	.669	86.0
.257 Weatherby	100	3650	2960	.217	.352	2040	930	.638	78.1
.334 B-J Express	250	2970	4900	.322	.525	1970	2160	.732	103.0

NOTE: All bullets assumed to be 6 calibre radius spitzers, soft point or small hollow point similar to Barnes, Norma, Nosler, Sierra, Speer and WTCH, to which are assigned a coefficient of form of .615 which is conservative. Ballistic factors from "Exterior Ballistic Charts" by Wallace H. Coxe and Edger Bugless, E. I. duPont and Company, 1926; and the "Hodsock Ballistic Tables," recomputed by O. Weston, Bisley, 1946.

Paul vonRosenberg, P. E.

For that reason I certainly would not like to ever go on record as even hinting that 4831 could be used in reduced loads. We have both seen guns that should be junked and certainly waiting for the excuse to blow up being used. We both also know that no matter what causes a gun to injure someone, is just more ammunition for the anti-gun nut.

I certainly hope you realize I am only trying to pass on information that I feel I would welcome should I be in your place. I realize you know your subject, but I've had some real knot heads hand me useful information and hope this has been useful. Lt.Col. BSS

ANSWER: I certainly appreciate the information that you sent about the reduced loads of 4831. You would be surprised at the arguments that this problem has kicked up and Bruce Hodgdon, who supplies this powder, has really been taking Jack O'Connor, Lee Parkinson, myself and others to task for warning handloaders about this phenomenon. I have received many many letters similar to yours stating that high pressures have been experienced with reduced loads of 4831 in cartridges like the .30/06.

On the other hand I have never had reports of a gun being blown up and most of them have been like yours which indicates that blown primers can occur. There have been two reasons why I have been really careful not to warn about common cartridges. The one is that it has not been brought to my attention that guns have actually been wrecked, and the other is that Hodgdon so loudly proclaims that this whole thing is absolutely impossible no matter what size cartridge is used. I have a large file here of correspondence from various individuals like yourself, Jack O'Connor and myself, who agree that this does happen but our big difficulty is that when we try to reproduce this in a laboratory it seems to be practically impossible to do it which is the reason that Hodgdon has an argument. What he fails to take into consideration is the fact that when reduced charges of slow burning powder are used, that usually the shooter has carried the rifle around with the loaded cartridges in it and finally the powder assumes some particular position in the case. When the cartridge is fired with the powder so positioned, it apparently results in a detonating effect. As I have so many times tried to point out to Bruce, we may be using the wrong word when we say "pressure" because obviously a half charge of powder is not going to produce the volume of gas that a full charge does, so there may be some other word which we should use. I am completely satisfied that this phenomenon does occur in almost all sizes of cartridges although in the smaller ones with a better ratio between case and bore capacity, the condition does not seem to be so dangerous.

QUESTION: In reading your loading manual, I noticed one comment which puzzled me . . . that is, your statement that fire forming modern brass was a risky operation. I am currently loading for three cartridges which require fire forming, the 6.5 Spence Special, the .219 Donaldson Wasp and the .219 Improved Zipper. Admittedly, forming the Spence Special is no trouble at all under any conditions, but the Zipper is one you specifically mentioned as being difficult. My system is this: simply load the new cartridges with about 10 grains of 2400 and fill it up to the top with Cream of Wheat, or corn meal. Cap it with a graphite wad to prevent spilling, and fire in the improved chamber. Using this method, I have fire formed 100 Wasp, 40 Improved Zipper and 60 Spence Special cartridges from brand new Winchester brass in the last five months without the loss of a single cartridge. This method was passed on to me by my good friend Harry Creighton, a local (Nashville, Tennessee) gunsmith of some repute, and as I said has been most satisfactory. WTW, III

ANSWER: I do not know where you noticed the statement in my book about fire forming being risky, but there are certain conditions under which the practice is more risky, and that is pulling the bullets out of the case far enough so that they make contact in the throat of the barrel. I have seen guns completely demolished when using this method. In other words, headspace must be minimum whether it be a magnum, rimless or rimmed cartridge. For example, if every case splits with the .219 Zipper, there is no danger connected with the operation, but there is a great deal of danger fire forming rimless cartridges which are much shorter than the chamber. There are several owners of Improved Zippers who have reported the same method that you have been using for fire forming cases.

QUESTION: I have been told that a rifle can be sighted in at 12-1/2 or 25 yards more easily than at longer ranges. Is this true? J.D.

ANSWER: Yes. I personally always sight my rifles in at short range. Jack O'Connor explained the system very nicely in the October issue of *Outdoor Life.* He pointed out that it is a lot easier to tell what is going on at 25 yards than it is at 100, 200 yards or farther. He explained that a .30/06 sighted to strike point of aim at 25 yards with a 180 grain bullet will shoot 1 inch high at 50 yards, 3 inches high at 100 yards and will be dead on again at 225 yards, which means that a .30/06 so sighted would be relatively accurate up to 300 yards without holding over. A .270, .300 Magnum or other flat shooting cartridges would be dead on again out around 275 yards and about 4-1/2 inches low between 325 and 350 yards.

QUESTION: Is the land and groove diameter and twist of the Colt single action 44 barrel suitable for .44 Magnum pistol conversion? If not, what barrel specifications do you recommend? F.G.

ANSWER: As far as I know, the dimensions of the .44 Colt Magnum barrel are the same as for the .44 Special. There is some disagreement as to what the specifications of the .44 barrel should be. Smith and Wesson use a groove diameter of .431 while others use .429, but apparently either one works all right.

QUESTION: What do you consider the correct amount of twist for the following calibres out of a 20 inch barrel (if length makes any difference) .218 Bee, .357 Magnum and .44 Magnum? G.F.

ANSWER: .218 Bee barrels are usually made with a 14 inch twist, but a 16 inch twist works all right. The standard twist for the .357 as used by Smith and Wesson is 18-1/4 inch while Colt standardized on the 16 inch twist and I believe this also applies to the .44 Magnum. My experience has been that twists from 16 to 24 inches all seem to work all right with these two cartridges.

QUESTION: I have heard that you make the .357 and .44 barrels for Numrich Arms Company. The .357 is one turn in 16 inches and the .44 seems to be one turn in 32 inches. Why the great difference for bullets that are not so different in speed? There are so many contradictory statements made concerning the correct twist to properly stabilize a bullet. Could you clarify the whole confusing thing for me? Is there a formula for figuring the correct twist or do you have to arrive at the numbers by experimentation? F.G.

ANSWER: I do not know who makes the barrels for Numrich Arms Company. I have never made any for them, but I assume that some barrel maker in the East is doing it. With the advent of the Ruger .44 Magnum rifle which has a very slow twist, something over 30 inches, some barrel makers have been stretching the twist over like this and they still seem to be all right, so apparently twist is not too much of a factor with these short stubby bullets. It would be hard to figure why a company would sell the .357 and .44 magnum with such a wide variation in twist when most old line hand gun manufacturers still stay with their original twist. As a barrel maker I get into lots of arguments about twist, or perhaps I should not say arguments, but criticism for some customer who believes that twist is the all important thing. For example, lately I rebored a barrel for a customer for a .358 Winchester with a 14 inch twist and he claimed that his barrel was ruined because I didn't use a 16 inch twist which must make Winchester wrong because they use a 12 inch twist. My conclusion is that this customer didn't know what he was talking about and he would probably have gotten equal results with a 12, 14 or 16 inch twist. About the only thing that I could tell you definitely about the twist problem is that the twist must be quick enough in the average barrel to handle all available bullets for the calibre for which the barrel was made. For example, many people will order a 14 inch twist in the .25 calibre barrel which seems to be fine for bullets around 90 grains in weight or lighter, and then they try to use 117 and 125 grain bullets and these long bullets appear to leave the barrel crosswise while if he had ordered the barrel with a 10 inch twist, it would handle all available weight bullets reasonably well, especially the medium and

and heavy weight bullets. So if we use a twist which is just a little bit fast we usually do not run into any trouble, but if we use one as slow as we can for some given bullet, then very often it will not handle the other weights of bullets and the owner has a barrel of very limited use.

QUESTION: What are the advantages of button rifling? RSG

ANSWER: I would say that the main advantage of button rifling is the much lower cost of production. Claims are made that button rifle barrels last longer because of the ironing effect of the button which has a tendency to close the pores as it passes through the barrel and also in some kinds of steel a work hardening action may take place which very slightly hardens the surface of the grooves, all of which probably are pretty far fetched claims. I would say that the two main advantages of button rifled barrels is the cost of production and the ease of holding tolerances. Rifling buttons are made of tungsten carbide and if the same kind of steel is used, or at least steel of the same uniform hardness the groove diameter can be held to much closer tolerances than is possible with the older methods. What I mean is that a carbide button when it is made to a certain size, and has been proven to produce a certain groove diameter, will continue to produce exactly the same groove diameter for a long period of time so long as the same kind of steel is used with a uniform hardness and I might add that there is nothing to some claims which would have us believe that it is necessary to use only relatively soft material for the button rifling method. It seems to be possible to rifle steel even harder than you can with a regular cutter.

QUESTION: I have been actively interested in shooting rifles and pistols for about two years now. Despite this relatively short time I have learned quite a bit about it. However, I have a few questions I need answered so that I can fully comprehend the articles in the various magazines. What does the two numbered calibre designation mean? Example .30/06, .25/06, .30/30?

What is meant by swagging?

Also please describe the theory of a bullet's trajectory.

QUESTIONS AND ANSWERS

Lastly, what is "bore sighting" when zeroing in a rifle? How is this done? T.C.T.

ANSWER: There seems to be no rule for the nomenclature of cartridges and calibres. .30/06 for example indicates that the bullet is .30 calibre but that the cartridge was introduced in 1906. .25/06 simply indicates that the cartridge is the regular .30/06 necked down to .25. .30/30 is also a standard .30 calibre indicated by the .30, but the second .30 indicates 30 grains of powder. In other words, there is no rule, you simply have to know these things.

Then we have other complications caused by the fact that many calibres are designated by the groove diameter. For example, a .25 calibre cartridge can be called the .25/250, .250 or .257. The first two numbers designate the bore, the third one is the actual diameter of the bullet, so in the .25 line we have such calibres as the .25/35, 35 indicating 35 grains of powder. .250/3000 Savage, the 3000 indicating the velocity. The .257 Roberts which means that it is the standard .25 calibre but the name of the originator identifies it from other .25 caibres. Then we have other systems like the .45/70/500. These figures indicating .45 calibre, 70 grains of black powder and a 500 grain bullet.

The definition of swaging found in the dictionary is quite difficult to apply to bullets. When we think of swaging in connection with bullets it usually is that we are either expanding the bullet in a die by applying pressure, or cutting the size of the bullet down by the same means, and it would be quite synonymous to what we would think of as sizing a bullet.

Trajectory of a bullet is simply the path that the bullet takes from the muzzle to the target, and that is actually an arc.

Bore sighting is simply done by holding a rifle stationary then looking through the barrel and getting the bore aligned perfectly on some object at the required distance and then setting the sights so that they also align on the same object. This does not necessarily mean that the bullet will strike that point, but it is sufficiently accurate to easily get the bullet on the paper so that the sight can then be adjusted correctly. I have an idea that the value of bore sighting is badly overrated by many.

Colonel Whelen's book, *Small Arms Design and Ballistics,* by Colonel Townsend Whelen available from the Small Arms Technical Publishing Company, Georgetown, South Carolina, is of great value to anyone interested in these subjects.

QUESTION: I have a story to tell and questions to ask, and I hope that you can help me. In 1955 I purchased a FN barrelled action with a FN medium heavy barrel in .30/06 calibre. I stocked it myself and had wonderful results as I out-shot some old time bench resters at the Torrance Police Range and at Bob Hutton's ranch. I apparently was loading quite hot, 57.5 grains 4320 behind a 150 grain Sierra Spitzer. I was shooting large groups of silver dollar size and when I was right, quarter size year after year. I could shoot for money at the 100, 200, 300 and 500 yard gong and most always won. I also killed eight bucks with 11 shots and all long shots.

Now my story of woe, I had an opportunity to go Elk hunting in 1960 and the group I was going with said the '06 wasn't enough so I ran my rifle over to Roy Weatherby's place and had it altered to .300 Weatherby. Then glassed the action and loaded up 100, .300 H&H for fire forming. Using normal loads and the 180 grain Sierra boat tails. The rifle shot almost as good as ever but since I didn't take my normal care in loading, I had 2-1/2 inch groups, I thought.

I then loaded 78 grains of 4350 behind the 180 grain Sierra Boattail and went back to Huttons. I squeezed off the first, never looking and the second, then looked and saw nothing on the paper. I then pulled out the bolt and bore sighted and squeezed off another and again nothing. Bob seeing me confused asked for the rifle and checked all screws etc. which were right, checked the mount and tried to sight it in on his special short range. He then handed it back and said there was something wrong and it probably was my mount. I disagreed and told him my story and bought a factory pack of .300 H&H from him to prove my story, at the price of $6.60 and that hurt too.

I climbed back on the bench and sighted in and to my amazement I saw in the two targets next to mine high and low my previous Weatherby shots, a nice tight four foot group.

Well, I squeezed off a .300 H&H and whamo 3 inches high at 100 yards in the center. I then put a Weatherby in and it never hit the paper. I then proceeded to shoot a .300 H&H every other shot and the .300 H&H shot a 3 inch group and the Weatherby never hit the right target, I was quite nervous as I was leaving for Colorado in five days.

By this time a couple of bench resters were onlookers and offered help, each loading my brass to their favorite Weatherby load. Same thing. So I tried the 150 grain Nosler that I had loaded for deer and found a 2-1/2 inch group, so off I went to make one-shot kills with 150 grain Nosler on a nice 5 point elk and a couple of nice four point bucks. I should have kept my '06 as I would have at least had confidence.

I am now shooting 180 grain Hornady Spire point and 82 grains of 4831 and the magnum primers and can only get 2-1/2 to 3 inch groups and I am unhappy.

Now I would like to know if it would be feasable to rebore to .338 Winchester Magnum or rebarrel to something other like your .300 Ackley Magnum.

By the way I had the rifle chambered for Weatherby even after reading your book, I should have eaten the pages I guess, but time was short.

Please let me know what happened, whether it was over spin or boat tails or worn bore, or just what. And also what you would advise to remedy my problem.

By the way I went back to Colorado and got a Royal bull and a seven point buck and also a four pointer. It is inaccurate as hell, but its a meat getter. But still no confidence as I took my .270 along just in case. J.K.

ANSWER: Problems such as yours are extremely hard to explain and anything that I could say would simply be a guess, but my guess is that the Weatherby loads were producing a little more velocity than the bullets which you were using will stand. Had you reduced the load in the Weatherby cases so that the velocity would have been the same as the .300 H&H factory loads, which incidentally, was quite low since they were being fired in so much a larger chamber, then the results would have been the same with both cases. Overgrown overbore capacity cases seem to have an adverse effect on bullets, probably due to the excessive amount of powder and sometimes a bullet which has been giving perfectly good results in a smaller case will not work at all in a large one even though the velocity is only a little higher. There are two things that can be done.

One is to use a bullet which is equal to the higher velocity and the other is to use a smaller and more efficient case. Another way of saying it is that there was too much spin on the bullet imparted by the higher velocity which creates too much centrifical force within the bullet itself which, in turn, causes the bullet lead core to expand to a point where the thin jacket will no longer contain it and either blows up entirely or starts leaking lead through cracks which appear along the case made by lands in the barrel. When a bullet like this is just leaking a little bit black tails will appear around the bullet hole in the paper.

High velocity cartridges are more or less defeated now days by the bullets which are available, especially the ordinary custom bullets which are so highly touted. If you stop to think about it, these bullets are the same as those which were available in 1890 simply being composed of a thin weak jacket and a hunk of lead. But in 1890, 2000 feet seconds was extremely high velocity but we have doubled that and try to use the same bullet. This is the reason why I am trying to get my old controlled expansion bullet back on the market which I hope to do soon.

Your barrel could be rebored to .35 calibre and then leave the chamber the way it is except to neck it up, but this results in a miniature cannon unpleasant to shoot and unnecessarily powerful for anything in North America. Very likely the best bet is to re-barrel the rifle or cut the velocity as mentioned above, which can be done in two ways. First, the powder charge can be cut provided the correct powder is used, such as 4064 or 4895. The other way is to use a heavier bullet which automatically slows things down even with the hottest charges. The problem is to cut the velocity in some way to a point where the bullets at hand will take the gaff.

I also might add that very likely the .300 H&H factory loads were not producing the velocity that you were originally getting with the .30/06. I think Bob would be able to explain this if you happen to see him and mention what I have said.

QUESTION: I recently purchased a U. S. M-1 calibre carbine in "like new" condition. This gun consistently groups 9 inches to the right shot at 75 yards from a bench rest and requires about 16 clicks of left windage to correct. A local "gunsmith" looked at it but "couldn't see anything wrong" with the sights or rifling to account for it. Could the barrel be out of alignment with the receiver due to a poor fitting job and cause this inaccuracy? J.P.S.

ANSWER: It is not uncommon to find a receive with the threads a little cockeyed. Neither is it uncommon to find a barrel which is not perfectly straight and either condition can cause your carbine to shoot to one side. It is no fault of the fitting job, and I wouldn't worry about the condition provided you have enough adjustment in the sights to compensate for it. The only solution would be to bend the barrel in the opposite direction until the rifle zeroes correctly. This of course, would not affect accuracy.

QUESTION: I have a .300 Ackley Improved Magnum that I have a question about. I would like your opinion on the number of rounds one could get out of this rifle and still have good hunting accuracy. I realize this would be hard to answer because so many things enter into it.

I worked an awful lot with this gun and really like it. I finally settled on a load of 80 grains of 4831 and the 180 grain Nosler (Remington case and primer) bullet. This load in this gun gives good accuracy and good case life and doesn't seem to give any pressure signs. I also would like to know if you freebore your rifles. As far as I can tell this one isn't (which I like) but you rechambered it, so would know. D.J.

ANSWER: The Improved .300 Magnum which you have has a life expectancy of about the same as the .300 Weatherby and at best it is relatively short. Barrel life for such rifles is quite unpredictable because for some reason when we get up in these very badly over bore capacity cartridges some rifles will shoot out in 500 rounds or so while others will go three times that long, but I am sure that the average will be under 1,000. I have seen some of these rifles like some of the radical .25 Magnums which were worn out before the owner found a load which was accurate. Of course, this boils down to the thing that we are always harping about that you have got to have a cartridge which has a well adjusted bore and case capacity ratio. For .30 calibre we know that 70 grain capacity is maximum for good results. Then too we must consider the fact that so many of these cartridges are so badly overrated or overadvertised by the originators and actually something like these big blown out Magnums are doing very little more than something like the Improved '06.

Of course, a rifle like yours, if used for hunting big game only would last a lifetime, but if you start shooting varmints with it, it probably won't stay with you very long, but once it has been shot out it is a simple matter to run it up to a larger size and simply neck the chamber up to take the larger diameter bullet and in that way it is not necessary to buy a new barrel.

I never free bore rifles unless the customer so orders because I have found free boring does no good. However, it does aid materially in some of the high powered advertising because it allows the use of considerably more powder which seems to be the measuring stick used by some shooters. For example, if you have a .300

Magnum which produces 3100 foot seconds with a top load behind the 180 grain bullet, the barrel can be free bored about 1-1/2 inches and then four or five more grains of powder can be used. When this is done, it is not necessary that the owner be told that his velocity drops at the same time and when he has built up his new loads to the original pressure, the velocity is the same as before.

I must add, however, that when we chamber barrels for the .300 Weatherby we do free bore them the same as Weatherby does for the reason that the factory loads would probably not work in a conventionally chambered barrel.

QUESTION: In 1956 I acquired a fine old hi-wall with heavy barrel and Winchester double set triggers that had been re-barrelled and chambered by Hervy Lovell for an Improved .219 Zipper. I have been reloading only since 1957 and am probably out of line writing to an old master but I have read other articles to the effect that .219 Zipper cannot be fireformed, but I have found a way after about 98% failures in conventional fire forming. My method, and I cannot believe no one else has used it. First, I pull the bullet and pour the powder into a suitable container, I use small druggist prescription bottles, one for each case, then measure 10 grains of 2400 into each case with no bullet, chamber the case, point the muzzle up, shake the powder down good and fire – perfect case!

Reprime, neck size and return the original powder charge if suitable, reseat the bullet and you are in business.

I used 2400 because it was handy and the charge will need to be adjusted to the gun and I guess the weather affects it also. 9 grains of 2400 will not completely shape the case and 11 grains of 2400 will cause it to stick. I don't have a full length die; use the Lyman 310 tool, so can't afford to overload; but have loaded a few cases more than a dozen times with from 30 to 34 grains 3031 and 50 grain Sierra bullet and have had none stick or fail. REB.

ANSWER: Since some of the comments that I made about fire forming Zipper brass have been printed, I have received all sorts of methods to form cases and I have been passing the information along whenever necessary, but your method is the most unique one I have ever heard of. The Improved Zipper is one of the best .22 calibre cartridges ever designed and this applies to the various versions like the K Zipper, my own, Mashburn and others which are all quite similar and equally good.

QUESTION: What in your personal opinion is the finest long range varmint cartridge. Be it wildcat or standard, I am looking for something for an extreme shot that is presented once in a while. Have tried quite thoroughly .22/250, 243, .244, .25/06, .257, .257 Weatherby, .264 Winchester .270 and can find none can make consistent hits beyond 400 yards. I have just finished putting together one of your .300 Ackley Improved Magnums on an Enfield, 28 inch barrel, full heavy. So far I have only had it out one day. Best group, 1-1/4 inch 15 shots, 84 grains 4831, 180 grain Sierra spitzer. Maybe this is my answer? AR

ANSWER: There is no cartridge that will do any better than the ones that you have tried for long range shots. At least that is my opinion and all you have proven is that very few people can make competent shots over 400 yards and most everyone is pretty well done a long time before that. Also we only find competent varmint shooting done at 600 yards, etc., when the proper sighting equipment is put on the guy's typewriter.

If you can take the recoil, your Improved .300 Magnum would probably outshoot the others that you have tried at these extreme ranges, but it is going to take some elimination of the human element to put much consistency into the program.

QUESTION: I am considering making up a couple of rifles for African game and will appreciate your help on the following:

How does a Magnum Mauser action differ from the ordinary standard length action? Is the FN Mauser action a true Magnum action capable of handling the .458 Winchester Magnum cartridge with an ample margin of safety? Where can I get loading data for the .458?

QUESTIONS AND ANSWERS

Where can I obtain a Brevex Magnum action barrelled for the .505 Gibbs cartridge and loading data and components for the .505?

Finally, can the .458 Winchester be loaded a bit hotter than the factory round? J.R.P.

ANSWER: The FN Mauser Magnum action is exactly the same as the other FN models except that it has a longer magazine and the receiver is cut out to accept this longer magazine and of course the bolt face is cut out for the Magnum cartridge head.

Here we have exactly the same situation as we find in the Model 70 Winchester. All Model 70 Winchester receivers are the same. That is, the .22 Hornet is the same as the .30/06, which is also the same as the .300 Magnum, so that it simply amounts to a plugged up action for the Hornet and a cut out action for the Magnum.

The true Magnum Mauser action is a larger action, or at least a longer action, than the standard and had the so-called pot-bellied magazine for the large Magnum cartridges and was long enough so that the receiver did not have to be cut out for the longer cartridge, thus weakening it.

The Brevex action is just another overgrown Mauser action which can be termed a true Magnum action because it is long enough for the longest Magnum cartridge.

I don't know where you could get a .505 Gibbs barrel, but you could try Apex Rifle Company of Sun Valley, California. You can get the action from Tradewinds, Inc., P. O. Box 1191, Tacoma 1, Washington, and I believe the present cost of the action is around $115.00.

The following are the only loads that I have for the .505 Gibbs and all are for the 525 grain bullet:

98 grains of 4064 powder		1970 fs.
100	HiVel #2	2250
105	HiVel #2	2390

This is not enough better than the .458 Winchester to make all the trouble worthwhile because the .458 Winchester will shoot all the way through the largest elephant and it will work through standard actions like the standard FN, Springfield, Enfield or Model 70 standard length actions.

The Terhaar Gun Works, P. O. Box 2753, Jacksonville, Florida, can furnish three leaf sights. The Burton Arms Company, 7834 Brecksville Road, Brecksville, Ohio, can also furnish three leaf sights, but it is quite difficult to get the genuine English type because these come in blank form so that when the rifle is completed the notches can be filed slowly until the rifle zeroes correctly for each leaf. This type of blank sight is available from Victor Sarasqueta, S.L., Eibar, Spain, or Holland and Holland, Ltd., 98 New Bond Street, London W.1, England.

You can steam up the .458 somewhat. In fact, you can load it hot enough so if you hit an elephant under the tail you will bulge his eyeballs.

QUESTION: I am interested in having a rifle made in the Ackley 7x57mm Improved. I have read that the pressure of this calibre can be as high as 60,000 psi or more. Do you feel that this pressure is on the high side regardless of case shape?

Do you feel that the FN Mauser action is suited to this calibre or would you recommend some other action? How does the recoil compare with the .30/06?

What do you think of muzzle brake for reducing recoil. If you think they are good, would you recommend which one to get. I would like one which would not increase muzzle blast.

Please tell me, if you can, the comparative recoil figures on the following calibres: .30/06, .280 Remington, 7x57mm and the 7x57mm Improved. A.C.

ANSWER: Pressure is a subject about which a great deal is written mostly by people who do not consider all of the factors or who do not understand the problems encountered in the gun business, because as you can readily understand, the pressure of any hand loaded cartridge is exactly what the hand loader makes it, which could be anything from zero to 100,000 pounds if he is so minded.

When authentic loading data tables are available, these tables contain loads which are supposed to be within safe pressures not exceeding 55,000 psi, but invariably any loading data must be accompanied with a warning to the effect that maximum loads should never be used until they have been worked up to carefully by starting a few grains under the recommended maximum load. This holds true for any cartridge, standard or "wildcat."

The improved 7x57 mm is a very good cartridge for anyone who intends to hand load his own ammunition. Naturally, it is not a calibre which is recommended for use with factory ammunition exclusively even though it will handle factory loads, which is the way the cases are formed.

I personally prefer the Improved 7x57mm to any 7mm Magnum regardless of whose version it may be and it is my opinion that it is one of the very best of the so-called "improved" cartridges.

I am not particularly in favor of recoil eliminators. My opinion is that anyone who is that conscious of recoil should concentrate on rifles of recoil which he can handle without flinching. However, recoil eliminators do help recoil a little bit even though they do make things very unpleasant from the standpoint of muzzle blast. Almost all of the recoil eliminators, at least to some extent do what is claimed for them. What is not said about them is what interests me. There are numerous makes all of which could be considered equally good.

Recoil is greatly dependent upon the bullet weight. For example, if you should use a 175 grain bullet in the improved 7x57mm it will give approximately the same recoil as the same bullet weight in a .30/06 provided the velocities are the same.

QUESTION: I have recently seen an advertisement in several magazines offering Model 95 or 98 Mausers, presumed to be the small ring type, barrelled in a variety of calibres such as .22/250, .220 Swift, .243 Winchester, .244 Remington, .250 Savage, .257 Roberts, 7mm and .308 Winchester calibres. Is the model 95 Mauser strong enough for the safe use of say, factory Swifts or equivalent hand loads. These are offered only as barrelled actions.

I am now in possession of a pre-war model .219 Savage in .22 Hornet calibre. Can this gun be chambered for the .219 Donaldson Wasp providing that I use .30/30 cases to offset the fire-forming problem? P.E.

ANSWER: The Model 95 Mauser is strong enough for most of the cartridges which you mentioned. I don't think I would be too happy with one for the .220 Swift, but it would very likely hold it safely. It would be my opinion that anyone buying a barrelled action of this kind would make a good investment by spending slightly more for the 98 type, preferably a genuine 98, for which parts are available anywhere. I might add that it is my opinion that no matter what the ads may lead you to believe, any surplus action is no bargain. If you investigate the cost of having one of these actions completely modernized to be anywhere near equal to the FN or some other new action, you will find that it will cost just as much but you wind up still having an old used obsolete action.

A good Model 98 Mauser is always a good basis to use for a custom rifle and it is safe for any modern cartridge with hand loads or factory ammunition, but the above opinions still hold true about the surplus actions being a bargain.

The .219 Savage can be rechambered for the .219 Donaldson Wasp, .219 Zipper and similar cartridges.

QUESTION: I would appreciate any information you could give me on 1920 system Mannlicher/Schoenauer rifles made by Steyr or Breda for the Greek government. I would like to know what pressure the action was designed for and what length cartridge the magazine was designed for. I would also like to know if there is any current publication listing specifications including how much pressure the actions were designed for and the maximum cartridge length the action was designed to handle and all or most of foreign military arms currently being imported.

ANSWER: The Greek Mannlicher is a fairly good action except that it is limited to its original calibre, which is the 6.5 Mannlicher. It is extremely difficult and quite impractical to try to convert these actions for any other cartridges, except perhaps a recreational project or student training project where time is no object.

These actions are quite strong and would be strong enough for larger cartridges, but the older Mannlicher actions were all made for a specific cartridge and do not work well in any other one.

QUESTION: I have a Ruger single six revolver in .22 WMR calibre with a 6-1/2 inch barrel. My problem is this: I would like to mount or have a scope mounted on it. I have never yet seen any information on pistol scopes or mounts in any of the well known gun magazines. Would you please tell me which scope and mount would be best for this handgun. Also who makes them.

Also, could you tell me if any method has yet been devised for reloading these powerful but expensive cartridges or any .22 calibre rim fire, for that matter? RVS

ANSWER: For pistol scope mounts write to Maynard P. Buehler, Orinda, California, for complete information on their mounts to fit pistols. For pistol scopes, try Bushnell.

There is no way to reload rim fire cartridges.

QUESTION: I have one of the 03A3 Springfield surplus Army rifles, and as I already own one .30/06 Model 70, I would like to have this rifle converted to handle the new .308 Norma Magnum cartridge. That is, if it would be suitable, or advisable. Could I expect satisfactory performance from such a conversion and how about the barrel life as compared to the .30/06? Does RCBS make dies for reloading the .308 Norma Magnum?

Also I would like your expert opinion on casting bullets for reloading the .30/30 Winchester for the Model 94 carbine. Can you expect to get as much velocity with cast, gas check bullets as the data listed in the Lyman Handbook and is there liable to be damaging effects by leading with cast bullets if they are properly lubricated? Some have informed me that cast bullets are better for deer loads than the jacketed bullets that are used in factory loads or bullets made by the custom bullet makers.

One more question. Could I improve the value, for deer hunting purposes of the Savage 219 in .30/30 calibre by having it rechambered to .30/30 Improved and what kind of accuracy may I expect? TEH

ANSWER: The 03A3 Springfield rifles work very well for the .308 Norma conversion and performance is quite satisfactory. Barrel life, naturally, will be shorter than with the .30/06 case, but so far I have had no reports or complaints about the barrel life for the .308 Magnum, therefore I assume that it at least is as good or better than the standard .300 H&H.

You can get almost as much velocity out of a cast gas check bullet in the .30/30 as you can with the standard factory jacketed bullet. I doubt very much if you have any loading problems if the bullets are properly lubricated. You can get considerably more power out of the Improved .30/30 in the .219 Savage, but the accuracy will remain unchanged. It will not harm or improve the accuracy.

QUESTION: I have a Savage sporter in .25/20 calibre. Can this rifle be converted to the .22 Hornet or the .218 Bee. This rifle has a 4 or 5 shot removable magazine. Will the Hornet or Bee work in it. How about the so-called Improved Hornet. JWS

ANSWER: The .25/20 Savage sporter could not be converted to .218 Bee. These rifles all have the receiver made in one piece which makes it near impossible to convert them at anything like a reasonable cost.

QUESTION: I have a Winchester Model 88 lever-action chambered for the .308 cartridge. Can this rifle be safely rechambered for the .308 Norma magnum?

ANSWER: It would not be practical to try to convert the Model 88 Winchester for a cartridge longer than the .308 Winchester.

7mm Remington Magnum

The 7mm Remington magnum is the latest factory introduction of a magnum cartridge and it could be described as a short 7mm magnum quite similar to the original .270 Ackley magnum, 7 x 61 S & H magnum, the short Mashburn magnum, Weatherby magnum and many other similar ones.

This new Remington cartridge is simply the .264 Winchester necked up to 7mm which in itself should be an improvement, since a cartridge case of this capacity is more efficient with a larger bore. It is still badly overbore capacity and suitable mostly for slow burning powders and probably in many ways is not as practical as the older .280 Remington which itself is a very good cartridge and one of maximum capacity for best results with a 7mm bore.

The following is a partial list of the loading data which has been developed by the Hornady Manufacturing Company. More complete information can be obtained from the Hornady Manufacturing Company, Box 906, Grand Island, Nebraska.

Bullet	Powder charge	Powder	Velocity
120 gr. bullet	55.8 gr.	4064 powder	3200 fs
	58	4064	3300
	54.5	4895	3100
	56.6	4895	3200
	58.4	4320	3200
	58.7	H380	3200
	66	4350	3200
	70.6	4831	3400
	72.3	H450	3400
139	55.4	4064	3000
	55.8	4895	3000
	60.3	4320	3100
	61.5	H380	3100
	66	4350	3200
	69.8	4831	3300
154	52.4	4064	2800
	53.1	4895	2800
	56.8	4320	2900
	58.1	H380	2900

MAXIMUM LOAD LISTED SHOULD BE APPROACHED WITH CARE

LOADING DATA

154 gr. bullet	62.6 gr.	4350 powder	3000 fs
	67.1	4831	3000
	68.2	H450	3000
175	53.2	4320	2700
	52.1	H380	2600
	58.8	4350	2800
	62.6	4831	2800
	64.7	H450	2800

120 gr. bullet	71 gr.	4831 powder	3321 fs
140	69	4831	3175
	72	H570	2825
160	64	4831	2915
	70	H570	2778

MAXIMUM LOAD LISTED SHOULD BE APPROACHED WITH CARE

NOTES

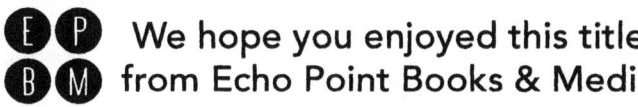 We hope you enjoyed this title from Echo Point Books & Media

Before Closing this Book, Two Good Things to Know

1. Buy Direct & Save

Go to www.echopointbooks.com (click "Our Titles" at top or click "For Echo Point Publishing" in the middle) to see our complete list of titles. We publish books on a wide variety of topics—from spirituality to auto repair.

Buy direct and save 10% at www.echopointbooks.com

 DISCOUNT CODE: EPBUYER

2. Make Literary History and Earn $100 Plus Other Goodies Simply for Your Book Recommendation!

At Echo Point Books & Media we specialize in republishing out-of-print books that are united by one essential ingredient: high quality. Do you know of any great books that are no longer actively published? If so, please let us know. If we end up publishing your recommendation, you'll be adding a wee bit to literary culture and a bunch to our publishing efforts.

Here is how we will thank you:

- A free copy of the new version of your beloved book that includes acknowledgement of your skill as a sharp book scout.
- A free copy of another Echo Point title you like from echopointbooks.com.
- And, oh yes, we'll also send you a check for $100.

Since we publish an eclectic list of titles, we're interested in a wide range of books. So please don't be shy if you have obscure tastes or like books with a practical focus. To get a sense of what kind of books we publish, visit us at www.echopointbooks.com.

If you have a book that you think will work for us, send us an email at editorial@echopointbooks.com

www.ingramcontent.com/pod-product-compliance
Lightning Source LLC
Chambersburg PA
CBHW050416170426
43201CB00008B/431